# HOW IT WAS
# IN THE WAR

# HOW IT WAS
# IN THE WAR
*An Anthology edited by*
## Godfrey Smith

PAVILION
MICHAEL JOSEPH

For Ken

First published in Great Britain in 1989 by
PAVILION BOOKS LIMITED
196 Shaftesbury Avenue, London WC2H 8JL
in association with Michael Joseph Limited
27 Wrights Lane, Kensington, W8 5TZ

Compilation, introduction and commentary copyright
© Godfrey Smith 1989. Copyright information for individual
extracts is given on pp. 313-4

All illustrations are by Fougasse
and are taken from
*A School of Purposes,*
*Fougasse Posters, 1939-1945*
introduced by A P Herbert
and first published by
Methuen and Co. Ltd., in 1946

Designed by Tom Sawyer

A CIP catalogue record for this book is
available from the British Library

ISBN 1 85145 363 6

10 9 8 7 6 5 4 3 2 1

Printed and bound in Great Britain by
Butler & Tanner Ltd, Frome and London

'Do not let us speak of darker days; let us rather speak of sterner days. These are not dark days: these are great days – the greatest days our country has ever lived; and we must all thank God that we have been allowed, each of us according to our stations, to play a part in making these days memorable in the history of our race.'

Winston Churchill
Harrow School, 29 October, 1941


Soldiers who want to be a hero
Are practically zero
But soldiers who want to be civilians
Jesus, they run into millions.

Anon (c. 1940)

# CONTENTS

INTRODUCTION

# THAT'S HOW THE POOR SOD DIED

# ARE WE DOWNHEARTED?

## A HOBNAIL LOVE ACROSS YOUR HEART

## SHALL I TELL MY HUSBAND?

## TORA! TORA! TORA!

## THE SWEET BREATH OF FEAR

# INTRODUCTION

How was it in the war? Obviously, at the outset, it is at one level an impossible question to answer. There were millions of wars. Every human being involved saw it through a different perspective. Moreover the range of experience it engendered was infinitely vast, ranging from the horrific to the comic, from the dramatic to the humdrum, and from the majestic to the bizarre.

For many, manifestly, it was a time of unquantifiable horror; sometimes the slow hell of Belsen or Buchenwald, sometimes the sudden catastrophe of Hamburg or Hiroshima. Sometimes it was a grievous assault on human dignity, as when the Russian troops, rampaging through East Germany, looted and raped at will; and sometimes it was the collision of grotesquely disparate cultures, as in the Japanese conquest of Singapore. Yet there were other kinds of war. Thus, the RAF aircrew flying home after the first thousand-bomber raid on Germany felt light-hearted enough to sing; and even in the maelstrom of the D-Day landings there was a Scottish piper gallant or foolhardy enough to play his pipes on the beaches.

If you were a recruit, like Michael Green, life could be both strenuous but comic; if you were a prisoner of war, like Robert Kee in Germany, your central problem was boredom. War was not all bad all the time for many of those involved: that gallant and brilliant fighter pilot Pierre Clostermann confesses freely that he wept in the cockpit of his plane the day he left the RAF. The war was a kind of black farce for P.G. Wodehouse, swept up like flotsam by the Germans from his plesaunce at Le Touquet and dumped unceremoniously in Berlin, there to be labelled a traitor. For millions of women, war involved both domestic privation and emotional stress, while for some, like the Land Girl whose story we tell, it had a tragi-comic dénouement. Things were not what they seemed. Jean-Paul Sartre, in his long, complex, and riveting account of Paris in the Occupation, makes it clear that even here the experience was perceived at different levels. At one, Sartre testifies, life to all intents and purposes went on normally; contrary to received opinion, the Germans did not behave like brutes and were generally both disciplined and moderate. If French girls went out with them they did so entirely of their own volition. At another level, though, there was the dark world of the Gestapo. Films like Le Chagrin et la Pitié have only recently been able to show the unending variousness of people's lives and attitudes in Occupied France.

The British experience was quite different; first, because they were at war longer than any other single people, second, because they fought that war for a year alone; third, because the very fact of conducting world war from an island lent both insularity and unity. The British were bombed, certainly; they were deprived of many things – food, clothes, travel – and the sort of freedom they had enjoyed in peace. On the other hand in one sense it was also a curiously carefree era. People were given jobs and had no choice but to get on with them. 'These are not dark days,' Churchill told the boys at Harrow in 1941. 'These are great days.' No doubt for the boys at Harrow and their greatest living old boy that was no more or less than the truth. Yet Churchill had his dark moments too, as we see in his own account of the worst day of the war, when he heard that the Prince of Wales and the Repulse had been sunk, thus leaving the Indian Ocean and the Pacific at the mercy of the Japanese. And all this only three days after the best day of the war:

when he knew that America had entered it and that, whatever catastrophes lay ahead, we had won.

The war brought death and bereavement to many in Britain as it did elsewhere, but it also brought glamour and preferment, change and excitement to many who in peacetime had been marooned in dead-end jobs. The man in the street had far more money in real terms than he had in the bleak Thirties, and all the statistics show that the health of the country improved dramatically from 1942 onwards. There was no drug epidemic. There were no football hooligans or lager louts. Neither alcohol nor tobacco were yet the public enemies they have become; they were scarce, that was all. Bombing proved a great leveller. The rich had to do without servants, travel and expensive clothes; the whole nation, as A.J.P. Taylor noted, lived roughly on the standard of the skilled artisan. There was no unemployment.

The sense of unity, of all being in it together, is dramatically exemplified by the fates befalling German spies landed in these islands; not one remained a free man more than a few hours. There was little or no moral debate about the rightness of what we were doing. If German cities were flattened by our bombs that was just too bad; what about Coventry? If a hundred thousand Japanese were to die in Hiroshima it seemed a perfectly acceptable price to pay for the end of the war in which another million or more Allied troops (and no one knew how many Japanese) would otherwise have died. They should have thought of that before Pearl Harbor.

Nevertheless, the passage of half a century has changed our perspective. The hatred that informed the testimony of seamen like Frank Laskier has long since gone; the Germans are our allies and partners, more noted for economic miracles and green politics than for the unpleasant concepts they gave the world then: Blitzkrieg, Übermensch and Herrenvolk. The Japanese have been transmuted from the sadistic psychopaths who used our men as slave labour to build the Burma railway into the brilliant race who have flooded us with their Sony radios, their Hitachi television sets, their Toshiba microwave ovens and their Honda motorbikes.

At this range, we can see the war much more clearly and much less emotionally than we did then. Fifty years is not a bad benchmark from which to try to take a fresh measure of it. In a world which seems increasingly unlikely to allow a catastrophe of that sort to happen again, the interest shifts. What seems more to the point now is not what the war did to the world, but what it did to us. There is a sense in which, as Robert Kee eloquently puts it, everything that has happened since is somehow secondary to it. This is in no way to celebrate war; only to respect its transmuting power. The stories gathered together in these pages can only be a sliver of a vast mosaic that will never be totally assembled; but even in their small ambit they show the astonishing range of experiences that befell the human race in its most cataclysmic and, we must trust, its final world war.

Godfrey Smith
Malmesbury, January 1989

14

# IT'S THAT MAN AGAIN

However small the job you do,
don't forget that
EYERY LITTLE HELPS!

ONE AIRCRAFT NOW
IS WORTH TWO NEXT YEAR

One of the first unsung casualties of the war was television. We tend to forget that in 1939 some 350 cinemas had been showing big-screen television reports of national news. All that had to go – and so, at first, did all the cinemas. Soon it became clear that people would need diversion and escapism as they buckled down to the grim imperatives of war. The radio became the principal pabulum and a show like ITMA permeated the whole nation with its corny catchphrases. Meanwhile, Lord Haw-Haw did his very best to spread gloom and defeatism from his studio in Germany, but remained a joke throughout the war.

## ENTERTAINERS – FRIENDLY AND HOSTILE

### E. S. TURNER

To foreigners, perhaps the most baffling feature of the late 1939 theatrical season was a revival of Young England, the impossibly patriotic play which had been ragged into an outstanding success in 1934. The venerable author, Walter Reynolds, wrote it in an effort to stir the laggard blood of his fellow-countrymen, but succeeded only in inciting them to mirth; it was little consolation that the play was a great success financially. Whether the original backers knew just what they were backing may be in doubt, but the audiences who went along to see the revival knew exactly how they were expected to behave. When the heroine put a whistle to her lips, the faithful in stalls, circle and gallery sounded an appropriate blast. When the telephone rang, the audience cried to the villain, 'Answer that phone, you cad!' As the villain robbed the safe, the audience warned him, 'Don't forget to wipe the handle' – and he obeyed. A scoutmaster dashed into a little wooden hut and out again, and this was the cue for cries of 'No paper.' So it went on, right to the flag-filled finale. Miss F. Tennyson Jesse supplied the appropriate comment when she wrote: 'We are fighting to be able to laugh at these things if we so choose.'

The cinema industry was in a state of anarchic depression. Even in normal times, backers were nervous of lending money to British studios, and in war they were more nervous still. Too many giant cinemas had been built, but there seemed a fair chance that the Luftwaffe would trim the circuits to a more economic size, always supposing it did not wipe them out altogether. The Government had no interest in, and no plans to harness, the industry, though it was quick to seize many of the huge studios, stuffing Pinewood and much of Denham with food. Sir Michael Balcon nearly lost his Ealing Studios; Associated British were turned out of Elstree, which became a war factory, and withdrew to Welwyn. If, in 1940, the erratic Gabriel Pascal had not taken such a long time to make Major Barbara, J. Arthur Rank's last foothold at Denham might have been lost. As it was, Rank jokingly credited Pascal with being the saviour of

British films. After a very groggy three months, the film industry, both British and British-American, began to mount a creditable production programme. The first notable film to be made during, and about, the war was *The Lion Has Wings*, with Ralph Richardson and Merle Oberon.

From this distance, nothing is more surprising than the off-hand way in which the BBC's television service was closed down and forgotten. The *Radio Times* made no mention of its disappearance until more than a month later, when this not-very-apologetic paragraph appeared:

> It has been pointed out to us that nobody said a word in the *Radio Times* about the passing of television. That is quite true, but so many things were passing, too, on that ominous week-end at the beginning of September, that television was at least not singled out for neglect. As a matter of fact we ourselves as viewers miss television as much as anyone could.

Alexandra Palace went off the air at noon on 1 September. No closing announcement was made to viewers, who for the rest of the day twiddled their knobs in a vain effort to tune in the advertised attractions: a cabaret show, Mantovani, a visit to the Zoo and variety. The last voice heard was that of Elizabeth Cowell, the announcer, speaking from Radiolympia. That morning Mr Val Gielgud was rehearsing a company in Somerset Maugham's *The Circle*, which was to have been produced on the day war was declared.

Various reasons were given for the shut-down. The principal one was that the short-wave transmission would help to guide enemy bombers. It was also pointed out that the cost of operating the service was very high in proportion to the number of set-owners, who totalled only about 20,000, and that, by closing the service down, skilled technicians would be freed to maintain sound radio (television used ten people for every one engaged on sound). Disgruntled viewers who had just paid between thirty and sixty guineas for their sets began to study the small print of the hire-purchase contracts to see whether they could suspend payments, but found they could not. In the next few months there was sporadic agitation, both from viewers and from the industry, for television to be resumed. An advisory committee under Lord Cadman went so far as to advocate a two-hour programme daily. Manufacturers pointed out that Britain was a year ahead of America in technical progress. In the First World War, Americans had captured the world film market; now they would seize the world television market. If there were defence objections against short-wave transmissions, argued one manufacturer, why not put out programmes over wires? None of these arguments prevailed. Ruefully, the industry took stock: there were sets worth £750,000 in the hands of the public; there were sets worth £70,000 in the shops; and there were 15,000 sets in process of assembly. These were scrapped.

The loss of television was also a loss to the film industry. In 1939 some

350 cinemas of the Gaumont-British group had been showing big-screen television reports of national events. There had been considerable pressure on the Government to allow television to develop independently of the BBC, but this was to some extent offset by the radio retail trade, which wanted to see television developed as a home entertainment. Today the cinema industry has probably forgotten that it ever took this noisy bantling under its wing.

Listeners to sound radio had no sympathy to spare for television viewers. Hitherto they had enjoyed the choice of eight regional programmes; now, on security grounds, these were cut down to one – the Home Service. The Forces Programme did not start until early in 1940.

In an emergency issue, the *Radio Times* congratulated listeners on the splendid service they would continue to receive. London would no longer be the centre of British broadcasting but three separate radio cities had been set up 'somewhere in England'. One was a variety centre, where numerous stars on long-term contracts, all carefully screened by Security, 'would find complete scripts and scores of shows and ideas – enough to provide as many as forty programmes a week – all ready to be produced.' These stars included Tommy Handley, Vera Lennox, Ernest Longstaffe, Sam Costa, Webster Booth, Charles Shadwell, Doris Arnold and Leonard Henry. The Features and Drama Department had in readiness the scripts of 330 plays and 200 features; and the musical centre had a concentration of orchestras – symphony, light, theatre and variety.

This was all very encouraging, but the programmes which ushered in the Home Service were singularly depressing. The Corporation at this period looked on itself as primarily a news service, for there were bulletins every hour, on the hour, coupled with endless official exhortations. In between were programmes of gramophone records and organ recitals by Sandy Macpherson. The public spirit of Mr Macpherson was never in doubt, but many thought, after the first few days of war that they had heard enough organ music for the duration. (Two other leading organists, Reginald Foort and Harold Ramsay, were in the habit of touring the country with mobile organs, which made an impressive sight on the roads; but with the temporary shut-down of theatres they were left without audiences.)

The BBC's Variety Department was evacuated to Bristol, effectively dispelling any breathless hush which still lingered in the Close at Clifton College. In the Clifton Parish Hall, which became the BBC's 'Garrison Theatre', the 'ITMA' programme was born, or rather re-born, for the idea had been tried out just before the war and then discontinued. This, the best-remembered radio show of the war and probably its finest morale-raiser, has been described by its producer, Francis Worsley, as 'all unconsciously the *commedia dell'arte* of modern times', and has been hailed elsewhere as, technically, the most perfect use of the radio medium. Those who remember this quick-witted nonsense will hardly need to be reminded of it; those who read a bald account of it will wonder how it ever became a national obsession.

The first wartime 'ITMA' programme went out on 19 September. Its title, 'It's That Man Again', had originally done service as a press headline alluding to Hitler; now it referred to the comedian Tommy Handley in his capacity as Minister of Aggravation and Mysteries at the Office of Twerps. Initially, it was a show designed to poke timely fun at wartime restrictions, exhortations and pomposities. Among its early characters were the spy Funf (Jack Train) who kept ringing up in a doom-laden voice to prophesy disaster, and the civil servant Fusspot. In later editions appeared Mrs Mopp, the indomitable charwoman (Dorothy Summers) and Colonel Chinstrap (Jack Train). Handley left the Minister of Aggravation and Mysteries to hold a variety of other appointments, among them that of Mayor of Foaming-at-the-Mouth. Always, he was the slick swashbuckler whose plans went awry.

'ITMA' was a triumph of professionalism. Handley and his script-writer, the New Zealander Ted Kavanagh, had been fellow toilers in the radio vineyard since 1924. The show was written for a formula which called for copious word-play, topical allusions and catch-phrases. Few of the catch-phrases were funny in themselves, but repetition by one and all made them seem so. They appealed to those who found comfort and even solidarity in thinking in *clichés* and also, as Worsley has pointed out, to those who were tongue-tied in company. The phrases included 'This is Funf speaking' (for leg-pulling on the phone); 'After you, Claude – No, after you, Cecil' (for collisions at doors, or baling out of aircraft); 'I don't mind if I do' (for the bar); 'I go – I come back' (for anyone temporarily excusing himself from company); 'TTFN' (Ta Ta For Now – for longer absences); 'It's me noives' (to excuse any clumsiness); 'Boss, boss, something terrible's happened' (for softening adverse news); 'Well, for ever more' (to express moderate surprise) and 'Can I do you now, sir?' (applications various). It was possible to raise a laugh merely by saying *à propos* of nothing, 'Don't forget the diver' or, in a mournful tone, 'It's being so cheerful as keeps me going.' Presumably the 'ITMA' program-mes were monitored by the enemy and the transcripts must have caused total bewilderment on the Wilhelmstrasse.

When 'ITMA' began, another fount of catch-phrases, the 'Band Waggon' programme, with Arthur Askey, Richard Murdoch and Syd Walker ('What would you do, chums?') was already soundly established. Jack ('Blue Pencil') Warner was the leading performer in 'Garrison Theatre', his most potent catch-phrase being 'Mind my bike.' Seen from this distance, it all seems curiously infantile; and, to be sure, there were intellectuals at the time who found it peculiarly harrowing.

The most solemn event in the listener's day was the Nine O'Clock News. It was preceded by Big Ben striking the hour, a portentous operation which lasted about a minute. This, according to Mr Maurice Gorham, was a compromise between a demand for a minute's silence and a demand for a daily prayer. During this minute it was up to the listener to dispose his thoughts in some suitable manner – if he was not too busy counting the strokes. The news readers (who did not identify themselves until after Dunkirk) had a difficult task. As the war progressed, they had to read increasingly sombre bulletins without sounding depressed, cheerful, casual or newly commissioned. They had to switch from reading details of disasters to a recital of the racing results without causing more offence than was inevitable. Each new campaign brought them a crop of tongue-twisting place names.

Those British listeners who had lived in fealty to commercial stations in France and Luxembourg found that most of these sources of culture were off the air. Luxembourg shut down in the interests of neutrality, because 'foreigners' were misusing its wave-length. One notable exception was Fécamp Radio, which for long resisted the efforts of Mr Noël Coward, then serving in an intelligence branch in Paris, to close it down on security grounds. Mr Coward's account in *Future Indefinite* of his one-man campaign against the commercial operators of Fécamp Radio makes odd reading.

There was, indeed, a profusion of overseas programmes in English. Germany offered not only mendacious news bulletins but programmes of cross-talk in which chuckle-headed Englishmen were converted by sweet reason to the cause of tyranny. Moscow had an English announcer with a Cockney accent. Chungking's English programme ended with 'The British Grenadiers' played on Chinese instruments. At this time a body calling itself the British Long-Distance Listeners Club issued special certificates to all members who could produce 'verification cards' issued by transmitting stations in all five continents. These cards were passed round among enthusiasts who were more keen to plaster their dens with impressive paper than to identify Quito and Saigon by their own efforts. Not until the summer of 1940 did it become illegal to send reports of transmissions out of the country to receive verification cards from overseas.

It required no high-powered set to pick up William Joyce ('Lord Haw-Haw'), a former British Fascist then actively engaged, 'within the German realm', in 'broadcasting to the subjects of our Lord the King propaganda on behalf of the enemies of our Lord the King'. In no other war had the British enjoyed the novelty of being cajoled and hectored by renegades in their own sitting-rooms. For many, the experience was distasteful; it was an abuse of their beloved 'wireless', and they did not tune in the enemy a second time. Mostly, those who listened to Haw-Haw excused themselves on the ground that he was the best entertainer on the air. Others listened so that they might be in the conversational swim next day. Others again argued that one ought to hear both sides and, after all, Haw-Haw sometimes told the truth. Even those who scoffed the loudest often gave credence and currency to the misinformation he circulated. Not everybody laughed derisively when he asked, 'Where is the *Ark Royal*?' Even when the Admiralty, at last, turned the laugh against him, revealing that the *Ark* was sailing the seas undamaged, his reputation was not exploded. When, by quoting from nerve tonic advertisements in the British press, he proved that the nation was in a bad state of jitters, nobody was deceived; that was just a good joke. But his ventilation of grievances and inequalities in Britain, his parading of skeletons from the colonial cupboard, led some to regard him as the voice of conscience. A reader wrote to a Scots newspaper to say that Lord Haw-Haw performed a valuable service by citing Britain's deficiencies and it would not help the cause of freedom and democracy if people were to be banned from listening to him.

Lord Haw-Haw was a very dangerous entertainer. At his most malevolent, as he rang a mock Lutine Bell to announce more sinkings of British merchantmen, his influence was not only depressing but uncommonly sinister. It was his custom to refer to local conditions in Britain, to impending evacuations or requisitionings, in such a way as to suggest that he had received his information from agents on the spot, when in fact he had obtained it from reading the British press. Among tales of his omniscience, the most popular one was that he had mentioned the time at which a certain town clock had stopped. A great many statements of this type were never made by him. According to Miss Rebecca West they were part of a whispering campaign by Fascists in Great Britain. Mr Peter Fleming considers they were 'a natural by-product of the human imagination and the human ego, interacting upon each other under stress'. There were, indeed, citizens who, without being evilly intentioned, were temperamentally unable to prevent themselves from making up and passing on good stories.

The Haw-Haw nickname was not really apt. It sugggests the one-time aristocratic habit of interjecting 'haw-haw' into every sentence (the seventh Earl of Cardigan was once dubbed 'Lord Haw-Haw' by a novelist); but while Joyce had arrogance it was not that kind of arrogance. 'Lord Hee-Haw' would have served as well, but Mr Jonah Barrington of the *Daily Express* hit on 'Haw-Haw' and that was that. As for Joyce's accent, readers of *The Times* floundered hopelessly when they tried to identify it (possibly not all were thinking of the same broadcaster). It was 'public school Yorkshire', said one; others thought it bore traces of Edinburgh University, Chicago, Manchester and even Oxford. In fact Joyce was Anglo-Irish, American-born. Many comedians, including the Western Brothers, mimicked his 'Jairmany calling' that winter, but not always with success.

1961

*Gavin Ewart – now one of our most entertaining and fecund poets – served in the war as a young artillery officer. In 'Officers' Mess' he vividly captures the conviviality and the banality of its life. Walter Andrewes, on the other hand, succeeds by depicting the juxtaposition between the boozy camaraderie of the mess and the aching sense of loss it conceals. I think Andrewes improved this poem. When I read it in the war it read: 'And a slightly drunk two-pipper, Who had been in insurance, said'. Clearly, 'travelled in hardware' comes off the tongue better.*

## OFFICERS' MESS

### GAVIN EWART

It's going to be a thick night tonight (and the night before was a thick
     one);
I've just seen the Padre disappearing into 'The Cock and Bull' for a
     quick one.
I don't mind telling you this, old boy, we got the Major drinking –
You probably know the amount of gin he's in the habit of sinking –
And then that new MO came in, the Jewish one, awful fellow,
And his wife, a nice little bit of stuff, dressed in a flaming yellow.
Looked a pretty warmish piece, old boy – no, have this one with me –
They were both so blind (and so was the Major) that they could
     hardly see.
She had one of those amazing hats and a kind of silver fox fur
(I wouldn't mind betting several fellows have had a go at her).
She made a bee-line for the Major, bloody funny, old boy,
Asked him a lot about horses and India, you know, terribly coy –
And this MO fellow was mopping it up and at last he passed right out
(Some silly fool behind his back put a bottle of gin in his stout).
I've never seen a man go down so quick. Somebody drove him home.
His wife was almost as bad, old boy, said she felt all alone
And nestled up to the Major – it's a great pity you weren't there –
And the Padre was arguing about the order of morning and evening
     prayer.
Never laughed so much in all my life. We went on drinking till three.
And this woman was doing her best to sit on the Major's knee!
Let's have the blackout boards put up and turn on the other light.
Yes, I think you can count on that, old boy – tonight'll be a thick night.

                                                                              1942

## MESS

### WALTER ANDREWES

How many, before war-ending,
Good or evil winds? –
How many, asked the young captain,
Leaves or wounds?

I had a friend: they
Tore his gentle flesh.
How many, asked the young captain,
Of us will this war finish?

There was a careful silence
After the captain spoke,
Till the Colonel made things decent
With an indecent joke –

And a slightly drunk two-pipper,
Who had travelled in hardware, said:
Better to die living
Than to live dead.

1943

---

14487348 Green *is better known to us nowadays as the author of the splendid* Art of Coarse Rugby *and many other hilarious books. Then, he was an 18-year-old trooper in the Royal Armoured Corps. His adventures as a recruit, though by no means untypical, are marvellously and minutely recalled here. Being packed so close together that you shaved somebody else's face may be poetic licence but it was not that far from the truth.*

---

## 14487348 GREEN

### MICHAEL GREEN

An old school chum, Alec Ford, who lived near us, joined up the same day as me, although he was a year older. We'd been to Miss Cooke's Dancing School together and served in many a Second XV battle at the Wyggeston. But Alec was more a credit to the school than myself, having set a new record in the mile and taken his Higher Certificate with glowing results. Now he is Professor of Economics at Warwick University and I am godfather to his children. That is the second teenage friend of mine to become a professor. Alec was posted to Northumberland and left on an overnight LMS train. As we said goodbye there was the inevitable feeling we might never meet again, and in fact it was to be nearly three and a half years before we did so.

I returned to the Midland Station next morning to catch the 6.30 a.m. to London. Father insisted on seeing me off, which meant being roused more or less in the middle of the night. He was not a man to catch a train by the skin of his teeth and on most family holidays we arrived in time to get the preceding service. The habit has transferred itself to me. To this day, I never fly to Dublin, Paris or Edinburgh without arriving at the airport as the last call goes up for the flight before.

At St Pancras I took a tube to Waterloo. I'd only been to London three times before – once on holiday with Uncle Will in Osterley, the day Warsaw was bombed in 1939 and once on my day trip from Northampton. The train from Waterloo to Wool, in Dorset, station for Bovington Camp, was crammed. Not just uncomfortably full, like a peacetime train at Christmas, but bulging with servicemen and women. They lay on luggage racks and filled even the guard's van. I felt sorry for the service girls, in particular the ATS. The stupid War Office had issued them with the same canvas kitbags as the men and it was pitiful to see them trying to drag these great clumsy things about, trailing them through the dirt and quite unable to lift them aboard the train. The men helped as best they could, but they might be burdened with full marching kit and rifle, steel helmet and gas mask.

Pressed like a sardine in the corridor, I stood all the way to Dorset, holding a little cardboard suitcase and feeling more and more apprehensive as the train got nearer to Wool. On arrival it emptied. Several hundred soldiers of both sexes poured out and either clambered into lorries or walked up the hill to Bovington Camp, which stood isolated in the middle of the heath. A small group of young men in civilian clothes were left behind – the new recruits. A corporal with a cane walked up and herded us on to lorries. After we reached camp they divided us into huts, gave us a meal, and issued everyone with a number. I remember mine to this day, more than forty years later. It was 14487348, and the 144 indicated I was a volunteer, not that the strength of the British Army had reached 14 million. A nervous cup of tea in the NAAFI (canteen), aware of the mocking glances of the real soldiers in uniform, and then we were ordered to bed.

Next moment it seemed I was awoken by somebody brutally banging the end of my two-tier bunk with a stick and shouting at me. It was the corporal. I shot out of bed, crashing five feet to the floor in my haste, fearful I'd be punished on my first day for not getting up at reveille. I needn't have worried. The corporal had roused us half-an-hour before reveille to make sure we would be ready in time. As reveille was at six this meant it was 5.30 a.m., still pitch dark and a bitterly cold, drizzly morning. We 'marched' in chaos to breakfast and returned to be divided into squads and transferred to new huts. They kitted us out, issued paybooks and blankets and made us tie up our civilian clothes in brown paper parcels for sending home.

At the end of the day the sergeant-major addressed us and said, 'You've left your mother's apron strings behind. I don't want to hear any snivelling. You're men now. In six months' time you'll be fighting Jerries. Now get back to your huts and get that new equipment clean. I want to see my face in those brasses.'

Bovington was the home of the tanks, where the Royal Tank Regiment had been born in 1916, and one of the first monsters stood on a plinth in the camp. The Primary Training Wing for recruits was situated in the old original wooden huts, unchanged since 1916. They were named after animals and birds for some reason and I was in Buzzard. The day began with reveille at six. Like most soldiers I shall never forget the horror of training-camp reveilles. Tired though I was, I was usually woken by apprehension or cold about 5.30 and lay shivering in the unheated and unventilated hut waiting for the agony to begin. The long room was pitch-dark and the windows boarded up for black-out. I was in an upper bunk. For those below was the added fear of waking up covered in urine if the soldier above wet his bed, a permanent hazard in the army. In service units the man above might be drunk; in training regiments the cause was usually the youth of the recruit, who at seventeen or eighteen might not have outgrown childish habits.

That period so much praised by poets, the first sign of day, came about quarter-to-six when the loudspeaker suddenly became live, as the orderly sergeant switched on the public address system in the camp office. He was not pleased at having to get up so early himself and muttering, blaspheming and cursing could be heard *sotto voce*, together with persistent coughing as he lit up a Woodbine. Occasionally he could be heard groaning 'bloody hell' or 'Christ' to himself. At six he cleared his throat with a noise like somebody being sick and shouted: 'Attention! Attention! Reveille! Reveille! Get up! Get up!' With a ghastly, rasping cough he then switched over to music. This was always the American Forces Network, who played Bing Crosby singing 'Would You Like to Swing on a Star' thirty times a day.

There were no pyjamas or sheets and we slept under the regulation four blankets, ingeniously folded to get the maximum thickness between us and the cold, kit piled on top for extra warmth. For night attire we wore the uncomfortable, hairy and collarless shirts issued to rankers in those days. As soon as reveille was announced we leaped out of bed and fought for a shave. King's Regulations insisted every man must shave every morning. Unfortunately the army provided only six wash-basins between eighty men, so we crowded three deep around them, occasionally shaving someone else's face by mistake. To make sure conditions were as vile as possible the army made it an offence to shave at night, because of the risk of getting impetigo off their filthy blankets. Luckily I was too young to need a shave every day. In fact I'd had a special shaving lesson from father just before I joined up, so I'd know what to do.

At 6.30, bleeding from a thousand cuts, we mustered outside in the rain or frost and marched to breakfast. This often contained a special meat known only to the British army: liver, full of enormous tubes. I have never seen liver like it since. It followed me round the army, right through my service. Rumour said it wasn't liver but slices of something more private. This was fried until hard as leather, left to cool, and served on a cold plate with a spoonful of congealing fat. We also had porridge without sugar, bread and a scrape of butter, and tea. There was no choice of food. But it was warm in the cookhouse and we were young and for fifteen blessed minutes you could put your numbed hands round the great pint mug of tea until the corporal marched you back to the hut again.

Back in the hut there was cleaning and sweeping to do. The hut might be freezing, with a coat of ice inside the windows, but we dared not light the stoves because the army insisted they must be cleaned and polished with black-lead before parade every morning. There was no time to do this, and get rid of the ash, so they remained unused except at weekends. Blankets had to be folded in a special way and squared up mathematically, with kit laid out on top, the spare boots sole upwards to show they did not need repair. Some units made soldiers polish the soles of their spare boots but we were spared this. Razor and mess tins would be examined for rust and it was an offence if any was found. At 7.30 we paraded for a day of drill, arms instruction, marching, P.T. and being shouted at.

Not surprisingly the first desertion came after only three days. A thin, dark chap named Lewis, he'd been boasting in the train from Waterloo about what he was going to achieve in the army. Alas, it was whistling in the dark and, on the second day, as the squad lined up for the first inoculations and vaccinations, he fainted at the thought of the needle.

'Drag him in here quickly,' shouted the Medical Officer as Lewis heeled over in the queue, and inoculated him while unconsicous.

Lewis simply ran away, taking no kit. At the time we hadn't been issued with proper battledress and were wearing denim overalls, but he did have boots, beret, gaiters and a greatcoat and dressed in these he caught the train from Wool to seek his home in London. He never had a chance, of course. Waterloo was alive with Military Police and they asked for his pass. He didn't have one and was promptly arrested.

Back at camp, rumours about his fate were rife. He had been shot by a firing-squad for desertion in wartime ('There's a special place in the Guard's Barracks where they do it against a wall'); he was doing five years' field punishment in the dreaded Aldershot military prison; he was being given a compassionate discharge; he'd eluded them all and gone on the run. But two Military Policemen brought him back after three days and he was charged with being absent without leave.

The punishment was lenient – three days' stoppage of pay by Royal Warrant (as they phrased it officially) and a severe reprimand. It was no good, though. The wretched Lewis couldn't face the army and took to his bunk with a mysterious back disorder. He simply lay there all day, staring at the ceiling and hardly talking. The NCOs ignored him. Occasionally somebody brought him food but otherwise he remained like a sick sheep, the outcast of the flock.

One day he vanished. He was lying on his bunk at first parade and when we came back an hour later to change into PT kit he wasn't there. The NCOs refused to enlighten us. 'He's been posted,' was all they said. We never heard of him again, although the platoon was full of theories.

'They come for you when nobody's about,' said the platoon alarmist. 'They come and take you away to a special punishment centre.' I think perhaps Lewis went to hospital. I hope.

Apart from him, nobody succumbed. The unit was specially for Armoured Corps volunteers so all were young and motivated, to use current jargon. A surprisingly large number were public schoolboys and included two Old Etonians in James Hay and Dickie Davidson. That was the unique thing about the wartime services, the mixture of types to be found in the ranks, and I met more Old Etonians (five) in the army as a trooper or private than I have met since, in more exalted circles. I also met more lorry drivers and fitters. The two Etonians made an instant impression of supreme self-confidence. They were afraid of nobody, not even the NCOs. Working-class recruits were suspicious of authority but obeyed it. Middle-class lads had been brought up to both obey and respect it (it was a long time before they could stop us calling even the corporals 'sir' and saluting them). But these boys had been brought up to be authority. They didn't answer back. They didn't need to. The NCOs, themselves experts in judging degrees of power, knew instinctively.

After an afternoon of specially severe bullying by the sergeant on the heath, James Hay once threw a clod of earth at him when his back was turned. We gasped in horror. The whole squad was petrified with fear as the sergeant raved at us. 'I know who it was and I will break him. Who was it? If I don't find out in five seconds the whole lot of you will be court-martialled. I know who it was, so don't think you can hide. . . .' James remained calm and impassive.

'Weren't you scared?' we asked when we got back to the hut, having run all the way as a punishment.

'What of him? You must be joking,' came the reply.

I suppose that's why Etonians used to dominate any British Cabinet, even with a Labour government.

Our immediate CO was Desmond Walter-Ellis, a tall, gangling captain in the Sherwood Foresters, who was unfit for active service because of a back injury. Later he became a well-known actor, appearing in the West End and on films and TV. By a coincidence his ATS girlfriend was to be my secretary twenty years later and marry one of my chums. He spent most of his time organizing the Bovington Camp Dramatic Society and playing all the best parts. A group of us went to see him in *Rope* and had to admit he was very good. He was pleasant and amiable, if somewhat aloof, but unfortunately we saw little of him. Day-to-day instruction was in the hands of a swaggering little sergeant and the corporals of the permanent camp staff. They bullied and chivvied us unmercifully but without much malice and we got to know the corporals quite well. It was Corporal Wilson, our own platoon NCO, who gave me my first practical lesson in sexual morality. Knowing he was married, we ragged him about being seen with an ATS girl.

'Listen, son,' he said, 'it doesn't matter who you see me with, my prick belongs to my wife. That's what the marriage ceremony means.'

While the Archbishop of Canterbury might disagree with Corporal Wilson about the meaning of marriage service, I think it was a much better summing-up of sexual morality than the vague wufflings of my old headmaster, with his talk of mystic communions. Corporal Wilson was lucky to be alive. He'd been fired on at a range of a few feet by a German machine-gun in North Africa and hit in the arm. But he survived to be posted home and tell the tale, doubtless with embellishments, one of which was that he was so near the German he could have reached out and grabbed the barrel of his machine-gun. At least his stories made a change from the First World War anecdotes I'd heard all my life.

The chief agent of torment was the RSM, a huge, red-faced man from the Guards, with a row of medals on his chest. Every morning he took us for an hour's drill on the vast barrack square. His favourite phrase was, 'Strike those rifles!' It was an effort to make our rifle-drill crisp and smart by slapping the weapons sharply as we ordered or sloped arms.

'Strike those rifles!' he bellowed. 'If you break one I'll buy you a new one. But my money's safe. Strike those rifles!'

One of our squad, however, actually did succeed in breaking his rifle. He struck it hard, as ordered, and a bit fell off and tinkled to the ground. I think it was the brass butt-plate. It was too much for everybody and we all burst into laughter, which was quelled by the sight of the sergeant-major swelling like a turkey-cock in rage. He advanced majestically to the hapless soldier and said in a low voice, which would carry about five hundred yards, 'If I thought you'd done that deliberately, son, I would have . . . I would have . . .' words failed him – 'been somewhat displeased.' His powers returned, and he added: 'I would have cut off your balls, son. WHAT WOULD I HAVE DONE?'

This rhetorical question was one of the great stock tricks of drill NCOs. A favourite wheeze was to insult the soldier, and then make him repeat the abuse, thus:

'You stupid, silly little man. What are you?'

'A stupid, silly little man, sergeant.'

'Right. Don't you forget it.'

Eventually, we could translate the shouted commands, which bore no relation to normal English. Thus, although the sergeant-major would refer to a rifle by its proper name in conversation, as part of an order it became a thing called a Hipe.

'Platoon . . . platoon . . . wait for it . . . platoon, slope Hipes! Present

28

Hipes! Order Hipes!'

Mercifully, the RSM's bark was worse than his bite. Jim Chamberlain, who slept in the bunk underneath me, was scrubbing some steps when the RSM walked up them. In his eagerness to stand to attention he jumped up and knocked a bucket of soapy water over the RSM's mirror-like boots. 'Take it easy, son,' was all the RSM said.

An old regular soldier, the RSM claimed to have been an intimate friend of Col. T. E. Lawrence, otherwise Lawrence of Arabia, Trooper Shaw, Aircraftman Ross, legendary figure of World War One and author of *The Seven Pillars of Wisdom*. Lawrence, in one of his periods of self-abasement, was a trooper in the Tanks Corps at Bovington during the thirties, in the same way as he'd joined the RAF as an aircraftman.

''E would come on parade in the morning dressed in filthy overalls,' the RSM said. 'But of course everybody knew 'e was Colonel Lawrence and said nothing. Then one day we 'ad a new second lieutenant to inspect the troop and 'e stops before Lawrence and 'e says. "What's all this, my man, you are filthy." Naturally, we was all horrified at him speaking to Colonel Lawrence like that and the sergeant tried to warn him, but Lawrence replied, "Sorry, sir, I was up late last night." "Up late?" says the officer. "And may I ask you what you were doing?" And Lawrence replies, cool as a cucumber, "I was translating a chapter of one of my books into Arabic, sir."'

The RSM claimed to have warned Lawrence of his death. Lawrence, who lived at Cloud Cottage, near the camp (we passed it on our route marches), was killed when his motor cycle crashed trying to avoid an errand boy. 'I told 'im, "You won't come to no good on that motor cycle, Mr Lawrence,"' said the sergeant-major, '"not the way you ride it." But he just laughed. He was scared of nothing.'

Gradually, almost against our will, we became soldiers, although those of us under eighteen were still graded as young soldiers, which entitled us to half a pint of milk every day, just like schoolboys. If somebody shouted 'You!' we would automatically snap to attention; our rifles, so difficult and clumsy to work with at first, became as familiar as a favourite cricket bat; like dogs we responded automatically to the appropriate stimulus, whether it was a shouted order or a jammed Bren gun.

Recruits weren't allowed out of camp for a fortnight and social life was restricted to a Spam roll (no butter) and a cup of tea in the huge YMCA by the square, or a sausage in the NAAFI, but on the third weekend the troops were adjudged smart enough for a precious day pass. I went to Bournemouth with Jim from the bunk below. We caught a train from Wool and drank a pint of Bass in a small hotel (Jim had worked in a brewery in Birmingham and appreciated good beer). I was still under eighteen and not old enough to be in a pub, but a uniform was a magic passport. Then we had lunch – rabbit stew and lucky to get it in wartime. Afterwards the two of us listened to a concert by the Bournemouth Symphony Orchestra and walked miles along the cliffs and beaches, covered in barbed wire against the vanished threat of invasion. The pier was closed and blown up halfway along so enemy troops couldn't use it as a landing-stage.

Tea was taken at the inevitable YMCA and then another glass of beer before joining the packed crowd of troops at Central Station. While waiting for the overcrowded train, we drank tea out of jam-jars from a WVS stall on the platform, run by a little old lady. On the way back in the train everyone in the compartment sang 'Bless 'em All'.

I couldn't buy a day like that now for ten thousand pounds.

Although as private soldiers we earned only a guinea a week (£1.05), I don't remember being short of money. Even the pitiful wages were raided. Sixpence a week (2½p) was deducted for barrack-room damages, whether the barracks were damaged or not. Another sixpence was deducted for haircut, whether the hair was cut or not. It was shorn by the regimental barbers under a big notice, 'The barber has orders to cut all hair to the regimental style'. This meant shaving it off. They treated customers with all the consideration of a New Zealand sheep-shearer and pleas from arty-crafty recruits to leave a little at the sides were brutally ignored. Other odd sums might be deducted from pay for loss of kit, etc.

Soldiers were expected to cringe for their guinea and a lesson was devoted to teaching the squad how to parade for their pay. The soldier marched in when his name was called and banged to attention in front of the pay clerk and an officer. The clerk then doled out his few shillings. In theory the soldier was expected to check it, but in practice he was told off unless it was immediately scooped up and thrust into his pocket. He then had to bellow, 'Nineteen shillings and sixpence pay correct, sir,' salute, turn right and march out.

The army's capacity for making simple things difficult never ceased to astonish. Even a window couldn't be cleaned without shouting and stamping. At least the formalities of pay parade led to some cash in hand, although recruits seemed to have enough money, mainly because there was nothing to spend it on and we were too young to have developed expensive tastes. A pint of beer was an evening out; I had never drunk spirits in my life and in any case we weren't allowed them.

Absence of sexual desire was a strange phenomenon of these first weeks. This was put down to a cunning wheeze by the army, who were rumoured to doctor the tea with bromide to sedate troops and make them more docile. The Great Bromide Rumour was one of the most persistent of the war and the most widely believed. Yet nobody knew for certain if there was any truth in it. In hundreds of cookhouse fatigues I never saw any bromide put in tea or porridge. While potato-peeling at Bovington, I scoured the cookhouse for traces of bromide, looking for a huge bag labelled BROMIDE – OTHER RANKS FOR THE USE OF, but found no clues. The cooks, who could have settled the whole controversy, were always evasive when asked.

'There's no telling what goes into army tea, mate,' they'd reply.

The cooks probably got a kick out of being mysterious. Thus the fantasy went unchecked and plenty of men will swear they have actually seen bromide shovelled out with a spoon.

However, lack of sexual desire was real enough. An uninhibited group from one hut sat round in a circle trying to get an erection, urged on by their comrades' erotic suggestions. Not surprisingly, they all failed. The male organ is a petulant beast at the best of times and does not like performing in public. I'm sure the real reason for the sexual hang-up was hard work and fear. We were on the go from 6 a.m. to lights out at 10 p.m., frantically changing from PT kit to battledress and to denims as the occasion demanded. In the evenings we had weapons to clean, kit to polish, fatigues to do, letters to write and sleep to catch up on. There was never enough sleep.

Men lived in permanent fear of punishment. Most of the crimes were invented by the army, which had a fiendish trick of making it impossible to obey its own regulations. Typical was the rule that ordered daily shaving and provided six wash-basins for eighty men. Another lunatic regulation said one pair of boots should be highly-polished and the spare pair dubbined. Any fool who turned up on parade in dubbined boots, however, was simply asking for punishment. At times we got the impression the War Office was staffed by people who set out to make life as difficult as possible for the private soldier.

The bromide rumour was only one of many, seized on avidly by barrack-room lawyers. There was a whole series of legends about soldiers' 'rights'. There was someone in every squad who'd advise, 'Don't do it, mate, they've no right to make you do it. It's in King's Regs.' In particular I remember a rumour which said every soldier was entitled to his dinner. 'Your breakfast is a parade and your dinner is a right' ran the fairy-story. Despite encouragement from many a khaki barrister I never dared test this and missed dozens of dinners in the army without complaint. I'm not sorry. The military prisons were full of soldiers who'd stood out for their rights. One difficulty was that soldiers were refused access to King's Regulations, yet were supposed to know them. In the face of this, most of us gave up and assumed we had no rights at all and did whatever the army ordered. I think that was probably what they wanted.

Those who did penetrate to King's Regulations (perhaps some office clerk) told a fascinating story of the contents, most of which were compiled in the previous century, such as the section relating to disobedience of an order. The example quoted was of a man who threw down his rifle on parade and said, 'You may do what you will, I will soldier no more.' He was, of course, immediately to be manacled and dragged away by two comrades. There were many times when we wondered if we dare follow the mythical soldier of KRs and tell the sergeant-major, 'You may do what you will, I will soldier no more.'

The army was much criticized during the war for putting round pegs in square holes, professors of Greek cleaning latrines or skilled engineers rotting at coal dumps. In response to this, the War Office decreed psychological and aptitude tests for all recruits. The squad were interviewed by a bored officer from the Medical Corps who gave us all a bicycle pump in pieces and we had to beat the clock in putting it together. This was the mechanical aptitude test.

I'd never realized a bicycle pump was so complicated before. The room resounded to cursing and swearing as men struggled to get them working. Eventually I got mine together but it wouldn't blow any air out. Others gave off great wheezing and farting noises. A huge Irish lout named Paddy, who'd been a railway porter, broke the shaft of his pump trying to force it down the barrel. Out of thirty pumps, I doubt if half-a-dozen worked. Yet all passed the test. It was my first lesson that army tests were not designed to fail people but to pass them. Otherwise they'd be short of men all the time. Not that the army is alone in this. Thirty years later I took a teacher-training course on which 99 per cent of the students passed, including some of the worst teachers that ever disgraced a classroom.

During those early days I learned something which proved a permanent benefit throughout life. At the time, I was covering my belt with blanco, smearing a block of the filthy stuff with a wet brush to produce a khaki-coloured paste and plastering it all over the webbing equipment. This was known as 'cleaning' the belt, straps and packs, although covering it with dirt seemed a strange way of doing so. In true army fashion, the penalties for not blancoing were dire but no facilities were provided and it was forbidden in the washrooms, so I was kneeling on a path outside the hut in a thin drizzle of rain with a mess tin full of water. There were about ten of us shivering there when one of the soldiers, a tall, rather amusing chap called Mike Luton, started to sing a song. It was a rude version of a popular hit on the wireless at the time, 'Poor Little Angeline', and it was quite the most revolting song I have ever heard in my life.

I devoted the next twenty-four hours to learning it, all fourteen verses. It served me well later, in many a tight social corner, from Bovington to Trieste and Hamburg, and in civilian life at countless occasions. It earned me free meals from grateful army cooks who asked me to sing it and once got me off a serious charge. I was found dozing on guard in Germany but, when the sergeant recognized me, he said, 'I won't say anything about this if you write out all the verses of "Angeline" for me to sing at the sergeants' mess party.' But that was in the future. Then I'd no idea how useful it would become. It just seemed a good way of forgetting the army for a few minutes.

They wouldn't trust us as sentries yet, but we went on fire picquet. The orderly sergeant read out a long list of orders which sounded as if they'd been compiled in the nineteenth century (they probably had). One clause said, 'If any Government property is seen to be blazing the fire picquet will immediately surround it' or words to that effect. The sergeant had just read out something about air raids ('When the alert sounds the fire picquet will immediately put on steel helmets and double to the guardroom') when the air-raid sirens sounded. We started to rush to the guardroom but the sergeant stopped us with a shout.

'Come back, you horrible lot,' he roared. 'I haven't finished yet.'

An aircraft, probably German, droned overhead as he ploughed through the rest of the instructions and then inspected us. By now the camp could have been in flames. Eventually he finished and we rushed off to air-raid stations just as the all-clear went.

Fire picquet provided me with the classic army dilemma. I was listed in orders for fire duty; simultaneously I was down to play rugby. I approached the sergeant, who said the penalty for not parading for fire picquet was death. I went to an officer and he said the penalty for not playing rugby when ordered to do so was also death (I may be exaggerating slightly). Eventually I think I paraded for fire picquet and went straight off to play rugby, where unfortunately the sirens sounded just as I received a pass, so I ran away to the guardroom still carrying the ball.

Meanwhile training went on. We threw live grenades and they taught us to fire rifles and machine-guns. I was a good shot with a Bren and became top marksman in the platoon. We dug trenches, cooked pitiful little meals on fires of twigs, fixed bayonets, marched fifteen miles and repelled gas attacks. In these activities we were supervised by a maniacal sergeant, a strutting little bantam cock of a man, whose megalomania took a theatrical turn at times. His favourite occupation was to take us on a march in which every known military disaster was simulated.

As soon as the squad were out of sight of camp and marching through the desolate waste of Wool Heath, the sergeant would vanish. Suddenly he would reappear from behind a tree, shouting, 'Gas! Gas! I am a cloud of chlorine! What are you going to do? Are you just going to stand there? Get those gas masks out! Too late, you're all dead. You have died horribly.'

The column disintegrated into chaos as we struggled with gas masks and gas capes and, when some sort of order had been restored, we lurched on, wearing those First World War type of masks. But not for long. The next thing would be a shower of stones from behind a hedge and a maniacal shout: 'Grenades! Grenades! You have just run into a fucking German ambush! It's no use trying to take cover, you are all dead! You have been blown to pieces because you wouldn't keep a look-out!'

These crises always ended with us being 'all dead'. The sergeant would never admit anyone could come out alive from his ambushes. There could be up to half-a-dozen crises on the march and we became weary of unslinging our rifles, hurling ourselves behind the hedge and optimistically firing blanks in the general direction of our tormentor, who could simulate anything from shellfire to a Stuka attack. Aircraft were his forte and it was most impressive to see him leap up waving his arms and crying, 'Aircraft! Aircraft! I am a Stuka! You are all dead, I tell you.' With which he would vanish and reappear from some other vantage point, like a pantomime demon, with a new horror: 'I am a tank!

I am a tank! No, you fool, it's no use firing your rifle at me, I am a tank, I have six inches of armour plating. . . .' Sometimes men became confused and put gas masks on when attacked by aircraft or threw grenades when assaulted with gas.

Usually we returned from these expeditions with a few genuine casualties. We were always stabbing ourselves with bayonets, burnt with blank cartridges, deafened by the thunderflashes used to simulate explosions or spraining ankles. Frequently the squad would hobble back to camp looking as if it had just returned from an attack on the Siegfried Line.

A big problem, which dogged my army career, was a tendency to burst out laughing on parade. Laughter among young men is highly infectious and soon the whole squad would be a heaving mass. (How sad that now I am older this tendency has been replaced by a predilection for bursting into tears.) It was never quite certain what would set it off – anything from someone farting in the ranks to a peculiar order.

Once a few of us were fooling around before the officer came and the sergeant-major separated the guilty men from the rest for punishment. When the officer arrived the sergeant-major addressed us: 'Men-who-were-laughing-and-skylarking-on-parade. . . . men-who-were-laughing-and-skylarking-on-parade . . . wait for it . . . slope arms. Men-who-were-laughing-and-skylarking. . . .' But by now we were helplessly doubled up with mirth. Not even the threat of death could have stopped the men who were laughing and skylarking on parade from laughing until the tears came. They did come later. I seem to remember shovelling about ten tons of coal next Sunday morning.

The army taught us plenty of things unwittingly, such as comradeship, or 'mucking in', as the phrase went. When I lost my purse, containing all of ten shillings, Corporal Wilson organized a search-party and when that failed had a collection among the lads to replace the money. Once my razor, laid out on the bunk for inspection, vanished. 'Some bastard has swiped it,' I thought bitterly, but a friend returned it that evening. It was rusty and he'd pinched it to save the sergeant noticing. Better an absent razor than a rusty one. It wasn't all sweetness and light, of course. There were the usual tensions one would get among any group of young men and splits according to social class or character. But we rubbed along well enough. In that I was lucky. Some young soldiers were not so fortunate and found themselves in barrack-rooms dominated by bullies and thugs.

1988

---

*'Naming of Parts' is one of the best-known poems to emerge from the Second World War; it has indeed become a set piece for examinations. Its skill lies in the splicing together of two totally disparate experiences: the banal task of learning how to take a rifle apart, and the heady intimation that spring is coming. The bolt slides rapidly back and*

forth: this is easing the spring. The early bees move backwards and forwards assaulting
the flowers; they call this easing the Spring too.

## NAMING OF PARTS

HENRY REED

Today we have naming of parts. Yesterday,
We had daily cleaning. And tomorrow morning,
We shall have what to do after firing. But today,
Today we have naming of parts. Japonica
Glistens like coral in all of the neighbouring gardens,
    And today we have naming of parts.

This is the lower sling swivel. And this
Is the upper sling swivel, whose use you will see,
When you are given your slings. And this is the piling swivel,
Which in your case you have not got. The branches
Hold in the gardens their silent, eloquent gestures,
    Which in our case we have not got.

This is the safety-catch, which is always released
With an easy flick of the thumb. And please do not let me
See anyone using his finger. You can do it quite easy
If you have any strength in your thumb. The blossoms
Are fragile and motionless, never letting anyone see
    Any of them using their finger.

And this you can see is the bolt. The purpose of this
Is to open the breech, as you see. We can slide it
Rapidly backwards and forwards: we call this
Easing the spring. And rapidly backwards and forwards
The early bees are assaulting and fumbling the flowers:
    They call it easing the Spring.

They call it easing the Spring: it is perfectly easy
If you have any strength in your thumb: like the bolt,
And the breech, and the cocking-piece, and the point of balance,
Which in our case we have not got; and the almond-blossom
Silent in all of the gardens and the bees going backwards and
forwards,
    For today we have naming of parts.

1970

*Advertising in the war met mixed fortunes. On the one hand, it was pointless to encourage a demand for things that were now in short supply; on the other hand, the man in the street had to be shown how to play his part in the war and encouraged when his spirits flagged. So equally did the woman. So a memorable portfolio of wartime advertising soon accumulated. The ad for Rose's Lime Juice stylishly catches the echo of a class structure that was already archaic and neatly conveys the humorous resignation of the island race to the exigencies of war. While Rose's Lime Juice could still be rustled up, the line still held.*

## AUSTERITY HALL

### ROSE'S LIME JUICE

'Good gracious, Hawkins, whatever's gone wrong? You look like a pantomime elephant after a fifty per cent cut in staff.'

*'I'm extremely sorry, Sir. I have not worn these garments for eighteen months. But, seeing you were on leave, Sir, I though it would be more like old times. I had not realized that I had become so – er – svelte.'*

'I appreciate the thought, Hawkins. Home Guarding and digging for victory have certainly wrought havoc with the perimeter of your breadbasket.'

*'I view the matter, Sir, with mixed feelings. Speaking as a butler, I deplore the loss of poise. As sergeant in the Home Guard, however, I find it all to the good. May I carve you a little more Spam?'*

'About two cubic millimetres. Tell me, Hawkins, do you remember the way you carved the ox the night Gerald came of age?'

*'Indeed I do, Sir. I still treasure the account in the local paper. As a matter of fact, Sir, I obtained these garments for that very occasion, and they fitted me like the proverbial onion skin.'*

'So you did. Good party that night, wasn't it?'

*'Indeed it was, Sir. A remarkably good time was had by all. Yet not a single morning-after, as far as I could learn. In those days we were amply supplied with Rose's Lime Juice.'*

'Well, let's be thankful we can still lay hands on the occasional bottle of Rose's. And now, hop along and change into mufti. We'll be able to get in an hour's digging before dark.'

The role of the conscientious objector was by no means always an easy one. If drafted to non-combatant duties with the army, he could end up in far worse physical danger than other front-line troops. If he got on the wrong side of military law and fell into the hands of the military police he could have a rough time indeed. Nevertheless, there was a machinery of tribunals through which candidates for conscientious objection could pass, and roughly four times as many went through it as in the First World War. No such recourse was available to conscientious objectors in Germany; they were clapped into prison.

## WHAT WOULD CHRIST HAVE DONE?

### E. S. TURNER

If the cruder expressions of patriotism were lacking at the start of the war, so was any overt contempt for conscientious objectors; but there was shocked surprise at the way pacifists gathered to rehearse their pleas before mock tribunals. It was clear that objectors were much more highly organized than in the First World War. They tended to form cells and the cells grew, often rapidly.

In the earlier war Britain had some 16,000 conscientious objectors. In the second it had four times that number. Many were adherents of the Peace Pledge Union, founded by the Rev. H. R. L. Sheppard and supported by George Lansbury. The idea of this body was devastatingly simple: if enough people signed a pledge saying they would not fight, war would become impossible. When war came, a good many members forgot their pledges and joined the Colours; which was what the founder of the movement, in his more realistic moments, had forecast.

The Churches, in the main, supported the right of the State to call its men to arms, while insisting that the individual who honestly believed it wrong to shed blood should be allowed to contract out. In the Church of England view, when justice and decency were being obliterated by tyranny a Christian might conscientiously spill such blood as was necessary to overthrow the tyrant. Without the earthly administration and discipline of the State, no one would be able to fight for anything, whether spiritual or material.

Just after the declaration of war the Archbishop of York complained that he had been wrongly reported as saying that it was a Christian's duty to fight. 'No such sentence occurred in my sermon,' he protested. 'On the contrary, I expressly said that I believed some Christians are directly called to be pacifists. I added that this is not a general obligation of Christians; but that to attempt to maintain goodwill, even while using force to check evil, is such a general obligation.'

Dr Temple's biographer says that while disagreeing strongly with the outlook of pacifists, the Archbishop treated them with unfailing consideration. They knew he would resist any attempt to reintroduce the cat-and-mouse tactics of the First World War. . . .

The tribunals began to function soon after conscription came in. Choosing the members was an unusually delicate task for the Minister of Labour and the Lord Chancellor. There were plenty of fire-eaters who would have delighted in the appointment, just as there were plenty of 'liberals' who would have welcomed it for the opposite reason. Mr Ernest Brown, Minister of Labour, told how he approached an eminent individual who said, 'It is a public duty and it is so disagreeable that I cannot refuse to do it.' The rule was that the chairman must be a county court judge or, in Scotland, a sheriff. On the first tribunal to sit, at Birmingham, the judge was supported by a trade union official, an ex-lord mayor of Nottingham, a professor in economics and a former town councillor.

It was open to objectors to bring anyone – a relative, a friend, a schoolmaster, a clergyman, or a Member of Parliament – to assist them to state their case. Many turned up accompanied by their mothers. After the pleas had been heard, the tribunal could take one of these courses: retain the applicant's name unconditionally on the register of conscientious objectors; retain it, on condition that he performed specified civilian work, or non-combatant work in the Forces; or strike it off the register. Once struck off, an objector was required to undergo a medical examination by Service doctors; and if he refused he was liable to imprisonment.

The tribunals' task was, and always will be, an impossible one. No man can say for certain whether another is sincere in his beliefs. An individual is not necessarily sincere merely because he thinks he is. Nor is he necessarily insincere because he holds foolish ideas. The best the tribunals could hope to do was to eliminate the blatant humbugs, the over-rehearsed sophists, the self-evident shirkers and concede the claims of those who seemed genuinely to have 'a call' to be pacifists. The task was not simplified by the fact that the law allowed a man to have a political conscience as distinct from a religious one.

There were complaints, in Parliament and elsewhere, that the tribunals took a carping, bullying attitude, and threw Biblical texts at the heads of objectors as if they were throwing ashtrays. But the tribunals had to probe, and test, and when necessary match guile with guile if they were to reach a fair decision. It is not surprising that, occasionally, chairmen lost their tempers; what is surprising is that they did not lose their tempers more often. Not all the silly statements by objectors were elicited by trick questions; many were voluntarily offered. Sometimes there would be long dialectical battles between the chairman and an objector's legal representative, conducted with every courtesy on both sides; a daunting experience for the abject and inarticulate objectors waiting to put their own cases.

An objector seeking unconditional exemption had to convince the tribunal that he was doing, and would do, nothing to help the prosecution of the war. He might be asked:

Do you eat food convoyed by the Royal Navy?
Are you not compromising when you eat? Do you not compromise at a very convenient point?
Have you made any sacrifices for your conscience? Are you a non-smoker? Do you drink tea?
Do you pay income tax?
Do you realize that by buying even a postage stamp you are helping to prosecute the war?

After being questioned on these lines, an objector who appeared before the Appellate Tribunal for England and Wales admitted: 'There is only one logical solution. A conscientious objector who does not want to help the war must commit suicide.' The chairman cordially agreed: 'I think so, or else leave the country.' Logically, however, an objector could not commit suicide, since that involved taking life. If he went to prison, he was hampering his own country and thus assisting the enemy to wage war. Occasionally an objector would deduct from his income tax or rates a sum proportionate to the amount devoted to defence, as an earnest of good faith (a Harringay man who did so was told by the bench that what he needed was a jolly good hiding).

In the Appellate Tribunal an objector from the Southend town planning department was questioned by the chairman:

Supposing a number of hostile aircraft approached Southend tomorrow morning. Is it your view that no one ought to take any steps to prevent them dropping bombs on the town? – Not steps that would involve taking life.
Can you suggest any other method of stopping hostile bombers dropping bombs other than seeking to destroy them? – Yes . . . by not giving them any reason to come over here in the first place.

In the same court occurred this exchange:

You think that if a large fleet of enemy bombers approached these shores they should be allowed to go unmolested? – Rather than kill the occupants, yes.
Despite the fact that if they came hundreds if not thousands of your fellow citizens in this country would lose their lives? – Yes, because I do not see any difference between my fellow citizens in Germany and my friends in this country.
How do you resist an enemy bomber by non-violent methods? – At first you might have to submit to suffering, but after that the enemy bomber would desist.

Both the above appellants were admitted to the register on condition they undertook work in agriculture.

A self-styled minor poet was able to give the South-Eastern tribunal a striking proof of his integrity. As a GPO night telephonist he had refused to pass on an air raid warning. 'The result was that the siren did not sound and I jeopardized the lives of my kith and kin, among others,' he said. For this he had been dismissed. The tribunal registered him as an objector on condition that he laboured in forestry as well as minor poetry.

Many objectors said they would not tend the wounds of soldiers, even if it meant leaving them to bleed to death. As one of them explained at Norwich, it was God's will that a man trying to take life should be left to die when wounded. This sort of assertion sometimes brought the retort, 'Did not Christ heal the Centurion's servant?' A medical student told the Appellate Tribunal, 'I object to the Royal Army Medical Corps. To get a wounded soldier ready to fight again would be going against my conscience.'

> Do you really mean that as a medical man, if you were properly qualified, you would not help a wounded soldier? – I would not put myself in a position to help a wounded soldier.

In Glasgow an objector who was asked whether he would go to the aid of bombed women and children replied: 'I think it is more important that pacifists should continue to witness for pacifism than even to engage in ARP work.' At the South-East tribunal an applicant said he would help the civil defence to put out a fire, but not if it was a fire in a military establishment. At Carmarthen, a grocer's assistant was asked if he would serve soldiers who entered his shop, and replied that he would not. A Manchester warehouseman said that if called upon to pack and dispatch cigarettes to soldiers he would give up his job. Before the London tribunal, an objector said he would rather take his own life than that of another, but he saw nothing incompatible in working in the War Office.

The objector who professed to be against the use of force in all circumstances could expect to be asked a variant of the famous question of the First World War: 'What would you do if you saw a German about to rape your sister?' One such variant was: 'If you saw a drunken man beating a small child to death what would you do? Would you allow a child to be killed in order to preserve your conscience?' The objector, if he attempted any reply, would probably say that he would try to resolve the situation by peaceful means. In one of the pamphlets issued by the Central Board for Conscientious Objectors occurs the sentence: 'If a man attacks you, the chances are that you can deal with him without causing his death.' But such dealing calls, presumably, for a modicum of force.

Often a tribunal would suggest to an objector that if he disagreed with the taking of life he ought to be a vegetarian. Did he object to killing beetles? Did he get someone else to destroy the rabbits on his farm? A Lowestoft vegetarian obtained unconditional registration after explaining that he had been sacked because he could not bear to handle poultry and game in a kitchen. He had contemplated joining the police but abandoned the idea on hearing that police duties might involve the use of force.

A number of objectors were asked why they carried gas masks if they believed in taking no steps either of offence or defence. Out-and-out objectors refused to allow their families to take anti-gas precautions. At Eastwood, Renfrewshire, a boy was sent home from school daily because his father would not let him have a mask.

When pressed to explain what he was doing towards world peace, an absolutist objector might say that he hoped, by his bearing and testimony, to keep the public mind alive to the evils of war, to prepare an atmosphere in which conciliation would eventually be possible. Some objectors admitted, not necessarily in front of tribunals, that they did not favour agitation for peace at any price; if peace came prematurely it would only be a triumph for panic and selfishness. Yet they denied that they were illogical in refusing to take part in a war while acquiescing in its continuance. The analogy, they argued, was that of two doctors consulting over a patient, and failing to agree on a common source. It was thus necessary that one doctor should be allowed a free hand while the other stood clear; he might yet be called upon to save the patient. Thus, the contribution of pacifists might be in the future. It was to pacifists of this persuasion that the tribunals were apt to put the question: 'Would you allow yourself to be parachuted into Germany with peace terms?'

Tribunals varied greatly in their attitude towards political objectors. It is doubtful whether Parliament really intended to give them powers to exempt Fascists who objected to fighting Fascist states, or Welsh or Scots Nationalists who objected to fighting for Britain, or Socialists who objected to fighting for a capitalist state. Various members of the Independent Labour Party said they felt a sense of unity with the workers of all countries, and that the war, instead of uniting the workers, would only perpetuate their disadvantage. An objector who had served two years in the Spanish Republican Army said his Socialist convictions would not let him fight in the war against Hitler. Sometimes a political objector secured partial exemption, sometimes not. Questions which he had to face included these:

If a Socialist state were attacked by a capitalist state, would you be prepared to defend it?
If you are willing to kill capitalists, why not Germans?
In a democratic state oughtn't you to accept the decision of the majority?
Do you think the Labour Party is the right spiritual home for a person who prefers enslavement to fighting?

A former member of a conscientious objectors tribunal, Professor G. C. Field, has expressed the belief that the only genuine and legitimate conscientious objection on political grounds would have been that of a convinced Fascist, since Britain was avowedly fighting to destroy something that he believed to be good; but his view was not generally shared.

Sometimes the tribunals were confronted by an artistic conscience. 'War is contrary to my nature,' said an unsuccessful objector in London. 'I can speak only in terms of art. Art is international, recognizes no frontiers. War is a negation of the ideals of art. It is essentially national.' A Norwich art student said he hoped to spend the war teaching and lecturing in order to enrich the standard of culture in the world. The tribunal agreed that he should continue to do so.

The numerous pamphlets and leaflets issued by the Central Board of Conscientious Objectors were intended to help persons 'to clarify their own personal grounds of objection'. Obviously, the Board explained, it could not urge one particular attitude as the only true ground of objection, but it could help a man to express himself. There had been many requests for specimen answers to questions. These would not be provided since they might be too exactly repeated and would do the applicant no good; the idea was not to help an objector to get a better exemption than he deserved.

Among questions the applicant was invited to ponder in order to 'clear his mind' were these:

Are you not placing too much confidence in your judgement when national leaders disagree with you?
Did Christ not say, 'Render unto Caesar the things that are Caesar's'?
The Church says that you have a duty to your country. Do you set yourself up against the Church?
Christ's method of dealing with the evil-doer was to threaten him with Hell. Can you state any single instance when Christ won over the evil-doer by love?
What is there in the teaching of Christ that prevents you taking part in the production of food?
Is the life of the Devil sacred?
Why do you object to killing if you believe in the Resurrection?
Are you quite prepared to see the national standard of life extinguished?
Do you realize that other people work while you rant?
Do not the black-out regulations offend your conscience?
Do you regard soldiers as murderers?
Aren't you very conceited?

The Central Board also published information about prison life for the benefit of its less successful adherents. 'You will have no stripes or broad arrows and your hair will not be cropped,' said one pamphlet. 'In your room a chamber pot is provided which is usually carried at the "double" to the latrines in the morning'; and 'during the day you are not supposed to go to the latrines except at parade times.' It was possible to avoid helping the war effort, even in prison, by declining to work on projectile bags and insisting on mail bags.

A tribunal judge who was frequently in the news was Judge Richardson, at Newcastle. One day, he said: 'I am certain, as sure as I sit here, that if Christ appeared today he would approve of this war.' In the ensuing storm of hisses and boos he ordered the court to be cleared and left the bench. Later he expressed regret at having let himself be carried away, but said he was tired of hearing people say that Christ would not stir a finger to help people in uniform. By this retraction, said a correspondent of the *Methodist Recorder*, the judge 'recovered his manhood'. On another occasion an objector appearing before him said he was one of seven brothers of whom six were killed in the previous war. After a moment's silence the Judge said: 'I am one of seven brothers, of whom only two are alive. I lost five brothers in the last war and I have a son going up next week.' When faced with objectors bearing the name of Donald, Cameron and Douglas, he exclaimed, 'Good fighting names!' and said that some of the dead who bore these names would turn in their graves if they could hear the views of modern Donalds, Camerons and Douglases. 'A very improper remark,' was the opinion of a Member of Parliament.

Now and again there were touches of pure farce. At a Lancashire tribunal an applicant slammed the door on leaving the court. The judge, commenting that this objector appeared willing to use force in certain circumstances, directed that this fact be entered in his record. Afterwards the objector wrote to say that he had not meant to slam the door; it had stuck. The apology was accepted and the record expunged. At Caernarvon an applicant said he had been a conscientious objector until the moment he told his wife. 'I would rather be in an armed force for the rest of my life than stay at home with my wife for another month,' he said. His request to be called to the Colours was granted.

1961

*Diana Gardner's story 'The Land Girl' was published in* Horizon, *Cyril Connolly's wartime literary magazine, in December 1940. It catches beautifully the unexpected hazards for the girls who had hardly seen a cow in their life when they were drafted to help the farmers bring in the harvest.*

# THE LAND GIRL

### DIANA GARDNER

I have Jersey cream for breakfast here on the farm. It is thick enough to spread on my porridge. Unfortunately, there is not enough sugar to go with it because of the rationing, which is rather a curse. What I'd like would be oceans of brown sugar crystals of the kind we used to have at my guardian's. As it is, I have to take it surreptitiously when Mrs Farrant goes to the kitchen for the kettle. She's very severe and down on landgirls altogether. She's also against me because I'm a 'lady', or I am when compared with her. She's a hard-bitten, crusty, thin woman and I don't think she and her husband get on particularly well together. She never calls him by his name or anything else, and refers to him as 'Mr Farrant'.

They don't half work the landgirls. You are expected to do a man's work right enough. Not that I mind: it's fun being out in the open all day, even if it is blasted cold. Today we fallowed a field the size of the hall at college and it took five hours. About mid-afternoon Mr Farrant came over and gave me a cigarette. I'm not allowed to smoke at the farmhouse because of Mrs F., so I have one now and again in the fields. It's decent of him to understand. I should say he's a man of about fifty-six, tall, very thin and his face is lined with tiny red veins. He has whitish hair and blue, amused eyes. I wish he wouldn't wear leather gaiters: they make his legs look far too thin.

'We'll make you into a farmer yet, Miss Una,' he said.

I laughed at the idea. If there weren't a war on I'd never be doing landwork. I don't believe I've got the patience. Farming is a dull game: you have to wait so long for things to grow. I like action. It was that which got me expelled from school – I used to sneak into the town to buy sweets after 'lights-out'. I've also got strong feelings, with decided likes and dislikes. Which reminds me, I don't think I'm going to like Mrs F. at all.

There's a thick frost today. Miller, the cowman, says it went down to 27 degrees last night. I was late for breakfast because it was so hard getting out of bed. Mr Farrant was on the farm and Mrs F. was busy in the scullery. It was quite nice to eat alone. I didn't have to be endlessly on my best behaviour. Believe me I was in a rage when I discovered that Mrs F. had left only a teaspoonful of sugar in the bowl for both tea and porridge. Mean old pig! I thought. I'll pay you out. Before I went on the farm I upset my tea over the tablecloth.

Miller was detailed for two hours to teach me how to manage the tractor. When the weather breaks we'll be busy. Miller is a bad teacher, or I'm a dud. I expect I shall understand it in time.

Mr Farrant gave me my lesson this morning. He explains things very well. He took the whole carburettor to pieces and showed me how it worked.

The weather is still mid-winter. Today I felt very bored, going up and down among the cabbages. If the war goes on much longer I shall be sick of this game. Nobody of my own age to talk to, only the farmhands and their wives, and I bet they laugh and imitate me behind my back. To tell the truth I don't feel I'm all that popular, and this makes me seem affected. Am beginning to wonder why I ever came here at all.

This morning Mr Farrant took me in his gig to market. The town looked like a Christmas card by Raphael Tuck: people were climbing the hill bent double for fear of falling on the ice, and one or two women wore red woollen caps with lipstick to match.
    I enjoy going around with Mr Farrant. He's a nice old boy and treats me well. He was shy at first about taking me into the Drovers because he said I was a lady. It was very hot and farmerish in there. I must say I enjoyed drinking a glass of good old brown ale with the locals. These togs, breeches and coat, etc., are very comfortable. Thank goodness I don't bulge out in the wrong places.
    When we got home Mrs F. didn't seem particularly pleased to see us. She spilled my tea pouring it out, so I refused to thank her for it. When she went to lock up the fowls I am afraid I pulled a face at Mr Farrant, but he didn't seem to mind.
    There has been another fall of snow. My room is in the attic and after Mr Farrant called me to get up I lay quite a while looking at it reflected on the ceiling.
    Practically all day I was clambering about with Miller searching for a pair of ewes which have lambed too early. After we'd found them Mrs Miller made tea for us at their cottage. It was the queerest place inside. The 'parlour' was fixed from top to bottom with pictures of the seaside, and china 'gifts', mostly from Brighton. She was very pleasant and had only two teeth in the top front. I wonder what happened to the others. Miller is a robust, earnest sort of fellow, and good-looking, if you like the earthy type.

Mrs Farrant made a scene today. I have come to loathe her.

When I came in I shook off all the snow I could in the scullery before going into the sitting-room. Mr Farrant was doing accounts. I could see she was in a vile temper: her hair was screwed into a tighter knot than ever.

I sat in an armchair and took up the *Daily Mail*.

Presently she looked across.

'Why didn't you take off your boots?' she said.

Before answering I laid the paper down very deliberately, and looked her over.

'Because I've been out all day on the farm and I'm dog-tired. I shook the snow off as I came in.'

'The snow's all over the carpet, and you'll take off those boots,' she said.

She came and stood over me so menacingly that my gore rose.

'My good woman,' I said. 'I haven't taken up farming to be ordered about by you.'

'This is my house and I'll be obeyed in it.'

'No one could mistake that,' I replied curtly, and I admit I looked meaningly at Mr Farrant.

'You'll kindly leave this room,' Mrs F. said. She's certainly got a shrill voice.

'I'm going to, thanks,' I said, and I took the *Daily Mail* with me. As I climbed to my room I brushed off as much snow as I could on the stairs.

When I went down for supper I found Mrs F. had gone to bed. Mr Farrant was quiet all through the meal. I am afraid he was upset.

Mrs F. is scarcely civil when I address her now. She has also taken to giving me small helpings at meals. When I object she refers to the strict rationing. I don't believe it; we live on a farm where there's plenty of food, and I tell her so.

This morning she had taken away the cream and left no milk for the porridge. She was making her bed upstairs.

I must say I wouldn't like to have a wife like Mrs F.

Last night I went to a Temperance Dance with the Millers. Mrs Miller doesn't dance, so I waggled a toe with him. It was a tiring affair. It's hard to get drunk on lemonade. When we got back to the farm after a three-mile walk through the snow, I found that damned woman had locked me out. All the doors were bolted and the place in darkness. I threw snowballs at Mr Farrant's window – they have separate rooms – and presently he came down, looking very sleepy, poor man, and let me in.

As I passed her door her room was suspiciously quiet. I am afraid I made no apology for getting him out of bed. He ought never to have married a woman like Flo Farrant.

This morning when I accused her of locking up the house she had the rotten taste to reply, 'Oh, I thought you'd be out all night.'

'What the hell do you mean by that?' I asked.

I think she was frightened because she did not answer.

'Come on,' I said, 'Explain yourself.'

But she wouldn't.

I'm going to get even with her for this.

I spent the whole of today carting hay for the cattle. I can't help thinking of what that bitch said yesterday.

It's open war between Mrs F. and me in this house now. I don't know how Mr Farrant can put up with it. I talk only to him. Mrs F. and I have put each other into Coventry.

I must think clearly about this evening to know what exactly happened. I admit I did it in an inexplicable, mad moment and I suppose I shall live to regret it, but I do feel Mrs F. is entirely to blame for the atmosphere which has grown up between us.

As it was Sunday she caught the early bus into town and went by train to her mother's farm.

She was gone all day.

At lunch-time Mr Farrant and I got on particularly well together. We laughed a good deal at his jokes and he seemed relieved that she was out of the way, and shy that he and I were alone, which was funny, because around the farm and all the time we are at work he treats me as if I were a sort of refined workman. In the afternoon he dozed, the newspaper over his face and his gaiters off, I was dressed in a frock for a change and feeling no longer a farm labourer.

Over tea we got on still better. I know Mr Farrant likes me quite a lot: I'm sensible and reasonably attractive. I like him in lots of ways. He's friendly and has a sense of humour.

As I poured the tea, sitting in Mrs F.'s chair, I must admit I was glad she was out of the house for once.

But not a shadow of what happened later entered my head at any time during the afternoon. I wrote some letters to one or two of the people I'd met at the agricultural college and amused Mr Farrant with tales about them. He thought they sounded great jokes.

When supper-time came he insisted that he should prepare it.

'After all, we're both farmers,' he said, 'so why shouldn't I get a meal for a change.'

He opened a tin of tongue and made some sandwiches. The tea was dreadfully strong. Afterwards he smoked some of my cigarettes and told me about his youth. He must have been a lad. Why on earth he had to marry Flo Farrant only the stars can tell.

As she was due on the ten o'clock bus, I decided to go to bed before she arrived. Just before nine-thirty Mr Farrant made the fire up and went into the kitchen to make some tea. While he was gone I put the room to rights, and presently he returned with a thermos and laid it on the table.

It was then that something took possession of me. The sight of the old, chipped thermos on the orange tray and his spent, thin shoulders bent over it, caused my dislike of Mrs Farrant to well up into a sudden storm of hatred. I don't remember ever having experienced such rage and no one can accuse me of being sweet-tempered. I felt choked with hatred. As I watched the nape of his neck I gripped the back of a wooden chair so hard that my hands were bloodless. Yet despite the ferocity of this feeling I don't think it could have lasted a second. I relaxed my grip on the chair and sat down.

He looked up alarmed.

'Are you feeling all right?'

'Yes . . . th-thanks,' I stammered.

'Not ill or anything? You're so white.'

'It must be the heat of the room,' I said and pulled myself together. I got up. 'I'm going to bed.'

'Right you are,' he said. 'I'm turning in, too.'

He went into the kitchen and I heard him stoking the Ideal boiler.

Suddenly my brain began to work at a great speed. Now that I think about it I suppose my subconscious had already worked out a plan. My movements became swift and furtive. I went quickly to the door, looked to right and left in the hall and then, as softly as I could, sped up the stairs. The way I knew what to do next was quite peculiar. I went straight to Mr Farrant's bedroom and switched the light on. His bed was over in the corner. I went straight over and lay on it. I even shook off my shoes as I climbed up – a funny thing to do when I had only a few moments to spare. I could hear him moving about downstairs and I knew the bus with Mrs Farrant in it would be arriving at any minute. I lay on my back and rolled about from side to side to deepen my impression in the feather mattress. It very soon became disordered. Then I got up, took off a blue Tyrolean brooch I always wear and laid it beside his brushes on the dressing-table. Grabbing my shoes in my hand I made my way on to the landing and up the stairs to the attic.

Once in my own room I stood with my head pressed against the door, listening for the sound of his movements. I heard him lift the lid of the letter-box and let it drop. He paused by the stairs to wind the grandfather clock.

At that moment I heard the bus. It pulled up and then started off noisily. Mrs Farrant was at the gate.

He climbed the stairs softly. I don't think he heard the bus. As he came to the linoleum on the landing his steps grew louder. He crossed to his room and went in.

Hardly breathing I came out of mine and ran stealthily down the stairs. My eyes must have been fixed and frightening. When the front door handle turned I gave a little gasp: nothing must prevent my plan from succeeding. If I were not wrong, Mrs Farrant would say good-night to her husband before she drank her tea.

I slipped into his room as quickly and quietly as I could. Once inside I appeared to be in no hurry. He stood in the middle of the room in his shirt sleeves. He appeared not to have noticed the state of the bed, and was staring pensively at his feet. He looked up surprised.

'I'm sorry,' I said, and I can't think what I must have looked like, 'but I've left a brooch on your dressing-table.' I spoke slowly. 'It's a little Austrian brooch my guardian gave me years ago.'

I began to play for time.

'Stupid of me to have left it. There it is – on the little china tray' – I heard footsteps on the stairs – in a slightly higher key I said, 'On the china tray, beside your brushes.'

'Oh,' he said, vaguely, and took it up in his hands. He was stupefied and tired. 'I don't quite understand.' He looked down at it in the palm of his hand and then at me. 'How did it get there?'

But I had no need to reply. Mrs Farrant stood in the doorway, her dark clothes part of the shadow in the landing, her face compressed and challenging. She looked at her husband, at the brooch in his hand, at me, and finally at the disarranged bed.

I don't know what I looked like but I can remember a sensation of rising triumph as I met her eyes. He was too befuddled to know what to say and I made no effort to help him.

I waited an age for her to speak, but she said nothing. Her face became completely expressionless. She looked again at the brooch in Farrant's hand and then turned on her heel. We heard her cross the landing to her own room and close the door sharply behind her.

I must confess I didn't know what to do when he turned and looked at me in a bewildered sort of way. I snatched the brooch from his hand and rushed upstairs to my room.

This morning it is still very cold. As I lay in bed unable to sleep, a good deal of noise was going on in the house below. Eventually I got up and stared out at the outbuildings of this blasted farm. Presently, Miller led the pony out and harnessed him to the gig. Almost at once Mrs Farrant piled it high with some tattered luggage. Without saying anything to Miller she climbed in and jerked the reins. The pony moved forward, through the gate and on to the high road, his breath misty in the frozen morning air. I got cold watching her back view until it was out of sight: the thin body and that frightful bun. That was the last I shall ever see of her, thank God.

After that I dressed and went downstairs.

As I went into the kitchen with a jauntiness I was far from feeling, Mr Farrant was making his own breakfast. He looked up with a numbed expression. I had expected reproaches: it put me off my stroke not to get any.

'She's gone,' he said, wearily. 'Nothing I could say made any difference.'

I said nothing.

Here I am waiting for the bus. It's so cold I have to run up and down beside my suitcases to keep warm. I am in my best clothes, but I do not know where I am going or what I shall do. All I am certain of is: I must get out of that house.

After all, I couldn't stay there alone with Mr Farrant. Even though he's been an awful dear to me he's old enough to be my father. And my life has only just begun.

1940

---

One of the most distinctive features of the New Statesman has for many years been its weekly column 'This England', in which it collates and publishes some of the bizarre new items published the previous week in the British press. The selection we publish here gives some slight notion of the political and social extremities of the spectrum evinced then in these islands; incredibly enough, although the compacted chauvinism, xenophobia, insularity and snobbery they convey often beggar credibility, they're all genuine.

---

## THIS ENGLAND

### NEW STATESMAN

THE DIGNITY OF MAN

When I enrolled as a Special Constable I felt that I had at least volunteered for a man's job. From the *Daily Mail* I am surprised and almost disgusted to see that Bolton has just appointed its first woman Special Constable. Is there nothing sacred to man? For my part I shall not attend any lectures or instruction classes at which there are women; in fact, I am considering resigning. – Special Constable, Bolton. *Daily Mail.*

MARRIAGE RITES AT SOUTHAMPTON

When Mr Kenneth George Morgan, a veterinary surgeon, and Miss Dorothy Price were married at Southampton, the 2 cwt. wedding cake was decorated with iced models of an operation on a dog and a calf drinking milk from a bottle. *Daily Telegraph.*

A REMEDY FOR NERVOUSNESS

'One strange thing about my batting,' Lady Baldwin once said, 'was that I was frightfully nervous when I went in. But when I became engaged to Mr Baldwin I lost my nervousness; and in the year I was married I made my best batting average – 62.' *Daily Express.*

FETICHISM IN SOMERSET

Mrs Chamberlain was told that the members of the Burrington (Somerset) Women's Institute were anxious to make a patchwork quilt from shirts belonging to Cabinet Ministers. *Edinburgh Evening News.*

## AUDACIOUS IDEA

The head of the Speaker's Department of the Conservative Central Office, who conducted his 500th class a few months ago, will, it is stated, shortly commence a new series.

The idea that Conservative Members of Parliament should be able to speak their own minds is steadily gaining ground. *Evening News.*

## ENFANTS TERRIBLES

Up to the time of writing the children's prayers have been answered, and the fact that the Russian Pact also has not yet been signed I ascribe to the intercession of St Teresa. I quite understand the annoyance it must cause to you gentlemen who run the world from your printing machines to have your pet theories rudely upset by a pack of children and saints in heaven. Letter in *Picture Post.*

## PEASANT AND PHEASANT

One of the delegates mentioned a case in which cottagers had to drink from a ditch while, on their master's estate, a piped water supply was provided for pheasants. *News Chronicle.*

## GOOD ENOUGH FOR FATHER

Mr T. Belk, Clerk to the Middlesbrough Magistrates: Why have you not sent your child to school regularly?

Mr J. T. Howlett: Because he has no boots.

The Clerk: But you went to school without boots when you were young, did you not?

The Parent: Yes, sir.

The Clerk: Then why cannot your son do the same? It will not do him any harm. *Reynolds News.*

## LITTLE WOMEN

Miss Thora Silverthorne, Secretary of the Association of Nurses, tells the following story:

A matron of one of our leading London hospitals was horrified the other day to discover that several nurses under her charge either had joined the union or were thinking of doing so. So she called her staff together and addressed them.

'You are,' she told them, 'God's own little gentlewomen. And as such you will have nothing whatsoever to do with such horrible ideas as joining a trade union.' *Daily Worker.*

## PEER AT A LOSS

For my own part, I have always found it significant and interesting that the two greatest musical nations in the world, the German and Italian, have both adopted the same form of government.

What is the explanation? I am at a loss to understand it. Lord Rothermere in *Daily Mail*.

BETTER LATE THAN NEVER
I saw half of it (*Pygmalion*) when a beautiful young lady actress was caused to utter the vilest expression I have ever heard in a public meeting – 'Not Bl—dy likely.' I was so disgusted I walked straight out. The film is a disgrace to civilization. I hope you'll do your best to get it taken off. Letter in *Daily Herald*.

WHITEWASH
Sir Nevile Henderson, formerly British Ambassador in Berlin, speaking of Goering at Sleaford (Lincs), last night, said: 'He may be a blackguard, but not a dirty blackguard.' *News Chronicle*.

I REACH FOR MY REVOLVER
The Government gives £50,000 to help wartime culture.
    What sort of madness is this?
    There is no such thing as culture in wartime. *Daily Express* Opinion.

NO DEPRESSION
Sir. – I was surprised to read in the *Daily Sketch* a suggestion that we should resort to deceiving the enemy as regards our weather at home. Would not that be to lower our standard to that of the enemy? – Lover of Truth. Letter in the *Daily Sketch*.

PHLEGM
A ball moved by enemy action may be replaced as near as possible where it lay, or if lost or destroyed a ball may be dropped not nearer the hole without penalty. New golf rule reported in Daily Paper.

SOCIAL STANDING ROOM ONLY
The First Aid Nursing Yeomanry, known as the Fany, is a corps of voluntary mechanical transport drivers who serve their country in times of national emergency. They serve at home or abroad. Members must be British subjects and of good social standing. *Nursing Illustrated*.

STRINGING ALONG
After waiting six days for a passenger boat, Major L. Palmer travelled from Guernsey to Jersey in a Channel mail steamer as a parcel, bearing a label marked OHMS and accompanied by a postman. *Daily Telegraph*.

A MAN'S SOLUTION
There is a simple solution to the cigarette shortage problem . . . . Let women stop smoking. . . . If they gave up the habit their health would be better and tobacco would be available for those for whom Nature intended it. I refer to men. Letter in *Daily Telegraph*.

CHELTENHAM BOLD
Speaking of politics after the war, Wing-Commander Hargreaves said,
'You, the Conservatives of Cheltenham, and the Conservatives of
England, have made England what it is, and you have it in your power to
organize the future. I want you to say to the other parties, "We have
helped you to win this war, but now we are going to run the peace."'
*Gloucestershire Echo.*

1940-6

*Few events in the war carried a more shattering culture shock than the evacuation of
British schoolchildren from the great towns to the countryside. It dawned on the
comfortable middle class that millions of their fellow countrymen and women were living
in those cities in hardly credible squalor. Between 1939 and 1942 the hygiene committee
of the Women's Group on Public Welfare made a study of the conditions and published it
in March 1943. It was a sober document, but it packed dynamite. In a prosaic table, it
showed that just on half of all children examined in the industrial cities had nits or lice in
their hair at some stage: boys mostly at the age of two or three, then gradually fewer as
they grew up, while girls' longer hair, the fad for permanent waves, and the reluctance
therefore to use a comb meant that one in three girls was still infested at the age of
thirteen, and nearly one in five at sixteen.*

## LIVING BELOW STANDARD

### HYGIENE COMMITTEE OF THE WOMEN'S GROUP ON PUBLIC WELFARE

'The Incidence of Head Lice in England'. Dr Mellanby was led by his
observation of children admitted to hospitals, mainly for infectious
diseases, to believe that the rate of verminous infestation was far higher
than that shown by the reports of the Medical Officers for the schools
from which they came. The Board of Education therefore paid the
expenses of an enquiry in ten industrial cities (including six with a
population of over 400,000) and rural areas in four southern counties.
The sample is not entirely representative of the population of the area
served as it contains a more than average proportion of young children
from poor and overcrowded homes. Dr Mellanby considers, however,
that in view of the relatively small size of the more prosperous classes in
a city, his results are accurate to the extent of some eighty per cent. He
observes that ascertainment in hospital is particularly thorough, patients
being disinfested lest they be said to have picked up vermin there.

## INFESTATION WITH HEAD LICE IN TEN INDUSTRIAL CITIES.

| A. Males. | | | | | B. Females. | | | | C. Both Sexes. |
|---|---|---|---|---|---|---|---|---|---|
| | | % Infested. | | Total % | | | % Infested. | Total % | % Males |
| Age. | Total No. | Nits. | Lice. | Males infested. | Total No. | Nits. | Lice. | Females infested. | and Females infested. |
| Under 1 | 1,876 | 5·9 | 5·1 | 11·0 | 1,425 | 6·4 | 5·9 | 12·3 | 11·6 |
| 1 | 2,229 | 17·7 | 17·9 | 35·6 | 1,981 | 19·9 | 19·5 | 39·4 | 37·4 |
| 2 | 2,126 | 22·3 | 22·3 | 44·6 | 1,928 | 22·2 | 27·2 | 49·5 | 46·9 |
| 3 | 2,035 | 20·9 | 21·5 | 42·5 | 2,027 | 23·8 | 27·2 | 51·0 | 46·9 |
| 4 | 1,890 | 20·8 | 18·7 | 39·6 | 1,890 | 23·1 | 26·6 | 49·7 | 44·7 |
| 5 | 2,103 | 18·2 | 16·6 | 34·9 | 2,161 | 24·8 | 26·5 | 51·3 | 43·1 |
| 6 | 1,681 | 16·6 | 17·5 | 34·2 | 1,768 | 22·4 | 24·4 | 46·8 | 40·6 |
| 7 | 1,326 | 13·0 | 16·5 | 29·6 | 1,521 | 22·7 | 27·4 | 50·2 | 40·6 |
| 8 | 1,156 | 14·5 | 16·2 | 30·8 | 1,328 | 20·6 | 29·5 | 50·1 | 41·1 |
| 9 | 934 | 16·7 | 13·2 | 29·9 | 1,087 | 22·4 | 27·9 | 50·3 | 40·8 |
| 10 | 865 | 12·9 | 13·5 | 26·5 | 1,035 | 21·6 | 30·0 | 51·6 | 40·2 |
| 11 | 769 | 9·7 | 14·2 | 23·9 | 850 | 20·5 | 30·7 | 51·2 | 38·2 |
| 12 | 630 | 13·3 | 15·4 | 28·7 | 716 | 19·2 | 29·7 | 48·9 | 39·4 |
| 13 | 546 | 8·2 | 13·2 | 21·4 | 574 | 17·1 | 27·6 | 44·7 | 33·1 |
| 14 | 412 | 9·4 | 9·9 | 19·4 | 453 | 14·5 | 25·8 | 40·4 | 30·4 |
| 15 | 369 | 7·6 | 7·3 | 14·9 | 422 | 11·1 | 25·4 | 36·5 | 26·4 |
| 16 | 222 | 3·6 | 3·6 | 7·2 | 325 | 8·7 | 17·8 | 26·5 | 18·6 |
| 17 | 220 | 2·2 | 4·5 | 6·8 | 410 | 7·8 | 10·7 | 18·5 | 14·4 |
| 18 | 234 | 0·8 | 0·8 | 1·6 | 418 | 3·3 | 6·3 | 9·6 | 6·7 |
| 19–20 | 455 | 0·6 | 0·9 | 1·5 | 731 | 5·7 | 5·6 | 11·3 | 7·6 |
| 21–30 | 1,375 | 0·9 | 0·6 | 1·5 | 2,226 | 3·4 | 5·2 | 8·6 | 5·8 |
| 31–40 | 655 | 0·8 | 1·8 | 1·8 | 1,095 | 4·4 | 3·9 | 8·3 | 6·0 |
| 41–50 | 377 | 1·0 | 0·9 | 1·9 | 460 | 3·4 | 4·4 | 7·8 | 5·1 |
| 51–60 | 382 | — | 0·3 | 0·3 | 341 | 3·2 | 2·6 | 5·8 | 2·9 |
| 61–70 | 274 | 0·4 | 0·7 | 1·1 | 231 | 3·0 | 4·0 | 7·0 | 3·8 |
| 70 up | 146 | — | 0·7 | 0·7 | 133 | 2·2 | 2·2 | 4·5 | 2·5 |

1943

# THE FINEST SIGHT
# IN THE WORLD

Of all the accounts of Dunkirk, few are more vivid than John Austin's. It is the small detail which counts: the sadness at the loss of their prize theodolite; the major's reluctance to lose his suitcase, and the sleep that came to him as soon as he had done so; and the most beautiful sight in the world – Ramsgate.

Yet everything in John Austin's story is within the framework of some rough discipline and order. The account of the same catastrophe as told by Harry in Virginia Woolf's diaries is a different kettle of fish altogether. Here we have a thoroughgoing defeatist: Harry has had enough of war and is certain of defeat. He has also taken part in the looting of a Belgian shop. Not very admirable; and of course his story is filtered through Virginia Woolf's testimony, which may or may not have distorted it. Whichever, Harry rejoined his regiment and fought with it throughout the rest of the war.

Meantime Harold Nicolson, writing to his wife, Victoria Sackville-West, was recording the same momentous days from the corridors of power. (He was parliamentary secretary to the Minister of Information, Duff Cooper.) He had little illusion about his own fate should the Germans invade England, and he thought in terms of the 'bare bodkin' which would have enabled Hamlet to make his quietus. And yet, despite all the horror, he feels curiously light-hearted. And then there's Winston Churchill to hear in the House of Commons making what Nicolson calls the finest speech he ever heard. This of course was 'We shall fight on the beaches'.

## RETURN VIA DUNKIRK

### JOHN AUSTIN

We were now in the region of the dunes, which rose like humps in a deeper darkness. And these in their turn were dotted with the still blacker shapes of abandoned vehicles, half-sunk in the sand, fantastic twisted shapes of burned-out skeletons, and crazy-looking wreckage that had been heaped up in extraordinary piles by the explosions of bombs. All these black shapes were silhouetted against the angry red glare in the sky, which reflected down on us the agony of burning Dunkirk.

Slowly we picked our way between the wreckage, sinking ankle-deep in the loose sand, until we reached the gaunt skeletons of what had once been the houses on the promenade. The whole front was one long continuous line of blazing buildings, a high wall of fire, roaring and darting in tongues of flame, with the smoke pouring upwards and disappearing in the blackness of the sky above the roof-tops. Out seawards the darkness was as thick and smooth as black velvet, except for now and again when the shape of a sunken destroyer or paddle-steamer made a slight thickening on its impenetrable surface. Facing us, the great black wall of the Mole stretched from the beach far out into sea, the end of it almost invisible to us. The Mole had an astounding, terrifying background of giant flames leaping a hundred feet into the air from blazing oil tanks. At the shore end of the Mole stood an obelisk, and the high explosive shells burst around it with monotonous regularity.

Along the promenade, in parties of fifty, the remnants of practically all the last regiments were wearily trudging along. There was no singing, and very little talk. Everyone was far too exhausted to waste breath. Occasionally out of the darkness came a sudden shout:

'A Company, Green Howards. . . .'

'C Company, East Yorks. . . .'

These shouts came either from stragglers trying to find lost units, or guides on the look-out for the parties they were to lead on to the Mole for evacuation.

The tide was out. Over the wide stretch of sand could be dimly discerned little oblong masses of soldiers, moving in platoons and orderly groups down towards the edge of the sea. Now and again you would hear a shout:

'Alf, where are you? . . .'

'Let's hear from you, Bill. . .'

'Over this way, George. . .'

It was none too easy to keep contact with one's friends in the darkness and amid so many little masses of moving men, all looking very much alike. If you stopped for a few seconds to look behind, the chances were you attached yourself to some entirely different unit.

From the margin of the sea, at fairly wide intervals, three long thin black lines protruded into the water, conveying the effect of low wooden breakwaters. These were lines of men, standing in pairs behind one another far out into the water, waiting in queues till boats arrived to transport them a score or so at a time, to the steamers and warships that were filling up with the last survivors. The queues stood there, fixed and almost a regular as if ruled. No bunching, no pushing; nothing like the mix-up to be seen at the turnstiles when a crowd is going into a football match. Much more orderly, even, than a waiting theatre queue.

About this time, afraid that some of our own men might be tailing off, I began shouting: '2004th Field Regiment . . . 2004th Field Regiment. . . .' We were also having difficulty in finding our report centre.

'I wonder where this blasted report centre is,' said the Major. 'Give another shout. If they hear us they can shout back instructions and tell us what to do.'

So from this point I went along shouting. But the report centre failed to materialize, and soon we decided that hanging about any longer on the promenade looking for it might prove disastrous. Heavy shells commenced crashing into the tops of the ruined buildings along the promenade, bringing down heaps of brick and masonry almost on our heads.

'It'll be healthier on the beach,' said the Major.

A group of dead and dying soldiers on the path in front of us quickened our desire to quit the promenade. Stepping over the bodies we marched down the slope on to the dark beach. Dunkirk front was now a lurid study in red and black; flames, smoke, and the night itself all mingling together to compose a frightful panorama of death and destruction. Red and black, all the time, except for an occasional flash of white low in the sky miles away to the left and right where big shells from coastal defence guns at Calais and Nieuport were being hurled into the town.

Down on the beach you immediately felt yourself surrounded by a deadly evil atmosphere. A horrible stench of blood and mutilated flesh pervaded the place. There was no escape from it. Not a breath of air was blowing to dissipate the appalling odour that arose from the dead bodies that had been lying on the sand, in some cases for several days. We might have been walking through a slaughter-house on a hot day. The darkness, which hid some of the sights of horror from our eyes, seemed to thicken this dreadful stench. It created the impression that death was hovering around, very near at hand.

We set our faces in the direction of the sea, quickening our pace to pass through the belt of this nauseating miasma as soon as possible.

'Water . . . Water. . . .' groaned a voice from the ground just in front of us.

It was a wounded infantryman. He had been hit so badly that there was no hope for him. Our waterbottles had long been empty, but by carefully draining them all into one we managed to collect a mouthful or two. A sergeant knelt down beside the dying man and held the bottle to his lips. Then we proceeded on our way, leaving the bottle with the last few drains in it near the poor fellow's hand so that he could moisten his lips from time to time.

On either side, scattered over the sand in all sorts of positions, were the dark shapes of dead and dying men, sometimes alone, sometimes in twos and threes. Every now and then we had to pull ourselves up sharply in the darkness to avoid falling over a wooden cross erected by comrades on the spot where some soldier had been buried. No assistance that availed anything could be given to these dying men. The living themselves had nothing to offer them. They just pressed forward to the sea, hoping that the same fate would not be theirs. And still it remained a gamble all the time whether that sea, close though it was, would be reached in safety. Splinters from bursting shells were continually whizzing through the air, and occasionally a man in one of the plodding groups would fall with a groan.

The darkness, as I have said, was mercifully saving us from many a spectacle of horror. Moreover it was saving us from the additional danger of bombing. Seeing as much as we did see gave us every reason for thanking God that we had come down to the beach at night, and not in the daytime. There was still another dread haunting us. Should we be able to get off the beach before dawn discovered us, and those waves of German bombers that we had watched the previous day diving over Dunkirk had us for a target?

'I'm not too comfortable in my mind about things,' Boyd muttered to me as we proceeded along.

Comfortable! Were any of us?

I stepped over the corpse of a man who had been killed just as he was trying to take cover in a shallow depression he had evidently been frantically digging when the bombers appeared. He had flung himself forward flat on his face towards it, and half his body only lay in the saucer-like grave. The dry sand was slipping down from the sides in little streams, gradually burying his head.

Comfortable in my mind? I should think not. If I had been inclined to laugh at anything just then, it would have been at Boyd's colossal understatement.

On we trudged, occasionally passing a slightly wounded man who limped along supported by a comrade on either side. All the time shouts of people identifying one another broke the silence. I, too, was now continually shouting: '2004th Field Regiment.... 2004th Field Regiment....'

We came at last to the water's edge, where the wreck of a dive bomber, standing up on its nose like a war memorial, bore somewhat of the aspect of a happy augury. Along the margin of the sea, a little way out, could be distinguished at intervals the hulls of bombed rescue vessels – tugs, drifters, a destroyer, a hospital ship, and several lifeboats.

'We'll have a rest here,' said the Major. And the suggestion was very welcome to all of us. Particularly so to me, for I had marched the whole of the way in my greatcoat, which I was determined not to lose if I could possibly save it. The ACPO was similarly burdened, and had other woes, of which more anon. The CPO was giving, for some reason I have never quite been able to fathom, a very creditable impression of a padre on tour. It may have been the haversack slung across his shoulders. It may have been his big walking-stick. A bit of a mystery, but there it was. The Major, greatly daring, had encumbered himself with a suitcase. Of which, also, more anon.

We were now close to the Mole on the beach. While we rested Boyd and the CPO decided to walk a little farther on, in a last attempt to discover something about our report centre. The ACPO leaned wearily against me.

'Do you know,' he said, in an almost heart-broken tone, 'I think I shall have to part with Theo the Dolite after all. I had to admit it, but he's too much for me.'

I found nothing comic in the ACPO's grief. I understood what he was suffering. The ACPO had developed a fond affection for the Battery's theodolite, a very valuable instrument. No other theodolite in the army could stand up against this, in the ACPO's estimation. He had bestowed on it a pet name, Theo the Dolite, and never referred to it in any other terms. When the Battery was liquidated he had taken Theo under his protection, determined at all costs that it should not be left behind. No, not if he had to carry it all the way to England himself. Which was a valiant decision, in the circumstances. For the theodolite represented the weight of a well-filled suitcase.

'I'm sorry, very sorry, old fellow,' I said. 'But you've done your best.'

'Yes. I can't go on with it,' he replied mournfully.

He rose, and I watched him walk over to the water's edge, pause for a second or two, and then drop Theo the Dolite into the water. He let it fall gently so that it made hardly a splash. It was too dark to see his face when he returned, but it would never surprise me to learn that he had tears in his eyes.

In a quarter of an hour Boyd and the CPO returned. They had had no luck.

'In any case,' said the Major, 'I don't like the look of the Mole. You saw the shelling going on at the land-end. They know it's packed with troops waiting to be taken off. It's sure to get a bad time.'

To all of which we heartily agreed.

'Shall we try to get off from the beach?' said the Major. 'Wade into the water, and take our chance in one of the queues? That's my idea.'

No one had any criticism of this proposal to offer. It fitted in with the fears and desires of each one of us. After another five minutes' rest we stood up, fell-in the men, and led them down to the water's edge.

We tacked ourselves on to the rear of the smallest of the three queues, the head of which was already standing in water up to the waist. Half an hour passed. Suddenly a small rowing boat appeared. The head of the queue clambered in and were rowed away into the blackness. We moved forward, and the water rose to our waists.

Our only thoughts now, were to get on a boat. Along the entire queue not a word was spoken. The men just stood there silently staring into the darkness, praying that a boat would soon appear, and fearing that it would not. Heads and shoulders only showing above the water. Fixed, immovable, as though chained there. It was, in fact, practically impossible to move, even from one foot to another. The dead-weight of waterlogged boots and sodden clothes pinned one down. My breeches seemed to be ballooned out with water as heavy as mercury. I was filled with a dread that when the time did come I should be unable to move. Every now and then as we stood there rooted in the sea, a slight swell stirred the surface and the water rose to my chest, and up to the necks of the shorter men. We thanked Heaven that the night was calm. Had there been a strong breeze blowing the swell would have swamped us and, I suppose, many of us would have been drowned, for we were too exhausted to make any struggle against a heavy sea.

We glued our eyes in the direction whence was to come our salvation. Another lifeboat appeared but it halted at the head of the queue on our right. Enviously we watched as it filled up.

'Not too many on one side or you'll have her over,' came the cry.

Off went the boat, and again we resumed our vigil. Minutes became hours; and hours an eternity. After a long while we were attacked by a horrible dread that there would not be any more boats. That we should stand there half submerged in water throughout the night, and then, after all, have to spend the day on the beach. A leaden depression seized us, and our hearts became as heavy as our waterlogged bodies. The weariness of the wait was appalling. Try as we could we found it impossible to keep our eyes open. Half of us were asleep standing up. And every one of us kept waking with a start out of the sort of coma that descended on us.

The ACPO, standing beside me, suddenly turned his head towards me and nodded significantly. It was as if he read the thought that was passing in my own mind. I nodded back. The time had come for another sacrifice.

The ACPO and I had indulged ourselves in two expensive rain-proof map cases. We took great pride in these possessions, and clung on to them to the end. And now the end had come. In our exhausted state they seemed to weigh a ton. We hadn't the strength to carry them another minute.

We looked at one another mournfully, the ACPO and I. Then simultaneously we tossed our burdens into the water, without saying a word. They floated off, half-submerged, till they were swallowed up in the darkness. Almost at the same moment I heard a splash behind me. Half-turning I was just in time to see the Major's suitcase disappear beneath the water. He, too, had had to give in. And now, without the consciousness of the struggle to retain it to keep him awake, he immediately closed his eyes and began to fall asleep.

During all this time the German shells continued to rain upon the town. Stray hot splinters flew round our heads, hissing as they fell into the water. Still Dunkirk showed its long flaming front behind us. The red glare in the sky extended over us. Along the Mole, a quarter of a mile to our left crept the tiny figures of the soldiers being evacuated by the ships. Little black figures, silhouetted against red fire.

Ages passed – ages as one measured time in those fateful minutes. We began to give up hope of a boat. Our tired eyes hurt from straining to pierce the darkness.

Suddenly out of the blackness, rather ghostly, swam a white shape which materialized into a ship's lifeboat, towed by a motor-boat. It moved towards us and came to a stop twenty yards in front of the head of our queue.

'Hi! Hi!' we all hailed, dreading they hadn't seen us.

'Ahoy! Ahoy!' came the lusty response.

'Come in closer,' we shouted.

'We can't. It's unsafe. Might upset the boat.'

But they risked a few more yards.

There was a slight hesitation at the head of the queue. As I have said, the water already stood above our waists. So fearful was I that the boat might move off and leave us that I struggled to the head of the queue and waded forward crying: 'Come on the 2004th!' That set everyone moving, and soon I was caught up and passed.

Higher rose the water every step we took. Soon it reached my armpits, and was lapping the chins of the shorter men. The blind urge to safety drove us on whether we could swim or not. Our feet just maintained contact with the bottom by the time we reached the side of the boat.

Four sailors in tin hats began hoisting the soldiers out of the water. It was no simple task. Half the men were so weary and exhausted that they lacked strength to climb into the boat unaided. The sailors judged the situation perfectly, as being one for rough words, threats, and bullying methods. The only spur sufficient to rouse our worn-out bodies to one last supreme effort.

'Come on, you bastards . . .'

'Wake up, blast you . . .'

'Get a move on, Dopey . . .'

The gunwale of the lifeboat stood three feet above the surface of the water. Reaching up, I could just grasp it with the tips of my fingers. When I tried to haul myself up I couldn't move an inch. The weight of my waterlogged clothes, especially my cherished greatcoat, beat me completely, desperately though I fought. I might have been a sack of lead. A great dread of being left behind seized me.

Two powerful hands reached over the gunwale and fastened themselves into my armpits. Another pair of hands stretched down and hooked on to the belt at the back of my greatcoat. Before I had time to realize it I was pulled up and pitched head-first into the bottom of the boat.

'Come on, you b----- . Get up and help the others in,' shouted a sailor, as I hit the planks with a gasp.

It was all rough medicine. But the right medicine for the moment.

The boat was now getting crowded. I wondered who else of our party had made it. I shouted the Major's name. There was no reply. 'Boyd,' I shouted, and from somewhere in the darkness he answered. The ACPO replied: 'Here I am' from my very elbow. I continued shouting names of men. The good proportion of responses gladdened me.

The moment came when the lifeboat could not hold another soul.

'Carry on, Mr Jolly. Carry on,' cried the sailor at our helm to someone in the motor-boat.

And we got under way, leaving the rest of the queue behind to await the next boat.

From the very instant I landed on my head in that lifeboat a great burden of responsibility seemed to fall from my shoulders. A queer sense of freedom took possession of me. All the accumulated strain of the last few hours, of the last day or so, vanished. I felt that my job was over. Anything else that remained to be done was the Navy's business. I was in their hands, and had nothing more to worry about. There and then, on that dark and sinister sea, an indescribable sense of luxurious contentment enveloped me.

Again the hearty voice of our helmsman:

'Little bit more to the left, Mr Jolly. Little bit more to the left. Or we'll hit her in the backside.'

The unseen Mr Jolly so contrived as to avoid this disaster, and the grey flank of HM Medway Queen, paddle-steamer, loomed in front of us, her shadowy decks already packed with troops from the beaches. In a minute or two our boatload was submerged in the crowd.

Boyd, the ACPO and myself managed to keep together, and a little later who should appear but the Major.

'Pleased to see you got in, Major,' I said. 'I called your name, but there was no answer.'

'Who else got away?'

I gave him all the names I had.

'By the way,' he said, 'I've just been informed that our battery was the last battery in the BEF to come out of action.'

For some while now, ever since I entered the lifeboat, I had forgotten Dunkirk. Such thoughts as I did possess were monopolized by England. The Major's words swung my mind back again for a moment. I gazed beyond the stern of the vessel, back to that dreadful strip of shore from which I had been snatched to safety. There it was. One long line of flame on the horizon, suffusing the dark sky with its dull red, angry glare. Tortured, martyred Dunkirk . . .

'Let's go down to the wardroom,' said the Major, and passing stretcher-loads of wounded we stumbled along to a small compartment, thick with officers, and even thicker with an air you could cut with a knife. They were sitting around smoking ship's cigarettes, and munching ship's chocolate and meat sandwiches. Of the sixty or so, most were in various stages of dishevelment. One had nothing on except a towel; another wore clothes borrowed from a seaman. A Guards staff officer with a large gash in his tin helmet informed me that he had been on the beach for seven complete days organizing the embarkation.

'By George!' exclaimed the Major in the middle of this fog. 'How I could do with a drink.'

Somebody overheard and handed him a water-bottle. The Major put it gratefully to his lips and, thinking it was water, tossed his head back to take a long draught. He jerked his head back again even quicker, coughing and spluttering. It was rum.

The ACPO and I sat squeezed together on the settee that ran along the whole length of the wardroom, his head pillowed on my chest, mine on his shoulder. In the hot atmosphere our sopping clothes already emitted quite respectable clouds of steam. Irresistible drowsiness seized us.

Dimly-heard scraps of the conversations going on around penetrated my doze.

'Was he at Arras? . . .'

'Wish I could get my socks off . . .'

'Got a cigarette, old boy? . . .'

'The 1st Battalion took a bad knock . . .'

And then it was the ACPO's voice speaking peevishly, as it seemed, from my own chest:

'You needn't have put your foot in my eye when I was helping you into the boat . . .'

And Boyd in protest: 'Could I help my foot slipping? . . .'

Then no more voices.

'We're going into harbour!'

Not one voice, but the whole wardroom seemed to be shouting it.

The ACPO and I woke with a combined jerk. Everyone was streaming towards the deck in a great bustle and commotion. We jammed on our tin hats and pushed our way along with them.

It was a beautiful sunny June morning. Not a speck of cloud in the blue sky. And there in the pearly light that a slight haze created we saw the finest sight in the world.

'Ramsgate!' I exclaimed.

'England,' murmured the ACPO.

'And beds to sleep in!' I said.

1947

---

# THE DIARY OF VIRGINIA WOOLF

## VOLUME 5: 1936–41

Thursday 20 June 1940

London diary: just back; & dinner so close & events so crowded that I must abstract. The French stopped fighting: whats to become of me? Offered a Roumanian bookshop. Then what about Press? KM [Kingsley Martin] after dinner. Now we suffer what the Poles suffered. Fight in our fortress: are conquered: I have my morphia in pocket . . . . Ch[urchi]ll broadcasts. Reassuring about defence of England; not all claptrap. Now we're fighting alone first, then invasion . . . . Monday ended in charcoal gloom. KM says we must & shall be beaten. He says perhaps 4 more numbers of NS [The *New Statesman*, which Kingsley Martin edited] will come out.

Here, as soon as we begin bowls, Louie [her maid of all work] comes agog. Harry [Louie's brother] came back on Monday. It pours out – how he hadnt boots off for 3 days; the beach at Dunkirk – the bombers as low as trees – the bullets like moth holes in his coat – how no English aeroplanes fought; how the officer told them to take their shoes off & go past a pill box on all fours. Then went himself with a grenade & blasted it. At Dunkirk many men shot themselves as the planes swooped. Harry swam off, a boat neared. Say Chum Can you row? Yes, he said, hauled in, rowed for 5 hours, saw England, landed – didn't know if it were day or night or what town – didnt ask – couldn't write to his mother – so was despatched to his regiment. He looted a Belgian shop & stuffed his pockets with rings, which fell out in the sea; but 2 watches pinned to his coat survived: one is chased, & chimes. Mrs [Louie] Everest has them. He saw his cousin dead on the beach; & another man from the street. He was talking to a chap, who showed him a silk handkerchief bought for his joy lady. That moment a bomb killed him. Harry took the handkerchief. Harry has had eno' war, & is certain of our defeat – got no arms & no aeroplanes – how can we do anything?

## DIARIES AND LETTERS 1939–1945

### HAROLD NICOLSON

H.N. TO V.S.-W.                                                    22 May 1940
                                                        Ministry of Information

Of course we hope to pinch out the German bulge and throw them back from the Channel. They are not there in strength and we have already retaken Arras. I don't know whether the Government have prepared any scheme for evacuation, but you should think it out and begin to prepare something. You will have to get the Buick in a fit state to start with a full petrol-tank. You should put inside it some food for 24 hours, and pack in the back your jewels and my diaries. You will want clothes and anything else very precious, but the rest will have to be left behind. After all, that's what the French did in 1915 and we have got to do it ourselves. I should imagine that the best thing you can do is to make for Devonshire. This all sounds very alarming, but it would be foolish to pretend that the danger is inconceivable.

V.S.-W. TO H.N.                                                   23 May 1940
                                                                Sissinghurst

The only nice thing that comes out of the war is that we now have a guard on top of the tower. In a steel helmet and rifle he looks most picturesque in the moonlight over the parapet. Ozzy [A.O.R. Beale, tenant farmer of the farm at Sissinghurst Castle, where the Nicolsons lived] is in command of the local squad of Volunteer Defence [Local Defence Volunteers, later the Home Guard]. They have got 32 from Sissinghurst village. Not bad.

V.S.–W. TO H.N.                                                  24 May 1940

Ozzy came here yesterday with the officer in charge of all the searchlights in this district. He wanted to inspect the country from the top of the tower. He was very frank. It is not only parachutes that they are afraid of, but troop-carrying 'planes landing on our fields. If this happens, our tower-guard rushes downstairs, informs Ozzy who telephones, and shock-troops arrive. They have pickets all over the district. The young officer was obviously longing for German 'planes to choose Sissinghurst or Bettenham to land on. I wasn't so sure that I shared his longing. Nor was Ozzy. 'My wheat . . .,' he remarked ruefully.

H.N.'s DIARY                                                              24 May 1940

Up to Leicester where there is a huge dinner of the 1936 Club. I get an excellent reception and find that their morale is very good. It is not mere complacency, since I give them a test question to vote on, namely, 'Should the Derby be put off?' They voted some 88 per cent in favour of postponement. I notice the rather dangerous anti-French feeling and the belief that the French Army has lost its morale.

H.N.'s DIARY                                                              25 May 1940

Go down to the War Office to discuss with Ned Grigg the question of civilian morale in case of invasion. He feels pretty certain that the Germans will attempt to make an attack on London, and he says that the possibility of evacuating the Channel and East Coast towns is now being considered. He indicates on the map the area which they are thinking of evacuating, and although it does not include Sissinghurst, it is only some twelve miles off. This makes me feel rather glum inside.

The Germans occupy Boulogne and Calais. Our communications are almost completely severed, and it is possible that the BEF may be cut off. There is a belief, however, that Weygand will be able to re-establish his own line within two weeks. We may have to ask the French to send some Divisions across here to help us.

H.N. TO V.S.–W.                                                          26 May 1940
                                                          4 King's Bench Walk, EC4

What a grim interlude in our lives! The Government may decide to evacuate Kent and Sussex of all civilians. If, as I hope, they give orders instead of advice, then those orders will either be 'Go' or 'Stay'. If the former, then you know what to do. If the latter, we are faced with a great predicament. I don't think that even if the Germans occupied Sissinghurst they would harm you, in spite of the horrified dislike which they feel for me. But to be quite sure that you are not put to any humiliation, I think you really ought to have a 'bare bodkin' handy so that you can take your quietus when necessary. I shall have one also. I am not in the least afraid of such sudden and honourable death. What I dread is being tortured and humiliated. But how can we find a bodkin which will give us our quietus quickly and which is easily portable? I shall ask my doctor friends.

My dearest, I felt so close to you yesterday. We never need to put it all in words. If I believe in anything surviving, I believe in a love like ours surviving: it is all so completely unmaterial in every way.

V.S.–W. TO H.N.                                             27 May 1940
                                                           Sissinghurst

I could not trust myself to say much to you yesterday, but I expect you know what I felt. Every time we meet now, it must be in both our minds that we may possibly never meet again; but it must also be in both our minds (as you said) that we have known what few people know: a great happiness and a great unalterable love.

I am sending your diaries to Eric [Nicolson, Harold's elder brother], also my Will.

H.N. TO V.S.–W.                                             27 May 1940
                                                    Ministry of Information

I am afraid that the news this afternoon is very bad indeed, and that we must expect the Germans to surround a large proportion of our Army and to occupy the whole area of Belgium and Northern France. We must also face the possibility that the French may make a separate peace, especially if Italy joins in the conflict. I warn you of this so that you will prepare your mind for the bad news when it comes and be ready to summon all the courage that is in you. I think you had better keep this to yourself for the moment.

V.S.–W. TO H.N.                                             28 May 1940
                                                           Sissinghurst

God help us, I have just heard about the Belgians! [who had capitulated]. Well, we must wait. In the meantime, how deeply I agree with you about love and also about the bodkin. I promise you never to do anything rash or impetuous with the latter, but I should like to have it by me. So see Pierre Lansel [Nicolson's doctor] as soon as you can, for both our sakes, and get it for yourself and also post me a little parcel. There must be something quick and painless and portable. Oh my dear, my dearest, that we should come to this! Anyhow, we have had our lives, or at any rate more than half of them, so let us never repine. I won't write more. I know you are busy, and it is not necessary for me to say more than that I have loved you more than anyone or anything in all my life.

H.N.'s DIARY                                                29 May 1940

We are creating a Corunna Line along the beaches around Dunkirk and hope to evacuate a few of our troops. The Navy is superb. I find a passionate letter from the French Ambassador saying that our Press is

67

putting all the blame on the French Army. I take this to Walter Monckton's Committee and we hope to improve the situation. I then belatedly try to dictate correspondence. The work is as urgent and cumulative as during the Paris Peace Conference. But then we were happy in those days and not in a state of fear.

H.N. TO V.S.–W.                                                   31 May 1940
4 King's Bench Walk, EC4

Our Army has fought the most magnificent battle in Flanders. They have created what they call the 'Corunna Line' and are holding it. We never hoped to rescue more than 20,000, and we have already saved 80,000 and hope to do more. Moreover we are now able to supply them with some food and ammunition. It is a magnificent feat once you admit the initial misery of the thing. It is perhaps fortunate that the BEF is so good at retreating, since that is what it mostly has to do. But I am not sneering. They have done more than just rescue themselves. They have killed two dangerous legends: (1) that no army could stand up to German mechanized attack; (2) that complicated naval operations such as embarking troops under fire could not be undertaken in the face of air superiority.

My darling, how *infectious* courage is. I am rendered far stronger in heart and confidence by such bravery.

H.N.'s DIARY                                                      1 June 1940

We have now evacuated 220,000 men, which is amazing when I recall how we feared that we should lose 80 per cent. But there are few grounds for enthusiasm really, except moral grounds. We have lost all our equipment. The French have lost 80 per cent of their forces and feel that we deserted them. Gort [Lord Gort, Commander-in-Chief of the British Expeditionary Force] says that he offered to take more French off, but that they were too dead-beat to move and that all those who could be galvanized into marching a few miles further were in fact rescued. This may be true, but the French with their tendency to attribute blame to others will be certain to say that we thought only of rescuing the BEF and let them down.

I escape at 6.15 to Sissinghurst. Our train is 1½ hours late, because trains are pouring up and down the line transporting remnants of the BEF. We pass twelve trains packed with tired, dirty but cheering troops. I only see one man who is shell-shocked, and he sits staring in front of him with drooping eyelids, as if drugged. The others might have been returning from a two-days' route march.

H.N. TO V.S.–W.

4 June 1940
4 King's Bench Walk, EC4

I was terribly rushed yesterday as I had to get out a Memo for the Cabinet about invasion. We do not know whether to warn people now, or to wait till it becomes likely. It is 80 per cent probable that the enemy will attack France first and only go for us afterwards. Yet we must be prepared for the invasion when it comes and the public must be told what to do. We have got a long list of instructions, but do not like to issue them without Cabinet orders. As Duff was over in Paris, I had to do this all myself.

My dearest Viti, I suppose it is some comfort to feel that it will either be all over in August or else we shall have won. Hitler will not be able to go on into next year. The whole thing is, 'Shall we be able to stand it?' I think we shall. And if we win, then truly it will be a triumph of human character over the machine.

But actually I do not believe that invasion will come, especially if the French are able to put up some show of resistance on the Somme. How I long for the spirit of Verdun to revive! It may – you know what the French are. I feel so deeply grateful for having hard work to do in these days. And now comes Italy [Mussolini declared war on 10 June but his intention to do so was already plain]. My dearest, what a mean skulking thing to do. The French have offered them practically all that they want in Tunis etc., but they want more and more. They are like the people who rob corpses on the battlefield – I forget what these people are called. The Greeks had a name for it.

Bless you. Courage and hope. This afternoon Winston made the finest speech that I have ever heard ['We shall fight on the beaches. . . .']. The House was deeply moved.

V.S.–W. TO H.N.

5 June 1940
Sissinghurst

I wish I had heard Winston making that magnificent speech! Even repeated by the announcer it sent shivers (not of fear) down my spine. I think that one of the reasons why one is stirred by his Elizabethan phrases is that one feels the whole massive backing of power and resolve behind them, like a great fortress: they are never words for words' sake.

How strange it is to have no knowledge of what is about to befall us. In ordinary times one seldom thinks how odd it is to have no knowledge of what may happen even within the next hour, but now the consciousness of this ignorance becomes acute. I see the future only in terms of colour: scarlet and black. But as you say, courage and hope. And there is always the bare bodkin.

Between *Wednesday 5 June 1940* and *Sunday 20 October that same year, J. B. Priestley broadcast a number of talks on the BBC which at once commanded a huge audience. They were blunt, simple, direct; and they immediately struck a chord. It is said that Winston Churchill hated them on two counts: firstly, they upstaged his own grandiloquent speeches; secondly, they spoke of a people's war – the first – and were by implication critical of the governing class to which Churchill belonged. Both A.J.P. Taylor and Asa Briggs, reputed historians, believe that Churchill was instrumental in getting Priestley taken off the air; hard evidence on this does not seem to exist.*

*We print here the very first radio talk, about the evacuation from Dunkirk. Its homely qualities are at once plain; actually we know, with hindsight, that the role of the little ships was by no means as great as we then thought. Still, it was heroic and colourful enough.*

## POSTCRIPTS

### J.B. PRIESTLEY

Wednesday, 5 June 1940

I wonder how many of you feel as I do about this great Battle and evacuation of Dunkirk. The news of it came as a series of surprises and shocks, followed by equally astonishing new waves of hope. It was all, from beginning to end, unexpected. And yet now that it's over, and we can look back on it, doesn't it seem to you to have an inevitable air about it – as if we had turned a page in the history of Britain and seen a chapter headed 'Dunkirk' – and perhaps seen too a picture of the troops on the beach waiting to embark?

And now that this whole action is completed, we notice that it has a definite shape, and a certain definite character. What strikes me about it is how typically English it is. Nothing, I feel, could be more English than this Battle of Dunkirk, both in its beginning and its end, its folly and its grandeur. It was very English in what was sadly wrong with it; this much has been freely admitted, and we are assured will be freely discussed when the proper moment arrives. We have gone sadly wrong like this before; and here and now we must resolve never, never to do it again. Another such blunder may not be forgiven us.

But having admitted this much, let's do ourselves the justice of admitting too that this Dunkirk affair was also very English (and when I say 'English' I really mean British) in the way in which, when apparently all was lost, so much was gloriously retrieved. Bright honour was almost 'plucked from the moon'. What began as a miserable blunder, a catalogue of misfortunes and miscalculations, ended as an epic of gallantry. We have a queer habit – and you can see it running through our history – of conjuring up such transformations. Out of a black gulf of humiliation and despair, rises a sun of blazing glory. This is not the

German way. They don't make such mistakes (a grim fact that we should bear in mind) but also – they don't achieve such epics. There is never anything to inspire a man either in their victories or their defeats; boastful when they're winning, quick to whine when threatened with defeat – there is nothing about them that ever catches the world's imagination. That vast machine of theirs can't create a glimmer of that poetry of action which distinguishes war from mass murder. It's a machine – and therefore has no soul.

But here at Dunkirk is another English epic. And to my mind what was most characteristically English about it – so typical of us, so absurd and yet so grand and gallant that you hardly know whether to laugh or to cry when you read about them – was the part played in the difficult and dangerous embarkation – not by the warships, magnificent though they were – but by the little pleasure-steamers. We've known them and laughed at them, these fussy little steamers, all our lives. We have called them 'the shilling sicks'. We have watched them load and unload their crowds of holiday passengers – the gents full of high spirits and bottled beer, the ladies eating pork pies, the children sticky with peppermint rock. Sometimes they only went as far as the next seaside resort. But the boldest of them might manage a Channel crossing, to let everybody have a glimpse of Boulogne. They were usually paddle steamers, making a great deal more fuss with all their churning than they made speed; and they weren't proud, for they let you see their works going round. They liked to call themselves 'Queens' and 'Belles'; and even if they were new, there was always something old-fashioned, a Dickens touch, a mid-Victorian air, about them. They seemed to belong to the same ridiculous holiday world as pierrots and piers, sand castles, ham-and-egg teas, palmists, automatic machines, and crowded sweating promenades. But they were called out of that world – and, let it be noted – they were called out in good time and good order. Yes, these 'Brighton Belles' and 'Brighton Queens' left that innocent foolish world of theirs – to sail into the inferno, to defy bombs, shells, magnetic mines, torpedoes, machine-gun fire – to rescue our soldiers. Some of them – alas – will never return. Among those paddle steamers that will never return was one that I knew well, for it was the pride of our ferry service to the Isle of Wight – none other than the good ship 'Gracie Fields'. I tell you, we were proud of the 'Gracie Fields', for she was the glittering queen of our local line, and instead of taking an hour over her voyage, used to do it, churning like mad, in forty-five minutes. And now never again will we board her at Cowes and go down into her dining saloon for a fine breakfast of bacon and eggs. She has paddled and churned away – for ever. But now – look – this little steamer, like all her brave and battered sisters, is immortal. She'll go sailing proudly down the years in the epic of Dunkirk. And our great-grandchildren, when they learn how we began this War by snatching glory out of defeat, and then swept on to victory, may also learn how the little holiday steamers made an excursion to hell and came back glorious.

# THAT'S HOW THE
# POOR SOD DIED

Pierre Clostermann – an only child – was separated from his parents for four years by many thousands of miles. The mail between London, where he had come to serve with the Free French Air Force in 1941, and Brazzaville, where his father was a captain in the French army, was erratic. So he kept a daily journal in an Air Ministry notebook. He wanted his parents to live every fighting day with him, even if he did not live to tell the tale. Between March 1942 and the end of the war he filled three books. He took a notebook with him everywhere – into the cockpit, stained with tea in the mess, beside him at long hours waiting at Dispersal. In them he jotted down exactly what happened. He says they have no pretension to be literature. In fact they make in sum a story that now seems hardly credible. The short snatches, the vivid telegraphese, the gallicism that pervades his prose like garlic, lend his testimony the ring of verisimilitude. He flew no fewer than 420 operational sorties, was credited with the destruction of 23 enemy aircraft, won a DFC and bar, and ended up commanding a fighter wing. Here, he tells how it all began.

## MY FIRST BIG SHOW OVER FRANCE

### PIERRE CLOSTERMANN

1325 hours. A white rocket rose from the control tower. Deere raised his arm and the thirteen aircraft of 611 Squadron started forward. In his turn Mouchotte raised his gloved hand and slowly opened the throttle. Eyes fixed on Martell's wing-tip, and my hands moist, I followed. The tails went up, the Spitfires began to bounce clumsily on their narrow undercarriages, the wheels left the ground – we were airborne.

I raised the undercart and locked it, throttled back and adjusted the airscrew pitch. We swept like a whirlwind over the road outside the airfield. A bus had stopped, its passengers crowding at the windows. I switched over to auxiliary tanks and shut the main tank cocks. Handling the controls clumsily and jerkily, I contrived to keep formation. The Spitfires slipped southward at tree and roof-top level in a thunderous roar which halted people in the streets in their tracks. We jumped a wooded hill, then suddenly we were over the sea, its dirty waves edged with foam and dominated on the left by Beachy Head. A blue hazy line on the horizon must be France. We hurtled forward, a few feet above the water.

Some disconnected impressions remain vividly impressed on my memory – a British coastguard vessel with its crew waving to us; an Air Sea Rescue launch gently rocking with the swell and surrounded by a swarm of seagulls.

Out of the corner of my eye I watched the pressure and temperature – normal. I switched on my reflector sight. One of the 611 aircraft waggled its wings, turned and came back towards England, gaining height. Engine trouble, probably.

1349 hours. Over the radio we could hear in the far distance shouts and calls coming from the close escort squadrons – and suddenly, very distinctly, a triumphant: 'I got him!' I realized with a tightening of the heart that over there they were already fighting.

1350 hours. As one, the 24 Spitfires rose and climbed towards the sky, hanging on their propellers, 3,300 feet a minute.

France! A row of white cliffs emerged from the mist and as we gained height the horizon gradually receded – the estuary of the Somme, the narrow strip of sand at the foot of the tree-crowned cliffs, the first meadows, and the first village nestling by a wood in a valley.

Fifteen thousand feet. My engine suddenly cut out and the nose dropped violently. With my heart in my mouth and unable to draw breath I reacted instinctively and at once changed to my main petrol tanks. My auxiliary was empty. Feeling weak about the knees I realized that through lack of experience I had used too much power to keep my position and that my engine had used proportionately more fuel. A second's glide, a splutter, and the engine picked up again. At full throttle I closed up with my section.

'Brutus aircraft, drop your babies!' sounded Deere's clear voice in the earphones. Still considerably shaken, I pulled the handle, hoping to God that the thing would work . . . a jerk, a swishing sound, and all our 24 tanks fell, fluttering downwards.

'Hullo, Brutus, Zona calling, go over Channel C Charlie.'

'Hullo, Zona, Brutus answering. Channel C. Over!'

'Hullo, Brutus. Zona out!'

I pressed button C on the VHF panel. A crackling sound, then the voice of Squadron Leader Holmes, the famous controller of Grass Seed:

'Hullo, Brutus leader, Grass Seed calling. There is plenty going on over target. Steer 096° – zero, nine, six. There are 40 plus bandits 15 miles ahead, angels 35, over to you!'

'Hullo, Grass Seed. Brutus answering. Steering 096°. Roger out.'

Mouchotte put us in combat formation:

'Hullo, Turban, combat formation, go!'

The three sections of four Spitfires drew apart. Below to my right the Gimlets did the same.

'Brutus aircraft, keep your eyes open!'

We were at 27,000 feet. Five minutes passed. The cloudless sky was so vast and limpid that you felt stunned. You knew that France was there, under the translucent layer of dry mist, which was slightly more opaque over the towns. The cold was painful and breathing difficult. You could feel the sun, but I could not make out whether I was being burnt or frozen by its rays. To rouse myself I turned the oxygen full on. The strident roar of the engine increased the curious sensation of being isolated that one gets in a single-seater fighter. It gradually becomes a sort of noisy but neutral background that ends up by merging into a queer kind of thick, heavy silence.

Still nothing new. I felt both disappointed and relieved. Time seemed to pass very slowly. I felt I was dreaming with my eyes open, lulled by the slow rhythmical rocking movement up and down of the Spitfires in echelon, by the gentle rotation of the propellers through the rarefied and numbing air. Everything seemed so unreal and remote. Was this war?

'Look out, Brutus leader, Grass Seed calling. Three gaggles of 20 plus converging towards you, above!'

Holmes' voice had made me jump. Martell now chimed in:

'Look out, Brutus, Yellow One calling, smoke trails coming 3 o'clock!'

I stared round and suddenly I spotted the tell-tale condensation trails of the Jerries beginning to converge on us from south and east. Christ, how fast they were coming! I released the safety catch of the guns.

'Brutus calling. Keep your eyes open, chaps. Climb like hell!'

I opened the throttle and changed to fine pitch, and instinctively edged closer to Martell's Spitfire. I felt very alone in a suddenly hostile sky.

'Brutus calling. Open your eyes and prepare to break port. The bastards are right above!'

Three thousand feet above our heads a filigree pattern began to form and you could already distinguish the glint of the slender cross-shaped silhouettes of the German fighters.

'Here they come!' I said to myself, hypnotized. My throat contracted, my toes curled in my boots. I felt as if I were stifling in a strait-jacket, swaddled in all those belts, braces and buckles.

'Turban, break starboard!' yelled Boudier. In a flash I saw the roundels of Martell's Spitfire surge up before me. I banked my aircraft with all my strength, opened the throttle wide, and there I was in his slip-stream! Where were the Huns? I dared not look behind me, and I turned desperately, glued to my seat by the centrifugal force, eyes rivetted on Martell turning a hundred yards in front of me.

'Gimlet, attack port!'

I felt lost in the mêlée.

'Turban Yellow Two, break!'

Yellow Two? Why, that was me! With a furious kick on the rudder bar, I broke away, my gorge rising from sheer fear. Red tracers danced past my windshield . . . and suddenly I saw my first Hun! I identified it at once – it was a Focke-Wulf 190. I had not studied the photos and recognition charts so often for nothing.

After firing a burst of tracer at me he bore down on Martell. Yes, it certainly was one – the short wings, the radial engine, the long transparent hood: the square-cut tailplane all in one piece! But what had been missing from the photos was the lively colouring – the pale yellow belly, the greyish green back, the big black crosses outlined in white. The photos gave no hint of the quivering of the wings, the outline elongated and fined down by the speed, the curious nose-down flying attitude.

The sky, which had been filled with hurtling Spitfires, seemed suddenly empty – my No. 1 had disappeared. Never mind, I was not going to lose my Focke-Wulf. I was no longer afraid.

Incoherent pictures are superimposed on my memory – three Focke-Wulfs waggling their wings; tracers criss-crossing; a parachute floating like a puff of smoke in the blue sky.

I huddled up, with the stick hugged to my stomach in both hands, thrown into an endless ascending spiral at full throttle.

'Look out! . . . Attention! . . . Break!' – a medley of shouts in the earphones. I would have liked to recognize a definite order somewhere, or some advice.

Another Focke-Wulf, wings lit up by the blinding flashes of its cannon firing – dirty grey trails from exhausts – white trails from square wing-tips. I couldn't make out who or what he was firing at. He flicked – yellow belly, black crosses. He dived and fell like a bullet. Far below he merged into the blurred landscape.

Another one, on a level with me. He turned towards me. Careful now! I must face him!

A quick half-roll, and without quite knowing how, I found myself on my back, finger on firing button, shaken to the marrow of my bones by the roar of my flame-spitting cannon. All my faculties, all my being, were focused on one single thought: I MUST KEEP HIM IN MY SIGHTS.

What about deflection? – not enough. I must tighten my turn! More . . . more still . . . more still! No good. He had gone, but my finger was still convulsively pressed on the button. I was firing at emptiness.

Where was he? I began to panic. Beware, 'the Hun you haven't seen is the one who gets you!' I could feel the disordered thumping of my heart right down in my stomach, in my clammy temples, in my knees.

There he was again – but a long way away. He dived, I fired again – missed him! Out of range. Raging, I persisted . . . one last burst . . . my Spitfire quivered, but the Focke-Wulf was faster and disappeared unscathed into the mist.

The sky had emptied as if by magic. Not one plane left. I was absolutely alone.

A glance at the petrol – 35 gallons. Time to get back. It was scarcely a quarter past two.

'Hullo, Turban, Yellow Two. Yellow One calling. Are you all right?'

It was Martell's voice from very far away.

'Hullo, Yellow One, Turban Yellow Two answering. Am OK and going home.'

I set course 320° for England, in a shallow dive. A quarter of an hour later I was flying over the yellow sands of Dungeness. I joined the Biggin Hill circuit. Spitfires everywhere, with wheels down. I wormed my way in between two sections and landed.

As I taxied towards Dispersal I saw Tommy, with arms raised, signalling and showing me where to park.

I gave a burst of throttle to clear my engine and switched off. The sudden silence dazed me. How odd to hear voices again undistorted by the radio.

Tommy helped me out of my harness. I jumped to the ground, my legs feeling weak and stiff.

Martell came striding towards me, and caught me round the neck.

'Good old Clo-Clo! We really thought you had had it!'

We went over to join the group by the door round Mouchotte.

'Hey, Clo-Clo, seen anything of Béraud?'

Béraud, it appeared, must have been shot down.

Bouguen's aircraft had been hit by two 20-mm shells. 485 Squadron had brought down two Focke-Wulfs. Mouchotte and Boudier had severely damaged one each.

I was now voluble and excited. I told my tale, I felt light-hearted, as if a great weight had been lifted from me. I had done my first big sweep over France and I had come back!

That evening, in the mess, I felt on top of the world.

1951

---

*The poetry of the Second World War has nothing like the emotional intensity of that spawned by the First World War. Still, it is a mistake to dismiss it. The Second World War lasted two years longer and spread much more widely over the world's surface; so a far wider range of experience was there to be recorded.*

*It ranged, as we have seen, from the wry social observation of Gavin Ewart (still with us and writing well) to the beautiful poetry of John Pudney, for many people the most memorable the Second World War produced. Everyone who saw the film The Way to the Stars remembers the two short poems 'For Johnny' and 'Missing'; but, because it is longer and somewhat more complex, a poem like 'Combat Report' is less well known. No one mixes elegance with vernacular more assuredly than Pudney.*

## COMBAT REPORT

JOHN PUDNEY

*Just then I saw the bloody Hun.*
You saw the Hun? You, light and easy,
Carving the soundless daylight. *I was breezy*
*When I saw that Hun. Oh wonder*
Pattern of stress, of nerve poise, flyer,
*Overtaking time. He came out under*
*Nine-tenths cloud, but I was higher.*
Did Michelangelo aspire,
Painting the laughing cumulus, to ride
The majesty of air. *He was a trier*
*I'll give him that, the Hun. So you convert*
Ultimate sky to air speed, drift, and cover:
Sure with the tricky tools of God and lover.
*I let him have a sharp four-second squirt,*
*Closing to fifty yards. He went on fire.*
Your deadly petals painted, you exert
A simple stature. Man-high, without pride,
You pick your way through heaven and the dirt.
*He burnt out in the air: that's how the poor sod died.*

## MISSING

JOHN PUDNEY

Less said the better.
The bill unpaid, the dead letter.
No roses at the end
Of Smith, my friend.

Last words don't matter,
And there are none to flatter.
Words will not fill the post
Of Smith, the ghost.

For Smith, our brother,
Only son of loving mother,
The ocean lifted, stirred,
Leaving no word.

79

# FOR JOHNNY

JOHN PUDNEY

Do not despair
For Johnny-head-in-air;
He sleeps as sound
As Johnny underground.

Fetch out no shroud
For Johnny-in-the-cloud;
And keep your tears
For him in after years.

Better by far
For Johnny-the-bright-star,
To keep your head,
And see his children fed.

# ARE WE DOWNHEARTED?

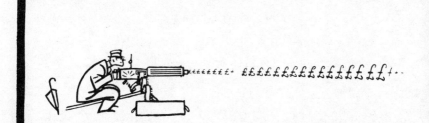

NOW — give em all you've got !!!

KENSINGTON "SALUTE THE SOLDIER" WEEK — MARCH 25TH TO APRIL 1ST

Ed Murrow was one of the greatest American broadcasters of his time. Born in 1908, he began to work for the Columbia Broadcasting System in 1935 and came to London for them two years later. His terse, authoritative and highly descriptive broadcasts from London in the Blitz brought the war home to Americans as little else did. He went on to a distinguished career in television, made a doughty stand against the activities of Senator Joseph McCarthy, and was appointed head of the US Information Agency by President John F. Kennedy in 1961, remaining in the post until the end of 1964. He died the following year.

## THIS IS LONDON

### EDWARD R. MURROW

[On 7 September, the mass air attacks on London began.]

8 SEPTEMBER, 1940

Yesterday afternoon – it seems days ago now – I drove down to the East End of London, the East India Dock Road, Commercial Road, through Silvertown, down to the mouth of the Thames Estuary. It was a quiet and almost pleasant trip through those streets running between rows of working-class houses, with the cranes, the docks, the ships, and the oil tanks off on the right. We crossed the river and drove up on a little plateau, which gave us a view from the mouth of the Thames to London. And then an air-raid siren, called 'Weeping Willie' by the men who tend it, began its uneven screaming. Down on the coast the white puffballs of anti-aircraft fire began to appear against a steel-blue sky. The first flight of German bombers was coming up the river to start the twelve-hour attack against London. They were high and not very numerous. The Hurricanes and Spitfires were already in the air, climbing for altitude above the nearby aerodrome. The fight moved inland and out of sight. Things were relatively quiet for about half an hour. Then the British fighters returned. And five minutes later the German bombers, flying in V-formation, began pouring in. The anti-aircraft fire was good. Sometimes it seemed to burst right on the nose of the leading machine, but still they came on. On the aerodrome, ground crews swarmed over those British fighters, fitting ammunition belts and pouring in petrol. As soon as one fighter was ready, it took the air, and there was no waiting for flight leaders or formation. The Germans were already coming back, down the river, heading for France.

Up toward London we could see billows of smoke fanning out above the river; and over our heads the British fighters, climbing almost straight up, trying to intercept the bombers before they got away. It went on for two hours and then the 'all-clear'. We went down to a near-by pub for dinner. Children were already organizing a hunt for bits of shrapnel. Under some bushes beside the road there was a baker's cart. Two boys, still sobbing, were trying to get a quivering bay mare back between the shafts. The lady who ran the pub told us that these raids were bad for the chickens, the dogs, and the horses. A toothless old man of nearly seventy came in and asked for a pint of mild and bitter, confided that he had always, all his life, gone to bed at eight o'clock and found now that three pints of beer made him drowsy-like so he could sleep through any air raid.

Before eight the siren sounded again. We went back to a haystack near the aerodrome. The fires up river had turned the moon blood red. The smoke had drifted down till it formed a canopy over the Thames; the guns were working all round us, the bursts looking like fireflies in a southern summer night. The Germans were sending in two or three planes at a time, sometimes only one, in relays. They would pass overhead. The guns and lights would follow them, and in about five minutes we could hear the hollow grunt of the bombs. Huge pear-shaped bursts of flame would rise up into the smoke and disappear. The world was upside down. Vincent Sheean lay on one side of me and cursed in five languages; he'd talk about the war in Spain. Ben Robertson, of PM, lay on the other side and kept saying over and over in his slow South Carolina drawl, 'London is burning, London is burning.'

It was like a shuttle service, the way the German planes came up the Thames, the fires acting as a flare path. Often they were above the smoke. The searchlights bored into that black roof, but couldn't penetrate it. They looked like long pillars supporting a black canopy. Suddenly all the lights dashed off and blackness fell right to the ground. It grew cold. We covered ourselves with hay. The shrapnel clicked as it hit the concrete road near by, and still the German bombers came.

Early this morning we went to a hotel. The gunfire rattled the windows. Shortly before noon we rang for coffee. A pale, red-eyed chambermaid brought it and said, 'I hope you slept well, sirs.' This afternoon we drove back to the East End of London. It was like an obstacle race – two blocks to the right, then left for four blocks, then straight on for a few blocks, and right again . . . streets roped off, houses and shops smashed . . . a few dirty-faced, tow-headed children standing on a corner, holding their thumbs up, the sign of the men who came back from Dunkirk . . . three red buses drawn up in a line waiting to take the homeless away . . . men with white scarfs round their necks instead of collars and ties, leading dull-eyed, empty-faced women across to the buses. Most of them carried little cheap cardboard suitcases and sometimes bulging paper shopping-bags. That was all they had left. There was still fire and smoke along the river, but the fire-fighters and the demolition squads have done their work well.

9 SEPTEMBER 1940

I've spent the day visiting the bombed areas. The King did the same thing. These people may have been putting on a bold front for the King, but I saw them just as they were – men shovelling mounds of broken glass into trucks, hundreds of people being evacuated from the East End, all of them calm and quiet. In one street where eight or ten houses had been smashed a policeman stopped a motorist who had driven through a red light. The policeman's patience was obviously exhausted. As he made out his report and lectured the driver, everyone in the street gathered round to listen, paying no attention at all to the damaged houses; they were much more interested in the policeman.

These people are exceedingly brave, tough and prudent. The East End, where disaster is always just round the corner, seems to take it better than the more fashionable districts in the West End.

The firemen have done magnificent work these last forty-eight hours. Early this morning I watched them fighting a fire that was obviously being used as a beacon by the German bombers. The bombs came down only a few blocks away, but the firemen just kept their hoses playing steadily at the base of the flame.

The Germans dropped some very big stuff last night. One bomb, which fell about a quarter of a mile from where I was standing on a roof-top, made the largest crater I've ever seen, and I thought I'd seen some big ones. The blast travelled down nearby streets, smashing windows five or six blocks away.

The British shot down three of the night-bombers last night. I said a moment ago that Londoners were both brave and prudent. Tonight many theatres are closed. The managers decided that the crowds just wouldn't come. Tonight the queues were outside the air-raid shelters, not the theatres. In my district, people carrying blankets and mattresses began going to the shelters before the siren sounded.

This night bombing is serious and sensational.

---

*Colin Perry was born in South London in February 1922. On leaving school he started work as an office boy in the City of London at fourteen shillings a week. When war broke out in September 1939 he was working for the California Standard Oil Company and living with his parents in a Tooting flat. He kept a diary through the Blitz which is remarkable for its freshness, candour and simplicity. On 10 September 1940, he was to rub shoulders with greatness.*

# BOY IN THE BLITZ

### COLIN PERRY

It is 1.10 p.m. on Tuesday, 10 September 1940. I am sitting in my office on the second floor of the Royal Bank of Canada building in Lothbury. An air-raid siren sounded ten minutes ago. As I write under a grey sky, under a pall of 'acidy' smoke, within a few seconds walk of wrecked and burning buildings, I take heart from the news I am to record.

I left the office this lunch hour at twelve precisely. I walked to the corner of King Street and Cheapside. My ABC was closed. Cheapside was a mass of charred debris; of firemen on ladders, hoses pouring jets of water into the charred and burning remains of elegant buildings of yesterday. Fire units, engines, troops in steel helmets move in the dense, choking clouds of smoke. Until the police move me along I stay and watch. The smoke rises high above St Paul's, obliterated the dome for minutes on end. Cheapside, in the heart of London, was stabbed. I moved along . . . .

I saw a crowd, milling, cheering, near the Mansion House Station. More people rushed to the spot . . . . I tore headfirst. What a crowd. Throbbing with anticipation, I fought my way through, jumped a police barrier, and heading off the crowd found the core of the excitement. Winston Churchill! I cheered, I yelled. I fought harder, and finally established myself in between Winston and his escort of the Commissioner of Police and an Officer of the Army. The crowd pressed on either side, but whether they mistook me for one of the party or not I cannot say; the fact remains I kept next to Churchill the whole route from the Mansion House Station to the Bank. I had my photograph taken countless times, and once had my hand on Churchill's coat. He looked invincible, which he is. Tough, bulldogged, piercing. His hair was wispy, wiry, tinted gingery. As he made his way through the smoke, through the City workers all crying 'Good old Winston' – 'Give 'em socks' – 'Good Luck' – and the culminating cry of 'Are we down-hearted?' to the heaven rising response of 'Nooooooo' which echoed round the City, round the world indeed, and warmed the 'cockles of our British hearts' and of all the free men in the world. It was magnificent, tremulous, stirring, dramatic. Amongst the 'ashes of London' stepped the man, his people, acclaimed, assured, and fulfilling the declaration that we will fight in the streets, in the fields, on the seas, in the air – that we should rather see London in ashes, but free and ours, than standing under the will of Hitler.

Churchill bought a flag outside the broken-windowed Mansion House, and I squeezed myself into the photo. He mounted the Mansion House steps and shook hands, presumably with the Lord Mayor; the people stood cheering themselves hoarse below, and we all stuck our thumbs up and yelled louder than ever for the Press photographers – and I guess I am in every one of their pictures. Next, Winston crossed to the bomb crater outside the Bank of England, and threw his cigar down upon the notice 'No Smoking – Danger Escaping Gas.' I could easily have retrieved the butt, but I had no desire to acquire such a souvenir – the sight, the memory is sufficient, and, I hope, the pictures. Winston stood on the bomb crater, waved, took off his bowlerish hat (how typical of the Churchill of the Sidney Street siege), sported his walking-stick, dug his left hand deep in his overcoat pocket. Approaching once again the crowds a young boy dashed up with an autograph album – Churchill signed. As he did so I had my hand on his sleeve, indeed I could not help myself, the crowd's pressure and enthusiasm was so terrific. Into his car and away – my hat, I certainly do seem to wangle my way into things – right by his side throughout his tour, the records of which will find space in every future book of history . . .

Well I must buy all the papers for the next few days, and if I am lucky enough to have come out OK I will buy the plates and send one to Binnie [a girl pen-pal] . . . with my friend Winston!

1972

American coverage of the war they were not yet in was substantial and expert. Life magazine had two men in London – Allan Michie and Walter Graebner – who put together a lively book of first-hand testimony about a wide variety of war experiences ranging from an RAF squadron leader fighting in the sky over Dunkirk to a fireman's account of his job during the London Blitz. Yet their own story is as vivid as any. One night there was an uninvited visitor in the Bloomsbury square where they lived: a crashing German bomber. It is not, after all, every night that a Junkers comes unexpectedly to dinner.

Curiously enough, the great Thirties poets – Auden, MacNeice and Spender – did not publish a great quantity of poetry that directly bore on the war, but Spender – honourably employed in fighting fires – has given us some, notably this poem about an air raid on Plymouth which exactly recalls the geometric patterns made by searchlights in the sky.

## AIR RAID ACROSS THE BAY AT PLYMOUTH

STEPHEN SPENDER

I

Above the whispering sea
And waiting rocks of black coast,
Across the bay, the searchlight beams
Swing and swing back across the sky.

Their ends fuse in a cone of light
Held for a bright instant up
Until they break away again
Smashing that image like a cup.

II

Delicate aluminium girders
Project phantom aerial masts
Swaying crane and derrick
Above the sea's just lifting deck.

III

Triangles, parallels, parallelograms,
Experiment with hypotheses
On the blackboard sky,
Seeking that X
Where the enemy is met.
Two beams cross
To chalk his cross.

IV

A sound, sounding ragged, unseen
Is chased by two swords of light.
A thud. An instant when the whole night gleams.
Gold sequins shake out of a black-silk screen.

V

Jacob ladders slant
Up to the god of war
Who, from his heaven-high car,
Unloads upon a star
A destroying star.

Round the coast, the waves
Chuckle between rocks.
In the fields the corn
Sways, with metallic clicks.
Man hammers nails in Man,
High on his crucifix.

1954

## THEIR FINEST HOUR – THE WAR IN THE FIRST PERSON

ALLAN A. MICHIE AND WALTER GRAEBNER

In the evening of 18 September 1940, a crippled Nazi Junkers bomber, hit repeatedly by anti-aircraft fire as it attempted to raid the centre of London, sailed silently into an unsuspecting Bloomsbury square. At least one bomb exploded in its rack as the plane was above the square, and a land mine aboard blew up with a terrific explosion as the plane crashed, levelling several houses, setting fire to others. Two American war correspondents were in their house, a few doors away, when the plane crashed. This is the story they cabled to America:

GRAEBNER: At a quarter to eight I left the *Daily Express* morgue, where I'd been gathering material on Prime Minister Churchill. My taxi whizzed recklessly through the darkened streets because the driver wanted to be out of Central London before the sirens wailed. I was just eating my dinner of lamb chops and baked beans – cooked on an electric fireplace since our gas supply had gone – when the raid started. The drone of German planes, clatter of anti-aircraft muck, the whistling and thuds of bombs grew so loud that I decided it was time to drift down to the basement, where we had improvised a shelter in a dirty wine cellar. I quickly changed into pyjamas, flannel trousers, and tweed jacket, grabbed the portable radio and my typewriter, and hurried down four floors. We lived in a charming seventeenth-century brownstone house in a quiet London square. The house was occupied by the Charles Laughtons until the war started. Laughton and wife, Elsa Lanchester, had spent a few thousand pounds modernizing it, and we certainly didn't want anything to happen to it.

MICHIE: I had dropped into a newsreel theatre in the late afternoon, to see a couple of Donald Duck cartoons in order to break the monotony of two weeks of almost continuous air raids, and decided to eat dinner in the West End instead of going home. I was just dawdling over my omelette and a half-bottle of lovely Sauterne when the waiter announced that the nightly Mona (the warning: the all-clear is Clara) had gone, a little earlier than usual. By the time I had finished dinner and started homeward the air was thick with muck, and the ack-ack flashes were so bright I could almost read my paper. It's almost impossible to get taxis during raids, so I didn't waste time trying, but hurried in the direction of our house in a half-walk, half-run, popping into doorways for a second whenever the stuff burst overhead. Londoners call this mode of travel door-hopping! I remember stopping outside a Lyons Corner House to buy a late paper, and was so amazed at the sight of an old newsboy calmly sitting selling his papers with a skyful of shrapnel that I gave him a sixpence for a penny paper.

Just as I reached our square the sky on my right suddenly lighted up in a bright red glow. Then came a terrific explosion. I was smack in the open, without a sheltering doorway to pop into, so I just stood still. Nothing fell around me, so I raced for our home. Inside I found Graebner in the shelter, and our housekeeper on the point of going out to meet her husband, who is quartered in London on army duty. My description of the fun and games outside quickly changed her mind. As soon as there came a lull in the ack-ack fire I raced upstairs to change into old clothes for shelter sleeping, and she followed to telephone her husband.

GRAEBNER: I had just comfortably propped myself up against pillows on top of a mattress and was listening to the nine o'clock news on the radio in my lap when there came a deafening crash which made me think that my world had come to an end. I could hear debris falling all over the place, but mainly above me, and an instant later the ceiling of the basement started cracking and bits of plaster cascaded to the floor. I was sure the whole house was coming down, and would be on top of me before I could escape. I was absolutely certain that Michie and the housekeeper were either dead or seriously injured.

For a few seconds I was too stunned to move. Then I remembered that I'd better clap on my steel helmet, but I was so jittery I couldn't find it for a minute. I groped in the brick cubicles of the wine vault over and over when I suddenly discovered I had had it in my hand all the time. Before going upstairs I decided to check on the two basement exits. If the upper part of the house was a shambles or aflame I wanted to be sure that I could get out from the cellar. The front basement door was still intact, but it was locked and I had no key. I rushed through to the back door, but when I opened it clouds of dust and the burnt smell of exploded bombs burst in and almost suffocated me. I slammed the door and raced upstairs, thinking that the worst had happened, but praying hard for the best. I wrenched open the door to the main floor passage and shouted 'Allan . . . Helene.' The male and female 'We're all right' that answered me were the six sweetest words I've ever heard.

MICHIE: I had changed into old trousers, wool shirt, and leather jacket, and was just standing in the fourth-floor bathroom when, without the usual bomb-swishing sound of warning, there came a terrific explosion in the square at the front of the house. I stood transfixed as the whole house swayed crazily from side to side. My brain kept shouting 'Get downstairs before the next one drops', but for some strange reason I persisted in going through the mechanical motions of flushing the toilet, buttoning my trousers, and putting out the bathroom light before I finally jumped and ran down to the third floor. I grabbed my typewriter and some paper from the hall table, and remember hearing the housekeeper cry over the phone to her husband, 'Something's happening to our house. I've got to go.' Before she could hang up the receiver the second explosion came. The blast blew in the hall window and the black-out paper wrapped itself around me as I was blown rump over teakettle into the kitchen, falling over Graebner's cocker spaniel Bepi and my typewriter on the way. The housekeeper was blown into the dining-room as its windows came tumbling down and the electric fire-place was flung across into the bookcase on the other side of the room. Furniture in both rooms went toppling crazily backwards, and a heavy mattress on top of a couch was lifted into the air. I scrambled to my feet and rushed into the dining-room and then dragged the housekeeper back into the kitchen, where she lay flat on the floor for safety. I thought we were finished. Planks, bricks and glass blown into the air by the explosion came tumbling down on the house, through the windows and roof, and clouds of smoke and bomb fumes rolled into the rooms. After what seemed an eternity the crashing stopped, and we heard Graebner's voice through the darkness.

GRAEBNER: We decided to go outside and see what had happened. Our massive front door stood wide open, its hinges sprung. The steel frame of the Yale lock had been blown clean off the door jamb. We stepped on to the porch and across the steps we saw a twisted mass of wreckage. We played our torches on it and then all chorused, 'It's a plane!' Sure enough, it was a hunk of the body of a Junkers bomber, about the size of a coffin. It looked like the wreck of an automobile after being hit by a locomotive, and every few inches it was pock-marked by fist-size ack-ack holes. A woman screamed from somewhere in the garden in the middle of the square, and Michie dashed across the street to help her while the housekeeper and I ducked inside our doorway to dodge the shrapnel that was raining down. The housekeeper was very worried and kept shouting, 'Mr Michie, come back inside. Think of your wife and baby in America.'

MICHIE: The street was littered with debris and ankle deep with glass, but I managed to stumble across into the garden, where I found a dazed woman, unable to find her way to the public shelter in the middle of the square. She sobbed that she had just escaped from the corner house, three doors away from us, in which the German plane had crashed. One of its bombs had exploded as it sailed across the square, and, we learned later, a land mine had gone off when it fell into the house. I must have been somewhat dazed myself, for, instead of leading her to the public shelter, I guided her across the street toward her demolished house. By this time her house and the ones next door and several others across the street were blazing fiercely. I realized what I was doing just in time and turned about and started back to the public shelter. At the garden gate I found two other women huddling, with blankets over their nightgowns, and led all three down the path to the shelter entrance. Then I ran for the house. When I saw the plane wreckage on the steps I determined that we had to have a souvenir for the evening's ordeal, so Graebner and I carefully carried Goering's little gift into our hall.

GRAEBNER: After a few minutes we reassembled in the cellar and, over three stiff shots of neat Scotch, discussed our next move. We quickly agreed that the combined danger of more bombs being dropped round the flaming target, unexploded time bombs which might be in the plane wreckage, and the possibility that our own house might go up in flames made it imperative to leave home at once. We didn't stop to collect any belongings, and Michie and I reluctantly agreed that we'd best leave my dog, who'd been shut in the kitchen after the second explosion, behind in the house. But our housekeeper begged us to take him, so we made a last dash upstairs for him. We had gone only a few feet into the street when we saw that they were so full of splintered glass and debris that he had to be carried.

MICHIE: We stumbled along the streets in the direction of a railroad station, where we hoped to find a taxi. By the light of the fires we could see pitiful groups of people running from their basement shelters to the undamaged public shelter in the square. Others stood helplessly in their doorways, not knowing whether to risk running through the streets or stay in their threatened homes. Halfway to the station another bright red glow suddenly lit up the street around the corner from us. I knew what was coming from experience. Just as the explosion came we threw ourselves into the doorway of a concrete building. The bomb made a direct hit on a building two doors away, but fortunately around the corner, so the blast didn't touch us. We hurried on, and in front of the station found a solitary cab, the driver of which was willing to risk a run to the Dorchester Hotel. We could have kissed him.

GRAEBNER: The lobby was thick with socialites and diplomats, with great and near-great Londoners, who eyed us as if we were refugees from a concentration camp. Even my old friend, Richmond Temple, the Dorchester's publicity chief, failed to recognize me through my coating of grime, but when I explained what had happened to us he beamed, 'The hotel is yours. Nothing is too good for the first Americans to bring down a German plane.' We didn't think we were that good, but, after packing the housekeeper off to bed, Michie and I took him at his word. We celebrated before we went to bed with the (familiar) symphony of the ack-ack guns blasting away overhead. Earlier, as we were sitting at the bar, my hand suddenly went to my pocket in a sort of post-hypnotic gesture and pulled out a teacup. I don't remember putting it there, but I must have picked it up before leaving the shelter.

MICHIE: In the morning we discovered that our housekeeper had taken a taxi to the house at five o'clock, before the 'all-clear' had sounded. The square and streets around were roped off because of the presence of delayed-action bombs, but she badgered her way past police and ARP men and made five trips upstairs to salvage a couple of suits, shirts and toilet articles for us. It wasn't until she'd finished her salvage job that she realized the risk she took; one big delayed-action bomb was buried in our back garden, four more were planted in adjoining gardens, and two were buried in the vegetable garden which ARP wardens had carefully cultivated atop the public shelter in the square.

1940

'Night Raid' *neatly conveys the strange argot of the shelters, but the last three lines lift it to a different level of achievement altogether. Novelist, editor and broadcaster, Desmond Hawkins went on to make a distinguished career as a BBC producer.*

## NIGHT RAID

### DESMOND HAWKINS

The sleepers humped down on the benches,
The daft boy was playing rummy with anyone he could get,
And the dancing girl said, 'What I say is,
If there's a bomb made for YOU,
You're going to get it.'
Someone muttered, 'The bees are coming again.'
Someone whispered beside me in the darkness,
'They're coming up from the east.'
Way off the guns muttered distantly.

This was in the small hours, at the ebb.
And the dancing girl clicked her teeth like castanets
And said, 'I don't mind life, believe me.
I like it. If there's any more to come,
I can take it and be glad of it.'
She was shivering and laughing and throwing her head back.
On the pavement men looked up thoughtfully,
Making plausible conjectures. The night sky
Throbbed under the cool bandage of the searchlights.

*While Ed Murrow was telling the Americans about the Blitz, the Canadians were receiving a first-hand account of the action from a programme called* Old Country Mail. *This was made up of a series of letters sent to Canada by friends and relations in the old country. By July 1941, when the hundredth such programme was broadcast, more than two thousand letters had been received and readings given from more than eight hundred. Many were published in book form, where they received an even wider audience. Here we give just two: an account of how a Nottingham housewife lost her house, but thought it of little consequence because her husband and baby were safe; and a graphic account of the London Blitz by a Canadian Sergeant. He candidly relates what is not often admitted: that the hellish cauldron of a major air raid can have its own lurid beauty.*

# THE HOUSE FELL ABOUT OUR EARS!

## A NOTTINGHAM MOTHER

Ours was a terrible experience. Fortunately we had moved the beds downstairs the night before the raid, as Jerry had been around all week. On this night the sirens went at nine o'clock, while we were listening to the news – but we didn't take much notice, as usually nothing happens. I was making some black-out curtains from material I had bought that day, and my husband went upstairs to the small back bedroom to watch the searchlights. About twenty minutes later we heard a Jerry circling round – but we still didn't bother. Then all of a sudden there were four terrific bangs, and I flew in and picked up baby and dashed into the pantry – which I thought was the safest place. But to my horror I saw flames spurting up outside the window. I called to my husband that there were incendiary bombs outside, and when he went out, the whole place was alight; there was one in every garden down our road, and the men around were busy putting them out. We thought the plane had gone for good, when suddenly we heard him coming back. I dived under the dining-room table; was standing by the door; when suddenly there was a terrible explosion that rocked the house. The next explosion put out the light; the third struck the house, and it all came down on top of us. The smell from the bomb was terrible – I thought we had been gassed. My next thought was that we should have to wait until we were dug out. I could feel the debris on my back – but just then my husband managed to reach me, and we tried to scramble out. I had put the baby right underneath me for protection; when it all fell, she just let out one awful scream, and was so quiet after that, I thought she must be hurt or something. But she was alright. G. and I, with the baby, ran along the road to a house we know that has a basement; there we sheltered until the all-clear sounded at four o'clock. What a night! The planes were going over every few minutes, and all of us in that basement crouched over our babies, in case anything else fell. Morning came, and we were able to see the damage. All the upstairs of our house was gone, and the front of the house was nowhere to be seen. The room we were in was the only room at all recognizable. Other houses near ours were either completely demolished, or else had their backs blown in, and all had their doors and windows blown out. At five o'clock in the morning, the wardens took everybody round to the church schoolroom for hot tea, and kept us there, as they suspected there were delayed action bombs about. Nearly all our stuff has gone – a lot we can never replace – but we have our lives, and the baby, and that is far more important.

# LONDON BURNING!

### A SERGEANT IN THE CASF WHO WAS IN LONDON DURING THE GREAT RAID OF MAY 1941

I had been taking supper with my sister, who is an ambulance driver, and at about half-past twelve I stepped outside to have a look round, in the hope that I'd be lucky enough to see one of our night fighters score a victory – and I was quite surprised to see fires of considerable size blazing about two miles away. I slipped a coat on and walked to the top of a hill, the better to see – and the higher I got, the more serious it looked. From where I stood, I could look over the Regents Park area to Baker Street Tube Station, and beyond to Marble Arch, Piccadilly, Hyde Park, and the West End in general. It was a holocaust of flames and smoke; bursting bombs, and more and more incendiaries starting more fires. Broken gas mains were flaming, and there was a veritable devil's tattoo of anti-aircraft fire and machine guns. It's awful to think that such a destructive and inhumane thing as an air-raid, in which people are dying and homes being blasted, *could* be beautiful – but actually from a distance it was a sight worth seeing. From my eminence, it was as though I was looking into a vast cauldron, from which arose a dull red glow, shot through with terrific, vivid white flashes; while clouds of smoke, dust and sparks billowed up and caused the moon to change from pale green to a rich orange tinge. On my left was a battery of three light guns, whose muzzle-blast reminded you of the yapping of a bad-tempered terrier dog. Dead ahead, another battery of heavier guns were going off with a report like a giant firecracker exploding in an iron drain-pipe. Then there was the crash of the heavy-calibre guns that might easily be mistaken for an exploding enemy bomb. Firing in groups of three, combined with all the other sounds you hear in an air-raid, it is like a sort of symphony orchestra. Through all the noise and confusion, there is a constant consciousness of *whistles*; as an inevitable background to any air-raid, there are always police whistles, wardens' whistles, signals from rescue parties, and other whistles that impress themselves on your mind by their constancy. They never seem loud or close at hand – yet you *always* hear them. One of my clearest remembrances of air-raids will always be of this particular sound. Well, anyway, I stood watching the great fire, and said to myself, 'I'll walk down to the next corner, to see if I can see it better from there.' When I got there, the next corner looked a better vantage point – and so on, until I was rushing up the street towards the area that had been paid particular attention by the *Luftwaffe*. On the way down, I stopped to talk to a group of fire-watchers, and we all suddenly heard the oddest sound – like the sound of old brass cow-bells at home, that go *clunk-clunk*, instead of ringing clearly. The sound was overhead and all around us, coming nearer. It was such a gentle sound that no one took alarm, and we finally started to *hear* things falling in the road. A policeman came up, and told us they were probably *booby-trap bombs* – that is, a tin of fifty De Reszke cigarettes – which explode when any attempt is made to open them! Several had been found already. We spent a fruitless ten minutes trying to locate them, and then I continued on down to the fire. Just as I was leaving the group, a big one started to come down, and it sounded as if it was landing fairly close – so the five special wardens flung themselves down on the ground like so many rag dolls! But when it did land, it didn't explode. I continued on down the street, past Lord's Cricket Ground, and rounding the curve, came in full sight of the fire. It was ghastly, yet magnificent. At the extremity of the street a broken gas main was flaming like fury. Flames towered up fifty feet or so and brought into sharp relief the tiny scurrying figures of the Auxiliary Fire Service and the other workers, as they raced between the flames and me. I hurried down, and the first job presented itself in the person of a girl, who asked me to help put out incendiaries that she had noticed in a row of flats round the corner. Several of us polished them off, and in the doing of it, I got drenched. I was flinging a pail of water at a blazing hole in the ceiling, just when a guy on the floor above was flinging a pail of water at a blazing hole in the floor – the consequences were staggering, as the pailful caught me squarely in the chest! All this time, *that man* was circling about overhead, dropping things on the fire. Strangely enough, you don't hear them explode if you're working hard – or else, it may be that you don't care! Further down the street I saw a fireman struggling to get a hose into a four-storey building, the top floor of which was well alight; so an Air Force bloke and myself gave him a hand, and up to the top we went, by a circular stairway. On reaching the top, the fireman said, 'Hold on to the hose, while I go down and start the pumper.' We were holding on like mad – but nothing happened. So the other chap, fearing that something had happened to the fireman, went to the window to have a look – and at that moment the water came on! The hose started leaping and bucking like mad, and as the first surge of water came spurting through, it bashed me up against the wall, as if I were a straw. We soon had it under control, though, and as three men trying to point a hose seemed to me one too many, I went down to the street, to see if I could help elsewhere. All I can remember of the next two hours is being on a roof, and my foot going through the slates and cutting my shin; climbing endless stairs with sand and water; kicking down locked doorways to gain access to houses on fire, and holding the hose. The house whose roof I struck my foot through we couldn't save – and yet the lady who owned it had the pluck to crack jokes and make us tea, while her top storey was blazing. Next I spotted a rescue party hacking at the indescribable wreckage of a house – mattresses, bird-cages, tables, linoleum, bedding, chesterfields, lumber, steel, bricks and dust, all welded into a seemingly immovable mass. 'There's three in that lot!' said a grim-looking old cuss – so off with the coat, and everybody tore into the pile, and miracle of miracles, we found the man of the house alive – shaken but unhurt – lying in a small groove-like space, sheltered by flooring boards from above. He was able to tell us exactly where to find his wife and mother, and although we could see them and hand them water, it was another hour and a half before we got them out – both almost completely unhurt. By now almost every other roof for blocks around was blazing. Not just small fires – but ones which everybody at home would turn out to see, if they occurred in London, Ontario. There were twenty fires to every fireman, and being old-fashioned buildings, with steep pitched roofs, thousands of gables and chimney-pots, it was very difficult to get at them. The houses all butted together, so that if one fire got out of control, it pretty well spelt finis to the others in that block. There were many unusual silhouettes, as churches and other buildings of unusual design would be a seething mass of flames inside, and the lovely arches, and odd corners with their gargoyles, etc. would stand out framed blackly against the angry red of the inner fire. At last it began to get light, and the last of the Hun raiders dropped his load and scooted. The anti-aircraft bursts pursuing him grew farther and farther away. I felt about done in, so I trudged home, tired but happy – glad to have been some help in London's biggest Blitz so far.

*England's greatest literary hedonist, Cyril Connolly, took the Blitz on London in 1940 surprisingly well. 'Really, you know,' he remarked to an apprehensive Peter Quennell as the bombs whistled down, 'we've all had interesting lives.' His new monthly magazine, Horizon, financed by his friend Peter Watson, was only six months old when the bombing started; but was to survive the worst Goering could do throughout the war. What Connolly could not stand was the V1 that followed in 1944. As he famously remarked to Harold Nicolson, who upbraided him for not thinking more about his dear ones at the front: 'Perfect fear casteth out love.' In fact Horizon played an important role in defining and strengthening the role of British intellectuals in the war; and in crystallizing their aching need for the European civilization from which they were cut off. It was, in sum, required reading for the age of longing.*

## PUBLISH OR PERISH

MICHAEL SHELDEN

In July 1940, Horizon published Goronwy Rees's 'Letter from a Soldier'. Formerly on the staff of the *Spectator*, Rees was now a military officer, and he took exception to Connolly's belief that 'war is the enemy of creative activity, and writers and painters are right and wise to ignore it'. In a scolding tone Rees accused Connolly of denigrating the common soldier, who could not enjoy the luxury of ignoring the fighting, and who was expected to face death so that civilians like Connolly could remain free. Rees complained, 'You say, in effect, to the artists: let the British and French soldiers protect you, but ignore them while they die for you and wait till they have killed the ogre that threatens.' Despite the conviction of this attack, it distorts Connolly's position. Concentrating on art rather than war does not mean that one ignores the sacrifices made by soldiers on the battlefield.

It would have been easy for Connolly to ignore Rees, or to bury his attack in small type at the back of the magazine. Instead he printed it, with a prominent heading, at the front – in the space normally reserved for 'Comment' – and put his response to it among the back pages. Furthermore, he admitted there was some justice to Rees's charges. *Horizon*, he confessed, had not taken the war seriously enough, and Hitler's recent victories on the Continent had made it clear that 'we cannot afford the airy detachment of earlier numbers. We have walked through the tiger house, speculating on the power and ferocity of the beasts, and looked up to find the cage-doors open.' But, he countered, the problem was really one of tone, not of substance, for 'the fact remains that war is the enemy of creative activity. . . . The point which *Horizon* has made is that though this war is being fought for culture, the fighting of it will not create that culture.' His position was essentially a sound one and, though he sometimes undercut it by treating the war too lightly, his critics were often guilty of taking his views too seriously, analysing them as though they had been printed in a government white paper instead of a literary magazine.

In the next number (August 1940) Connolly could not resist having some fun at the expense of those who thought *Horizon* should give more attention to the war. Squeezed in among short stories, a poem by C. Day Lewis, and articles on Racine and ancient music, was a solemn essay on military tactics: 'Generalship Old and New' by Major-General J.F.C. Fuller. Connolly gave the piece top billing on the cover of the magazine, and no doubt some readers assumed that General Fuller and his article were invented. But the general was a retired officer of the Oxfordshire and Bucks Light Infantry and a leading authority on tanks. Except for a brief remark at the end of 'Comment', Connolly presented the article without introduction, as though it belonged perfectly with the rest of the 'highbrow' contributions. But its turgid, rambling discourse on 'the requirements of generalship' needed no introduction; its outrageously bad style is better than any parody:

> Originality, not conventionality, is one of the main pillars of generalship. To do something that the enemy does not expect, is not prepared for, something that will surprise and disarm him morally. To be always thinking ahead and to be always peeping round the corners. To spy out the soul of one's adversary, and to act in a manner which will astonish and bewilder him, that is generalship. To render the enemy's general ridiculous in the eyes of his men, that is the foundation of success.

Perhaps a few readers, including the general, did not see the joke, but thought that finally 'highbrows' like Connolly were showing an interest in subjects which really mattered. But for those who recognized the joke, the point was clear enough – what mattered in Horizon was literature. Earnest discussions of tank tactics old and new might serve the war effort and show that the magazine was not ignoring what was happening in the 'real' world, but would hardly serve the needs of literature.

Connolly enjoyed the joke so much that he wrote a parody of the general's article and published it at the end of August in the New Statesman, identifying himself as 'Rear-Colonel Connolly'. Titled 'What will He Do Next?', it is almost as good as General Fuller's original. Like the general, 'Colonel Connolly' is a tank expert who has thought long and hard about the contributions 'a small highly mechanized strike force' can make to modern warfare. He has written specialized books on the subject, but he is not quite sure how to explain his views to the intellectuals who read the New Statesman. He does his best to put his theories into simplified form, though he is more successful at giving civilians advice on practical problems in the event of a German invasion, such as 'How to stop a tank':

> For a tank trap it is only necessary to remove the paving stones outside your house (borrow a wheelbarrow from the man next door) and dig a pit some forty feet wide by twenty deep. Place a sheet of wire netting over the road, cover it with cardboard or brown paper, and a top dressing of asphalt. Your trap is made.

'What will He Do Next?' was published as Connolly was returning to London from Thurlestone. Ironically, he had seen more German planes over 'peaceful' Devon than he would have spotted all summer long if he had stayed in London, which until the last week of August suffered only one significant raid.

There was considerable fear of invasion, and most Londoners assumed that large-scale air attacks were imminent. Indeed, early in the evening of 7 September the raids began, and for the next fifty-seven nights great waves of German bombers, averaging more than 150 planes each night, pounded London. On the first night Connolly and George Orwell were together at Athenaeum Court in Piccadilly, where Connolly had taken a furnished flat on the top floor. The worst bombing was in the East End, but from the rooftop of Athenaeum Court they saw the night sky ablaze over the river, where huge fires had engulfed the docks. Earlier, a few stray bombs had fallen near Piccadilly; Orwell had been forced to take cover from flying shrapnel. But it still seemed beyond belief, as though the explosions and fires were part of some imaginary spectacle. Feeling oddly detached, Orwell looked out over the scene from the rooftop and came away impressed 'by the size and beauty of the flames'. The only consolation for them was that Athenaeum Court was a sturdy modern building of steel and concrete, and was thought to be relatively safe as long as the bombs did not fall too close to it.

On the following night, the German attack spread to Bloomsbury, inflicting terrible damage on the district's elegant streets and squares. In Guilford Street, which ran next to Lansdowne Terrace, a bomb ruptured a gas main and set off a large fire, while another exploded in the playground opposite Horizon's office. No one was hurt, and the only damage to the office was a broken window pane. Virginia Woolf's house in nearby Mecklenburgh Square was not so fortunate. It survived the initial attacks, but unexploded bombs in the square went off a few days later, and the ceilings collapsed, leaving it a shambles. For a fortnight the area around Lansdowne Terrace was cordoned off because of unexploded bombs, and Horizon was without an office for a good part of September. (Spender still had many of his books and other belongings stored there, but it had long ago completed its transformation from a flat into an office.) To add to Horizon's problems, the Curwen Press was bombed at least three times. A raid in October destroyed two thousand copies of one issue. These were quickly replaced, but the printers had to work under a gaping hole in the roof of their building. In the December 'Comment' Connolly complained, 'The offices of Horizon would seem to be a military objective second in importance only to our printers.'

The same 'Comment' pointed out that the magazine's circulation had suffered a sharp decline since Dunkirk. After selling 8,000 copies of the April number, Horizon had a sale of only 5,000 at the end of 1940. Part of the problem was that fewer copies were being ordered by newsagents and booksellers. New restrictions designed to save paper prevented them from returning unsold copies of periodicals, so they ordered only what their shops were sure to sell. To keep its ration of paper secure, Horizon needed to build up its circulation by expanding its list of regular subscribers, but the Blitz had made that difficult. The disruptions in the postal service had caused endless problems with the subscribers the magazine already had, and cancellations from those people made it hard to gain ground from new subscriptions. Horizon needed all the help its friends could give. 'We exist to provide good writing,' Connolly told his readers, 'and we must not forget it. But we barely exist, and those who wish us well can help by getting us more readers and more subscribers.' He was not above shaming people into subscribing, if that would do the trick. In 'Comment' he declared, 'If we can go on producing a magazine in these conditions, the least you can do is to read it. The money Horizon loses would provide you with, if not a Spitfire, at any rate a barrage balloon. If you would rather have that, say so.'

Except for a short trip to Scotland in October, he stayed in London through the worst weeks of the Blitz. It would have been easy to evacuate the magazine and its staff to a remote spot in the countryside; but after the first few nights of bombing Connolly – like so many Londoners – became accustomed to the raids and the dangers, and was determined to carry on as normally as possible. Even during heavy and close raids, he surprised friends by his calmness. Peter Quennell remembers an occasion when he and Connolly were caught in the street, and he could not persuade his friend to take cover in a public shelter nearby. 'Bombs were going off all around us, and Cyril simply stood inside a doorway calmly waiting for the raid to end. I was visibly frightened, thinking any minute a bomb might hit us, but when Cyril saw the expression on my face he just looked at me and said, "Be calm. Really, you know, we've all had interesting lives."' (Much later, when the Germans began sending over the V1 flying bombs, Connolly's composure broke down. He admitted that he was utterly terrified by the new weapon, which killed so suddenly and randomly. When he spoke of his fear to Harold Nicolson, he was told that he ought to worry more about his 'dear ones' fighting in France, 'who are in far greater danger'. To which Connolly responded, 'That wouldn't work with me at all, Harold. In the first place, I have no dear ones at the front. And in the second place, I have observed that with me perfect fear casteth out love.')

In Peter Watson's case the Blitz brought one important change for the better: he acquired new respect and admiration for his country. He was deeply moved by the great courage ordinary people demonstrated every day in the streets of London, and gratified to see the unity of people of all classes in the face of the German attacks. He too remained in London during the grim autumn months of 1940, and did his best to ignore the dangers. His flat in Athenaeum Court might have been safer than most places, but it was still vulnerable to direct hits. He was resolved to accept all risks: 'I never go to a shelter,' he told Cecil Beaton. 'I would rather die in my sleep.' Unlike Connolly, he was even willing to accept the risks of military service. His elder brother, Sir Norman Watson, was an RAF officer, and Peter was also prepared to serve the RAF if he were needed. While waiting to be called up, he declared in a letter to Parker Tyler: '[I] am no pacifist, one must fight for anything worth having and rightly so.' His physical examination by RAF doctors in October showed, however, that he was seriously underweight and mildly jaundiced – he suffered from periodic attacks during much of his adult life – and he was therefore rejected.

As the Blitz dragged on, Watson developed a keen sense of pride in *Horizon*'s ability to keep going despite the hardships involved in preparing, printing, and distributing each issue. He was pleased to be a part of it all, and began to look upon his work as a kind of patriotic service – a defiant gesture for British culture against the German threat. He was no longer apologetic about the magazine or doubtful of its value. When it was reported to him that Cecil Beaton had called *Horizon* 'cowardly', Watson wrote, 'I wish you would write and tell me exactly why. I imagined we had been really rather morally courageous.' In a rare show of anger, he complained to Beaton that some of their wealthy French friends had lately shown true cowardice by fleeing France and then secretly giving their support to Pétain's puppet régime in Vichy: 'How I despise those super-rich (some of whom you and I have known very well) who sent all their money to England and America . . . and are now living over here feeling very pro-Pétain, not daring to say so openly and afraid to return in case Pétain came in against England.'

Horizon's 'courage' did not go unrecognized by its readers. Despite Goronwy Rees's complaints in July, it soon became clear that quite a few soldiers placed high value on the magazine's defence of culture. During the stay at Thurlestone, when the war was just beginning, Spender recalls that 'we received letters from pilots fighting in the Battle of Britain, often saying they felt that so long as Horizon continued they had a cause to fight for. Such letters could only make us feel unworthy and ashamed. Yet for these young men, Horizon, New Writing, and one or two other literary reviews, were the means whereby they felt that they, as well as we, survived the war.'

One young contributor to the June 1940 number, a pilot named Gully Mason, was shot down and killed just a short time after he visited the editors at Thurlestone during a brief leave. Later in the war the famous Spitfire pilot Richard Hillary, author of The Last Enemy, asked if he could contribute an article. His proposal was accepted, but he died in an air crash before it could be written. In 1942 Horizon published a story called 'The Pupil', submitted by a young fighter pilot stationed in Tunisia. Rollo Woolley, the author of the story, had been at Rugby and Oxford before joining the RAF, and his appearance in Horizon was warmly received. He placed another story in New Writing, but at the age of twenty-three he was killed in an air battle over North Africa. After his death, Connolly learned that a diary had been found in which Rollo Woolley had written in capital letters over a whole page: 'MY STORY ACCEPTED BY HORIZON!'

1989

---

*The Germans were nothing if not thorough. In 1941, at Leipzig, they printed a book which laid down the ordinances that the British would have to obey when they were under the jurisdiction of the German Military Commander. It contained few surprises.*

---

## GERMAN OCCUPIED GREAT BRITAIN

### ORDINANCES OF THE MILITARY AUTHORITIES

I.

All newspapers, pamphlets, publications, printed matter, reproductions obtained by mechanical or chemical methods, writings, pictures with or without words, music with words or explanations and cinematographic films, which are intended for public distribution and are of a nature to prejudice public order or endanger the security or the dignity of the troops of occupation, are forbidden, and may be seized by order of the Military Commander by the representative of the county. In the case of a daily publication, the representative of the county may order its exclusion from his area for a period of three days. If such publication is published in that area, he may order its suspension for the same period. The action taken will be reported immediately to the Military Commander who will give a final decision thereon.

II.

The Military Commander may order that any periodical publication which shall offend against this article shall be suspended or excluded from the occupied territory for a period not exceeding three months. Every such publication which shall have more than once been the subject of suspension or exclusion on the part of the Military Commander may, in the event of a subsequent offence, be suspended or excluded for a period exceeding three months or for an indefinite period.

III.

All theatrical or cinematographic performances, pantomimes, readings, recitations, concerts, lectures, or similar public manifestations of a nature to prejudice public order or affect the security or dignity of the troops of occupation are likewise forbidden. In case of urgency the county delegate of the Military Commander shall be entitled to prohibit performances and other manifestations of the above mentioned nature. Any action taken by such delegate shall be subject of immediate report to the Military Commander for a final decision.

IV.

The Military Commander may also order the closing for a period not exceeding three months of any establishment in which any newspaper or other publication, reproduction or film mentioned in section 1 above shall have been exhibited, sold or distributed. The Military Commander may similarly order the closing of any establishment in which any manifestation mentioned in section 3 above may have taken place.

*Not a single German spy landed in Britain lasted more than a few hours: a lively indication of the vigilance then being displayed by everybody in the beleaguered island. The truth is, though, that German attempts at espionage verged on the farcical. There was nothing farcical, however, about the fate of those caught. The confusion in the German mind between Tunbridge Wells and Mr Tunbridge the postmaster, however, is pure Beachcomber. It showed, too, that blacking out all place names was not an exaggerated precaution.*

# INVASION 1940

### PETER FLEMING

As the plans for 'Sea Lion' took shape, the extent to which they were hampered by lack of accurate intelligence came to be appreciated by the German Supreme Command, and the *Abwehr*, whose reputation at the time was high, endeavoured to remedy this state of affairs by large-scale improvisation. In September a shower of spies descended on the United Kingdom; all were taken into custody by the British authorities. They were for the most part low-grade agents who had not completed their training. The *Abwehr* seems to have realized that their chances of doing useful work or even of escaping detection were not high; but they were only expected to remain in the field for a few weeks, and it was hoped that any who got into trouble would be got out of it when the German troops arrived. At any rate a number of inferior spies were more likely to produce results than no spies at all, and early in September this clandestine traffic began in earnest. Let us follow the fortunes of two parties sent across; they give an adequate idea of the *Abwehr's* methods at this time.

On 2 September 1940 four German agents embarked at Le Touquet in a fishing boat which was escorted across the Channel by two mine-sweepers. According to one of the men the fishing boat's crew consisted, improbably, of three Russians and a Latvian; another said it was manned by two Norwegians and one Russian. All had confused memories of the voyage, and it seems possible that they were drunk.

The spies were to hunt in couples. One pair, after transhipping to a dinghy, landed near Hythe in the early hours of 3 September. They had a wireless set and an elementary form of cipher, and their orders were to send back information of military importance; they had been given to understand that an invasion of the Kentish coast was imminent. By 5.30 a.m. on the same morning both men, although they separated on landing, had been challenged and made prisoner by sentries of a battalion of the Somersetshire Light Infantry.

This was hardly surprising. The two men were of Dutch nationality. They were completely untrained for their difficult task; their sole

103

qualification for it seems to have lain in the fact that each, having committed some misdemeanour which was known to the Germans, could be blackmailed into undertaking the enterprise. Neither had more than a smattering of English; and one suffered, by virtue of having had a Japanese mother, from the additional hazard of a markedly Oriental appearance; he it was who, when first sighted by an incredulous private of the Somersets in the early dawn, had binoculars and a spare pair of shoes slung round his neck.

The other pair of spies consisted of a German, who spoke excellent French but no English at all, and a man of abstruse origins who claimed to be a Dutchman and who, alone of the four, had a fluent command of English. They landed at Dungeness under cover of darkness on 3 September, and soon after daybreak were suffering acutely from thirst, a fact which lends colour to the theory that on the previous night the whole party had relied on Dutch courage to an unwise extent. The English-speaker, pardonably ignorant of British licensing laws, tried to buy cider at breakfast-time in a public house at Lydd. The landlady pointed out that this transaction could not legally take place until ten o'clock and suggested that meanwhile he should go and look at the church. When he returned (for she was a sensible woman) he was arrested.

His companion, the only German in the party, was not caught until the following day. He had rigged up an aerial in a tree and had begun to send messages (in French) to his controllers. Copies of three of these messages survived and were used in evidence against him at his trial. They were short and from an operational point of view worthless; the news (for instance) that 'this is exact position yesterday evening six o'clock three messerschmitt fired machine guns in my direction three hundred metres south of water reservoir painted red' was in no way calculated to facilitate the establishment of a German bridgehead in Kent.

All four spies were tried, under the Treason Act, 1940, in November. One of the blackmailed Dutchmen was acquitted; the other three were hanged in Pentonville Prison in the following month. Their trials were conducted in *camera*, but short, factual obituary announcements were published after the executions.

Two men and a woman, who on the night of 30 September 1940 were landed by a rubber dinghy on the coast of Banffshire after being flown thither from Norway in a seaplane, had – and, except by virtue of their courage, deserved – no more luck than the agents deposited in Kent. They were arrested within a few hours of their arrival. During those hours their conduct had been such as to attract the maximum of suspicion. This – since both men spoke English with a strong foreign accent and the documents of all three were clumsily forged – they were in no position to dispel; and the first of them to be searched by the police was found to have in his possession, *inter alia*: a wireless set; a loaded Mauser automatic; an electric torch marked 'made in Bohemia'; a list of bomber and fighter stations in East Anglia; £327 in English notes;

and a segment of German sausage. Both men – one a German, the other a Swiss – were in due course hanged. Although 'Sea Lion' had for practical purposes been cancelled before they left Norway, one of them had been given, like the men in Kent, a purely tactical role connected with the invasion.

The one serious leakage of secret information known to have occurred during the period was not contrived by the German intelligence. The principal persons concerned in this strange episode were a young American born in China, the then Member of Parliament for Peebles and Midlothian, and the daughter of a former admiral in the Russian Navy. The American, Tyler Kent, was a thirty-year-old cipher-clerk employed in the United States Embassy. Five years earlier, while holding a similar position in Moscow, he had formed the habit of keeping copies of the more important messages which passed through his hands, and he resumed this practice when transferred to London in October 1939. According to his own story, his motives, though muddled, were pure. He disapproved of the manner in which American foreign policy was conducted, felt that the loyalty he owed to his country as a whole was at least equal to the loyalty he owed to whichever of her representatives he happened to be serving, and accumulated his hoard of documents against a day when he might feel it his duty to reveal their unsatisfactory contents to influential Congressmen. It seems quite possible that this explanation was more or less true.

In London Kent made the acquaintance of Anna Wolkoff, a lady some ten years older than himself, and was drawn into the orbit of the 'Right Club', a small, seedy clique of anti-semites, whose dedicated members went round in the black-out sticking up handbills which proclaimed, 'This is a Jews' War'. Prominent among these unbalanced cranks (but unlike some of them a staunch anti-Nazi) was Captain A.H.M. Ramsay, an old Etonian, a Member of Parliament and an officer with a good record in the First World War; Anna Wolkoff called herself his ADC.

By January 1940 Kent's collection of documents had begun to include copies of the messages exchanged between Churchill (then First Sea Lord) and President Roosevelt; these were despatched through the United States Embassy. Of those which came into Kent's possession, none was of the first importance but all would have been of value to the enemy. In February he applied for, but was refused, a transfer to Berlin. When at his trial Counsel for the Prosecution asked Kent whether, if his application had been granted, he meant to take the documents with him and make them over to the Germans, Kent replied that the question was hypothetical.

He had however begun to show these documents indiscriminately to his comrades in the fight against the Jews and the Freemasons, Captain Ramsay and Anna Wolkoff. The latter had a close association with an Assistant Military Attaché of the Italian Embassy. It was not proved that she transmitted to him any of the interesting information to which she now had access; but on 23 May the German Ambassador in Rome (Mackensen) telegraphed to Berlin an accurate summary of Roosevelt's reply to Churchill's first message in the 'Former Naval Person' series to be sent after he became Prime Minister. Churchill's message was transmitted on 15 May and included a request for 40 or 50 of 'your older destroyers'. The reply – a sympathetic one – was sent from Washington on the 16th but was not received by the Prime Minister until the 18th. Earlier messages in the same series had passed through Wolkoff's hands and had been photographed; and it seems probable that Kent had thus been indirectly instrumental in furnishing the Italians with copies of these important communications. Certainly the formula employed by Mackensen in prefacing his report. ('I am reliably informed from an unimpeachable source . . .') suggests that his excellent intelligence was derived from access to a verbatim version of the President's message; and this impression is strengthened by internal evidence in his telegram. This was a dangerous leakage. The secrets to which Kent (who for more than five years, without incurring suspicion, had been systematically betraying the trust reposed in him by the State Department) now had access really mattered. A grave threat to British security had come fortuitously into existence.

But it had come into existence under the microscope automatically focused by the authorities on such blatantly dubious organizations as the 'Right Club'. Kent and Wolkoff were arrested on 18 May (the American Ambassador having waived the former's title to diplomatic immunity as a member of the Embassy staff) and tried in *camera* at the Old Bailey. Kent was sentenced to seven years' imprisonment, Anna Wolkoff to ten. Captain Ramsay, who could not be shown to have broken any law by his fervent but tangential activities, was interned under Section 18 (B) of the Defence Regulations on 23 May. He continued at intervals, as was his right, to assert in written communications to the Speaker of the House of Commons the thesis that his detention constituted a breach of Parliamentary privilege. The House debated this matter in December 1940 and decided that no breach of its privileges was involved. Ramsay was not released until after the war; he died in 1955.

In 1940 the schisms, caused mainly by the internecine war between the *Abwehr* under Canaris and the *Sicherheitsdienst* under Himmler, which later reft and stultified German Intelligence, had not begun to provide an explanation for its inefficiency. Its standards, even so, were not high. Some idea of its limitations may be gained from a report dated 5 September 1940 and headed 'England: Fortifications on the South Coast', for which a place was found in the files of the Supreme Command of the German Navy. It read as follows:

*A secret agent reported on September 2:*

The area Tunbridge Wells to Beachy Head, especially the small town of Rye (where there are large sand-hills) and also St Leonards, is distinguished by a special labyrinth of defences. These defences, however, are so well camouflaged that a superficial observer on the sand-hills, bathing spots and fields, would not discover anything extraordinary. This area is extremely well guarded, so that it is almost impossible to reach there without a special pass.

In Hastings, on the other hand, most of the defences can be recognized quite plainly. In the town there are troops of every kind. The presence of numerous small and heavy tanks is most striking.

Numerous armoured cars were also seen in St Leonards and in a small locality where there is a famous golf-course, probably St Joseph.

*Comment by the Abwehr:*

The agent was not able to give a clearer account of the number of armoured cars in the different localities, or of the regiments he saw there.

From the position of Beachy Head (west of Hastings) and Rye (east of Hastings), it can be deduced that the place in question near St Leonards was the western villa-suburb of Hastings. Tunbridge, which lies on the railway line from Hastings to London, must, according to the sense of the report, also lie on the coast, but, as in the case of St Joseph, this cannot be confirmed from the charts in our possession.

Both Tunbridge Wells and Tonbridge are some thirty miles inland from Beachy Head. It is just possible that the spy's geography was bedevilled by an odd coincidence. In 1940 the post office at Camber-on-Sea (a small village about ten miles east of Hastings) was kept by a Mr Tunbridge, and after the obliteration of all place-names in May the sign over his premises read:

TUNBRIDGE
POST OFFICE AND STORES

1957

D. *Van den Bogaerde conceals the identity of the distinguished actor Dirk Bogarde. In 1943 he was an obscure soldier, but with a handy turn of phrase, as 'Steel Cathedrals' shows.*

## STEEL CATHEDRALS

### D. VAN DEN BOGAERDE

It seems to me, I spend my life in stations.
Going, coming, standing, waiting.
Paddington, Darlington, Shrewsbury, York.
I know them all most bitterly.
Dawn stations, with a steel light, and waxen figures.
Dust, stone, and clanking sounds, hiss of weary steam.
Night stations, shaded light, fading pools of colour.
Shadows and the shuffling of a million feet.
Khaki, blue, and bulky kitbags, rifles gleaming dull.
Metal sound of army boots, and smokers' coughs.
Titter of harlots in their silver foxes.
Cases, casks, and coffins, clanging of the trolleys.
Tea urns tarnished, and the greasy white of cups.
Dry buns, Woodbines, Picture Post and Penguins;
and the blaze of magazines.
Grinding sound of trains, and rattle of the platform gates.
Running feet and sudden shouts, clink of glasses from the buffet.
Smell of drains, tar, fish and chips and sweaty scent, honk of taxis;
and the gleam of cigarettes.
Iron pillars, cupolas of glass, girders messed by pigeons;
the lazy singing of a drunk.
Sailors going to Chatham, soldiers going to Crewe.
Aching bulk of kit and packs, tin hats swinging.
The station clock with staggering hands and callous face,
says twenty-five-to-nine.
A cigarette, a cup of tea, a bun,
and my train goes at ten.

It was the bizarre and unkind fate of a number of highly educated Central European refugees to be locked up by the British when they had come here to escape being locked up by the Germans. Intentions were honourable enough. In the aftermath of Dunkirk the British were hyper-sensitive about the infiltration of foreign spies and it says something for the solidarity and watchfulness of the island race that, as we have seen, not a single German spy stayed free for long in wartime England. Still, this admirable preoccupation meant that a number of distinguished men and women were rounded up and incarcerated in conditions, superficially at least, uneasily reminiscent of those they had left behind. Gradually it was sorted out. One prisoner was released to lecture at All Souls College, Oxford; others, like Arthur Koestler, were freed to write their books. One internee, Henry Prais, later to hold the chair of French in Jerusalem, had to fill up a form giving his past prison record. He duly completed it: 'November–December 1938: Buchenwald, on the charge of being a Jew; July–December 1940: Onchan, on the charge of being a German.'

# BRITAIN'S INTERNEES IN THE SECOND WORLD WAR

MIRIAM KOCHAN

In the summer of 1942 fewer than 5,000 enemy aliens remained in the Isle of Man. Of these, according to the Board of Deputies of British Jews, only 300–400 were refugees.

The vast majority who had been released began yet again to rebuild shattered lives, some of them with remarkable success.

For some, such as Klaus Loewald, the experience of internment had been a valuable one: 'To me, the two years had passed very quickly. Many windows had been opened in my mind, and I was conscious of having obtained the kind of education which attendance at school could not provide. My years of internment constituted a period of uninterrupted good fortune. I had entered them in a spirit of irresponsible youthful adventure, and at their end I had to remind myself that it was not wisdom which had guided my steps.'

Few retain the bitterness of the internee who wrote to me from America: 'The Germans overran France, and the English government was in a panic and had to show their people that they were on the alert. So they arrested friendly refugees and sent many of them by boat to Canada. When at the same time thousands of English citizens belonged to the Mosley party and were waiting for Adolf Hitler to invade England. It was the biggest farce and one of the most cowardly steps the English government took against the refugees.'

For some, internment had changed the course of their lives. 'If they hadn't interned me,' said Felix Darnbacher, 'I would not have come to Israel. I would have been so British.'

Others are so British. Eugen Glueckauf writes, 'A year after my release I got the offer of a McKinnon Research Studentship of the Royal Society which ran for two years, and I continued to do meteorological war research on the water content of the stratosphere. In 1944 I applied for a position with the Department of Scientific and Industrial Research, involving research on the separation of isotopes, in collaboration with Sir Francis Simon, who was Professor of Physics at Oxford. The work was to be done at Durham. After getting naturalized in 1946 I applied for a post with the Atomic Energy Research Establishment at Harwell, and we moved there in 1947. This proved to be a most important change of status. Though only recently naturalized I was accepted without reservation as a Principal Scientific Officer, and in due course was promoted to Deputy Chief Scientist and Head of the Physical and Radio-Chemistry branch. In spite of an audible accent, I assimilated well, was elected a Fellow of the Royal Society, and was elected and served for more than twenty years on our local parish council.

'It goes without saying that I never felt any resentment about the few months I spent in internment. My years as a British subject were the best I could have wished for, and this country has become our home.'

Others take a philosophical approach. 'When I was released,' Henry Prais told me, 'I had to fill in a form giving my past record. Had you ever been in prison before? November–December 1938: Buchenwald, on the charge of being a Jew; July–December 1940: Onchan, on the charge of being a German.

'From 1936 onwards you had become so accustomed to an insecure existence that you did not find injustice surprising. You were conditioned to the fact that life was going to be insecure from then on. The only thing that you felt bad about: for the Nazis to call you a Jew – well, that was all right. For the British to call you a German, that was unfair. But we used to say, "The poor buggers don't know any better." You made excuses for them. The Jews always say, "Perhaps we are to blame."'

'I hold no resentment,' Dr H. writes. 'The rounding-up happened in the panic of Dunkirk and, in spite of all the sufferings and inconveniences, we must not forget that we lived on the Isle of Man during the time of the worst bombing, which we (and later the children) were spared. How many people who were sent to concentration camps would have been happy to suffer the hardships of internment? Nevertheless it was at that time hard to understand that one had been classed with obvious Nazis, from whom one had tried to escape.'

'Now we understand it, of course,' Freda explains, 'but at the time we only thought, "Why did they do this to us?"'

1983

---

Some refugees went on to America. Louis MacNeice was in New York in September of 1940 when a shipload disembarked 'with prune-dark eyes'. He catches perfectly the friendless world they must inherit.

## REFUGEES

### LOUIS MACNEICE

With prune-dark eyes, thick lips, jostling each other
These, disinterred from Europe, throng the deck
To watch their hope heave up in steel and concrete
Powerful but delicate as a swan's neck,

Thinking, each of them, the worst is over
And we do not want any more to be prominent or rich,
Only to be ourselves, to be unmolested
And make ends meet – an ideal surely which

Here if anywhere is feasible. Their glances
Like wavering antennae feel
Around the sliding limber towers of Wall Street
And count the numbered docks and gingerly steal

Into the hinterland of their own future
Behind this excessive annunciation of towers,
Tracking their future selves through a continent of strangeness.
The liner moves to the magnet; the quay flowers

With faces of people's friends. But these are mostly
Friendless and all they look to meet
Is a secretary who holds his levée among ledgers,
Tells them to take a chair and wait . . . .

And meanwhile the city will go on, regardless
Of any new arrival, trains like prayers
Radiating from stations haughty as cathedrals,
Tableaux of spring in milliners' windows, great affairs

Being endorsed on a vulcanite table, lines of washing
Feebly garish among grimy brick and dour
Iron fire-escapes; barrows of cement are rumbling
Up airy planks; a florist adds a flower

To a bouquet that is bound for somebody's beloved
Or for someone ill; in a sombre board-room great
Problems wait to be solved or shelved. The city
Goes on, but you, you will probably find, must wait

111

Till something or other turns up. Something-or-Other
Becomes an expected angel from the sky,
But do not trust the sky, the blue that looks so candid
Is non-committal, frigid as a harlot's eye.

Gangways – the handclasp of the land. The resurrected,
The brisk or resigned Lazaruses, who want
Another chance, go trooping ashore. But chances
Are dubious. Fate is stingy, recalcitrant,

And officialdom greets them blankly as they fumble
Their foreign-looking baggage; they still feel
The movement of the ship while through their imagination
The seen and the unheard-of constellations wheel.

1941

When George VI became king in 1936 – the third to sit on the British throne that year – monarchy was at a nadir in the land; a substantial minority of Tories declared themselves converted to republicanism. The long climb back was undertaken by a man who had no desire to be king and few apparent qualifications. He had passed last out of his class at Dartmouth, had knock knees, a dreadful stammer, and a short temper. His elder brother David had been granted all the glamour by the fates. Nevertheless, despite – perhaps because of – these manifest shortcomings, George VI slowly won the affection of his people. In this he was immeasurably helped by his wife. The way they stayed to face the bombs like every other Londoner unquestionably was a key factor in their enormous popularity. The German pilot who made his famous bombing run up the Mall gave the royal family a totally unplanned bonus. Meantime, the Duke of Windsor fretted away the war in the Bahama sun, bitter at what he considered his inequitable exile, and probably not realizing to the end of his life the good turn he had done the country by deserting its throne in favour of Wallis Simpson.

## THE QUEEN MOTHER

### ANN MORROW

If there were still those who thought the Queen a 'sweet' little thing at the beginning of the war, by the end of it that slightly patronizing description would not do. 'Sweet' hardly applied to a woman who chased rats out of the bomb-blasted Palace, or coped with an intruder in the same magnificently cool way as her daughter did in 1982, and who had learnt to handle a .38 revolver and a .303 rifle.

Lord Halifax, the Foreign Secretary, who was allowed to take a short cut through the grounds of Buckingham Palace, was once practically scared out of his black jacket and striped trousers by the sound of rifle shots. It was the Queen practising rapid fire: 'I shall not go down like the others,' she told him. She had been horrified by the plight of European royals like the Grand Duke of Luxembourg and Queen Wilhelmina of the Netherlands, who arrived in Britain with nothing more than a tin hat and a handbag, driven out by the Nazis and given shelter at Buckingham Palace.

The Queen always liked the Foreign Secretary and sent him a nice note once about Hitler's book:

15 November 1939

My dear Lord Halifax,
I send you *Mein Kampf*, but do not advise you to read it through, or you might go mad, and that would be a great pity.

Even a skip through gives one a good idea of his mentality, ignorance, and obvious sincerity.

At the very first rumbling of war the Queen was with the two Princesses at their house near Ballater, Birkhall, but she refused to stay there in safety. George VI was in London. 'If things turn out badly I must be with the King,' the Queen told her lady-in-waiting, Mrs Geoffrey Bowlby, as she left Scotland by the first available train.

A soldier in the Cameronians, who still treasures a handwritten note from the Queen, remembers vividly her 'into battle look' when she visited Westminster Children's Hospital in Vincent Square on one of the last delicate days of 'phoney' war in 1939.

The King and Queen remained in London: 'We stay with our people,' the Queen said. In 1939, before the bombing really began, it was thought that the King and Queen might send the princesses abroad. Parents were sending children away with their nannies at a rapid rate of knots to the safety of Canada and America. The Queen listened to the arguments and was touched by the invitations from the Dominions. But, as she wrote: 'So kind, but no, there was no question of the royal family taking up their kind offer because the children could not go without me, I could not possibly leave the King and the King would never go.'

There was nevertheless a real fear that she might be killed. Hitler had marked the Queen when she scattered poppies at a war cemetery in Paris in the summer of 1938, and there was a 'Kamikaze' determination by many of the German Luftwaffe to score a direct hit on the Palace.

First, an unexploded bomb fell near the King's study, but it was defused. Then, on 13 September 1940, the King described how he and the Queen '. . . heard an aircraft make a zooming noise above us and saw two bombs falling past on the opposite side of the Palace and then heard two resounding crashes as the bombs fell in the quadrangle about 30 yards away . . . We all wondered why we weren't dead.' The German pilot must have been surprised, too: he had taken a huge risk, flying straight up The Mall underneath the camouflage of cloud to drop a stick of six bombs. Nobody was killed, but the Palace was damaged extensively. When the King and Queen went down to see if the staff were all right, a policeman said, rather foolishly, 'A magnificent piece of bombing, Ma'am'. He then had the wit to add, 'If you'll pardon my saying so.'

The Queen replied: 'I'm glad we've been bombed. It makes me feel I can look the East End in the face.'

When the Queen went to visit the East End she deliberately wore light and pretty clothes: no sombre black and no green. Norman Hartnell designed discreet outfits in inoffensive gentle pastel blues, greys and lilacs. She took great trouble with her appearance because, she felt: 'If the poor people came to see me they would put on their best clothes.'

'Some clothes do not like me,' she explained, and decided against wearing a uniform of any kind. It was not a frivolous decision; she knew that a mannish uniform on her would not cheer anybody up. Again and again, during the war, she was seen stepping nimbly over rubble in high heels; the men with the shovels would see her smile and one Cockney sang out: 'Ain't she just bloody luvverly?'

In 1941, she visited the decimated city of Sheffield. Lord Harlech, the Midlands Commissioner, described how, when her car stopped, 'the Queen nips out into the snow and goes straight into the middle of the crowd and starts talking to them. First they would just gape; then they all started talking at once. "Hi, Your Majesty! Look here!"'

Distressed Londoners, scrabbling through the debris, would suddenly look up and see the Queen standing beside them. One woman was trying to get her terrified dog to come out from under a pile of dusty rubble. 'Perhaps I can try,' the Queen suggested. 'I am rather good with dogs.' A mother with an injured arm was trying to dress her baby. 'Let me help,' the Queen said as she darted forward, leaving officials open-mouthed.

On another occasion in the East End someone digging in the ruins shouted, 'Thank God for a good King!' The King, deeply touched, replied: 'Thank God for a good people.' Now, they were cheering his wife too.

1985

# WE SANG
# ALL THE WAY BACK

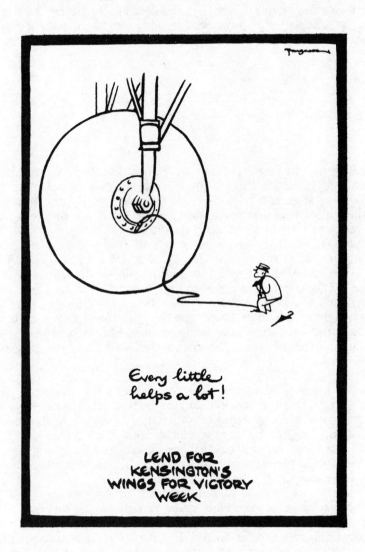

*RAF Bomber Command lost 56,000 British and Commonwealth aircrew during the war. Despite these grievous figures, morale was never in any doubt. A medical report at the end of the war showed that less than one man in 250 had to be taken off aircrew duties because of what the RAF called LMF – Lack of Moral Fibre. Yet of course they knew fear, as Max Hastings graphically demonstrates in his book Bomber Command. He chose six squadrons from different stages of the war, and sought out some hundred survivors from them to help him piece together a remarkable story. The difference an extraordinary man like Cheshire could make, with his almost messianic vision of flying, was incalculable. Lesser men had to struggle with their terrors as best they could.*

## BOMBER COMMAND

### MAX HASTINGS

Throughout the war, morale on British bomber stations held up astonishingly well, although there were isolated collapses on certain squadrons at certain periods – for example, during the heavy losses of the Battle of Berlin. Morale never became a major problem, as it did on some 8th Air Force stations during the terrible losses of 1943 and early 1944. An RAF doctor seconded to study aircrew spirit at one American station reported in dismay: 'Aircrew are heard openly saying that they don't intend to fly to Berlin again or do any more difficult sorties. This is not considered a disgrace or dishonourable.' Partly the Americans found the appalling business of watching each other die on daylight sorties more harrowing than the anonymity of night operations. Partly also, they were far from their homes, and many did not feel the personal commitment to the war that was possible for Englishmen . . . .

The Air Ministry never lost their conviction that gentlemen made the best aircrew, and a remarkable staff memorandum of late 1942 expressed concern about the growing proportion of Colonials in Bomber Command and suggested: 'There are indications in a number of directions that we are not getting a reasonable percentage of the young men of the middle and upper classes, who are the backbone of this country, when they leave the public schools.'

When Ferris Newton was interviewed for a commission, the group captain had already noted without enthusiasm that he owned a pub, and inquired whether it catered to the coach trade. Yet the Commonwealth aircrew, especially, believed that it was their very intimacy with their crews, their indifference to rank, that often made them such strong teams in the air. An Australian from 50 Squadron cited the example of a distinguished young English ex-public school pilot who was killed in 1943. This boy, he said, was a classic example of an officer who never achieved complete cohesion with his crew, who won obedience only by the rings on his sleeves and not by force of personality: 'He simply wouldn't have known how to go out screwing with his gunners in Lincoln on a Saturday night.' In his memoirs [Sir Arthur] Harris [C-in-C of Bomber Command] argues that the English made the best aircrew, because they had the strongest sense of discipline. It was a difference of tradition.

To the men on the stations, the RAF's attitude to their problems often seemed savagely unsympathetic. One day on a cross-country exercise before they began operations, the bomb-aimer of [the Norwegian pilot] Lindaas's crew at 76 Squadron fell through the forward hatch of the aircraft, which had somehow come loose. The rest of the crew thought at first that he had fallen out completely. Only after several moments did they realize that he was clinging desperately beneath the aircraft. Only after several more moments of struggle did they get the dinghy rope around him, and haul him back into the aircraft. When he returned to the ground, he said flatly that he would never fly again. He was pronounced LMF, and vanished from the station. Normally in such cases, an NCO was stripped of his stripes, which had been awarded in recognition of his aircrew status, and posted to ground duties. Only in incontrovertible cases of 'cowardice in the face of the enemy' as at one 5 Group station where one night three members of a crew left their aircraft as it taxied to take-off, was the matter referred to court-martial. A further cause of resentment against Permanent Commissioned Officers was that if they wished to escape operations, they could almost invariably arrange a quiet transfer to non-operational duties, because the service was reluctant to instigate the court-martial that was always necessary in their case, to strip them of rank.

It was very rare for a case to be open and shut. The navigator of a Whitley in 1941 ran amok and had to be laid out with the pilot's torch over Germany. The man disappeared overnight from the squadron – normal procedure throughout the war, to avoid the risk that he might contaminate others. But the pilot recounting this experience added: 'Don't draw the obvious conclusion. The next time I saw the man's name, he was navigating for one of the Dambusting crews.' Many men had temporary moral collapses in the midst of operational tours. The most fortunate, who were sensitively treated, were sent for a spell at the RAF convalescent home at Matlock in Derbyshire. A post-war medical report argues that many such men genuinely wanted to be rehabilitated and return to operations to save their own self-respect, while genuine LMF cases proved on close study to be those who should never have survived the aircrew selection process.

But the decisive factor in the morale of bomber aircrew, like that of all fighting men, was leadership. At first, it is difficult to understand what impact a leader can have, when in battle his men are flying with only their own crews over Germany, far out of sight and command. Yet a post-war 8 Group medical report stated emphatically: 'The morale of a squadron was almost always in direct proportion to the quality of leadership shown by the squadron commanders, and the fluctuations in this respect were most remarkable.' A good CO's crew pressed home attacks with more determination; suffered lower losses; perhaps above all, had a negligible 'Early Return' rate. Guy Gibson, the leader of the Dambusters, was one kind of legendary Bomber Command CO. Not a cerebral man, he represented the apogee of the pre-war English public schoolboy, the perpetual team captain, of unshakeable courage and dedication to duty, impatient of those who could not meet his exceptional standards. 'He was the kind of boy who would have been head prefect in any school,' said Sir Ralph Cochrane, his commander in 5 Group.

For the first four months of 1943, 76 Squadron was commanded by Leonard Cheshire, another of the great British bomber pilots of the war, of a quite different mould from Gibson, but even more remarkable. Cheshire, the son of a distinguished lawyer, himself read law at Oxford, then joined the RAF shortly before the outbreak of war. In 1940 he began flying Whitleys over Germany. By 1943, with two brilliant tours already behind him, he was a 26-year-old wing-commander. There was a mystical air about him, as if he somehow inhabited another planet from those around him, yet without affectation or pretension. 'Chesh is crackers,' some people on the squadrons said freely in the days before this deceptively gentle, mild man became famous. They were all the more bewildered when he married and brought back from America in 1942 an actress fifteen years older than himself.

Yet Leonard Cheshire contributed perhaps more than any other single pilot to the legend of Bomber Command. He performed extraordinary feats of courage apparently on impulse, yet studied the techniques of bombing with intense perception and intelligence, later pioneering the finest precision marking of the war as leader of 617 Squadron. At 76 Squadron there was a joke about Cheshire, that 'the moment he walks into the bar, you can see him starting to work out how much explosive it would need to knock it down'. He was possibly not a natural flying genius in an aircraft like [the famous Australian pilot] Micky Martin, but, by absolute dedication to his craft, he had made himself a master. He flew almost every day. If he had been on leave and was due to operate that night, he would go up for two hours in the morning to restore his sense of absolute intimacy with his aircraft. He believed that to survive over Germany it was necessary to develop an auto-pilot within himself, which could fly the aircraft quite instinctively, leaving all his concentration free for the target and the enemy. As far back as 1941 he had written a paper on marking techniques. He had always been an advocate of extreme low-level bombing.

Cheshire himself wrote, 'I loved flying and was a good pilot, because I threw myself heart and soul into the job. I found the dangers of battle exciting and exhilarating, so that war came easily to me.' Most of those he commanded knew themselves to be frailer flesh, and he dedicated himself to teaching them everything that he knew. He had never forgotten that Lofty, his own first pilot on Whitleys, had taught him to know every detail of his aircraft, and he was determined to show others likewise. He lectured 76's crews on Economical Cruising Heights, Escape and Evasion techniques, and methods of improving night vision. They knew that he was devoted to their interests. On a trip to Nuremberg they were detailed to cross the French coast at 2,000 feet. He simply told Group that he would not send them at that height. It would be 200 feet or 20,000. He made his point.

A CO who flew the most dangerous trips himself contributed immensely to morale – some officers were derisively christened 'François' for their habit of picking the easy French targets when they flew. Cheshire did not have his own crew – only Jock Hill, his wireless operator. Instead, he flew as 'Second Dickey' with the new and nervous. Perhaps the chief reason that 'Chesh' inspired such loyalty and respect was that he took the trouble to know and recognize every single man at Linton. It was no mean feat, learning five hundred or more faces which changed every week. Yet the ground crews chorused: 'We are Cheshire cats!' because the CO spent so much of his day driving round the hangars and dispersals chatting to them and remembering exactly who had sciatica. It was the same with the aircrew. A young wireless operator, who had arrived at Linton the previous day, was climbing into the truck for the dispersals when he felt Cheshire's arm round his shoulder. 'Good luck, Wilson.' All the way to the aircraft, the W/Op pondered in bewildered delight: 'How the hell did the CO know my name?' They knew that when Cheshire flew, it was always the most difficult and dangerous operations. He would ask them to do nothing that he had not done himself. By the end of the war, with his Victoria Cross, three Distinguished Service Orders, Distinguished Flying Cross and fantastic total of completed operations, he had become a legend.

Yet at 76 Squadron from the spring of 1943 onwards, there were a substantial number of LMF cases, matched by an 'Early Return' rate from operations which by autumn sometimes exceeded 25 per cent of aircraft despatched, and which caused Sir Arthur Harris to make an almost unprecedented personal visit to Holme in October to remind aircrew in the most forceful terms of their duty. 76 Squadron's moral had slumped. They felt neglected by the promotion and commissioning authorities, bruised by the transfer from the comforts of Linton to the gloominess of Holme, generally disgruntled with the Royal Air Force.

It had been an impossible task to find a successor as CO to match Cheshire when he left in April, but it was unfortunate that he was followed by an officer who had difficulty making himself liked or respected. On his occasional operational sorties, the new CO's aircraft was jinxed by repeated bad luck. When he went to Stuttgart, he was obliged to return early with a glycol leak, having lost an engine. Three nights later he had to come home with an engine failure, and crashed at Linton. On a subsequent occasion, the CO committed the oldest crime in the pilot's book by flying a 'red on blue' – a 180 degree Reciprocal Course which took him northwards towards the Atlantic for thirty-two minutes before he realized his error and was obliged to return to Linton and abort the operation. A month later he ran out of petrol on the way home from Mont Beliard, and crashed in a potato field near Scunthorpe. Although the CO completed a number of operations without incident, two of them to Berlin, his troubles were a matter of some mirth to most of the squadron. He was a regular officer who had never flown operations before, but by 1943 no one was disposed to make many allowances. The crews were not sufficiently afraid of his anger or sufficiently interested in his good opinion to complete an operation if they felt disinclined to do so. His appeals to their courage and determination were treated as cant. A consistent handful of pilots found themselves unable to take off at all because of 'mag drop', so easily achieved by running up an engine with the magnetoes switched off, oiling up the plugs.

A 76 Squadron wireless operator who completed six operations with one of the Norwegian crews before reporting sick with ear trouble and refusing to fly again over Germany said that he would never have had the courage to march into the CO's office to 'jack out' if Cheshire had been sitting in the chair. This man was reduced to the ranks, stripped of his flying brevet, posted to the depot at Chessington which dealt with such cases, and spent the rest of the war on ground duties. So did Alf Kirkham's rear gunner:

> After our first few trips together, which were very rough indeed [wrote Kirkham], he simply did not like the odds. He decided that he wanted to live, and told me that nothing anyone could do to him would be worse than carrying on with operations. He was determined to see the war out, and as far as I know he was successful.

Marginal LMF suspects, along with disciplinary cases who had broken up the sergeants' mess, been discovered using high-octane fuel in their cars, or been involved in 'avoidable flying accidents', were sent to the 'Aircrew Refresher Centres' at Sheffield, Brighton or Bournemouth – in reality open-arrest detention barracks – where they spent a few weeks doing PT and attending lectures before being sent back to their stations, or in extreme cases posted to the depot, having been found 'unfit for further aircrew duties'. They were then offered a choice of transferring to the British army, or going to the coal mines. By 1943 the 'Refresher Centres' were handling thousands of aircrew. One 76 Squadron rear gunner went from Sheffield to the Parachute Regiment, and survived the war. His crew were killed over Kassel in October.

A pilot who joined 76 Squadron in the autumn of 1943 wrote:

> There was something lacking in the atmosphere . . . The camaraderie between the aircrew was there just the same, and between aircrew

120

and groundcrew too. But the atmosphere of a squadron, like that of a ship, is hard to define. There are happy ships and happy squadrons. Our squadron was not happy, I thought . . . .

This officer, Denis Hornsey, was like very many of those who spent their war in Bomber Command fighting fear and a dread of inadequacy, without ever finally succumbing. At the end of the war Hornsey wrote an almost masochistically honest and hitherto unpublished account of his experiences and feelings. At thirty-three, he was rather older than most aircrew and suffered from poor eyesight – he wore corrected goggles on operations – and almost chronic minor ailments throughout the war. He hated the bureaucracy and lack of privacy in service life, and was completely without confidence in his own ability as a pilot. After flying some Whitley operations in 1941, he was returned to OTU for further training, and his crew was split up. He then spent a relatively happy year as a staff pilot at a navigation school. He felt that he was an adequate flier of single or twin-engined aircraft, and repeatedly requested a transfer to an operational station where he could fly one or the other. But by 1943 it was heavy-aircraft pilots who were needed. Everybody wanted to fly Mosquitoes. Hornsey was posted to Halifaxes. He knew that he was by now being accompanied from station to station by a file of unsatisfactory reports. He began his tour at 76 Squadron with two 'Early Returns', which made him more miserable than ever. Fear of being considered LMF haunted him almost as much as fear of operations.

> Each operation, in my experience, was a worse strain than the last, and I felt sure that I was not far wrong in supposing that every pilot found it the same. It was true that it was possible to get used to the strain, but this did not alter the fact that the tension of each trip was 'banked' and carried forward in part to increase the tension of the next. If this were not so, the authorities would not have thought it necessary to restrict a tour to thirty trips.

There were men who were stronger than Hornsey, even men who enjoyed operational flying, but his conscious frailty was far closer to that of the average pilot than the nerveless brilliance of a Martin or Cheshire. The day after 76 Squadron lost four aircraft over Kassel and George Dunn's crew completed their tour, Hornsey recorded a conversation in the mess:

> 'What chance has a man got at this rate?' one pilot asked plaintively. 'Damn it all, I don't care how brave a chap is, he likes to think he has a chance. This is plain murder.'
> 'Better tell that to Harris,' someone else suggested.
> 'You needn't worry,' I said, 'you represent just fourteen bombloads to him. That's economics, you know.'

As it transpired, operations were cancelled at the eleventh hour, when we were all dressed up in our kit ready to fly. It was too late then to go out, so I went to the camp cinema and saw *Gun for Hire*, a mediocre film portraying what I would have once thought was the dangerous life of a gangster. Now, by contrast, it seemed tame.

That night, I found it difficult to settle down. There was much going on inside my mind that I wanted to express. I felt lonely and miserable, apprehensive and resigned, yet rebellious at the thought of being just a mere cog in the machine with no say in how that machine was used.

But I was getting used to such attacks, which I had learned to expect at least once in the course of a day, as soon as I found myself at a loose end. As I could now recognize, without fear of it adding to my mental discomfort, they merely signified an onset of operational jitters. So composing myself as best I could, I went to sleep as quickly as I could.

Hornsey's tragedy was that he was acutely imaginative. He pressed the Air Ministry for the introduction of parachutes that could be worn at all times by bomber aircrew, so many of whom never had the chance to put them on after their aircraft was hit. He made his crew practise 'Abandon aircraft' and 'Ditching' drill intensively, and protested violently when he found the remaining armour plate being stripped from his Halifax on Group orders, to increase bombload.

The men who fared best were those who did not allow themselves to think at all. Many crews argued that emotional entanglements were madness, whether inside or outside marriage. They diverted a man from the absolute single-mindedness he needed to survive over Germany. When a pilot was seen brooding over a girl in the mess, he was widely regarded as a candidate for 'the chop list'. Hornsey, with a wife and baby daughter, was giving only part of his attention and very little of his heart to 76 Squadron.

Cheshire argued emphatically that what most men considered a premonition of their own death – of which there were innumerable instances in Bomber Command – was in reality defeatism. A man who believed that he was doomed would collapse or bale out when his aircraft was hit, whereas in Cheshire's view if you could survive the initial fearsome shock of finding your aircraft damaged, you had a chance. Yet by the autumn of 1943, many men on 76 Squadron were talking freely of their own fate. One much-liked officer came fresh from a long stint as an instructor to be a flight commander. 'You'd better tell me about this business, chaps,' he said modestly in the mess. 'I've been away on the prairies too long.' After a few operations, he concluded readily that he had no chance of survival. 'What are you doing for Christmas, Stuart?' somebody asked him in the mess one day. 'Oh, I shan't be alive for Christmas,' he said wistfully, and was gone within a week, leaving a wife and three children.

'The line between the living and the dead was very thin,' wrote Hornsey. 'If you live on the brink of death yourself, it is as if those who have gone have merely caught an earlier train to the same destination.

And whatever that destination is, you will be sharing it soon, since you will almost certainly be catching the next one.'

On the night of 3 November 1943, Hornsey's was one of two 76 Squadron aircraft shot down on the way to Düsseldorf. He was on his eighteenth trip with Bomber Command. It is pleasant to record that he survived and made a successful escape across France to England, for which he was awarded a DFC perhaps better deserved and more hardly earned than the Air Ministry ever knew.

At the end of 1943, 76 Squadron's CO was 'screened' and awarded the usual DSO handed out to squadron commanders at the end of their stint, regardless of operations flown. In his place came Wing-Commander 'Hank' Iveson, a pilot of much experience who had flown Whitleys and Halifaxes in 1941. Iveson began by sacking the most persistent 'Early Returners', whose crews were broken up and returned to OTU for reassignment. When the new Mark III Halifax arrived at Holme with a fearsome reputation for accidents, Iveson and his three flight commanders flew its first operation themselves. Despite the restriction on squadron COs flying too many trips, Iveson did fifteen in the next six months. He lectured the crews intensively on every aspect of operations, emphasizing three-engine flying, which had caused so many accidents. Within a month this big, bluff, jovial man who confessed that he found bomber operations 'fascinating' had drastically reduced the Early Return rate, and done much to rebuild morale. But even Iveson could do nothing about the losses.

1979

---

*Randall Jarrell's chilling little poem pays tribute to a member of the aircrew often overlooked: the lonely ball-turret gunner at the rear of the aircraft, whose fate could easily be as bloody as Jarrell tells us.*

---

## THE DEATH OF THE BALL TURRET GUNNER

### RANDALL JARRELL

From my mother's sleep I fell into the State
And I hunched in its belly till my wet fur froze.
Six miles from earth, loosed from its dream of life,
I woke to black flak and the nightmare fighters.
When I died they washed me out of the turret with a hose.

1971

---

How did it feel to take part in the first thousand-bomber raid over Germany? *The captain of a Stirling that flew to Cologne on Saturday night, 30 May 1942, recorded his impressions at the time. With the benefit of half a century's hindsight, we can see that he would probably not have sung all the way back with the peace of utter satisfaction if he had been able to see what his bombs had done. The moral dimension did not obtrude at that dark nadir of the war.*

## FIRE OVER COLOGNE

### CARL OLSSON

Saturday night, 30 May 1942, was a black night for Hitler's Reich. That night they glimpsed the shape of things to come. Within the space of ninety minutes more than 1,000 British bombers were put over the city of Cologne, second largest in Germany and a great armaments and war transport centre.

More than 1,500 tons of bombs were dropped and scores of thousands of incendiaries and reconnaissance aircraft reported that the city was still on fire two days after the raid. The largest number of night bombers ever used by the *Luftwaffe* on a single raid up to that time was just over 450 – against London, a target many times bigger than Cologne.

The Cologne raid was followed by other 1,000-plane raids. By the time these words are read there will probably, and with the added weight of American bombers, have been even bigger raids on German cities. But Cologne made history in the air war. The American press described it as 'the first pay-off for Warsaw and Rotterdam, Coventry and Plymouth'.

But it was also a testing ground for Bomber Command's theory that Germany's very efficient AA defences could be overwhelmed by concentrating a sufficiently large force of bombers over a given target in a short space of time. It was also a valuable exercise in the difficult technique of getting 1,000-plus bombers away from their aerodromes and home again within the limited area of this small island.

This is the story of one of the pilots who took part in the Cologne raid. The narrator, the captain of a Stirling, is a veteran at night-bombing Germany – from the days when sorties were made on less than a score of machines. So his impressions of that great night have a special personal value.

For some days before this biggest of all raids, most of us on the station guessed that something special was afoot.

For one thing the Intelligence and Operations people had been invisible except at meal times. And when they did appear among us they were much too excessively eager to talk about any subject on earth rather than 'shop' and Ops.

And for another, all squadrons had been brought up to total strength plus reserves, and the ground crews had been working sixteen hours a day to make every aircraft fully serviceable.

Some of the wise guys had been making side bets on the probable target and the poor 'weather man', sitting in his cubby hole surrounded by charts and instruments, had been getting his life pestered out of him by artfully phrased inquiries.

What's the weather going to be like over Germany tonight, "Met", old man?'

'Baltic area, probably heavy ground mist. Berlin, thick low cloud. Ruhr area, clearing, but doubtful.'

'And what's it going to be like elsewhere?'

'Well . . . in the extreme south it's still holding bright and clear.'

So back to the crew rooms and hangars the wise guys would go. 'It's going to be Turin, or Milan, or Munich.' Another day it would be Berlin or Dresden or Leipzig, according to these hunch riders and weather wizards. But it was all guessing.

We never knew till that Saturday morning of 30 May, the day of the big raid. I was in the mess ante-room with the others, turning over the morning papers after breakfast, and wondering whether I would be able to 'work' that night out for a local dance.

Suddenly the Tannoy speaker blared out from the wall: 'Attention everybody! This is Operations . . .'

There was a short pause and everybody stopped talking to listen.

Then the voice blared forth again: 'All flying crews – I repeat, *all* flying crews of squadrons will assemble in Operations Room at 10.00 hours . . .'

We looked at each other briefly and I know all of us felt a quickening of excitement. This is IT, I thought. And this is a big thing. A 10 a.m. call meant that.

For if it had been a call to a 'prayer meeting' (as we call the usual informal lectures on tactics, etc.) or if it was to be a briefing for the ordinary kind of raid, it would have been held in the crew room.

At 10.00 hours we were all in Ops. Room. The Station CO was there as well as the two Wing Commanders. Also there was an officer from Group HQ and the Intelligence and other experts in full strength.

Our 'Wingco' began his 'spiel' casually enough, and looking downwards at some papers on his table.

'You are going to be briefed for an absolutely "maximum effort" raid. You are going to a place where most of you have been before – but' (he added with a sudden grin) 'you'll find it's no trouble at all.'

Then he looked up suddenly, shuffling his papers and addressed us directly.

'It must have been obvious to you all that something special has been cooking. I can tell you now that you will be attacking Cologne, that more than 1,000 aircraft will take part, and that from the first machine "on target" to the last one off, the whole attack must be completed in ninety minutes.'

There must have been nearly two hundred of us packed into that room, but nobody made a sound as the 'Wingco' went on.

'Before I give you the "gen" (general information) I will read you this special letter to all taking part from the C-in-C.'

He then read that letter, some of which has been published, about letting the Hun have it 'right on the chin'.

After that he gave us the 'gen'. Take-off times and intervals (which had to be precisely adhered to), routes and heights for the journey out, the various types of bomb load and the heights at which the attack was to be carried out.

He suggested a medium altitude – subject of course to the conditions each pilot found over the target.

I heard that my squadron was to have the honour of being first on the scene. We were to be the 'pathfinders' – to start fires for the others to follow. My aircraft, for instance, was to be entirely loaded with incendiaries – nearly eight tons – and there were plenty more like me.

The Intelligence Officer followed the 'Wingco' with a talk on the target to which we had been assigned (it was an area in the centre of Cologne) and about the sort of opposition we should be likely to meet. The Weather man followed him and then the Signals Officer. Then the Station CO wound up the proceedings with a specially straight little talk which was much appreciated (the CO rarely says much at the briefings).

The briefing ended as simply and unemotionally as it had begun. There were no dramatics and no high-flown phrases – but all of us felt that we had been present at an historical moment in aerial warfare.

I know I felt, as I went through the routine of that day – working out courses with my navigator, thoroughly testing my bomber in flight, etc. – and in spite of the dragging tension of waiting for the take-off – that I wouldn't have changed places for any other job in Britain.

At last the time came when we drove out in the gathering dusk to our bombers waiting at the dispersal points, and after the usual preliminaries, with my ground crew (bless'em!) fussing around till the last minute to put the final touch of perfection on everything, we climbed aboard.

We took off with clockwork precision. I was fifth in place in my squadron and punctually to the minute I got my radio signal for the 'off'.

Climbing nicely, the rising moon swinging past my wing-tips as I circled to my course, I headed for the coast. On my course I plugged in 'George' (the automatic pilot) and then called up the rest of the crew to see if they were all set and comfortable.

First, to 'Rupe', my rear gunner, a tough Rhodesian who had just rejoined the squadron after a marvellously quick recovery from three bullet wounds, two in the throat and head, obtained in an encounter with a German night fighter (who, however, never lived to tell the tale). Rupe was cheerful as ever and ready for trouble.

Then to my navigator, an Australian flight sergeant, serious but keen and one of the best navigators I know. After him to my mid-upper gunner, a cheerful Cockney much addicted to song.

Then to my flight engineer, lugubrious like most engineers, but a sound man who can work miracles with a sick engine.

Also to my wireless operator, who thereafter would say nothing more unless he had to, being all the time intent on his instruments, and sharing the watch through the astrodome for night fighters with the engineer.

Lastly I spoke to Curly, my front gunner, who from his position has a better view than anybody except the bomb-aimer when actually over the target.

Curly is a disappointed man. He failed as a wireless operator, so it is now his pleasure to pick up beacons on the way home long before the wireless-op. reports his radio signals. But Curly also knows the night face of Germany as well as the streets of his native Lancashire town, and he is a great help in picking up landmarks.

I also had a passenger with me as second pilot – a squadron leader who was returning to 'ops' after a year's absence. He was coming along to get the 'gen' on any alterations made on the German defences since he was over there last. And to be in on the big party, of course.

Heading east across the North Sea, the brilliant moon shining out of a cloudless sky seemed to turn the night into day. And far away on my left hand the Northern Light, which holds perpetually at this time of the year, filled the horizon with radiance and put out the stars.

My Stirling was flying perfectly and I was in a trance, not thinking of what lay ahead, when the casual voice of the mid-upper gunner in my earphones brought me back to the present.

'Here's the reception committee, sir,' he said.

I looked up from my instruments and saw ahead of me on the Dutch coast the first 'flak' barrage coming up.

It was coming up in car-loads, much thicker than usual, miles of coloured tracer curving against a winking, flashing wall of shell-bursts.

And scores of searchlights pale against the moonshine waved and probed across the sky. 'Blackpool Front,' murmured the squadron leader in my ear. The searchlights seemed a trifle frantic in their erratic groping. And no wonder; I thought of the masses of 'plots' their radiolocation must be picking up from the approaching air armada. Enough to put the wind up anybody. And the Hun is notoriously easily rattled by anything that's off the straight line of the expected.

Kicking the rudders about, pushing and hauling at the control column, turning and diving and climbing in violent avoiding action, I passed through the first walls of the coastal barrage.

Inland over Holland there was no opposition, fields and rivers and small towns sliding peacefully below, clearly marked out in the light of the moon. If it's only like this over Cologne, I thought happily. But I warned the gunners to keep a sharp lookout for the expected night fighters and the radio-op. posted himself with his head in the astrodome (the glass bulge in the roof of the fuselage) to add his pair of eyes to the gunners'.

It was just here, a few miles inside Holland, that I got the full measure of what this terrific night's operation meant. For some minutes the intercom phones were busy with staccato calls from the gunners, 'Aircraft, red (port side), below . . . . Aircraft, green (starboard), astern.' And as fast as I swung the aircraft to help the gunners to get these strangers in their sights, back would come further reports: Wellington, or Whitley, Lancaster, Manchester, Stirling.

We looked out through the windows and saw the black shapes filling the sky, converging from all over England on our course for Cologne. You ought to appreciate what that sight meant to an ordinary bomber pilot. I have been on dozens of raids and never seen another one of our aircraft out or home. And here there were countless scores of bombers. It was hugely thrilling, and from the excited back-chat going on over my phones, everybody was thinking the same.

For another half-hour or more we rode on in this majestic company. What our sky-filling roar must have seemed like to the Jerries in Holland below, I don't know. But there was plenty of evidence of how we were catching them on the hop. Half-way across Holland I counted no less than three 'dummies' to represent fires or airfield flare-paths being hopefully and hurriedly lit to attract our bomb loads. We laughed and passed on.

Then Curly called out from his glasshouse in front that he was picking up the bend in the Rhine which was our run-in point to Cologne. The navigator passed me, tapping me on the shoulder, to go to his position forward over the bomb sight. As I banked to turn, all Germany was spread out dead and silent below, and the Rhine was a twisting band of shining ebony.

A few minutes more and the whole sky broke into a blinding blaze as the first belt of lights and gun defences swept into action. (I mentioned that my squadron was to be first into Cologne to start fires.) In a moment my cabin was lit up with the baleful blue glare of a 'master searchlight' and then a whole cone caught me. I slammed the hand lever down which lowers my seat, and then, sticking my head down to avoid being dazzled by the glare, I went hurtling and twisting down to lose the lights, listening the while to my navigator calling out changes of direction.

Out of one belt of defences and into another. Gusts of blast shook my Stirling as packets of 'flak' burst beneath. Once there was a heavy thud as something hit us, but I had eyes only for the dim-lit instruments panel, ears only for the chanted directions of the bomb-aimer in my earphones, 'Left, left . . . steady. R-i-g-h-t, steady,' as the target area wavered down his sights.

Then suddenly, 'Bombs going, hold her!' I could feel the little 'lifts' as the loads of incendiaries left her in succession laying a long trail across the target area. Then 'Bombs gone!' and I swung out and along the perimeter of the city.

Travelling thus outwards and away from the target there was one dreadful moment when a Wellington flashed across my nose less than fifty yards in front. The second pilot gave a convulsive gasp and kicked out as if he was striking at the rudder pedals. It was a shattering experience but some indication of how full the sky was that night.

My orders were to cruise round the city for a while after dropping my load, observing, keeping out of trouble as much as possible. And as I turned in again from the eastern ring of defences I saw an unforgettable sight below.

The whole city seemed a mass of myriad points of white light as the incendiaries started off. Hundreds were slowly changing to red as fires took hold. And in their midst there were thundering great flashes, as swift as rolling gun-fire, as the other bombers were unloading their H.E. I heard the second pilot (whose parents once lived in Coventry and who was in the Bath raid a few weeks ago) murmuring fervently, 'Hold that, you Hun, and that . . . and that . . .'

By the time I started in on my second circuit the whole field of view below was a mass of red glare marked by leaping flashes of bombs still raining down. Below and around were black silhouettes of our bombers still coming in, and above were many more, their undersides lit up in the red glow of the burning town. 'Out from under!' I heard the second pilot yelling. And I got out.

By the time I completed my third circuit of stooging round I could see that we had the defences completely foxed. A lot of lights were out and guns silent, probably knocked out by our hail of bombs. Others were shooting wildly and anyhow. The gunners must have thought that the end had come.

Near the western outer ring I went down in a great dive to give my gunners a chance at a specially big searchlight battery. Six flicked out and two stayed steady as if their crew had left or been hit.

And just here I ran into my first trouble. I heard my mid-upper gunner yell 'Fighter!' Then I saw a line of flashes streaming ahead of me. I thought at first he was firing forward and shouted to him. Then realized that it was cannon shell from the fighter astern just missing my roof and exploding ahead.

Phew! I dodged wildly, scrammed for the darkness and lost him. And now I turned away, heading north-west and home.

I heard the rear gunner call out that he could see Cologne Cathedral. Unbelieving I turned my head, but there were the twin towers standing out against a sea of fire. I wondered if St Paul's looked like that to the Luftwaffe pilots, the night they set the City of London on fire. Or if Warsaw and Rotterdam and Coventry looked like that to them.

I am not a bloodthirsty man. I have a job to do. But I can assure you that it was with the peace of utter satisfaction that I headed my bomber for home, knowing that at last we had been able to hand out a lesson that even a Hun can't forget.

We sang all the way back.

1943

---

The firestorms in cities like Hamburg created by Allied bombing created holocausts of unprecedented horror and precipitated a debate that still rages. The police president of Hamburg had no doubt about the reason for the gruesome catastrophe that had befallen his city: it was due to the murderous lust of a sadistic enemy.

## REPORT ON THE RAIDS ON HAMBURG IN JULY AND AUGUST 1943

### POLICE PRESIDENT OF HAMBURG

1 December 1943

The cause of the enormous extent of the heavy damage and particularly of the high death rate in comparison with former raids is the appearance of firestorms . . .

In Hamburg the firestorms originated in densely built-up and thickly populated areas, where, therefore, by reason of the type of building and the densely massed houses affected, conditions were favourable for the development of firestorms. In the affected areas in Hamburg there were mostly large blocks of flats in narrow streets with numerous houses behind them, with terraces (inner courtyards), etc. These courtyards became in a very short time cauldrons of fire which were literally man-traps. The narrow streets became fire-locks through which the tall flames were driven . . .

Only very shortly after the first H.E. bombs had fallen an enormous number of fires caused by a great concentration of incendiary bombs – mixed with H.E. bombs – sprang up. People who now attempted to leave their shelters to see what the situation was or to fight the fires were met by a sea of flame. Everything round them was on fire. There was no water and with the huge number and size of the fires all attempts to extinguish them were hopeless from the start . . .

The firestorm raging over many square kilometres had cut off innumerable people without hope of rescue. Only those got away who had risked an early escape or happened to be so near the edge of the sea of fire that it was possible to rescue them. Only where the distance to water or to open spaces of sufficient size was short, was flight now possible, for to cover long distances in the red-hot streets of leaping flames was impossible.

Many of these refugees even then lost their lives through the heat. They fell, suffocated, burnt, or ran deeper into the fire. Relatives lost one another. One was able to save himself, the others disappeared. Many wrapped themselves in wet blankets or soaked their clothes and thus reached safety. In a short time clothes and blankets became hot and dry. Anyone going any distance through this hell found that his clothes were in flames, or the blanket caught fire and was blown away in the storm.

Numbers jumped into the canals and waterways and remained swimming or standing up to their necks in water for hours until the heat should die down. Even these suffered burns on their heads. They were obliged to wet their faces constantly or they perished in the heat. The firestorm swept over the water with its heat and its showers of sparks so that even thick wooden posts and bollards burned down to the level of the water. Some of these unfortunate people were drowned. Many jumped out of windows into the water or the street and lost their lives. . . .

The scenes of terror which took place in the firestorm area are indescribable. Children were torn away from their parents' hands by the force of the hurricane and whirled into the fire. People who thought they had escaped fell down, overcome by the devouring force of the heat and died in an instant. Refugees had to make their way over the dead and dying. The sick and the infirm had to be left behind by rescuers as they themselves were in danger of burning. . . .

Speech is impotent to portray the measure of the horror, which shook the people for ten days and nights and the traces of which were written indelibly on the face of the city and its inhabitants.

And each of these nights convulsed by flames was followed by a day which displayed the horror in the dim and unreal light of a sky hidden in smoke. Summer heat intensified by the glow of the firestorms to an unbearable degree; dust from the torn earth and the ruins and debris of damaged areas which penetrated everywhere; showers of soot and ashes; more heat and dust; above all a pestilential stench of decaying corpses and smouldering fires weighed continually on the exhausted men.

And these days were followed by more nights of more horror, yet more smoke and soot, heat and dust and more death and destruction. Men had not time to rest or salvage property according to any plan or to search for their families. The enemy attacked with ceaseless raids until the work of destruction was complete. His hate had its triumph in the firestorms which destroyed mercilessly men and material alike . . .

The streets were covered with hundreds of corpses. Mothers with their children, youths, old men, burnt, charred, untouched and clothed, naked with a waxen pallor like dummies in a shop window, they lay in every posture, quiet and peaceful or cramped, the death-struggle shown in the expression on their faces. The shelters showed the same picture, even more horrible in its effect, as it showed in many cases the final distracted struggle against a merciless fate. Although in some places shelterers sat quietly, peacefully and untouched as if sleeping in their chairs, killed without realization or pain by carbon monoxide poisoning, in other shelters the position of remains of bones and skulls showed how the occupants had fought to escape from their buried prison.

No flight of imagination will ever succeed in measuring and describing the gruesome scenes of horror in the many buried air raid shelters. Posterity can only bow its head in honour of the fate of these innocents, sacrificed by the murderous lust of a sadistic enemy.

# I SURVIVED

CARELESS TALK
COSTS LIVES

How did it feel to live in France during the German Occupation? Fortunately, we have the testimony of one of Europe's greatest writers, Jean-Paul Sartre. In this subtle and complex analysis he makes it clear that at one level everything went on as before, but that at another level sinister and terrible things were happening. Nor were the Germans the bullet-headed louts of wartime film and fiction; generally they behaved admirably to children and old ladies. The general attitude, Sartre sums up, was that of the great Abbé Siéyès, during the Revolution: 'I survived'.

## PARIS UNDER THE OCCUPATION

### JEAN-PAUL SARTRE

Many Englishmen and Americans, on arriving in Paris, were surprised to find us less thin than they had expected. They saw elegant, and apparently new, women's dresses, and men's suits which, at a distance, still seemed quite presentable; rarely did they come across that pallor and general physical wretchedness, which is the usual sign of starvation. Frustrated pity is apt to go sour; I am afraid they were rather annoyed with us for not living up to the tragic picture they had imagined. Some of them, perhaps, wondered privately whether the occupation had really been so terrible after all, and whether France should not consider her defeat as a stroke of luck which removed her from the war and enabled her to recover her position as a great power at small cost. Perhaps they thought, like the *Daily Express*, that, compared to the English, the French did not have such a bad time during those four years.

It is for those people that I am writing this article. I should like to explain to them that they are mistaken. The occupation was a terrible ordeal; it is not certain that France will recover from it; there is not a single Frenchman who has not often envied the fate of his English Allies. But as I put pen to paper, I realize the great difficulty of the task. Once before, I encountered similar difficulties. It was when I returned from captivity in Germany and was asked about the sort of life led by the prisoners. How can anyone who has not lived in a prison camp be made to feel what the atmosphere is like there? A slight slip of the pen and everything could be made unduly sombre, or a false step in the other direction, and everything could appear jolly and gay. Nor was the truth to be found even by striking a balance between one and the other. A great deal of skill and inventiveness was required to depict it, and considerable imagination and goodwill to understand it. My present problem is of the same order. How can the people of the free countries be made to realize what life was like under the occupation? There is a gulf between us which words are powerless to bridge. When Frenchmen speak amongst themselves about the Germans, the Gestapo, the

Resistance Movement and the Black Market, they understand each other quite easily, because they have lived through the same events and are full of the same memories. But the English and the French have no longer a single memory in common; a past which fills London with pride was, for Paris, marked with shame and despair. We must learn to talk about ourselves without passion, and you must learn to understand us, and above all to grasp, behind the words used, what can only be suggested or signified by a gesture or by silence.

But even if I try to give only a glimpse of the truth, I come up against fresh difficulties. The occupation of France was an immense social phenomenon which affected thirty-five million human beings. How can one speak for them all? The small towns, the big industrial centres and the country districts did not share the same fate. In some villages, the Germans were never seen at all. They were stationed in others during the whole four years. Since I spent most of the time in Paris, I shall restrict myself to describing the occupation there. I shall not deal with physical sufferings, famine (which did exist, but was hidden), nor with the draining of our vitality and the increase of tuberculosis. These calamities, the full extent of which will be revealed later by statistics, are not, after all, without some parallel in England. No doubt, the standard of living remained definitely higher in your country than in ours, but you had to undergo bombing, V1's and military losses. We did not fight. But there are ordeals of another kind, and it is those that I would like to describe. I should like to show how Parisians *felt* the occupation.

First of all, we must discard all conventional pictures. The Germans did not stride, revolver in hand, through the streets; they did not force civilians to make way for them on the pavements. They would offer their seats to old ladies in the Underground. They showed great fondness for children and would often pat them on the cheek. They had been told to behave correctly and, being well-disciplined, they tried shyly and conscientiously to do so. Some of them even displayed a naïve kindliness which could find no practical expression. Nor should it be imagined that the French maintained an heroic stiffness, or an attitude of crushing contempt. True, the great majority of the population took care never to come into contact with the German Army. But it should be remembered that the occupation was part of our daily life. Someone who was asked what he had done during the Reign of Terror replied, 'I survived.' That is an answer we could all make today. For four years we went on living, and the Germans went on living, too – in our midst, submerged and absorbed in the life of the great city. I could not but smile at a photograph which I was shown recently in a copy of *La France Libre*. A broad-shouldered, thick-necked German officer was thumbing the books at a bookstall on the *Quais*, under the cold, sad gaze of a little old bookseller, with a typical little French beard. The bulky German seemed to push his frail neighbour almost out of the picture. And under the photograph, there was a caption which ran: 'A German pollutes the banks of the Seine, once the haunt of poets and dreamers.' Of course, there is no question of the photograph being faked; but it is only a photograph, that is, an arbitrarily chosen glimpse of life. The human eye could have seen a much wider view. The photographer must have seen hundreds of Frenchmen looking at dozens of bookstalls, and one solitary German, who no doubt appeared too small in the larger setting, turning over the pages of an old book. Perhaps he himself was a poet or a dreamer. In any case, he was perfectly harmless, and it was precisely the harmless side of the German soldiers strolling through the streets which we noticed every minute of the day. Their uniforms were caught up in the crowd, making a pale, dull-green unobtrusive stain, which one almost came to expect amongst the dark clothes of the civilians. And then, we were thrown against them by the necessities of everyday life; we were hustled along and tossed together in the stream and swirl of urban existence. We were squeezed against them in the Underground, and we bumped into them in the dark streets. No doubt they would have killed us mercilessly, had they been ordered to do so, and of course our memories were still loaded with resentment and hatred, but these feelings had become rather abstract, and eventually there arose a sort of indefinable, shamefaced solidarity between the people of Paris and the German troopers, who at bottom were so similar to French soldiers. No liking entered into this solidarity; it was rather the outcome of biological habit. At first, it hurt us to see them, and then gradually we learned not to see them, and they became something in the nature of an institution. Their ignorance of our language completed the inoffensiveness of their presence. Many a time I have seen Parisians in cafés discussing politics with the utmost freedom, only a few yards from a solitary German, sitting with vacant gaze over a glass of lemonade. We considered them more as part of the scenery than as men. Whenever one of them stopped us and asked the way with extreme politeness (for most of us, these were the only occasions on which we spoke to them), our feeling was more one of embarrassment than of hatred; in a word, we could not be *natural*. We remembered that we had decided once and for all never to speak to them, but at the same time the sight of a lost soldier aroused in us that old habit of helpfulness we had been taught in our childhood, and which prompted us to come to the rescue of any man in difficulties. We would reply, according to mood, either 'I don't know' or 'Take the second turning on the left,' but in either case we felt dissatisfied with ourselves. Once, on the Boulevard Saint Germain, a car in which a German colonel was driving overturned. I saw ten Frenchmen rush forward to his rescue. I am sure they all hated the occupation troops, and no doubt some of them later, as members of the FFI, took part in the fighting on the same boulevard. But what did that matter? Could the man lying there, crushed under his own car, be considered as a member of the occupation forces? What was the right thing to do? The idea of who is one's enemy is only clear and definite when the enemy is on the other side of the fighting line.

However, there was an enemy, of the most hateful kind, but his face was never seen. Or rather, those who saw it rarely came back to tell the tale. He could be compared, I think, to an octopus, which surreptitiously seized our best men and spirited them away. All around us, people seemed to be quietly swallowed up. One day you might ring up a friend and the telephone bell would throb for a long time in an empty flat. You would go round and ring at the door, but no one would open. When the porter finally forced the lock, there would be two chairs standing close together in the hall, and between them a few fag-ends of German cigarettes. If the wife or mother of the vanished man had been present at his arrest, she would tell you that he had been taken away by very polite Germans, like those who asked the way in the streets. And when she went to ask for news of her husband at the offices in the Avenue Foch or the Rue des Saussaies she would be very graciously received and might be given comforting reassurances. And yet all day and late into the night screams of pain and terror could be heard coming from the buildings in the Avenue Foch and the Rue des Saussaies. Everyone in Paris had at least one relation or friend who had been arrested, deported or shot. It was as if there were hidden leaks in the city and its life were gradually draining away through them. Paris was suffering from a mysterious internal haemorrhage. It was spoken about very little. Partly through prudence, partly through a sense of dignity, Parisians covered up this constant internal bleeding, even more than they did the food shortage. 'They have arrested——,' it would be said, and the they, like the pronoun that madmen use to describe their imaginary persecutors, designated not so much men as a sort of living impalpable pitch which darkened everything, even the daylight. At night, you could hear them. At about a quarter to twelve, there would be the scurrying footsteps of someone trying to reach home before curfew time, and then there would be silence. After that, we knew that any footsteps in the streets must be their footsteps. It is difficult to convey the impression given by the deserted city – the no-man's-land which lay just outside our windows, and where they were the only living beings. And houses did not afford much protection. The Gestapo often carried out its arrests between midnight and five a.m. It seemed that at any minute the door might open to admit a gust of cold, night air, and three soft-spoken Germans with revolvers. Even when we were not speaking about them, or even thinking about them their presence could be felt. In some way, inanimate objects seemed to belong to us less than before; they were stranger, colder, more public, so to speak, as if the intimacy of our homes were invaded by an alien watchfulness. The next morning, we would again see harmless little Germans hurrying to their offices with their despatch cases under their arms, and looking more like lawyers in uniform than soldiers. We would try to find on their familiar, expressionless faces something of that spiteful ferocity we had imagined during the night, but without success. And yet, the horror still remained. That was, perhaps, the most painful feature; the abstract, ambient horror, inspired by an invisible enemy. It was certainly the first effect of the occupation. Let the reader try, then, to imagine the perpetual co-existence of a hatred which could not find its object, and an enemy who was too familiar to be hated.

There were many other causes at the root of this horror. But before going any further, there is a misunderstanding we must avoid. This horror should not be thought of as a violent or devastating emotion. As I said before, we went on living; which means that we could still work, eat, talk, sleep, and even sometimes laugh, although that had become rare. The horror seemed to be outside us, in the external world. We could forget it for a while, and become absorbed in a book, a conversation or a piece of work, but we always came back to it and realized that it was still there. Steady, calm, almost discreet, it coloured both our day-dreams and our most practical thoughts. It formed the fabric of our consciousness and influenced the whole meaning of the world. Now that it has gone, we look back on it as one event amongst others, but when it was all around us, we were so used to it that it seemed to be the natural background to our moods. Will the reader understand me when I say both that it was unbearable, and that we managed to put up with it very well?

It is said that some madmen are haunted by the feeling that some terrible event has upset their lives. And when they try to understand the cause of this strong sensation of discontinuity between the past and the present, they can find no reason for it; nothing has happened. We were more or less in the same position. We were aware all the time that a link with the past had been broken. Our traditions were disrupted, our habits, too. And we could not quite grasp the meaning of the change, which the defeat could not wholly explain. Now, I can see what it was. Paris was dead. There were no longer motor-cars, or people in the streets, except at certain times and in certain districts. There was nothing but stone walls on all sides. We seemed to have been left behind after some great exodus. A little provincial life managed to cling to some corners of the capital. There remained the skeleton of a city, grandiose and motionless, too long and too wide for us. The over-wide streets stretched away to the horizon; distances were too great and every prospect too tremendous. We were lost in them. Parisians stayed at home or moved about only in their own district, not wishing to walk amongst those great, austere buildings which were plunged each night into absolute darkness. Here again, we must guard against any exaggeration. Many of us liked the rustic quiet and the quaint charm of the exhausted capital on moonlit nights. But our pleasure was tinged with bitterness: what could be more bitter than to walk down one's own street, past one's own church and town hall, and feel the same sad delight as if one were visiting the moonlit Coliseum or Parthenon. Everything was ruined; empty sixteenth-century houses with closed shutters, requisitioned hotels and cinemas marked off by white railings against which the passer-by would stumble, bars and shops shut for the duration of the war and whose proprietors had died, disappeared or been deported, empty stone bases on which statues had stood, gardens cut in two by barriers or disfigured by concrete pillboxes, and all the big dusty letters on the fronts of buildings – electric signs now extinguished. As one walked along one could read in the shop-windows advertisements which seemed to be engraved on tomb-stones: 'Choucroute always on sale', 'Viennese pastries', 'Week-ends at Le Touquet', 'All you need for your motor-car'. We experienced all that, too, you will say. There was the black-out and restrictions in London as well, I know. But these did not have the same significance for you. London, although mutilated and diminished, remained the capital of England. Paris was no longer the capital of France. Formerly, all roads and railway-lines had led to Paris; the Parisian felt himself to be in the centre of France and of the world. New York, Madrid, London, lay on the horizon of his ambitions and his loves. Although nourished by Périgord, Beaune and Alsace, and by the fishing fleets of the Atlantic coasts, the capital was not a parasitical city, as ancient Rome had been. It directed the life and commerce of the nation, turned raw materials into manufactured goods, and was a kind of central turntable for the whole of France. The armistice changed all that; the splitting up of the country into two zones cut Paris off from the country; the Breton and Norman coasts became forbidden areas; a concrete wall separated France from England and America. There remained Europe, but its very name was revolting and signified enslavement. With the setting-up of a puppet Government in Vichy, the City of Kings lost even its political rôle. France, divided up by the occupation into self-centred provinces, forgot Paris, which became merely a huge, useless and insipid urban centre, haunted by memories of its past greatness, and whose vitality only rallied from time to time under the influence of injections. Its languid existence depended on the weekly quota of trucks and lorries the Germans allowed to enter. Vichy had only to be a little stubborn, or Laval a little hesitant about despatching workers to Germany, for the injections to be completely interrupted. Paris would grow peaked and yawn with hunger under the empty sky. Cut off from the rest of the world, fed only through pity or for some ulterior motive, the town led a purely abstract and symbolic life. Dozens of times during those four years, on seeing bottles of St Emilion or Meursault wine stacked in grocery-shop windows, Parisians would hurry up to find, below the display, a notice saying 'All these bottles are dummies.' Paris, too, was a dummy. Everything there was hollow and empty; there were no pictures in the Louvre, no members of Parliament in the Parliament building, no senators in the Senate, no schoolboys in the Lycée Montaigne. The artificial life maintained by the Germans – the theatrical performances, the races, the feeble, mournful entertainments – had no other aim than to assure the world that France was safe since Paris was still alive. A strange consequence of centralization! At the same time, the English flattened-out Lorient, Rouen or Nantes with their bombs, but had decided to respect Paris. And so, in the moribund city, we enjoyed a deathly, symbolical peace. All around, steel and fire rained down from the sky, but just as we no longer shared in the work of the provinces, we were not allowed to join in their sufferings. The hardworking, quick-tempered city had become a symbol – nothing but a symbol. And we looked at each other and wondered whether we had not become symbols, too. The fact was that for four years we were robbed of our future. We had to depend on others, and for them we were merely an inanimate object. True, the English wireless and the English press showed great friendliness towards us, but we would have to have been very presumptuous or very naïve to imagine that the English were carrying on a bloody war with the sole aim of coming to our rescue. Manfully, sword in hand, they were defending their vital interests, and we all knew that we figured in their plans only as one factor amongst many others. As for the Germans, they were thinking out the best method of absorbing another piece of territory into the European *bloc*. We felt that our fate was no longer in our hands; France was like a flower-pot which is put out on to the window-sill when it is fine and brought in again at night-time, without its wishes being consulted.

Everyone has heard of the neurosis called 'depersonalization'. The patient suddenly imagines that everybody is dead, because he has lost the faculty of looking forward to his own future, and therefore cannot feel anyone else's future. That was, perhaps, the most painful thing – the fact that the people of Paris were depersonalized. Before the war, whenever we looked affectionately at a child, or a young man or a young woman, we were conscious of their future; we could guess it dimly from their gestures and the cast of their features. For a living man or woman is first and foremost a being in the making. But the occupation deprived all Frenchmen of their future. We could no longer gaze after a young couple and wonder what their future would be. We had no more future than a nail has, or a door-knob. All our actions were purely temporary, their meaning was limited to the day on which they were performed. In the factories, the workers might be busy one day and idle the next, because the current had suddenly been turned off. Or the Germans might stop all deliveries of raw materials, or suddenly deport all the workers to Bavaria or the Palatinate. Students would study for examinations, but who could tell them whether the examinations would be held, or they able to sit? We looked at each other, and felt we were looking at dead men. This dehumanization or petrification of mankind was so unbearable that to escape from it many people joined the Resistance movement. They thus acquired a strange future, bounded by torture, imprisonment and death; but at least it was one of their own making. But we knew all the time that the Resistance Movement could give no more than individual satisfaction. The British would have won the war without it; just as, in spite of it, they would have lost the war had such been their destiny. For us, the value of the Resistance Movement was mainly symbolical, and that is why many of its members, feeling themselves to be still symbols, were just as wretched as before. It was a symbolical rebellion in a symbolical city; only torture was real.

We felt, then, that we were in a backwater. Not only were we no longer fighting, but to our shame we no longer understood the war. While we were still ruminating over our 1940 defeat, we could see from a distance how the English and the Russians were adapting themselves to German methods. Our defeat had been too rapid and had taught us nothing. Those who congratulate us ironically on having escaped the war have no idea how ardently the French would have taken up the fight again. Day after day, we saw our towns being destroyed and our wealth being obliterated. Our youth was wasting away; three million Frenchmen languished in Germany, while at home the birthrate was falling. What battle could have done more harm than that? These sacrifices would have been made willingly, had we thought they would hasten our victory; but in fact they were meaningless, or only helped the Germans. Perhaps everyone can understand that the terrible thing is not to suffer or die, but to suffer and die in vain.

As we lived thus, in absolute abandonment, we would sometimes see Allied planes flying overhead. We were in so paradoxical a situation, that the sirens announced them as enemy aircraft. Definite orders had been given that we were to leave our offices, close our shops, and go down into the shelters. We never carried them out, but stayed in the streets, with upturned faces. Nor was this disobedience an empty gesture of revolt or stupid foolhardiness. We were gazing desperately at our only remaining friends. The young pilot, passing over our heads in his machine, was linked by invisible threads to England or America, and so the sky seemed full of the great, free world. But the only messages he carried were messages of death. It will never be realized how much faith we had to have in our Allies to go on loving them, and to wish for the destruction they carried out on our soil, and to salute their bombers, in spite of all, as the true expression of England. If bombs missed their target and fell on an urban centre, Frenchmen tried hard to find excuses for the airmen. Sometimes, even, the Germans were accused of having dropped the bombs in order to stir up feeling against the English, or of having deliberately given the warning too late. When Le Havre was having its heaviest bombing, I spent a few days there with the family of one of my fellow prisoners. On the first evening, we all sat down in front of the wireless set and the father turned the knobs with touching solemnity, as if he were performing a religious rite. Just as the BBC news bulletin was beginning, we heard the roar of planes in the distance. We well knew that they were coming to drop their bombs on us. It will be a long time before I forget the mixture of terror and delight with which one of the women murmured, 'Here come the English.' And, for a quarter of an hour, as the bombs crashed down outside, without moving from their chairs, they listened to the voice from London. It seemed to have come nearer, as if the squadrons passing overhead had made it incarnate. But such acts of faith implied constant nervous tension; they meant that a feeling of indignation had often to be repressed. We succeeded when Lorient was razed to the ground, when the centre of

Nantes was wiped out, and bombs hit the heart of Rouen. Perhaps the reader will guess what efforts were required. Sometimes anger got the upper hand, and we would try to reason it away as we would with any other passion. I remember coming back from Chantilly, in July 1944, in a train that was machine-gunned. It was a perfectly harmless suburban train. Three aeroplanes went by, and, in the space of a few seconds, three people were dead and a dozen were wounded in the first carriage. The passengers stepped down on to the railway line and watched the bodies being carried away – some on stretchers, but most on green station benches, which were used in the absence of anything better. Everybody was white with distress and anger. You were bitterly criticized and accused of inhumanity and barbarism: 'What do they mean by attacking a defenceless train? Haven't they enough to do on the other side of the Rhine? Why don't they go to Berlin? I suppose they are afraid of the anti-aircraft fire,' and so on. And then, suddenly, someone found the explanation. 'Wait a minute. Usually they aim at the engine and don't hurt anybody, but today the engine was at the back, and so they fired at the first carriage. At the speed they go, they mustn't have noticed that the engine wasn't there.' At once, all criticism was silenced. Everybody was relieved to know that the airmen had not committed an unforgiveable crime and that we could go on liking you. But the temptation to hate you was not the least of our difficulties and we often had to struggle to overcome it. And I can bear witness to the fact that we felt utterly alone when, under the ironical gaze of the Germans, we watched the smoke rising from the fires you had started on the outskirts of our city.

And yet we did not dare complain, because we had bad consciences. We were gnawed at by a secret shame which I first experienced when I was a prisoner. In the camp, we were unhappy, but could not be sorry for ourselves. 'Well,' the prisoners would say, 'we'll not half catch it when we get back.' Their sufferings were acrid, sour and unpleasant, being poisoned by the feeling that they were not unmerited. They were shamed in the eyes of France; and France had been shamed in the eyes of the world. It is sometimes soothing to weep over one's fate. But how could we take pity on ourselves, when we were surrounded with contempt. The Poles in my *Stalag* did not attempt to hide their disdain; the Czechs accused us of having deserted them in 1938; and I have been told that a Russian, who had escaped and was hidden by a *gendarme* in Anjou, would smile good-naturedly and say, 'Frenchmen, rabbits! rabbits!' You yourselves have not always been very lenient, and I remember a speech by Marshal Smuts that we were obliged to listen to in silence. After that, of course, we were inclined to insist doggedly on our humiliation and even exaggerate it. It might have been possible to find a defence; after all, it has taken the three greatest powers in the world four years to beat Germany; was it not natural that we should have given way beneath the first shock, when we had had to withstand it all alone? But we did not think of arguing. The best of us joined the Resistance Movement as a way of redeeming our country. The others hesitated uncomfortably, worrying over their inferiority complex. Does the reader not agree that the worst ordeal is that which cannot be deemed undeserved and yet cannot be considered as a means of redemption?

But at the very moment when we were about to give way to remorse, the Vichy Government and the collaborationists, by urging us to do so, caused us to hold back. Occupation meant not only the constant presence of our conquerers in our towns, but also the publication in all the newspapers, the plastering up on the walls, of the foul image they wished us to have of ourselves. The collaborationists began by appealing to our sense of honesty. 'We are beaten,' they said. 'Let us be sporting and admit our shortcomings.' And then, immediately afterwards, 'Let us agree that the French are frivolous, thoughtless, boastful, selfish and ignorant of other nations, and that the war caught our country in an advanced state of decomposition.' Mocking posters poured ridicule on our last hopes. Drieu la Rochelle insulted us in the *Nouvelle Revue Française*. Faced with such baseness, and such obvious trickery, we revolted; we felt the need to be proud of ourselves. But, alas! as soon as we raised our heads, we discovered in ourselves genuine reasons for remorse. And so we lived in the acutest distress, unhappy without daring to admit it; ashamed and yet disgusted with shame. To complete our misfortunes, we could not stir an inch, eat or even breathe, without becoming the accomplices of the enemy. Before the war, the pacifists had explained to us more than once that a country, when invaded, should refuse to fight and meet the enemy with passive resistance. This is easier said than done. For such resistance to be effective, engine-drivers would have had to go on strike and farmers refuse to plough the land; this might have hampered the invader, although, of course, he could obtain supplies from his own country, but it is certain that it would have destroyed the whole of the occupied nation in a very short time. We had, then, to work and maintain some semblance of national, economic organization, and ensure the provision of a bare subsistence, in spite of destruction and German depredations. But the slightest activity aided the enemy who had hurled himself upon us, was clinging to us like a leech and drawing his substance from us. Not a drop of blood formed in our veins but he took his share of it. There has been much talk of 'collaborationists', and it is true that there were actual traitors in France. We are not ashamed of them. In each nation there are dregs; a sediment of unsuccessful and embittered individuals who take advantage of disasters and revolutions. The existence of a Quisling or a Laval in any national group is a normal phenomenon, like the suicide rate or criminal statistics. But what seemed to us abnormal was the fact that the whole country both collaborated and resisted. The men of the *Maquis*, who were our pride, did not work for the enemy, but to feed them the farmers had to go on raising cattle; half of which was carried off to Germany. Everything we did was equivocal; we never quite knew whether we were doing right or doing wrong; a subtle poison corrupted even our best actions. I shall give only one instance; the railwaymen, firemen and drivers behaved admirably. Their calm courage and selflessness saved hundreds of lives, and enabled whole trainloads of food to reach Paris. Most of them belonged to the Resistance Movement, and proved it by their acts. And yet the zeal with which they tended our rolling stock helped the Germans; the engines which they had so miraculously kept in running order might be requisitioned overnight; amongst the lives they saved were those of German soldiers going to Le Havre or Cherbourg; food trains also carried war material. And so Frenchmen, whose only thought was to serve their fellow-countrymen, were forced by the nature of things to help our enemies against our friends; and when Pétain pinned medals on their tunics, they were really being decorated by Germany. All during the war, we did not *recognize* our own actions and could not take responsibility for all their consequences. Evil was everywhere; life was a constant choice between two evils, a choice we had to make on our own responsibility. With every heartbeat, we sank deeper into a welter of guilt, which filled us with horror.

Perhaps we would have been better able to tolerate the deplorable state to which we were reduced, had we been able to achieve against Vichy the unity that Vichy was always asking for in support of its policy. But it is not true that misfortune cements people together. In the first place, the occupation scattered families to the four corners of the globe. For example, a Parisian industrialist had left his wife and daughter in the free zone, and during the first two years of the occupation could neither see them nor communicate with them, except by postcard; his eldest son was a prisoner in an *Oflag* and the youngest was with the Free French Forces. Paris was peopled by the absent. One of the most characteristic features of our life during those four years was our cult of memories. As we thought of our distant friends, our minds harked back to a joy of living, a pride of living, which had now disappeared. In spite of our efforts, our memories faded a little more every day, and old faces vanished gradually one by one. At first, we talked a great deal about the prisoners, then a little less and then less still; not that we ever stopped thinking about them, but after being precise and painful memories that we carried within us, they became simply yawning, empty gaps, phenomena of the same order as the thinness of our blood; we felt them to be lacking as we lacked fats, sugar and vitamins, in the same complete and indifferentiated fashion. Just as the taste of chocolate or *pâté de foie gras* eventually disappeared, so did the memory of certain outstanding days – 14 July at the Bastille, a walk with a loved one, an evening on the sea-shore, or the greatness of France. Our demands diminished with our memories, and since it is possible to put up with everything, we experienced the shame of tolerating our wretchedness, the swedes which were served at meal-times, the tiny liberties we still had left and the desiccation of our inner-life. We grew less complex every day and finally spoke of nothing but food; less, no doubt, through hunger or fear of insufficiency than because of the fact that the hunt for food bargains was the only enterprise which was still within our scope.

In addition, the occupation resuscitated old quarrels and emphasized the disagreements within the nation. The division of the country into two zones revived the old rivalry between Paris and the provinces, between North and South. The people of Clermont-Ferrand, and Nice accused Parisians of coming to terms with the enemy, while Parisians thought the people of the free zone were very half-hearted and were blatantly and selfishly satisfied by the fact that they were not themselves 'occupied'. It must be admitted that in this connection the Germans did us a great service by disregarding the armistice clauses and extending the occupation to the whole country. They thus restored unity to France. But many other conflicts went on; for instance, the hostility between country people and town-dwellers. The country people had long been irritated by the contempt which they believed the townspeople felt for them, and now they took their revenge, and were very offhand with the townspeople, who, in turn, accused them of supplying the Black Market and starving the cities. The Government poured oil on the fire by publishing speeches, some of which praised the farmers up to the sky, while others accused them of concealing their harvests. Blatant luxury feeding in certain restaurants excited the workers against the upper classes. In actual fact, these establishments were frequented largely by the Germans and a handful of 'collaborationists'. But their existence was a constant reminder of social inequality. Also the working classes clearly realized that they supplied most of the men who were sent to help the German industrial machine. The upper classes were hardly affected at all. I cannot say whether this was, as some thought, a deliberate move on the part of the Germans to spread dissatisfaction or whether it resulted from the fact that the workers were more useful. But – and this is an example of the uncertainties which afflicted us – we did not know whether to be pleased by the fact that most university students escaped deportation, or regret that the measure did not weigh equally on all classes and thus strengthen national solidarity. Finally, to complete the picture, we should mention that our defeat increased hostility between the old and the young generations. For five years running, the veterans of the last war accused their juniors of having lost the war, while the young men reproached the old with having lost the peace.

But it should not be imagined that France was torn by dissensions. The truth is not so simple. What quarrels there were seemed to stand as obstacles to an immense, if clumsy, desire for union. Never, perhaps, has so much goodwill been displayed. Young people dreamed dimly of a new order, and employers, on the whole, showed a tendency to make major concessions.

Whenever two travellers came to blows in the Underground or there was a dispute between a pedestrian and a clumsy cyclist, one would hear the same murmur from the crowd: 'It's a downright shame for Frenchmen to fight amongst themselves. In front of the Germans, at that!' But the very circumstances of the occupation, the barriers the

Germans set up to divide us and the needs of the underground struggle, in most cases prevented this goodwill from finding any practical expression. And so, those four years were one long impotent dream of unity. That is what invests the present with such painful urgency. The barriers have been removed and our fate is in our own hands. Which will triumph, the old, resuscitated quarrels or the great desire for solidarity? But we must ask all of you who are watching us from London to have a little patience. The memory of the occupation has not yet disappeared; we are still only half-awake after the nightmare. If I run into an American soldier as I go round a corner, I recoil instinctively because I imagine he is a German. Conversely, a German soldier who had taken refuge in a cellar but was forced to give himself up when his food ran out was able, a fortnight after the liberation, to ride down the Champs Elysées on a bicycle without anyone stopping him. The passers-by were still so used to the German uniform that they simply did not see him. We shall need a long time to forget, and the France of tomorrow has not yet appeared in its true light.

But we would ask you in the first place to remember that the occupation was in many ways more terrible than war. In a country at war, each man can at least do his duty, whereas in our ambiguous situation, we could neither act nor even think. No doubt, during that time France – the Resistance Movement being excepted – did not always display greatness of conduct. But it should be remembered that active resistance was necessarily limited to a minority. And I think that that minority, by accepting martyrdom deliberately and without hope, has more than redeemed our weaknesses. Lastly, if what I have written has helped you to realize what our country had to suffer in shame, loathing and anger, you will, I think, agree with me that it is deserving of respect even when it is mistaken.

1944

'Children in Bondage' was a survey of child life in the occupied countries of Europe and in Finland that was published in 1942. Its import was so Orwellian that it still beggars credibility. Yet it was published under the sober auspices of the Save The Children Fund. Racial purity for Nazi Germany was no abstract principle; it was to be pursued in the most literal and most unhinged manner.

## CHILDREN IN BONDAGE

### SAVE THE CHILDREN FUND

Polish circles in Great Britain received, in June 1942, a description of the Helenowo Camp, near Lodz, for racial improvement, where young

Polish boys and girls, aged fifteen to eighteen of good physique and perfect health, are made to live in couples with German girls and boys of the same age.

By September every hut in the camp was inhabited by a young pair: a German boy and a Polish girl or a Polish boy and a German girl.

The camp day begins at 6 a.m. and finishes at 10 p.m. when lights must be put out in the little huts. There is no forced labour and the life is that of a well-run holiday camp. The boys and girls get meat every day, milk and fresh fruit as well as large quantities of white bread and fresh vegetables.

But in spite of the seemingly complete freedom and of the good conditions in the camp, there is one duty which is absolutely compulsory – a duty from which none can escape. The couples living in the huts must have regular sexual intercourse, and this is strictly controlled by the camp doctor. Boys and girls failing to carry out their 'duty' in this respect are severely punished.

'When Polish girls were forced to have relations with German boys there were attempts at suicide. In order to prevent them the spiritual leaders of the camp organized a series of special talks advocating sexual intercourse among the young people of the camp and showing the importance of racial purity in the German and Polish nations.

The camp at Helenowo has recently been enlarged and there are now over five hundred boys and girls, the majority of whom are Polish. The inmates are constantly being changed; the girls who become pregnant are sent to Germany where they are to remain for good. The fate of the Polish girls after the birth of their child can easily be imagined. At the best they are either sent to work on the land or in an armament factory, while at the worst they will go to swell the ranks of the 'women for the Army'.

1942

In 1941 listeners in Britain and America were astonished to hear the voice of P.G. Wodehouse, the greatest English comic writer then living, broadcasting from Nazi Germany. He was denounced as a traitor, and MPs called for his trial on the charge of High Treason. The BBC refused to broadcast any more of his work, and public libraries banned his books.

In 1944 and 1945 MI5 compiled a dossier on Wodehouse's wartime role. It remained secret until 1980 when Iain Sproat, MP for South Aberdeen and a devoted Wodehousian, persuaded the Home Office to let him see it. He at once saw that Wodehouse had been done a grave injustice. There was nothing in the five broadcasts that could remotely be called German propaganda, as the text of the first given here demonstrates. There had been no deal between Wodehouse and the Germans; his main motive in broadcasting had been to reply to the many thousands of well-wishers in America and thank them in the only way open to him; a secondary motive, he admitted rather self-consciously, was to show that he had managed to keep cheerful. Not all his time in German hands had been amusing. He was packed into a cattle truck with the other male internees and travelled three days and nights with nothing to eat but one small bowl of soup a day. He slept on thin straw on a stone floor for six weeks. Yet he met some kindly and amiable Germans. This fact, which hardly surprises us now, enraged gung-ho minds in Britain – notably Duff Cooper, then Minister of Information, and Cassandra, famed Daily Mirror columnist.

Happily, however, there were many wiser voices raised to testify that Plum was a political innocent: Evelyn Waugh amongst them. In the end the British saw the matter in the right perspective. They bestowed a knighthood on him before he died in 1975 at the ripe age of ninety-three.

## WODEHOUSE AT WAR

This is the German Shortwave Station. Here in our studio in Berlin tonight is Mr P.G. Wodehouse, the well known father [sic] of the inimitable Jeeves, of Bertie Worcester [sic], Lord Emsworth, Mr Mulliner, and other delightful persons. Mr Wodehouse has been in Germany for almost a year since German troops occupied his residence in Northern France. During that time he has finished a new novel which, I understand, is on its way to the United States for publication, and started with another one. We felt that his American readers might be interested to hear from Mr Wodehouse, so we have invited him to this microphone to tell you in his own words how it all happened.
Mr Wodehouse:

It is just possible that my listeners may seem to detect in this little talk of mine a slight goofiness, a certain disposition to ramble in my remarks. If so, the matter, as Bertie Wooster would say, is susceptible of a ready explanation. I have just emerged into the outer world after forty-nine weeks of Civil Internment in a German internment camp and the effects have not entirely worn off. I have not yet quite recovered that perfect mental balance for which in the past I was so admired by one and all.

It's coming back, mind you. Look me up a couple of weeks from now, and you'll be surprised. But just at the moment I feel slightly screwy and inclined to pause at intervals in order to cut out paper dolls and stick straws in my hair – or such of my hair as I still have.

This, no doubt, is always the effect of prolonged internment, and since July the twenty-first, 1940, I have been spending my time in a series of Ilags. An Ilag must not be confused with an Offlag or a Stalag. An Offlag is where captured officers go. A Stalag is reserved for the rank and file. The Civil Internee gets the Ilag – and how he loves it!

Since I went into business for myself as an internee, I have been in no fewer than four Ilags – some more Ilaggy than others, others less Ilaggy than some. First, they put us in a prison, then in a barracks, then in a fortress. Then they took a look at me and the rest of the boys on parade one day, and got the right idea at last. They sent us off to the local lunatic asylum at Tost in Upper Silesia, and there I have been for the last forty-two weeks.

It has been in many ways quite an agreeable experience. There is a good deal to be said for internment. It keeps you out of the saloons and gives you time to catch up with your reading. You also get a lot of sleep. The chief drawback is that it means your being away from home a good deal. It is not pleasant to think that by the time I see my Pekinese again, she will have completely forgotten me and will bite me to the bone – her invariable practice with strangers. And I feel that when I rejoin my wife, I had better take along a letter of introduction, just to be on the safe side.

Young men, starting out in life, have often asked me, 'How can I become an Internee?' Well, there are several methods. My own was to buy a villa in Le Touquet on the coast of France and stay there till the Germans came along. This is probably the best and simplest system. You buy the villa and the Germans do the rest.

At the time of their arrival, I would have been just as pleased if they had not rolled up. But they did not see it that way, and on May the twenty-second along they came – some on motor cycles, some on foot, but all evidently prepared to spend a long week-end.

The whole thing was very peaceful and orderly. Le Touquet has the advantage of being a sort of backwater, off the line of march. Your tendency, if you are an army making for the coast, is to carry on along the main road to Boulogne, and not to take the first turning to the left when you reach Etaples. So the proceedings were not marred by any vulgar brawling. All that happened, as far as I was concerned, was that I was strolling on the lawn with my wife one morning, when she lowered her voice and said, 'Don't look now, but there comes the German army.' And there they were, a fine body of men, rather prettily dressed in green, carrying machine guns.

One's reactions on suddenly finding oneself surrounded by the armed strength of a hostile power are rather interesting. There is a sense of strain. The first time you see a German soldier over your garden fence, your impulse is to jump ten feet straight up into the air, and you do so. About a week later, you find that you are only jumping five feet. And then, after you have been living with him in a small village for two months, you inevitably begin to fraternize and to wish that you had learned German at school instead of Latin and Greek. All the German I know is 'Es ist schönes Wetter', I was a spent force, and we used to take out the rest of the interview in beaming at one another.

I had a great opportunity of brushing up my beaming during those two months. My villa stands in the centre of a circle of houses, each of which was occupied by German officers, who would come around at intervals to take a look at things, and the garden next door was full of Labour Corps boys. It was with these that one really got together. There was scarcely an evening when two or three of them did not drop in for a bath at my house and a beaming party on the porch afterwards.

And so, day by day, all through June and July, our quiet, happy life continued, with not a jarring incident to mar the serenity. Well, yes, perhaps one or two. One day, an official-looking gentleman with none of the Labour Corps geniality came along and said he wanted my car. Also my radio. And in addition my bicycle. That was what got under the skin. I could do without the car, and I had never much liked the radio, but I loved that bicycle. I looked him right in the eye and said 'Es ist schönes Wetter' – and I said it nastily. I meant it to sting. And what did he say? He didn't say anything. What could we have said? P.S. He got the bicycle.

But these were small things, scarcely causing a ripple on the placid stream of life in the occupied areas. A perfect atmosphere of peace and goodwill continued to prevail. Except for the fact that I was not allowed out of my garden after nine at night, my movements were not restricted. Quite soon I had become sufficiently nonchalant to resume the writing of the novel which the arrival of the soldiery had interrupted. And then the order went out that all British subjects had got to report each morning at twelve o'clock at the Kommandantur down in Paris Plage.

As Paris Plage was three miles away, and they had pinched my bicycle, this was a nuisance. But I should have had nothing to complain of, if the thing had stopped there. But unfortunately it didn't. One lovely Sunday morning, as I was rounding into the straight and heading for the door of the Kommandantur, I saw one of our little group coming along with a suitcase in his hand.

This didn't look so good. I was conscious of a nameless fear. Wodehouse, old sport, I said to myself, this begins to look like a sticky day. And a few moments later my apprehensions were fulfilled. Arriving at the Kommandantur, I found everything in a state of bustle and excitement. I said 'Es ist schönes wetter' once or twice, but nobody took any notice. And presently the interpreter stepped forward and announced that we were all going to be interned.

It was a pretty nasty shock, coming without warning out of a blue sky like that, and it is not too much to say that for an instant the old maestro shook like a badly set blancmange. Many years ago, at a party which had started to get a bit rough, somebody once hit me on the bridge of the nose with an order of planked steak. As I had felt then, so did I feel now. That same sensation of standing in a rocking and disintegrating world.

I didn't realize at the time how much luckier I was than a great many other victims of the drag-net. All over France during that Sunday, British citizens were being picked up and taken away without being given time to pack, and for a week those in Boulogne had been living in what they stood up in at the Petit Vitesse railroad station. For some reason, Le Touquet was given a substantial break. We were allowed to go home and put a few things together, and as my home was three miles away, I was actually sent there in a car.

The soldier who escorted me was unfortunately not one of those leisurely souls who believe in taking time over one's packing. My idea had been to have a cold bath and a change and a bite to eat, and then to light a pipe and sit down and muse for a while, making notes of what to take with me and what could be left behind. His seemed to think that five minutes was ample. Eventually we compromised on ten.

I would like my biographers to make careful note of the fact that the first thing that occurred to me was that here at last was my chance to buckle down and read the complete works of William Shakespeare. It was a thing I had been meaning to do any time these last forty years, but somehow, as soon as I had got – say, *Hamlet* and *Macbeth* under my belt and was preparing to read the stuffing out of *Henry the Sixth*, parts one, two and three, something like *The Murglow Manor Mystery* would catch my eye and I would weaken.

I didn't know what internment implied – it might be for years or it might be for ever – or it might be a mere matter of weeks – but the whole situation seemed to point to the complete works of William Shakespeare, so in they went. I am happy to say that I am now crammed with Shakespeare to the brim, so, whatever else internment has done for me, I am at any rate that much ahead of the game.

It was a pang to leave my novel behind, I had only five more chapters of it to do. But space, as Jeeves would have pointed out, was of the essence, and it had to go, and is now somewhere in France. I am hoping to run into it again one of these days, for it was a nice little novel and we had some great times together.

I wonder what my listeners would have packed in my place – always remembering that there was a German soldier standing behind me all the time, shouting 'Schnell' or words to that effect. I had to think quick. Eventually what I crammed in were tobacco, pencils, scribbling blocks, chocolate, biscuits, a pair of trousers, a pair of shoes, some shirts and a sock or two. My wife wanted to add a pound of butter, but I fought her off. There are practically no limits to what a pound of butter can do in warm weather in a small suitcase. If I was going to read the complete works of William Shakespeare, I preferred them unbuttered.

In the end, the only thing of importance I left behind was my passport, which was the thing I ought to have packed first. The young internee is always being asked for his passport, and if he hasn't got it, the authorities tend to look squiggle-eyed and to ask nasty questions. I had never fully realized what class distinctions were till I became an internee without a passport, thus achieving a social position somewhere in between a minor gangster and a wharf rat.

Having closed the suitcase and said goodbye to my wife and the junior dog, and foiled the attempt of the senior dog to muscle into the car and accompany me into captivity, I returned to the Kommandantur. And presently, with the rest of the gang, numbering twelve in all, I drove in a motor omnibus for an unknown destination.

That is one of the drawbacks to travelling, when you are an internee. Your destination always is unknown. It is unsettling, when you start out, not to be sure whether you are going half-way across Europe or just to the next town. Actually, we were headed for Loos, a suburb of Lille, a distance of about a hundred miles. What with stopping at various points along the road to pick up other foundation members, it took us eight hours.

An internee's enjoyment of such a journey depends very largely on the mental attitude of the sergeant in charge. Ours turned out to be a genial soul, who gave us cigarettes and let us get off and buy red wine at all stops, infusing the whole thing [with] a pleasant atmosphere of the school treat. This was increased by the fact that we all knew each other pretty intimately and had hobnobbed on other occasions. Three of us were from the golf club – Arthur Grant, the Pro., Jeff, the starter, and Max, the caddie master. Algy, of Algy's bar in the Rue St Jean, was there, and Alfred, of Alfred's bar in the Rue de Paris. And the rest, like Charlie Webb and Bill Illidge, who ran garages, were all well-known Paris Plage figures. The thing was, therefore, practically a feast of reason and a flow of soul.

Nevertheless as the evening shadows began to fall and the effects of the red wine to wear off, we were conscious of a certain sinking feeling. We felt very far from our snug homes and not at all sure that we liked the shape of things to come.

As to what exactly *was* the shape of things to come, nobody seemed to know. But the general sentiment that prevailed was one of uneasiness. We feared the worst.

Nor were we greatly encouraged, when, having passed through Lille, we turned down a side lane and came through pleasant fields and under spreading trees to a forbidding-looking building which was only too obviously the local hoose-gow or calaboose. A nasty-looking man in the uniform of the French provincial police flung wide the gates and we rolled through.

Next week – the Rover Boys in Loos Prison.

That was Mr Wodehouse in the first broadcast of a series of weekly talks which he will give from this station.

1981

The Germans who occupied the Channel Islands were, on the evidence of this witness, stolid, unimaginative, disciplined and humourless – but not bad fellows. They did their utmost to win the confidence of the islanders, and sometimes succeeded. Some went out with local girls, but if so, it was entirely because the girls wanted it. Crime among the occupying force was virtually unknown. Many of these Germans fell in love with the beauty of the island, and vowed to come back after the war with their families. Few did. Towards the end of the war, though, a new note was heard among them: dissent. The pamphlet printed here is translated from the original German, and was circulating in Jersey by March 1945. By then, even these obedient and disciplined men could see the war was lost. 'Death to all Nazis' ran the slogan of Free Germany.

## SWASTIKA OVER GUERNSEY

### VICTOR COYSH

What of the Germans? It has already been said that, in the main, they adopted a 'correct' attitude, which is to their credit, but their behaviour warrants more than this terse description.

They arrived in Guernsey in arrogant mood. They believed that the conquest of Britain was imminent (indeed some thought that this was the Isle of Wight!) and they could afford to be truculent. Hence the severe orders which they issued on the first day of the Occupation.

At the same time they were prepared to be friendly. They sought to ingratiate themselves with the islanders and some of them succeeded in doing so. It is difficult to account for this approach even as it is hard to believe that British folk would surrender to their advances.

Their military discipline was rigid and this accounted for the very small number of crimes committed by Germans against the community. There was a certain degree of liaison between the troops and some young women but this was entirely voluntary on the part of the girls. There was no compulsion about it.

This military severity had its grimly humorous side. If one happened to catch a German stealing roots from a field or otherwise breaking the law one could assault him freely for, were he to report the civilian, the soldier would receive worse punishment for his offence.

It is on record that a German, answering a telephone call, found that he was speaking to a superior officer. The call over, the soldier stepped back two paces, gave the Nazi salute, and cried, 'Heil, Hitler!'

They had no sense of humour as we know it. Islanders could hoodwink them with ease and the Germans, stolid, would accept what they were told. Some of them even believed that Britain would win the war, when islanders told them so.

Many of them understood English. They improved on this knowledge while they were here, and the longer they remained in the island the better were they pleased. They all loved Guernsey and several declared that, when the war was over, they would return with their families on holiday. Hardly any seem to have done so.

They expressed wonder at seeing palms and pines growing in a small island, for the one is semi-tropical and the other semi-arctic. They marvelled at our blending of English and French, at our constitution, the variety of scenery within so small a compass, at the quaintness of the town and the simplicity of our way of life.

They did not seek to change these things. The alterations they made were, on the whole, military necessities. They did not interfere with our worship (although, absurdly, they banned meetings of the Salvation Army because they wore uniforms), they allowed us our traditional form of government (subject to their supervision), and for a time they permitted radio sets. All this was reasonable and it is fair to record it.

Later they certainly did alter our way of life when some of us were deported, but this may have been dictated from higher quarters, for some occult reason. They imposed such innovations as traffic keeping to the right and the introduction of German time, but these were not unreasonable. . . .

No such epoch as the Occupation could occur without its amusing side. Dozens of humorous anecdotes have been told – most of them true, no doubt – which prove that the Guernseyman, even in adversity, did not forget to smile. The German, on the other hand, appeared to be unable to do so.

The story is told of the lady who concealed her radio crystal set where no gentleman would ever attempt to look for it, when Germans arrived to search a house for hidden wireless sets. Another good lady, faced with the same difficulty, plunged the crystal into a saucepan on the fire. The set was lost but the situation was saved.

There was a certain irony in the number of petty regulations the Germans made, the breaking of which meant a prison sentence. So many islanders were sent to jail that they were obliged to wait their turn. The small prison proved quite inadequate, and they were notified by postcard when it was convenient to receive them.

A prison sentence in the Occupation was not, therefore, anything of which to be ashamed and certainly no social stigma was attached to it. Indeed, going to jail could be an honourable experience, as in the case of those who were caught with radio sets, spreading the news or other meritorious practices.

To their lasting shame there were some (not many) islanders who betrayed their fellows to the Germans. Those nursing a grievance or wishing to curry favour with the invaders saw their chance and seized it. Probably the Germans felt as disgusted as every decent islander at such behaviour. Fortunately, it was rare.

Troops billeted on civilians were not always the burden one might suppose. Some of them were decent fellows, most behaved themselves, and the householder received certain privileges which he could accept with honour. These included additional rations of food and fuel, as well as payment.

It is easy to state that the islander should have had nothing to do with the enemy, and that he should have done all in his power to sabotage the German war effort. Some have even suggested that the population should have openly revolted.

Those who reason thus have never had the enemy within the gates. Had they experienced this they would realize that any show of resistance would have meant death to many others besides themselves, that such action would neither further the British cause nor hamper the enemy's, and that whereas resistance movements were possible on the Continent they were impossible in little Guernsey.

Before the Occupation there were opportunities for all who so wished to evacuate. Those who remained did so voluntarily and were obviously prepared to accept the consequences of their decision. Had everybody left the island, Guernsey at Liberation would have been in a terrible state, for the Germans would have had a free hand. Alderney, which was completely evacuated, was in a dreadful condition in 1945, though it certainly recovered after a few years.

Guernsey, however, was deemed to be of greater military importance than Alderney. Indeed, it was probably more heavily fortified and garrisoned than any of its neighbours. Without the restraining influence of a civilian population (even though it was half its original size) who knows what havoc the Germans might have wrought? It might have taken Guernsey a decade to revert to her former prosperity whereas, as events were, this occurred in a surprising short time.

Therefore those who were prepared to endure the Occupation could not be blamed for making the best of a bad job. They had no idea how long it would last (though few expected it to be for five years), nor were they at all certain that Germany would not win the war, especially in 1940. So the islanders accepted the Germans, not gladly, but with resignation.

Collaboration there was, but it was trivial. The average Guernseyman is British to the core and he refused to heed the blandishments of his unwelcome 'guests'. He, too, was 'correct' in his attitude towards them, treating them with wary formality.

The average German was not really a bad type. He was stolid, unimaginative, discipline's slave and without humour. Yet he was kind to children and animals, he appreciated Guernsey's charm, if he was severe with foreign workers he did his utmost to win the islanders' friendship. After all, he was not in Guernsey by choice and missed his fatherland as the exiled islander grieved for his.

Like most tribulations the Occupation had its virtues, bitter though they may have been in the assimilating thereof. Those five years taught the exile how much his island meant to him, of the blessings of home, relatives and friends and of the futility of war. The captive islander realized what freedom meant only when he had lost it, and appreciated Liberation only when, at last, that glorious morning dawned.

---

*Copy of a pamphlet translated from German and distributed among the German troops on the Island of Jersey, to the men who are in favour of overthrowing the Nazis and making an end to the siege.*

27/2/45

COMRADE:

The Russians are before the gates of Berlin, the Anglo-Americans stand on German soil in the West, their planes day by day lay more German cities in dust and ashes, each day kill more of our wives and children. WHY?

Hitler began this War, Hitler wished to conquer the world, he wished to annihilate English cities, he wanted to exterminate all peoples. This great guilt of a maniacal visionary and his accomplices has to receive bitter vengeance. The most stupid begins to realize by degrees that all Hitler's promises were a fraud. We have only him and the Nazi high priests to thank for the immense sorrow that has befallen all mankind, and above all, the German people.

SOLDIERS OF THE ISLAND OF JERSEY.

How long will you continue to join with this greatest deceiver of all times, how long do you wish to starve here?

The War is lost, we can do nothing here to avert the total disaster, on the contrary by holding out longer we are spoiling for ourselves the last possibility of a future regulated to a certain extent by ourselves. We appeal to you, make an end, join with us against the irresponsible officer-clique and their satellites. A great part of the Island Garrison is preparing for the insurrection against our tormentors. Will you help also? Be watchful, the day is coming when we shall show that not all Germans are blind to their destiny. Give the world a good example and our future will be secure. Close the ranks, organize yourselves into bands and companies from strongpoint to strongpoint. You will not be alone, a number of experienced officers are on our side. Here on the island of Jersey accounts will be settled, and that thoroughly, upon that Messrs the Nazis may depend.

Remain quiet until you receive further information.

Death to all Nazis.

Long live free Germany.

# DEATH HAD COME
# TO FETCH THEM

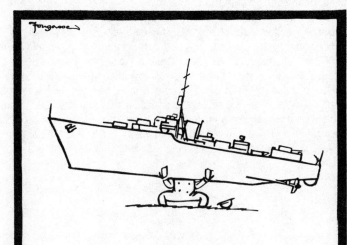

THIS REALLY
**DOES**
NEED YOUR SUPPORT

**KENSINGTON WARSHIP WEEK**
March 21 - 28

*Pursuit* – the story of the chase and the sinking of the Bismarck – is one of the great sea epics. Ludovic Kennedy, as a young officer on the destroyer Tartar, took part in that enormous action which raged from the Baltic to the Arctic to the Atlantic to the Bay of Biscay and all in the space of only eight days. More than four thousand sailors, British and German, were killed. I have chosen here the death of the Hood since it seems to me one of the most stupendous and chilling of all such losses. The fact that there was no perceptible sound as this great battleship blew to pieces is hard to believe nearly fifty years on, but well-authenticated. And still chilling are the figures: of all the fourteen hundred men who sailed in the Hood that day, just three survived.

Bismarck's end was also terrible in its majesty: she went down with her colours still flying, and only after eight battleships and battle-cruisers, two aircraft carriers, eleven cruisers, twenty-one destroyers and six submarines had been engaged – not to mention the three hundred air sorties. But at least 107 Germans were picked up from the two thousand who sailed in her; it could have been more had not the Dorsetshire, busy picking up survivors, noticed a smudge of smoke on the starboard bow. Captain Martin had no choice but to ring down for full speed; no one would have thanked him then for losing his ship to a U-Boat. So hundreds of Germans were still left in the sea. All but five of these – picked up later by German ships – died.

## PURSUIT

### LUDOVIC KENNEDY

And so the two admirals, Lütjens and Holland, riding on their great chargers, came at each other like knights of old, with guns for lances and armoured bridges for visors and pennants streaming in the wind. And beneath their feet, on the airy decks and in the warm bellies of their mounts, were their six thousand young seconds, half on either side, who felt no personal ill will towards each other at all, who in different circumstances might have played and laughed and sung together, kissed each other's sisters, visited each other's homes, but now, because of this time and place, were at each other's throats, concentrating as never before to ensure that they killed first, that their knights' lances toppled the other in the tourney.

In the gun turrets of the four ships, the first shells and cartridges and silken bags of cordite had been sent up from shell rooms and magazines far below, were even now rammed home in the barrels of each gun, the breeches had been closed and locked, the gun ready lamps were burning: the guns of Hood and Bismarck were over twenty yards long, weighed 100 tons apiece. The range-finding ratings leaned heads forward on rubber eye-cushions: the German range-finders were stereoscopic, which meant centring the little yellow *Wandermark* on the base of the enemy's superstructure; British range-finders were co-incidental, presenting an enemy vessel in two images which required merging into one. The British Navy had considered stereoscopic equipment after the first war, for it was deadly accurate, especially at initial ranges; but it required special aptitudes and a cool head which might be lost in the heat of the battle, so in the end they rejected it. The ranges both visual and radar were fed by electrical circuits to computers in transmitting stations deep below each bridge, along with own course and speed, enemy's course and speed, wind velocity, air density, rate of range-change, and, thus programmed, the computers fed to the gun-turrets an ever changing stream of directions for the training and elevation of the guns. In four gunnery control positions above each bridge, the four gunnery control officers – Schneider, McMullen, Moultrie and Jasper saw the gun ready lamps burn in front of them, stood by to open fire.

For a few moments then, as the two squadrons raced towards each other in that cold, pale dawn, with the eastern sky pink and violet on the low cirrus and a hazy blue above, there was in all the ships a silence made more striking by the knowledge of the thunder that was to come. Men's voices and hands had done all they could by way of preparation: the only sounds now were sea sounds, bows slicing the water, whistling wind and spray.

On Hood's bridge a man with headphones on his ears began singing out softly the closing ranges as given from the gunnery control position, like the conductor of a Dutch auction. And at about the same time as Admiral Holland's Chief Yeoman of Signals was hoisting the preparatory signal to open fire to Prince of Wales, Admiral Lütjens was ordering his Chief Yeoman to hoist JD, the signal to open fire to Prinz Eugen. When the range was down to thirteen miles, Admiral Holland said, 'Execute.' The Chief Yeoman shouted to the flag deck, 'Down Flag 5', Captain Kerr said, 'Open fire' and in the control tower the gunnery officer said 'Shoot!'

There came the tiny, tinkly, ridiculous ding-ding of the fire gong, like an overture scored for triangle, for a moment the world stood still, then the guns spoke with their terrible great roar, the blast knocked one almost senseless, thick clouds of cordite smoke, black and bitter-smelling, clutched at the throat, blinded the vision, and four shells weighing a ton apiece went rocketing out of the muzzles at over 1,600 miles an hour. To Busch in the Prinz Eugen, Hood's gun flashes appeared as 'great, fiery rings like suns', and Jasper beside him called out 'Damn it, those aren't cruiser's guns, they're battleships', just as Bismarck's second gunnery officer Lieutenant Albrecht was telling Schneider the same. Now it was Prince of Wales's turn, Esmond Knight in his air defence position was deafened by the crash of the forward turrets, felt the breath squeezed from his body, was unable to see for the smoke. As it cleared, he saw an orange ripple of fire run down the length, first of Bismarck, then Prinz Eugen.

In the tightly-shut armoured control position on Bismarck's bridge Lütjens and his staff rocked to the roar of Bismarck's opening salvo. This battle was not of his choosing, for his instructions were to shun any engagement with enemy forces not escorting a convoy, and he had delayed permission to open fire so long that there were some in *Bismarck* and *Prinz Eugen* who thought he was hoping to avoid it. But with the ice to the west of him, the two cruisers to the north, and Holland's force to the east, there was no escape; and in that situation his orders were to fight all out.

Now the shells were in the air, like flights of arrows, and men on either side, counting the seconds until their arrival, asked themselves anxiously where they would fall. Some believed they were directed to them personally, had their name on them as the saying went, felt the first stirrings of panic. 'He's fired,' came the agitated voice of a petty officer on *Prinz Eugen*'s bridge, and Captain Brinkmann said quietly, 'Keep calm, man. Of course he's fired. Now let's see what comes of it.' With a shriek and a roar the shells fell, great geysers of water leapt in the air, high as Hiltons, white as Daz. *Hood*'s shells landed in the vicinity of *Prinz Eugen*, but not dangerously so, *Prince of Wales*'s were a thousand yards short of *Bismarck*; but the shells of *Bismarck* and *Prinz Eugen* were deadly accurate, they enveloped *Hood* in a curtain of splashes, the men of *Prince of Wales* saw it with horror and relief.

If Admiral Holland's plan of the night before had worked, and he had come upon Lütjens unseen, he might already have won a great victory. But now everything had gone sour on him, he had the worst of every world. By steering at this angle he was denying his own force the maximum of fire-power and yet giving the enemy more to aim at than necessary. He had reduced his initial superiority in heavy guns of eighteen against eight to ten against eight, which was about to be reduced to nine against eight, as one of the *Prince of Wales*'s forward guns had a defect which would render it inoperative after the first salvo. Further, while the British fire was divided between *Bismarck* and *Prinz Eugen*, the German fire was concentrated on *Hood*. It would have helped if *Norfolk* and *Suffolk* had closed up on *Bismarck*, worried her from the rear, drawn the fire from her after turrets: this was Holland's intention, and orders to Müllenheim-Rechberg in *Bismarck*'s after control to keep his eyes fixed on the two cruisers show that Lütjens was expecting it. But Holland had failed to give Wake-Walker the necessary orders; the opportunity was lost.

There were other handicaps. The Germans had what sailors call the weather gauge, which meant the British ships were steaming into wind, the spray drenching the lenses of the forward turrets' two thirty-foot range-finders, necessitating use of the small range-finders in the control tower instead. And by keeping *Prince of Wales* close to him, making her conform to his movements rather than let her vary her course and speed, Holland was making it easier for the Germans to range-find, more difficult for the British ships to observe each other's fall of shot.

The shells went to and fro, east and west. One from *Hood* landed just ahead of *Prinze Eugen*, the water rose in a tall, white column and, falling, drenched fo'c'sle and upperworks, smeared the lenses of periscopes and telescopes that jutted out from the armoured control position on the bridge. Other splashes rose on the port bow, and Captain Brinkmann ordered the helmsman to steer towards them, knowing that salvoes never land in the same place twice. Then he opened the heavy door, went outside with Friebe to see through dry binoculars. *Prinze Eugen*'s first salvo had been a little short, now she was firing her second. Twenty seconds went by, Brinkmann saw the white fountains shoot up, some short, some over – a straddle – and then a flame leapt up on *Hood*'s boatdeck amidships. 'It's a hit,' shouted one of Jasper's crew excitedly, 'the enemy's on fire.' Busch saw the fire as 'a glaring blood-red rectangle which began to emit thick fumes', Captain Leach in *Prince of Wales* as 'a vast blow-lamp', Captain Phillips in *Norfolk* as 'a glow that pulsated like the appearance of a setting, tropical sun'.

On *Hood*'s bridge the fire was reported by the torpedo officer as being caused by a shell-burst among the 4-inch anti-aircraft ammunition. Able Seaman Tilburn, one of the 4-inch guns' crews, was ordered with others to put the fire out, was about to do so when ammunition in the ready-use locker started exploding, so they all lay flat on the deck. Then another shell, or perhaps two, hit *Hood*, killing many of the gun crews now sheltering in the aircraft-hangar; and part of a body, falling from aloft, struck Able Seaman Tilburn on the legs.

Now Holland decided, whatever the risks to *Hood*, that he could no longer afford to keep half his gun-power out of action. He had already made one small alteration back to port, and to bring the after turrets of both ships to bear, he hoisted the signal for another. While some on *Prince of Wales*'s bridge were looking at the fire in *Hood*, and others had their eyes fixed on the enemy, one man's telescope had never wavered, despite the smoke and confusion of battle, from the flagship's yardarm. 'From *Hood*, sir,' shouted the Chief Yeoman of Signals as the flags went up. 'Two Blue. Turn twenty degrees to port together.' Captain Leach and Lieutenant-Commander McMullen heard the news with joy: now at last the four-gun after turret with its frustrated crew would be brought into action.

The executive signal came down, the two ships began to turn. Then the incredible happened. When Schneider in *Bismarck* saw the fire on *Hood*'s boatdeck, he ordered an immediate broadside, and presently, and for the fifth time in four minutes, *Hood* was hidden by a curtain of shell splashes. But at least one shell of that broadside made no splash: it came plunging down like a rocket, hit the old ship fair and square between centre and stern, sliced its way through steel and wood, pierced the deck that should have been strengthened and never was, penetrated to the ship's vitals deep below the water-line, exploded, touched off the 4-inch magazine which in turn touched off the after 15-inch magazine. Before the eyes of the horrified British and incredulous Germans a huge column of flame leapt up from *Hood*'s centre. One witness in *Norfolk* said it was four times the height of the mainmast, another that it 'nearly touched the sky'. Busch saw it as a red and white funnel-shaped glow, Esmond Knight as a long, pale red tongue, Lieut-Commander Havers in *Suffolk* as a stick of red rhubarb, Lieutenant Schmitz, the war artist in *Prinz Eugen*, as in the shape of a sinister fir-tree. It was followed by a thick mushroom-shaped cloud of smoke which to Lieut-Commander Towell in *Prince of Wales* had the appearance of steam, but which Esmond Knight described as 'dark yellow, like the smoke from a gorse fire'. One of the oddest things about the explosion was that it made no noise. On *Hood*'s bridge Midshipman Dundas and Signalman Briggs heard nothing unusual, and Esmond Knight said, 'I remember listening for it and thinking it would be a most tremendous explosion, but I don't remember hearing an explosion at all.' As the smoke welled upwards and outwards bits and pieces of *Hood* could be seen flying through the air – part of a 15-inch gun turret, the mainmast, the main derrick. Captain Brinkmann noticed the ship's shells exploding high up in the smoke, bursting like white stars. To Esmond Knight it seemed the most famous warship in the world was blowing up like a huge Chinese Christmas cracker.

In all disasters, however unexpected and dramatic, there is often a moment, maybe no longer than a fraction of a second, when those about to die comprehend dimly that something unusual has happened, that things are not as they should be. On *Hood*'s bridge, after the great flame had shot up, there was time for Signalman Briggs to hear the officer of the watch report the compass had gone, the quartermaster to report the steering had gone, the captain to order a switch to emergency steering: then the ship fell sideways like a collapsing house. On the boat-deck Able Seaman Tilburn was conscious of a most extraordinary vibration. He saw a man beside him killed, another's side ripped open by a splinter and the guts coming out, went over to the side to be sick, found the deck level with the water. And elsewhere in the ship there were others calmly watching dials or adjusting levers who suddenly were aware that something very strange was happening to them, who, as they were lifted off their feet, and plates and bulkheads collapsed around them, sensed for one terrible, brief moment, no longer than it takes a flash of lightning, that death had come to fetch them.

In *Prince of Wales*, *Bismarck* and *Prinz Eugen* only a handful of men saw *Hood*'s end with their own eyes: the vast majority were below decks and to them the incredible news came on inter-com and by telephone, second hand. Some simply did not believe it. *Prinz Eugen*'s executive officer, Commander Stoos, on duty in the lower command post, hearing his captain's voice announcing the news, said quietly, 'Some poor fellow up there has gone off his head.' In *Bismarck*'s after transmitting station Leading Seaman Eich heard Commander Schneider's joyous shout, 'She's blowing up,' and would remember the long drawn out 'uuup' for the rest of his life. In the after director tower Müllenheim-Rechberg heard it too, and despite orders to stick to the two cruisers, couldn't resist swinging round to see for himself. The smoke was clearing to show *Hood* with a broken back, in two pieces, bow and stern pointing towards the sky. As he watched, he saw the two forward turrets of *Hood* suddenly spit out a final salvo: it was an accident, the circuits must have been closed at the moment she was struck, but to her enemies it seemed a last defiant and courageous gesture.

Now Prince of Wales, turning to port to obey Holland's orders, had to go hard a-starboard to avoid the wreckage ahead, and Jasper, through Prinz Eugen's main range-finder, saw on the far side of Prince of Wales a weird thing – the whole forward section of Hood, rearing up from the water like the spire of a cathedral, towering above the upper deck of Prince of Wales, as she steamed by. Inside this foresection were several hundred men, trapped topsy-turvy in the darkness of shell-room and magazine. Then Prince of Wales passed, both parts of Hood slid quickly beneath the waves, taking with them more than 1,400 men, leaving only a wreath of smoke on the surface. 'Poor devils, poor devils!' said Jasper aloud, echoing the thoughts of those around him; for as sailors they had just proved what sailors do not care to prove, that no ship, not even Hood, is unsinkable, and that went for Bismarck and Prinz Eugen too.

1974

One of the best wartime poets, still happily with us and still writing poetry as well as editing the London Magazine, is Alan Ross. He served in the Arctic and the North Sea before going into naval intelligence, and wrote some fine poetry there: '. . . the sea curdles and sprawls, / liverishly real, and merciless all else away from us falls.'

## DESTROYERS IN THE ARCTIC

### ALAN ROSS

Camouflaged, they detach lengths of sea and sky
When they move; offset, speed and direction are a lie.

Everything is grey anyway; ships, water, snow, faces.
Flanking the convoy, we rarely go through our paces:

But sometimes on tightening waves at night they wheel
Drawing white moons on strings from dripping keel.

Cold cases them, like ships in glass; they are formal,
Not real, except in adversity. Then, too, have to seem normal.

At dusk they intensify dusk, strung out, non-committal:
Waves spill from our wake, crêpe paper magnetized by gun-metal.

They breathe silence, less solid than ghosts, ruminative
As the Arctic breaks up on their sides and they sieve

163

Moisture into mess-decks. Heat is cold-lined there,
Where we wait for a torpedo and lack air.

Repetitive of each other, imitating the sea's lift and fall,
On the wings of the convoy they indicate rehearsal.

Merchantmen move sideways, with the gait of crustaceans,
Round whom like eels escorts take up their stations.

Landfall, Murmansk; but starboard now a lead-coloured
Island, Jan Mayen. Days identical, hoisted like sails, blurred.

Counters moved on an Admiralty map, snow like confetti
Covers the real us. We dream we are counterfeits tied to our jetty.

But cannot dream long; the sea curdles and sprawls,
Liverishly real, and merciless all else away from us falls.

---

*Frank Laskier was a twenty-year-old merchant seaman when he was discovered by a BBC reporter called Terence Domani. At that time the BBC was trying to find someone to record at first hand the Battle of the Atlantic, then at its height. Although Domani had spent six weeks as an ordinary inmate of the Seamen's Home at Liverpool, sleeping, eating and drinking with its shifting population, he had not found the man he wanted. He heard many good stories but not the ace story and the ace speaker he felt sure would turn up in the long run. After some weeks he heard about a seaman with a bee in his bonnet about using petrol for joyrides – then, of course, it was in very short supply and cost lives to bring into Britain by sea. This was Frank. They met, sat down at a table in a Liverpool café with a recording car outside and began to talk. The first story Frank told us was that which we publish here. It caused a sensation and to many remains the greatest broadcast of the war.*

---

## MY NAME IS FRANK

### FRANK LASKIER

I am a sailor, an Englishman, and my first name is Frank. I am quite an ordinary sort of individual – all we sailors are. We have our job to do and we do it. You can see me or my mates anywhere in the whole world; you can find us in Jovey's Saloon in Montreal, or you can find us dancing in the Trocadero in Brisbane, or you can find us getting slightly kettled in Jack Dempsey's Bar in New York. We don't wear any uniform. We have a small silver badge.

Well, when this war first started the Navy sent round asking us what we would like to do – whether we would want to have Navy personnel on board our ships to man the guns; or whether we would like to train and handle them ourselves. Well, naturally, we said we would defend our own ships. And so we all went to schools started all over in the seaports of England, and we learnt how to handle the 4-inch gun and the anti-aircraft gun, and everything going.

We started this war – we entered into this war – we, the sailors, with a distinct understanding in our own souls that we would fight clean. Well, all sorts of things happened to us; some of us did long and unpleasant trips in prison ships, others were torpedoed and spent – one man I know spent as much as forty-three days in an open boat. But we didn't mind; we were young and we were strong and we were healthy. And then things started to happen to us.

I found a ship in Liverpool and I found out, as we will on board ship before we sail, that she was taking evacuee children to Canada. I was so scared at the thought of taking those children, and I was so scared of anybody getting to know about it, that I even gave my allotment note to the Post Office with the instructions that they would send it to my mother five days after I had sailed. So that even my poor old mother wouldn't even know the name of the ship that I was on.

Well, we sailed out from Liverpool; we scouted round the coast of England, and one night we picked the children up and we went out. It was the happiest and yet the most dreadful trip I had ever done in my life. Of course those children, they were ordinary children, boys and girls in between nine and twelve; the little boys and little girls so pathetically seasick at first, and so wonderfully bright afterwards. They used to come up on the gun and look on us with awe, astonishment and fear, and ask us to open the breach so that they could look up the muzzle. And generally we had a beautiful time.

We wore our eyelids out, looking for submarines; we did watch and watch and watch and watch, and finally we got them safely into Montreal. We sailed up the St Lawrence and we handed them over to the kind care of friends who were waiting for them; and we rubbed our hands together and we said: 'Boys, that was a good trip, that's over', and we went into Joey's, and we bought ourselves a few beers. We loaded up with food and we came back to England. We had no children on board for the return journey.

Five days out from England I was on watch on the poop, and I saw a boat. We trained the gun on it, because the Hun has a very nice habit of hiding a submarine behind a boat. We saw no one in the boat – no sign of life. We sailed right up to it. We made a lee, and I was one of the men who went down over the side, and we put grapples on the lifeboat and swung her inboard.

In that boat, laying in the bottom, there were sixteen dead children; ordinary children, may be the little boy or girl who lived next door to you. Children! And their faces were blue and pinched with the cold, and

165

their little hands and knees were covered with scratches and blood where they had gone down the ship's side into that boat. Some of them had little nightdresses on; others were half-dressed, others were fully dressed. Their lifebelts had cut rings and grooves and chafed with saltwater round their necks; and we stood – the men of that ship, looking at that lifeboat, and we swore by everything we held holy that we would be avenged.

Because we know – we sailors know since – they had waited for the *City of Benares*. I am sorry if anybody listening to me had children on the *City of Benares* – it's opening up old wounds I know, but it's infinitely better that these wounds should be opened and remain open to the end of the war than we who are left, strong and healthy, should forget about it. Sixteen dead children! On a cold winter's evening, 500 miles from land. Dead! I can't forget it. Will you ever forget it?

We came back from the *City of Benares*. We buried our cargo at sea; we separated and we went on other boats, and stranger and even more horrible things happened to us.

Then we did another trip. I came back, and one evening in a pub I was talking to an old shipmate of mine, and he told me of something that had happened. He was on a boat; he had said good-bye to his wife knowing that he was going out on a benzine tanker – and, believe me, even in peace-time a benzine tanker is no picnic. They went over to America and loaded her up with benzine and they brought her back. Those men sat on top of 15,000 tons of benzine – 15,000 tons of benzine that had to be taken straight out of the ship and put straight into a bomber.

Coming back their convoy was attacked; a German raider appeared on the horizon, and with their superior guns and their superior range, she shelled the convoy. Five shots landed on board the ship and the midship house, and burst it into flames, ripped it wide open. Another shot landed on the after well-deck and burst the tank tops open. The ship was ablaze – she was flooded with benzine – and the captain ordered 'Abandon ship'. They went over the side and into one boat filled with about fourteen survivors under the charge of the second mate, a man named Hawkins.

Well, as they got into the boat, Hawkins was looking out and he saw the last man coming down the ladder. He was a greaser and his name was Boyle or Doyle, I am not sure which, and as he came down the gangway he slipped and he fell across the gunwale of the boat, and he picked himself up and his face was the colour of a bucketful of ashes.

They pushed the boat off and left their blazing ship, and went out into the waters of the Atlantic – mid-Atlantic – the Atlantic in a gale; and for two days those men were adrift on the Western Ocean in that boat. They were safe, as safe as I am sitting here, as safe as you are in your homes, because that was the *Jervis Bay* convoy, and they knew that they were going to be picked up – that destroyers were out looking for them. And during that time Harry Boyle had stayed in the boat; he'd never shirked his watch, he'd bailed, he'd steered, he'd kept a lookout, and he had never complained.

After two days they came across the San Demetrio. She was still ablaze but she was still floating, and those men – those fourteen men – went back on board and they put the fire out; and they sealed the decks up, and with the aid of a lifeboat compass and a Philips' Atlas, without stores, without radio, and without help, they brought that ship back to England with 12,000 tons of benzine on board her. And Paddy Boyle was an engine-room man, and he crawled up the ladder on board the Demetrio and he went down into the engine room and he watched for two days and for two nights without rest or respite, or sleep, and he never complained.

And in the evening of the second day, Paddy went up aloft to his room, and laid down on his bunk, and died. And when they went to pick him up he just hadn't any ribs; when he'd fallen across the gunwale of the boat he'd stove them in.

They buried him at sea, under the Union Jack – a sailor's grave, a sailor's death.

But they brought 12,000 tons of aviation spirit home for England, and that same spirit was intended to go into a bomber that would scream over Berlin and scream over Hamburg, and blast the daylight out of them and leave them in the misery and desolation that they have caused all over the world. That benzine will go into tanks that will go down the Unter-den-Linden; and those men who have been chased out of Dunkirk and tricked and cheated will be behind those guns on the day of Victory, on the day of the sailor's vengeance. But they didn't bring that benzine back to put in joy-riding cars.

That point is one that's a sore point with me. If you people will only realize that no matter what you are doing, the food you eat, that the petrol you use, that the clothes you wear, that the cigarettes you smoke and matches that you strike to light the cigarettes, that the plush on the cinema seats – that everything – everything in England, is brought over by the sailors. We will never let you down; we will go through trials unimaginable; we'll fight and we'll fight and we'll sail, and we'll bring back your food.

If I were merely sitting here giving this – can we call it talk? – merely to ask you for money, how easy it would be. You'd merely dig into your pockets or your cheque-books, and you'd give me all the money I wanted. But we don't want money. There's a scheme on foot these days; all over the world you see the letter 'V'. All over occupied Europe, all over England, is that 'V'. We have brought you your food. But for us the 'V' stands for Victory, and for Vengeance.

A long time ago I had four friends, four shipmates, four schoolmates. In 1938 we came back and we decided that as we were all friends we would have a holiday ashore. We had a marvellous time; we were happy and we were sunburned, and Charlie had his wife. And I always look back on that as a sort of calm before the storm, of this storm. You see, to digress for one moment, Charlie and I were very great friends and we both fell in love with the same girl. Well, she was a very, very wise girl; she chose the infinitely better man – she chose Charlie. Okay! I came to their wedding, I was Charlie's best man; we had a marvellous time and they were both happy.

Out of those four men I sit here now, with a funny little grotesque stump where a perfectly good right foot used to be. Billie was blown to hell on a minesweeper; George went down with the *Courageous*. Let me tell you what happened to Charlie.

Charlie was on my ship with me, and we signed on, and he was very, very unhappy when we had to push off. We went out in convoy and we faced the dive-bombers and we faced the submarines, and twenty-one days out the convoy sort of broke up and we went our various ways.

We settled down to the ordinary routine life of a ship at sea, and one night – eight hundred miles from land – I was on watch on the gun. At half-past six it was pitch dark on a tropical night. Suddenly there was a shot and a bang, and into the air there shot an enormous great yellow flare. I turned round and made one wild dash for the gun, and as I got to the gun, suddenly a hell, an absolute holocaust of shells burst around us. They were firing on the starboard beam, complete broadsides, those six 11-inch guns and eight 5.9-inch guns.

Quick, up to the gun, open the breech, ram the shell, ram the charge home, close the oven door, stick the tube in, run to the trainer, train her round, quick, quick, and crash the shells are banging into us.

Round she's trained, the lights are there, try to get on the searchlight, duck under the muzzle, put your range on, bring it down, bring it down; pull the trigger. Bang went old Mildred! It was heaven.

Back aft, open up again, put the shell in, and then . . . there was a crash like the opening of the Gates of Hell!

I was thrown about six feet. I picked myself up and there was just no gun worth speaking of left. Up to my feet, round the poop, down the ladder, across the well-deck, stepping on a bloody gruel of men's bodies who had been smashed as they came out of the poop; up the ladder, along the upper deck. God, where's the bridge? There isn't any. The captain is shouting: 'Abandon ship.' The great glaring eye of a searchlight is blazing down on us. I turn to go aft and there on the deck is Charlie.

I never thought that any man could be so horribly wounded, and still live.

If you are listening, Mary, I have to apologize to you. I told you that Charlie died quickly and quietly, with a bullet through his head; but it doesn't matter, Mary, there are a lot of people listening to this, in the fo'c'sles of ships, and they will remember; remember that 'V'; remember the *Vengeance*. Remember; remember what we have been through; remember what we're going through; and fight, and fight, and never, never, never give in!

The name of Frank's ship was *Eurylochus*. The raider that sank her was the *Von Scheer*.

1941

# A HOBNAIL LOVE
# ACROSS YOUR HEART

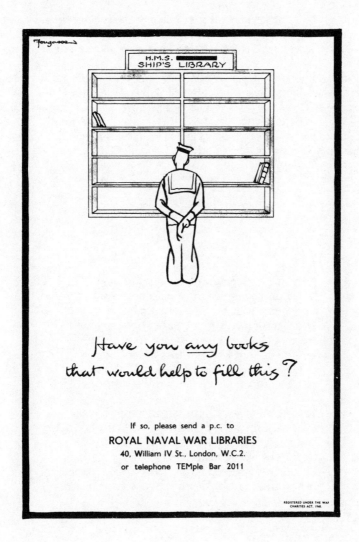

Now for three very different poems about wartime life in Oxford. J. D. James was a barrister of distinction whose later years were troubled by illness; but who had another life as a poet. '48-Hour Pass' has an emotional undertow both romantic and elegiac, but will probably only punch its full weight to those who know that the Park to which he refers was Heaton Park, then a desolate limbo in Greater Manchester where redundant aircrew waited to hear what their future fates would be on remustering for other trades when the war ended.

Gavin Ewart, as we have already seen, can unerringly capture the smoky, gin-sodden atmosphere of a wartime officers' mess. He is equally at home in the saloon bar of an Oxford hotel. Indeed, we can almost feel we know some of those faces he remembers only too well.

Finally, in this set, Mary Wilson. She was born in Diss, the daughter of a congregational minister, and married Harold Wilson, later Prime Minister, while still in her teens. Three collections of her poems have been published and she has also edited an anthology of poetry, published in 1982. Her 'Oxford in Wartime' is not exactly a distinguished poem – she is sometimes held to be a kind of female McGonagall – and yet it does convey with simple candour the feel of wartime Oxford.

## 48-HOUR PASS (FOR A.C.B.)

### J. D. JAMES

Almost I had forgotten how you smile.
Leave and green corduroys seemed months ago,
And memories of you improbable:
You had grown strange after so short a while.
Here in the Park the days were oddly dull,
The measurement of hours meaningless:
Useless parades, the endless talk of 'Joe',
The Squadron NAAFI's crowded emptiness . . .

To drip of trees the misty morning dawns,
My schoolboy heart sings Oxford and I come.
Rain falls in Manchester as I depart
(A Forces ticket, via Birmingham)
To print my studded boots on College lawns
And tramp a hobnail love across your heart.

## OXFORD LEAVE

### GAVIN EWART

'The Lamb and Flag' was closed, so I went to the Budolph Hotel
And saw there several faces that I remember too well,
Wartime and peacetime faces, RAF operational types,
Girls who were arty and tarty – and several blokes with pipes.
Young undergraduate faces and over there by the door
Under a smart and once fashionable hat what might (perhaps) be a
    whore.

I stood there like Charles Madge, observing, with the ginger beer I had
    bought
(The war had done away with the beer) and to myself I thought
Et ego in Arcadia vixi and worn undergraduate clothes,
No one here is different from me essentially, I suppose, . . .
Plus ça change . . . and a donnish type, a rather middle-aged queen,
Gave me a look, not a dirty look, and I knew what that look could mean.

Behind my back was a shocker with a handlebar moustache
Treating a blonde to a Dubonnet sec and his laugh was loud and harsh.
A rather passé arty woman invited a boy to her home
'We're going to have fish and chips, my dear, really we'd like you to
    come.'
On my left two rich young men were busy discussing the tart,
Two well-fed minds without, I should say, a single constructive thought.

Ah, youth! and how time passes! Was it really five years ago
That I left my Alma Mater? Yes, Time is not so slow.
It takes the loves and the parties but nostalgically in the brain
And even in the Army, their memories remain
And these are all real people, not the distortion of dream,
And though one might not believe it, they're all of them what they seem.
1942

## OXFORD IN WARTIME

MARY WILSON

The silenced bells hang mutely in the towers,
The stained-glass windows have been taken down
To Wales, to shelter underneath the mountains;
And battledress has shouldered-out the gown.
And undergraduates waiting for their call-up,
And feeling restless and dissatisfied
Are fighting with Australians in the Milk Bar;
Yet soon they will be serving side by side.
Flapping in tattered fragments from the billboards,
Torn posters advertise an old Commem,
And some who danced all night have gone for ever –
The Roll of Honour will remember them.
The colleges are full of Civil Servants
Trucking and jiving when the day is done,
And as the evening mists rise over Isis,
The RAF flood in from Abingdon
To the King's Arms, to play bar billiards;
Laughing and talking, flirting, drinking beer
No shadow from the future clouds their faces,
Only a heightened sense of danger near.
The pencil searchlights swing across the darkness,
The bombers throb above through driving rain,
We know that Woolton pie is on the menu
In the new British Restaurant at the Plain.
So tiring of the dreary wartime rations,
To dine at the George Restaurant we go,
Where high above the scene of shabby splendour
The punkas waver slowly to and fro.
The Barrel is rolled out beneath my window,
Deep purple always falls with falling night,
And here, in the enemy's encampments
Lili Marlène stands by the blacked-out light.
She shines a tissued torch upon her nylons
And ties her hair up in a Victory Roll.
Washing is hanging in the Fellows' Garden,
Evacuees live in the Metropole.

And in the crowded daytime roads of Oxford,
The shifting costumes make a masquerade
As men and women officers, all polished
Mingle with cloaked exquisites from the Slade.
In blue suits and red ties, the walking wounded
Hobble with sticks to help their bandaged feet,
And prisoners-of-war, with yellow circles
On their brown battledress, dig in the street.
And we all live as if there's no tomorrow –
Indeed, for some of us, there will not be –
And 'til the bugle calls us to the conflict
We sit in the Cadena, drinking tea.

Those wartime years have gone, and left no traces,
Fresh tides of youth have swept them all away;
New buildings have arisen by the river,
And there are few who think of yesterday;
Yet sometimes, in the middle of September
Though Spitfires scream no more across the sky,
As dusk comes down, you cannot see the pavement
Where ghosts in blue are walking down the High.

# SHALL I TELL
# MY HUSBAND?

For those who
are fighting
the Battle of the Fields,
the Women's Land Army Benevolent Fund
urgently asks your help.

Please send a donation to The Women's Land Army, 6 Chesham Street, London, S.W.1

or to

The W.L.A. County Office

War brought women new freedoms and new headaches. For the young woman, it might mean drudgery on a farm, boredom in a factory, or adventure on an airfield. For older women it meant keeping families going through rationing, bombing, shortages and black-outs. There was the strain of long separations; the question of fidelity; the problem of pregnancy in a world where the pill had not yet been invented and an abortion was still illegal. Not surprisingly, the agony aunts were in constant demand.

## WOMEN IN WARTIME

### JANE WALLER

With such attitudes to be found at the highest levels, it is not surprising that throughout the land there was resistance on the part of many men to any changes in the *status quo*.

Such changes put the relationships between men and women under strain. But they also affected young women who were still living at home.

Before the war most young middle-class girls would have stayed at home, or been allowed to take up a limited number of jobs. These would, for the most part, have brought them into contact with few people outside their own class. As the war went on, however, women from all backgrounds found themselves working, sometimes living, together. Who knows what these well-brought-up girls might not pick up from the riff-raff they were forced to associate with! That parents often felt such alarm was clear from the letters sent to Leonora Eyles [of *Woman's Own*].

Some were from the parents themselves:

DAUGHTER OUT LATE
'I have two daughters and a son married, and I have always brought them up strictly and made them mind me. But my daughter of sixteen, who has just started in business, won't come in at night. Often she is out till 11.00 and as there are lots of soldiers about, this worries me.' (Woman's Own, 13 April 1940)

HARD TO HANDLE
'I am so worried about my daughter of sixteen; she has started to make up to look much over twenty and stay out till after midnight. She is often a little the worse for drink when she comes home. She was a nice girl till she started to work in a factory, but now I don't know how to manage her. Her father is overseas.' (Woman's Own, 16 June 1944)

Others were from daughters:

SO DEPRESSED
'Ever since I had to register I have longed to belong to one of the many organizations in

*our town; I have a job on essential war-work but have to get home every evening straight from work, and if I work overtime Father phones the firm to make sure it is true. This shames me before others, and I am so depressed and fed up.'* (Woman's Own, 5 May 1944)

There was also much debate about how much young girls should know about the 'facts of life'. When young women wrote to Leonora Eyles, revealing their ignorance, she used to send them some information. This didn't always please the girls' mothers:

SHOCKED
*'I am very shocked at your advocating telling girls the facts of life before they get married. It is soon enough then for them to find out the dreadful lot of women.'* (Woman's Own, 20 March 1942)

PROTEST
*'I am very indignant. My daughter of eighteen wrote to you asking the facts about sex, marriage and babies; and a letter and a booklet came to the house which I burned immediately. I think young people should be protected from people who take away their innocence this way.'* (Woman's Own, 23 October 1942)

Leonora Eyles sympathized with worried parents, but suggested they make their homes more welcoming for their older children. She encouraged the children to stand up for their rights to 'friendship and brightness'.

But she had no time for those who would hide from the realities of life. To the mother who destroyed her daughter's booklet she thundered:

*'Have you any idea of the dangers of the world in which your young people are living today? Unless they know the things I try to teach them, they may form friendships which will ruin them for life. Ignorance is not innocence; innocence is knowledge protected by a good code of behaviour.'*

And the dangers were very real. By early 1943 there had been a spectacular increase in pre- and extra-marital sex, and its consequences of illegitimacy and the spread of venereal disease. Magazine articles warned that it was not only girls of 'a certain class' who were affected: the mixing of young people from all backgrounds spread both knowledge and temptation, and a mother's first duty to her daughter was to tell her the facts of life before she went out into the world.

Some men, affected by the rumour-mongering of 1941, worried about what might happen to their girlfriends or fiancées in the women's services. One wrote to Leonora Eyles in March 1942 saying:

*'I and my girl have been keeping company for four years now. I expect to be sent abroad very shortly and I look forward to the day when I shall come home and we*

*shall be able to marry. What worries me – and I cannot bring myself to discuss it with her – is the fact that she is going to join one of the services soon. She will be meeting all kinds of men, perhaps getting in with the wrong kinds of girls. How can I be sure she will be true?'*

In her reply Leonora Eyles referred disparagingly to the 'grossly exaggerated talk about so-called "immorality" in the women's service' and wished the two of them luck. But what she failed to mention was that such women were likely to be in greater 'moral danger' from their boyfriends or fiancés than from casual acquaintances.

War appears to bring with it an inevitable loosening of sexual restraint, and many servicemen, knowing that they were going off to possible death, brought pressure on their women to give them a special memory to take away with them. Some women wondered if they should do so.

TRIAL WEEKEND
*'I am in love with a man – we have known each other for four years – but there is no hope of getting married as he has only just qualified as an architect; and now he is being called up. He wants me to go away with him for his last weekend and I long to go, but somehow I don't think it's right. Yet, why should we be penalized because we can't afford to get married? . . . And am I, like hundreds of other women, to spend perhaps the rest of my life regretting what might have been?'* (Woman's Own, 19 September 1940).

And others regretted that they hadn't given in:

HIS IDEAL
*'Some months ago my boyfriend asked me to do wrong, but I would not. He then said he was only testing me to see if I was worth fighting for. Now I have had news that he is missing and I am heartbroken because I think that I ought to have given him what he wanted.'* (Woman's Own, 30 June 1944)

Leonora Eyles consoled the second writer with the thought that she had 'sent that boy to his duty with a dear and lovely vision of a girl he loved and felt was worth all he could give or do'. And to the first she simply said, 'But why not get married, my dear . . . If you are sure of your love for each other, then that is the only answer.'

But it was far from certain that such wartime marriages would survive into peacetime. As the war went on, the average age of brides dropped. Woman's Own reported in August 1941 that, according to the Rector of St Andrews, Mottingham, 'in twenty-four weddings, seventeen brides were twenty-one or under, one was seventeen, two were eighteen. The tendency for girls to be married so young is lamentable.'

It wasn't just that they were young; people who hardly knew each other were getting married. Lengthy courtships and engagements were becoming things of the past. As Woman's Journal said in May 1943:

'No one would begrudge the youngsters their hour of happiness or their dreams, but there will be many bitter awakenings when they go back to civil life and find they are from different backgrounds.'

And the war meant that for many couples the opportunities to get to know each other were rare. A man back on leave would be unlikely to want to hear about his wife's problems, and would probably expect to assume the role of head of the family as a matter of right. Small wonder, then, that such leave time was not always happy. One woman wrote that:

'We were married at the beginning of the war and have scarcely been together. Every time my husband comes home on leave I am terribly thrilled, and he writes me lovely letters beforehand. But when we meet it is nothing but silly little squabbles. After his last leave we thought we had better part and get a divorce; yet I love him very much and I know he loves me.' (Woman's Own, 16 June 1944)

Leonora Eyles counselled patience and the need to keep faith. It was just 'one of those unfortunate things brought about by the awful conditions of wartime life'. But wartime marriages were often under strain even when the husband was in a reserved occupation:

WAR STRAIN
'I am so unhappy; my husband was so much in love with me for the first three years of our married life but lately . . . he never seems to want to make love to me. I worry in case he is in love with another woman, though how he can spend any time with her I don't know, as he is working all day and doing Home Guard duty two nights a week. Is there something wrong with me?' (Woman's Own, 7 July 1944)

Leonora considered that in such cases the strain of war, added to heavy work, was to blame, not another woman.

But in many cases, there was 'another woman' involved; or, increasingly, 'another man'.

JEALOUSY
'My wife is working on a farm, and I am in the Army. Each time I come home I see her being very friendly with the farm men, taking tea out to them and so on; and people tell me she always does this. Last time I came home unexpectedly she said she could not get off, as they were harvesting, and I ordered her home. I feel angry and suspicious.'
'Dear, dear! Fighting to end tyranny – and having a spot of it in your own home! Don't be so silly, my friend. It is your wife's job to take tea out to the men and be friendly with them; a smile and a bit of friendliness are worth a lot nowadays. Stop ordering your wife about; and do be loyal to her. Next time someone tells tales on her, I hope you will stick up for her and tell them to mind their own business.' (Woman's Own, 14 September 1940)

The problems of infidelity were not evenly balanced between the sexes. Men away in training camp or overseas could be as unfaithful as they wished and no word of it would get back to their wives. It was only if they volunteered information, or left evidence about, that wives would become suspicious. Many women wrote of their suspicions to magazines, requesting advice. The typical reply stressed the need not to make a fuss, not to do anything to disturb the husband's leave, and suggested that friendships with other women – if they existed at all – were natural, and likely to be innocent.

Even when infidelity on the part of the man was admitted, there was a tendency to go easy on him. In March 1940 Leonora Eyles chose this as *Woman's Own* 'Problem of the week':

'*A wife of 29 had to leave her husband at the outbreak of the war and settle the two children with her mother, as this was a danger area. While there her mother was taken ill and she had to stay for six weeks and nurse her. On her return home her husband had been unfaithful and admitted it. He said he had been lonely. She feels she cannot forgive him such disloyalty, although he now says he is very sorry.*'

'Well this seems to be a case where tolerance and understanding are the only way to save the situation. It *was* lonely, and many people at the beginning of the war felt very distressed and off their balance. Even if she doesn't forgive him, what can she gain except the ruin of her married life? I would forgive him and never mention it again. He will be so grateful and so full of admiration for his wife's loving understanding that probably they will be happier than they ever were.'

In August 1941 an infuriated reader accused her of showing too much sympathy to men who strayed, but she defended herself on the grounds that 'one isolated mistake' should be forgiven while 'it is obviously impossible to make a life' with a man who is 'persistently unfaithful and extravagant'. Despite this rebuttal, a great degree of tolerance towards errant husbands was preached in the magazines. But when it came to wives being unfaithful then the words could be somewhat harsher, the condemnation more forceful.

## WOMEN AND FIDELITY

Among the most moving of letters were those from young women struggling to remain faithful to fiancés or husbands whom they had not seen for years. And these received for the most part, particularly tender replies:

KEEPING FAITH
'*Please help me, you can't imagine my trouble. My boy has been a prisoner in Japan for three years and I can't go out with other boys when I think of what he may be*

*suffering. My girl friends are courting now and I am so lonely I don't know what to do.'*
'Poor little girl, it is terrible that this, which should be your happiest time, should be so clouded. But I am glad that you are keeping faith with your boy. . . . Isn't there a youth club you could join and make new friends? Or how about volunteering at any local canteen several nights a week?' (*Woman's Own*, 7 July 1944)

And where the man was missing, perhaps dead, the problems of loyalty were even greater. Evelyn Home of *Woman* chose such a case in June 1944:

*'Separation has immensely increased the problems of human relationships. I have a letter from a girl whose fiancé has been reported missing at sea. This happened some months ago, since then no further news has been received of him, and the girl has been approached by another young man who wants to marry her. The girl tells me that she is still in love with the man who is missing. Would it then be wrong for her to marry the second man – and devote her life to trying to make him happy?'*

'Personally, I don't think this girl has waited long enough, either to know whether her fiancé is truly gone beyond recall or whether she is really ready for marriage with another man . . . I advise this girl to wait another six months at least before she makes up her mind. She may find that there is no need to make up her mind – circumstances and people may have changed in the meanwhile, and her problem may have vanished.'

But on occasion women were told that they could go out with other men, provided that they knew where to draw the line. They should remain scrupulously faithful, not even allowing a kiss. And most 'decent' women were considered to be loyal and true by nature. A single case of infidelity on the part of a woman was not necessarily seen as the end of a marriage:

SOLDIER'S WIFE UNFAITHFUL
*'I am a soldier and recently got 48 hours unexpected leave. I went home feeling on top of the world but I found that my wife had been associating with another man. I have every reason to believe she has been unfaithful. What ought I to do about it?'*
'Everything depends on how things were before you went away; were you both happy and in love? Is this – if your suspicions are correct – likely to have been a temporary lapse? Talk the matter over now the first shock has worn off – perhaps she could come to where you are stationed. Give her another chance if you feel she has learned her lesson; but, if not, go to your chaplain; he will tell you what legal steps to take, if any.' (*Woman's Own*, 27 March 1942)

But confessions of persistent infidelity received little sympathy from the agony aunts.

SHALL I TELL MY HUSBAND?
'I have been married for five years, and six months ago my husband went overseas. Just recently I have met a young man and we find we are falling in love with each other. He wants me to write and tell my husband this and ask him to give me my freedom when he comes home so that we can get married. I have no children to consider. Do you think I should tell my husband of this affair now, or wait until he comes back?'

'I am going to speak plainly to you, partly because I think that you, and others like you, who seem to have a very sketchy idea of loyalty, need to face facts. Your husband has gone overseas. Do you realize what this means – danger, privation, loneliness, possibly pain and death? Do you realize that he and all those with him are facing all this cheerfully and for your sake so that you, and all of us here at home, can live in safety and comfort? So that we can go out and about freely and safely – so that we may have enough to eat, and so that our homes shall remain homes, and not targets for an invading enemy? Do you think you are worth it? Can you believe that you, and others like you, who have no idea of remaining loyal to their marriage vows, who talk lightly of "being in love" with another man, are worth the lives of all our gallant men? I strongly advise you to sit down and do some hard thinking about this. Cut out this affair, give up seeing this man; avoid him as you would the plague, and you will soon get over it. You certainly should not say anything to your husband about it; you don't want to add to his hardships.' (*Woman's Weekly*, 24 July 1943)

Almost without exception the columnists were insistent that a husband should not be told of his wife's infidelity while serving abroad. But when the man was due to return home to find that his wife had borne a child to someone else, they usually suggested how the news could be broken as gently as possible:

DON'T TELL YET
'My husband is a prisoner of war, and I was dreadfully depressed and lonely until I met two allied officers who were very sweet to me. Now I realize that I am going to have a baby, and I don't know which is the father. My husband is shortly to be repatriated, and I don't know how to tell him.'

'It is very difficult for me to advise you. I appreciate the loneliness and depression you were suffering, but that you could do such a thing – and with two men – passes my comprehension. But now the main thing to do is to avoid hurting him, isn't it? I advise you, as soon as you know he has reached the country, to write to the matron of the hospital, or the commander of the next camp to which he is sent, tell them the truth, and ask them how you can arrange some way of not seeing him until your condition is not apparent. Wait until his health is better before you tell him the truth. It might be the finish of everything for him if he knew it now.' (*Woman's Own*, 10 December 1943)

Some readers questioned whether the truth should be withheld from a man serving abroad, and to one of these Leonora replied:

> 'Try to see his point of view; he is, perhaps, thousands of miles away, fighting for his life and thinking of home and wife. Surely it is unfair to let him have such a ghastly shock when he can do nothing about it? I am appalled at the infidelity of a serving soldier's wife, my dear, but I cannot see that the situation is improved by his suffering. Let her wait till he comes home and can face the position with his time and mind at his own disposal, not taken up by the business of fighting for life.' (Woman's Own, 27 August 1943)

But it was a man, Stephen Francis, writing in *Woman and Beauty* in November 1943, who produced the fiercest condemnation of such would-be confessions – 'what untold harm a foolish, unthinking woman can do with a scrap of paper, a pen and ink.' He described as 'fifth columnists' those wives 'who are unfaithful and want to ease their conscience with confessions'. He quoted a war correspondent as asking:

> 'Are half the wives in Britain demented? Won't they realize the men out here have a job on that's more important than the heart-burnings and soul-searchings of all the silly females who have nothing better to do than pour out on paper their wretched "confessions"? Don't they know what they're doing to the morale of the men?'

And he went on to say that he knew that kind of letter well:

> 'It begins . . . with some such stock phrase as "I don't know how to write this to you . . ." Well, why write the cursed thing? Keep it. Tear it up. Wait till the war's over – you may have learned more sense by then. Or, if not, perhaps he'll have died happy.
> Cruel? Possibly. But not so cruel as the pen of a thoughtless woman. The amount of damage to morale and to the war effort that some thoughtless women are doing daily in their letters to their men in the Services is probably greater than that done by the whole of Dr Goebbels' propaganda machine . . . I accuse all such women of activities dangerous to the prosecution of the war. I suggest they think twice before they dip their pens in this poison and ask themselves: Do I write this because I love him or because I love myself? Is it devotion or downright selfishness? Am I being forthright or fifth column? Their husband's happiness – perhaps his life – depends on their answer.'

## PREGNANCY

Today it is difficult to understand how narrow the choices were at this time for a woman who wanted to avoid having children. The contraceptive pill had not been invented; abortion was strictly illegal, and only carried out, for the most part, by back-street practitioners whose medical training was usually minimal. And a woman could not even offer a baby for adoption, since this needed the consent of her husband, whether he was the father or not.

183

Many women in such positions wrote to the magazines for help and advice, but little could be said other than tell him the truth and ask his forgiveness. A lot of men would not forgive. The divorce rate rose from 10,000 in 1938 to 25,000 in 1945, most proceedings being brought by husbands and usually on grounds of adultery. Some men accepted the new child; others were prepared to resume their marriage on condition the child was put out for adoption. And the 'Homes', as Leonora told one distraught woman in 1944 'will take a baby on condition the marriage is not broken'.

## TRADITIONAL VALUES

From all this it might be inferred that the vast majority of women in wartime Britain were having a wild time with their fiancés or husbands away. And it is true that traditional values were severely shaken. But the majority just struggled on, though few people wrote about them. One such woman wrote to *Woman's Own* in March 1945 to say that:

'One hears so much these days about broken marriages due to the separations brought about by the war, that it sometimes comforts me to consider the cases of my friends. There are about half a dozen who spring to mind at once. All have been married for four years or longer; some have children, some not; one has unfortunately lost her husband in this war; another's husband has been a prisoner in Japanese hands since the loss of Singapore. For those of us still fortunate enough to have our men within letter distance, our greatest pleasure is in writing to and hearing from them, and we all long eagerly for their return. Surely there must be thousands like us in England – faithful, loving wives? But one reads so much of the others that the fact that there are many happy marriages in spite of war difficulties is apt to be overlooked.'

And of course she was right. There were thousands like her. But, sadly, for many of them, their menfolk would come back broken in mind or body; if, indeed, they came back at all.

Some men feared that they would never come back or, if they did, would be a burden on their wives. And this caused many of them to wish to put off marriage until the danger was over. One woman who wrote to *My Home* in April 1940, complaining of her fiancé's reluctance to marry, was told:

'You are up against a very big obstacle – a man's sense of honour. He is certainly thinking along these lines: "Marriage means undertaking the responsibility of a girl's future, of guarding and protecting her as well as giving her companionship and support. And to do this I must be able to count on a reasonable amount of security in our joint lives. War makes all this impossible, as well as bringing inevitable risks for myself of being maimed or even killed. Risks which I would face alone, but to which I cannot subject the woman I love."'

'That is the way he is reasoning, and a very manly way, too. But he leaves out one important factor, the kind of love you have for him . . . In a true woman's heart there is a passion for giving. Giving all sorts of lovely things. Things like patience, self-devotion, sympathy and inspiration . . . But in order to give them fully to the man she loves she must belong to him, and have the proud name of wife. Can you make him understand this? Make him see how empty the months and years will be for you and how, if the worst comes to the worst, the great consolation for you would be to have been his?'

A disturbing letter was sent to Leonora Eyles in early 1943 by a wounded air gunner, sent home on sick leave, who wrote that his wife:

'. . . who has been everything to me for six years says that the sight of me makes her sick because I have murdered innocent people. She has fallen for a civilian, and wants to leave me and take the child. Is this what we are fighting for?'

And perhaps the saddest she received was:

'Three of us have lost our fiancés in the war and look like being spinsters. A friend has told me that spinsters deteriorate mentally and physically. Another friend says that spinsters should learn to sublimate. What does this mean?'

Leonora Eyles, and her counterparts in the other magazines, did what they could to advise, console and, where necessary, admonish the thousands who wrote to them. Nearly fifty years on some of what they wrote may seem quaint, old-fashioned and occasionally misleading. But at a time when people were more reluctant than nowadays to talk about their deepest worries, the agony aunts were perhaps the only escape-valve for many of the women of Britain.

---

Mass Observation had already proved its worth in the 1930s. Led by Tom Harrisson, it had conducted sociological surveys into the habits of the industrial northern working class of Britain with stunning effect. Books like The Pub and the People have recently been republished and still have the same clout. Harrisson's method was to infiltrate himself and his colleagues into the town disguised as lorry drivers, ice cream vendors or whatever, so that they melted into the background and were free to observe the subject matter as if it were a rare tribe in the South Seas.

Celia Fremlin was already one of its most valued observers; she had made her name before the war with a book on domestic service called Seven Chars of Chelsea; and she had also worked as a waitress at a Lyons Corner House during the London Blitz. She had been closely involved in the study of morale and wartime production between 1940 and 1941, and was therefore no stranger to factory life when she presented herself for duty on 7 February 1942 at Malmesbury in Wiltshire. Her placement had been arranged by the Ministry of Labour; strings had been pulled by Harrisson to get her there. The report that she published in October 1943 – War Factory – was enthusiastically received. The Guardian called it 'a remarkable study', and The Sunday Times 'fascinating'. Celia Fremlin herself said that she would never have written with quite such frankness had she appreciated that the report would end up in the hands of management. But perhaps it is as well that she didn't know and that she wrote as frankly as she did.

Here we examine just one aspect of the lives these conscripted women lived in this tiny Saxon town in the middle of the war as exemplified by their weekly budgets. An ordinary unskilled girl was getting £2 14s (£2.70) in her pay packet each week including overtime. That may not seem a great deal, but it was substantially more than they would probably have earned in the various forms of domestic work then available around the town, where 23s (£1.15) a week would have been a more normal wage. The details Celia Fremlin gives of their spending habits with the money left over after paying their keep gives us a vivid insight into the lifestyle of the time. Whatever happened to Glymiel jelly? Do people still buy Milk of Magnesia tablets? And is iron tonic still bought? Halibut oil is certainly now an endangered species and, as a present to send a boyfriend in the army, Swiss roll also has a quaint period touch.

## WAR FACTORY

### CELIA FREMLIN

We will now go on to give some details of the way in which the girls' money is spent, on these afternoons and otherwise.

THE WEEKLY BUDGET

An ordinary unskilled girl gets about £2.14s in her pay packet each week, including overtime. Naturally enough, the girls we are discussing in this chapter – i.e. those living at home – are better off financially than those in lodgings. They do, of course, pay something into the general family fund, but – with a few exceptions – they pay no more now than they did before, when they had much lower-paid jobs. Thus a girl who was formerly getting 23/- a week for some sort of domestic work, and paid her mother 10/- of this, will in all probability, still pay her mother 10/- out of her new wage of £2 14s. Most parents who are at all in a position to do so, accept, and indeed encourage this state of affairs, feeling that after working such long hours, the girl deserves to keep the money herself. On the average, then, the basic weekly expense of a girl living at home will be:

| | |
|---|---:|
| To mother, | 10/- to 15/- |
| To canteen (if not provided with sandwiches from homes), | 10/- |
| Fares, | 3/- |

She will thus be left with more than a pound to spend as she likes. About three or four shillings of this will probably be spent on pictures or dances; about five shillings saved – usually for some special coveted article, like a summer coat, or a new pair of shoes. The rest is spent on the Saturday afternoon shopping expeditions referred to above.

As this seems to account for a big share of the weekly money – anything up to fifteen shillings or one pound – it seemed worth while to get some idea of exactly how the money was being spent on these expeditions. So some typical individual shopping lists were recorded – partly from observation, and partly from conversation:

(1) F25C (unmarried):

| | |
|---|---:|
| Tube Glymiel jelly | 1/9 |
| Cigarettes | 6½ |
| Tube of wine gums | 2 |
| Small tin Milk of Magnesia tablets | 7 |
| Large bottle of cough mixture | 1/9 |
| 1 pair of stockings | 4/11 |
| | 9/8½ |

(The stockings turn out to be already laddered, so she has to go out during the dinner hour on Monday to change them.)

(2) F25D (married):

| | |
|---|---:|
| Nail varnish | 1/4 |
| Card of hooks and eyes | 4 |
| Jar of cold cream | 2/6 |
| Shampoo | 6 |
| Tablet of soap | 4 |
| 4 stamps | 10 |
| Pair of No. 9 knitting needles | 8 |
| Cigarettes | 1/6 |
| | 8/- |

(3) F25C (unmarried):

| | |
|---|---:|
| Shampoo and set at hairdresser | 4/6 |
| Pair of dance shoes | 12/11 |
| Polish remover | 1/9 |
| Ornamental flower for dance dress | 2/6 |
| Writing pad | 7½ |
| | £1 2 3½ |

(4) F20D (unmarried):

| | |
|---|---:|
| Knitting pattern | 3 |
| No. 8 needles | 8 |

| | |
|---|---|
| Hand cream | 2/6 |
| Pair of stockings | 3/1 |
| Iron tonic | 1/7 |
| | 8/1 |

(5) F20C (unmarried):

| | |
|---|---|
| 8 oz. Wool for jumper | 7/5 |
| Pair No. 10 needles | 6 |
| Pair of stockings | 3/6 |
| Shoes from mender | 5/11 |
| Jar cold cream | 2/6 |
| Jar vanishing cream | 1/6 |
| Box of powder | 1/6 |
| Tube of toothpaste | 7½ |
| Tube of camphor ice | 10½ |
| Cigarettes | 2/5 |
| Mending wool | 8 |
| Ribbon | 1/5 |
| Toffee | 5 |
| Shoe laces | 7 |
| | £1 9 10 |

(6) F25D (unmarried):

| | |
|---|---|
| *Woman's World* | 3 |
| Ankle socks | 2/1 |
| Knickers | 4/11 |
| Cold cream | 1/3 |
| Soap | 3 |
| | 8/9 |

(7) F30C (married):

| | |
|---|---|
| Knitting wool for little boy's jersey | 5/11 |
| Safety pins | 2 |
| Packet of needles | 2 |
| Bias binding | 7 |
| Shampoo | 3 |
| Lipstick | 1/1 |
| Halibut oil | 2/- |
| Packet of rusks (tried to get biscuits) | 1/4 |
| Cigarettes | 2/1 |
| | 13/7 |

(8) F20C (unmarried):

| | |
|---|---|
| Writing pad and envelopes | 1/11 |
| Knitting pattern | 3 |

| | |
|---|---:|
| Box of powder | 2/- |
| Jar of night cream | 1/7 |
| Stamps | 1/8 |
| Reel of cotton | 2 |
| Bottle of ink | 6 |
| Swiss roll (to send to boyfriend in Army) | 9 |
| Cigarettes | 2/9 |
| | 11/7 |

(9) F25D (married):

| | |
|---|---:|
| Box of throat lozenges | 6 |
| Embroidered tablecloth | 18/5 |
| | 18/11 |

Says: 'It's my sister's birthday tomorrow, and I wanted to get her something she wanted, and she told me she wanted a pretty tea cloth. I didn't know it could cost all that; I don't know what I'll do for next week, I'll have nothing left.'

Even from this small number of lists, it is possible to see clearly the emphasis on cosmetics, knitting, cigarettes, etc. There would also be a heavy emphasis on sweets, if there were any to be had; one of the staple topics of conversation on Saturday mornings is whether or not there will be any sweets left in the shops by the afternoon. There rarely are.

Cosmetics also are much discussed. There is always great excitement when the news goes round that some particularly popular brand of any kind of cosmetic is in stock somewhere:

'They've got some Coty powder in J's.'
'What do you mean, real Coty? In the Coty boxes?'
'I think so. I haven't been but Lil went dinner time, and she got a lovely box.'
'What shades have they got?'
'I don't know . . .'
'Are there any dark shades? I want a dark powder for the summer.'
'I shan't worry about the colour. So long as it's Coty, that's all I care. I'll mix it to make the right colour.'
'Will it still be there tomorrow? Was there a lot?'
'I don't know. Lil said . . .'
'I'm not going to chance it. I'm going to get off early tonight.'
'It's worth it for Coty, isn't it? You don't see that much now.'

There are practically no housekeeping goods bought at all on these expeditions. The reason, of course, is that, from the nature of their work, none of these women, married or single, are able to look after their homes themselves, and so whoever it is who looks after the house for them also does the household shopping during the week.

1943

James Lansdale Hodson was a kind of sub-Priestley figure; he travelled many thousands of miles across Britain during the war and recorded his impressions in a series of diaries which were enormously popular at the time. H. G. Wells, no less, said of one of his earlier books, Towards the Morning: 'It is the best reading I know of just now and I think it will always be good reading.' And the poet Edward Shanks said of another, War in the Sun: 'A war diary which has no exact parallel. Future generations are likely to find a place for it near the diaries of Pepys, Greville and Hickey.' Today Hodson is well-nigh forgotten; but his diaries repay re-reading. The extract on the life and hard times of gently born girls in the services may strike us as a little bizarre today fifty years on; but no doubt it was a true culture shock for these young women to have their heads examined for lice. The short extract about the WAAF admiring the fliers is one example among thousands of the hero worship in which aircrew were then held. But six years of war were to end without a single girl taking to the air in combat as Hodson thought they might. The third extract gives us a salutary correction to the notion that all war workers were dedicated; no doubt many of them were much as Hodson's anonymous correspondent describes.

And finally, from his diaries, a vivid heart-wrenching account of the pain of bereavement.

## HOME FRONT

### JAMES LANSDALE HODSON

15 July 1942

A young friend in the WAAF has been giving me a few eye-openers about the less happy side of service life for women. She and other recruits (she was a professional woman) had a head inspection for lice when they arrived at their depot at eleven p.m. on a winter's night. Finally, they were put to sleep in huts – no heat of any kind, shoddy blankets, having weight but little warmth (I know them well). For several days the girls were kept hanging about in wind and rain drawing various bits of kit, and lugging large pieces of it from one end of the camp to the other. One girl caught a chill, travelled up to Lancashire, caught pneumonia and died. Yesterday an ATS girl told my wife that in her batch they were inoculated with a needle that was blunt and which was not sterilized between one girl and the next, and that, in consequence, some girls got very bad arms indeed. Now these are charges which may be a bit exaggerated, which most officials would deny, but which any serviceman knows may well be true. The bully and the careless person and the grossly inefficient are by no means extinct; it would be odd if they were.

The chief greenkeeper on the golf links told me yesterday that his daughter in the ATS is batman to three officers, that she buys the material for cleaning their belts and kit out of her own money (being reimbursed monthly), that she stays up late cleaning their belts, etc., and gets up at six a.m. to get their shaving-water. If I am asked how I should like my daughter to be batman to three officers, I reply I should resent it. And yet it might happen. War is war. Our daughters go into the services, and chance pretty well decides what becomes of them. In the Wrens none can have a commission before the age of twenty-one (perhaps rightly), but it means that for three years she can fetch and carry. Boys can occasionally have a beastly time in the ranks as I know, but for gently-nurtured girls to be suddenly hurled among girls of all sorts, the clean and the dirty, the well-bred and the foul-mouthed, gentlefolk and riff-raff, all herded together and treated alike, is a business that can be tough. My young friend didn't know there were such sides to life as she has now been – and roughly – made acquainted with.

In passing, she said she now does the same work as men, but gets half their pay. (This on radiolocation.) Three nights a week she is on night duty. She works in an atmosphere akin to the London Underground. They have fans, but don't use them because they prevent you from hearing the spoken word, and the spoken word is highly important on their work. 'We blink like pit ponies when we come up into the fresh air.'

16 July 1942

A young friend in the WAAF said today, as we watched a couple of our heavy bombers come back from France: 'I do envy those men who fly – it must be thrilling.'

I said: 'You'll probably be alive at the end of the war and they may not be.'

To which she answered: 'I don't mind not being alive. I don't mind being bumped off tomorrow – it's got to come, sometime. I'd much rather take the risks and have the thrills than do my boring job.'

Maybe, before this war ends, we shall see our girls as wireless operators and navigators in aircraft. Apart from the chance of being maltreated after being shot down, or baling out over enemy country, I see no insuperable objection. They possess the courage and, some of them, the endurance.

2 August 1942

Another correspondent, anonymous this time, and in green ink, begins: 'Oh, you writers! You, among others, descended to the shipyards via the managerial offices. Next time, if you are a genuine truth-seeker, put on overalls and be one of the crowd of Heroes. . . . If you want to see the art of scrounging and clock-watching as practised by experts, then get on the ships after launching. The tempo changes from a slow foxtrot to a whining lament. This wicked waste of man-power is not by any means altogether the fault of the workman. I think the management is to blame for about seventy per cent. I honestly believe that, apart from piece-workers, the average work per man per day is three hours. Ye gods! I am an electrician and I say there are twice as many here on the

Tyne, as are necessary. I don't suppose you can alter things, but you can refrain from patting us on the back.'

3 August 1942

Ros rang up last night and mentioned that she's had bad news – Jock is missing. (Jock is a New Zealand pilot, DFM, with whom Ros is friendly.) I keep hearing of lads gone. I met an old doctor friend and asked after his Squadron-Leader son. He said with deadly quietness: 'We lost him a year ago.' Col. B., whom I met in Brussels and in Syria, has lost his son. My friend, H.W.P., has lost all three sons – one killed, two missing. T.L.G. has lost a son; my wife's dentist has lost his son-in-law; Sir Basil Clarke's son-in-law is missing. So it goes on in my small circle. Sometimes I feel sick at heart. A. said the other day she's quite reconciled to being killed as a fire-watcher on the roof of her office. We were already a nation with too many old people. How can we bear the loss of our finest sons? And yet, how can we not go on bearing it? For the alternative is a tyranny of wickedness. A level-headed friend said to me: 'Nothing can justify this horrible slaughter.' Who will build the new world with the flower of our manhood gone? Sir John Orr, who has just written a good book, *Fighting For What——?*, inscribes it to his son and all the other boys killed in the war and adds: 'May the Lord do so to us and more also if we fail to build the new world you fought and died for.'

# TORA! TORA! TORA!

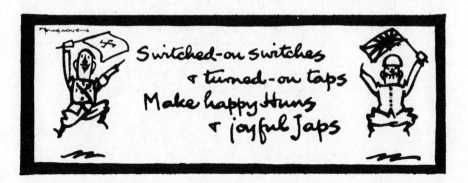

7 December 1941, was a well-nigh perfect morning at the great American naval base in Pearl Harbor; so perfect indeed, that one doughboy there joked to a buddy that it was one for the tourists. The sun shone, the clouds were high, and the naval community woke sleepily to another peaceful day. It was true that the US destroyer Ward had sunk an unknown submarine just outside Pearl Harbour an hour earlier. Fourteenth Naval District Headquarters had been informed; but nobody else knew. A launch was taking one group ashore for church, two small boys were fishing, one sailor sat down to a heroic breakfast of four eggs and bacon, another read the Sunday comics. The only excitement due that day was the arrival of twelve new B17s from the mainland. On board the battleship Nevada, bandsmen assembling for the ceremony of morning colors noticed a number of small specks in the sky far to the southwest. The clocks stood at 0755.

## DAY OF INFAMY

### WALTER LORD

The large and the small, the mighty and the meek, they all added up to 96 warships in Pearl Harbor this Sunday morning.

Assembled together, the US Pacific Fleet was a big family – yet it was a small family too. Most of the men knew everybody else in their line of work, regardless of ship. Walter Simmons, who served a long hitch as mess attendant on the Curtiss, recalls that it was almost impossible for him to board any other ship in the fleet without meeting someone he knew.

In these pre-war days everybody stayed put. Chief Boatswain's Mate Joseph Nickson had been on the San Francisco nine years; Chief Jack Haley on the Nevada twelve years. Ensign Joseph Taussig, brand-new to the ship, thought that several of the chief petty officers on the Nevada had been there before he was born. These old chiefs played an important part in keeping the family spirit. They were almost like fathers to the young ensigns – taught them beer baseball in the long, dull hours when nothing was happening; called them 'Sonny' when no one else was listening. But they were also the first to accept an officer's authority, and believed implicitly in the Navy chain of command.

For the officers it was a small world too. Year after year they had come from the same school, taken the same courses, followed the same careers, step by step. They too knew one another's service records and 'signal numbers' by heart. They all shared the same hard work, wardroom Cokes, starched white uniforms, Annapolis traditions. Like all true professionals, they were a proud, sensitive, tightly knit group.

A number of the men turned their thoughts to Christmas – there were only fifteen more shopping days left. Yeoman Durrell Conner sat in the flag communications office of the California wrapping presents. Seaman Leslie Short climbed up to one of the Maryland's machine-gun stations, where he wasn't likely to be disturbed, and addressed his Christmas cards.

On every ship there were men still at breakfast. Captain Bentham Simons of the *Raleigh* lounged in a pair of blue pyjamas, sipping coffee in his cabin. On the *Oklahoma*, Ensign Bill Ingram, son of the Navy's great football coach, ordered poached eggs. Quartermaster Jim Varner took a large bunch of grapes from the serving line on the repair ship *Rigel*, then retired below to enjoy them properly. He hung them from the springs of an empty upper bunk and climbed into the lower, lay there happily plucking the grapes and wondering what to do the rest of the day.

The shoreside breakfasts offered more variety, fewer restrictions. At the target repair base, Seaman Marlin Ayotte's meal showed real faith in his cooking – four eggs, bacon, two bowls of cereal, fruit, toast, three cups of coffee. At the civilian workers' cantonment – affectionately known to the residents as 'Boystown' – Ben Rottach entertained a couple of friends from the *Raleigh* at a breakfast of ham and eggs with whisky chasers.

Everybody who was in the know wanted to see the B17s arrive from the mainland. They were new, fabulous planes; to have twelve of them come at once was a big event indeed. Down on the field, Captain Andre d'Alfonso, medical officer of the day, prepared his own special welcome. As soon as they arrived, his job was to spray them with Flit guns.

Elsewhere hardly anything was going on. Sergeant Robert Hey began dressing for a rifle match with Captain J. W. Chappelman. Captain Levi Erdmann mulled over the base tennis tournament. Nurse Monica Conter – in between dates with Lieutenant Benning – took pulses and temperatures at the new base hospital. Private Mark Layton squeezed under the 7.45 breakfast deadline, but most of the men didn't even try. At the big new consolidated barracks, Staff Sergeant Charles Judd lay in bed, reading an article debunking Japanese air power in the September issue of *Aviation* magazine.

Five miles farther up the coast lay the Kaneohe Naval Air Station, the only other post on the windward side of Oahu. Thirty-three of the Navy's new PBYs operated out of here. This morning three of them were out on patrol. The others were in the hangars or riding at anchor in the choppy blue water of Kaneohe Bay.

At 7.45 this lazy Sunday morning Kaneohe looked as serene as any of the Army airfields. Mess Attendant Walter Simmons was setting the table in the officers' wardroom, but nobody had turned up to eat. Lieutenant Commander H.P. McCrimmon, the post medical officer, was sitting in his office with his feet on his desk, wondering why the Sunday paper was late.

That was what the people in Honolulu were wondering, too. Normally they counted on the *Advertiser* as an indispensable part of Sunday breakfast, but this morning the presses had broken down after running off only two thousand copies. The papers already printed had gone to Pearl Harbor for distribution among the ships. Everyone else was simply out of luck. Getting something repaired on Sunday in Honolulu was a tall order, although Editor Ray Coll worked hard at the problem.

Across town, Editor Riley Allen of the *Star-Bulletin* had no press troubles and his afternoon paper didn't come out on Sunday, but he was miles behind on his correspondence. This morning he hoped to catch up, and now sat in his office dictating to his secretary, Winifred McCombs. It was her first day on the job, and at 7.45 a.m. she perhaps wondered whether she had been wise in leaving her last position.

Most of the people in Honolulu were enjoying more civilized hours, many of them sleeping off the island's big football weekend. Saturday afternoon the University of Hawaii beat Willamette 20–6 in the annual Shrine game, and the victory had been celebrated in standard mainland fashion. Now the fans bravely faced the morning after. Webley Edwards, manager of radio station KGMB and a popular broadcaster himself, tackled a grape and soda. It looked like a constructive way to start the new day.

In sharp contrast to Oahu's Sunday morning torpor, the destroyer *Ward* scurried about off the entrance to Pearl Harbor. A lot had happened since she polished off the midget sub. At 6.48 a.m. she sighted a white sampan well inside the restricted area. She scooted over to investigate, and the sampan took off. Quickly overhauled, the sampan's skipper, a Japanese, shut off his engines and waved a white flag. This struck [Lieutenant] Outerbridge [Skipper of the *Ward*] as rather odd – these sampans often sneaked into the restricted area for better fishing, but when caught the surrender was rarely so formal. On the other hand, the skipper had already heard plenty of firing and might be just emphasizing his own peaceful inclinations. In any case, the *Ward* started escorting the offender towards Honolulu to turn him over to the Coast Guard.

At 7.03 a.m. the *Ward* picked up another sub on her sound apparatus. Outerbridge raced over to the spot indicated, unloaded five depth charges, and watched a huge black oil bubble erupt three hundred yards astern. Then back to the sampan. Everyone remained at general quarters, and Outerbridge alerted Fourteenth Naval District Headquarters to stand by for further messages.

At headquarters, all of this fell into the lap of Lieutenant Commander Harold Kaminsky, an old reservist who had been in the Navy off and on ever since he was an enlisted man in the First World War. Regularly in charge of net and boom defences, he took his Sunday turn as duty officer like everyone else. This morning he held down the fort with the aid of one enlisted man, a Hawaiian who understood little English and nothing about the teletype.

Due to various delays in decoding, paraphrasing, and typing, it was 7.12 by the time Commander Kaminsky received the *Ward's* 6.53 message about sinking the submarine. First he tried to phone Admiral Bloch's aide but couldn't reach him. Then he put in a call to the admiral's chief of staff, Captain John B. Earle. The phone woke up Mrs Earle, and she immediately put her husband on the wire. To Kaminsky, the captain sounded astonished and incredulous. Captain Earle later recalled that he first felt it was just one more of the sub 'sightings' that had been turning up in recent months. On the other hand, this did seem too serious to be brushed off – it was the first time he heard of a Navy ship firing depth charges or anything else at one of these contacts. So he told Kaminsky to get the dispatch verified, also to notify the CINCPAC duty officer and Commander Charles Momsen, the Fourteenth Naval District operations officer. Earle said he would take care of telling Admiral Bloch.

The admiral was on the phone by 7.15. Captain Earle relayed the news, and the two men spent the next five or ten minutes trying to decide whether it was reliable or not. In the course of passing from mouth to mouth, the message had lost the point Outerbridge tried to make by saying he 'fired on' the sub, hence must have seen it. Now neither Bloch nor Earle could tell whether this was just a sound contact or whether the *Ward* had actually seen something. Finally they made up their minds. Since they had asked the *Ward* to verify, since Commander Momsen was investigating, and since they had referred the matter to CINCPAC, they decided (using Captain Earle's phrase) 'to await further developments'.

Meanwhile Kaminsky had notified CINCPAC Headquarters over at the sub base. The assistant duty officer, Lieutenant Commander Francis Black, estimated that he got the call around 7.20. He relayed the report to the duty officer, Commander Vincent Murphy, who was dressing in his quarters on the spot. Murphy asked, 'Did he say what he was doing about it? Did he say whether Admiral Bloch knew about it or not?'

Nothing had been said on these points, so Murphy told Black to call back and find out. He dialled and dialled, but the line was always busy. By now Murphy was dressed and told Black, 'All right, you go to the office and start breaking out the charts and positions of the various ships. I'll dial one more time, and then I'll be over.'

The line was still busy, so Murphy told the operator to break in and have Kaminsky call the CINCPAC office. Then he ran on down to get there in time for the call.

Small wonder Kaminsky's line was busy. After talking to Black, he had to phone Commander Momsen, the district operations officer. Then Momsen said to call Ensign Joseph Logan. Then a call to the Coast Guard about that sampan the *Ward* caught. Then Momsen on the line again at 7.25 – have the ready-duty destroyer *Monaghan* contact the *Ward*. Then a call to Lieutenant Ottley to get the Honolulu harbor gate closed. Phone call by phone call, the minutes slipped away.

Commander Murphy dashed into his office a little after 7.30 to find the phone ringing. But it wasn't the call that he expected from Kaminsky; it was a call from Commander Logan Ramsey, the operations officer at Patrol Wing (Patwing) 2, the Ford Island headquarters for all Navy patrol plane work. Ramsey was bursting with news – a PBY reported it had just sunk a sub about a mile off the Pearl Harbor entrance. Murphy told him he already had a similar report, and for the next minute or so the two men compared notes.

The PBY message had been sent by Ensign Tanner. It was logged in at seven o'clock, but there had been the usual delays in decoding, then the usual incredulity. Commander Knefler McGinnis, who was Tanner's commanding officer and in charge of Patwing 1 at Kaneohe, felt it must be a case of mistaken identity. He checked to make sure that all information on US subs was in the hands of the patrol planes. Ramsey himself received the message around 7.30 from the Patwing 2 duty officer, and his first reaction was that some kind of drill message must have gotten out by mistake. He ordered the duty officer to request 'authentication' of the message immediately. But to be on the safe side he decided to draw up a search plan and notify CINCPAC – that was what he was doing now.

As Murphy hung up, the phone began ringing again. This time it was Kaminsky, finally on the wire. He assured Murphy that Bloch had been told . . . that the ready-duty destroyer was on its way to help . . . that the stand-by destroyer had been ordered to get up steam. Murphy asked, 'Have you any previous details or any more details about this attack?'

'The message came out of a clear sky,' Kaminsky replied.

Murphy decided he'd better call Admiral Kimmel, and by 7.40 CINCPAC himself was on the telephone. The admiral, who had left Mrs Kimmel on the mainland as a defensive measure against any diverting influences, lived alone in a bare new house at Makalapa, about five minutes' drive away. As soon as he heard the news, he told Murphy, 'I'll be right down.'

Next, Ramsey phoned again, asking if there was anything new. Murphy said there wasn't, but warned him to keep search planes available, in case the admiral wanted them.

Now Kaminsky was back on the wire, reporting the *Ward*'s run-in with the sampan. He had already told Earle, and the captain regarded it as evidence that nothing was really the matter – if there was a submarine around, what was the *Ward* doing escorting a mere sampan to Honolulu? He apparently didn't realize that the submarine incident was at 6.45, and the *Ward* had considered it definitely sunk.

Commander Murphy thought the sampan report was sufficiently interesting to relay to Admiral Kimmel, and he put in another call about 7.50.

Out in the harbor, Lieutenant Commander Bill Burford made the best of things as skipper of the ready-duty destroyer *Monaghan*. She was due to be relieved at eight o'clock, and Burford had planned to go ashore. In fact, the gig was already alongside. Then at 7.51 a message suddenly came in from Fourteenth Naval District Headquarters to 'get under way immediately and contact *Ward* in defensive sea area'. The message didn't even say what he should prepare for, but obviously it might be a couple of hours before he would be free again to go ashore.

Whatever was in store for the *Monaghan*, the other ships in Pearl Harbor had only morning colors to worry about. This ceremony was always the same. At 7.55 the signal tower on top of the Navy Yard water tank hoisted the blue 'prep' flag, and every ship in the harbor followed suit. On each ship a man took his place at the bow with the 'jack', another at the stern with the American flag. Then, promptly at 8.00, the prep flag came down, and the other two went up. On the smaller ships a boatswain piped his whistle; on the larger a bugler sounded colours; on the largest a band might even play the National Anthem.

As the clock ticked towards 7.55, all over the harbor men went to their stations. On the bridge of the old repair ship *Vestal*, Signalman Adolph Zlabis got ready to hoist the prep flag. On the fantail of the sleek cruiser *Helena* at 1010 dock, Ensign W. W. Jones marched to the flagstaff with a four-man Marine honour guard. On the big battleship *Nevada*, the ship's band assembled for a ceremony that would have all the trimmings. The only trouble was, the officer of the deck, Ensign Taussig had never stood watch for morning colors before and didn't know what size American flag to fly. He quietly sent an enlisted man forward to ask the *Arizona* people what they were going to do. While everybody waited around, some of the bandsmen noticed specks in the sky far to the southwest.

Planes were approaching, and from more than one direction. Ensign Donald L. Korn, officer of the deck on the *Raleigh*, noticed a thin line winging in from the northwest. Seaman 'Red' Pressler of the *Arizona* saw a string approaching from the mountains to the east. On the destroyer *Helm*, Quartermaster Frank Handler noticed another group coming in low from the south. The *Helm* – the only ship under way in all of Pearl Harbor – was in the main channel, about to turn up West Loch. The planes passed only a hundred yards away, flying directly up the channel from the harbour entrance. One of the pilots gave a casual wave, and Quartermaster Handler cheerfully waved back. He noticed that, unlike most American planes, these had fixed landing gear.

As the planes roared nearer, Pharmacist's Mate William Lynch heard a *California* shipmate call out, 'The Russians must have a carrier visiting us. Here come some planes with the red ball showing clearly.'

Signalman Charles Flood on the *Helena* picked up a pair of binoculars and gave the planes a hard look. They were approaching in a highly unusual manner, but all the same there was something familiar about them. Then he recalled the time he was in Shanghai in 1932, when the Japanese Army and Navy invaded the city. He remembered their bombing technique – a form of glide bombing. The planes over Ford Island were diving in the same way.

In they hurtled – Lieutenant Commander Takahashi's twenty-seven dive bombers plunging toward Ford Island and Hickam ... Lieutenant Commander Murata's forty torpedo planes swinging into position for their run at the big ships. Commander Fuchida marked time off Barbers Point with the horizontal bombers, watching his men go in. They were all attacking together instead of in stages as originally planned, but it would apparently make no difference – the ships were sitting ducks.

A few minutes earlier, at 7.49 a.m., Fuchida had radioed the signal to attack: 'To . . . to . . . to . . . to . . . .' Now he was so sure of victory that at 7.53 – even before the first bomb fell – he signalled the carriers that the surprise attack was successful: 'Tora . . . tora . . . tora. . . .'

Back on the *Akagi*, Admiral Kusaka turned to Admiral Nagumo. Not a word passed between them. Just a long, firm handshake.

1957

*For Winston Churchill – and indeed for most British people at the time – the best and worst moments of the war fell close together. On 7 December 1941, when the news of Pearl Harbor came through, Churchill knew that we had won. It might take time, all sorts of catastrophes might lie ahead; but of the end he had no doubt at all. The fates take care to deal mortal men buffets to balance their favour; and it was only three days later that he was awoken from sleep to be told by the First Sea Lord, Sir Dudley Pound, that Japanese aircraft had sunk the Prince of Wales (on which only a few months before he had voyaged to his historic parley with President Roosevelt) and the Repulse. The Pacific and Indian Oceans were at the mercy of the Japanese. 'I was thankful,' he confesses, 'to be alone.'*

## PEARL HARBOR!

### WINSTON S. CHURCHILL

No American will think it wrong of me if I proclaim that to have the United States at our side was to me the greatest joy. I could not foretell the course of events. I do not pretend to have measured accurately the martial might of Japan, but now at this very moment I knew the United States was in the war, up to the neck and in to the death. So we had won after all! Yes, after Dunkirk; after the fall of France; after the horrible episode of Oran; after the threat of invasion, when, apart from the Air and the Navy, we were an almost unarmed people; after the deadly struggle of the U-boat war – the first Battle of the Atlantic, gained by a hand's-breadth; after seventeen months of lonely fighting and nineteen months of my responsibility in dire stress. We had won the war. England would live; Britain would live; the Commonwealth of Nations and the Empire would live. How long the war would last or in what fashion it would end no man could tell nor did I at this moment care. Once again in our long Island history we should emerge, however mauled or mutilated, safe and victorious. We should not be wiped out. Our history would not come to an end. We might not even have to die as individuals. Hitler's fate was sealed. Mussolini's fate was sealed. As for the Japanese, they would be ground to powder. All the rest was merely the proper application of overwhelming force. The British Empire, the Soviet Union, and now the United States, bound together with every scrap of their life and strength, were, according to my lights, twice or even thrice the force of their antagonists. No doubt it would take a long time. I expected terrible forfeits in the East; but all this would be merely a passing phase. United we could subdue everybody else in the world. Many disasters, immeasurable cost and tribulation lay ahead, but there was no more doubt about the end.

Silly people, and there were many, not only in enemy countries, might discount the force of the United States. Some said they were soft, others that they would never be united. They would fool around at a distance. They would never come to grips. They would never stand blood-letting. Their democracy and system of recurrent elections would paralyse their war effort. They would be just a vague blur on the horizon to friend or foe. Now we should see the weakness of this numerous but remote, wealthy, and talkative people. But I had studied the American Civil War, fought out to the last desperate inch. American blood flowed in my veins. I thought of a remark which Edward Grey had made to me more than thirty years before – that the United States is like 'a gigantic boiler. Once the fire is lighted under it there is no limit to the power it can generate.' Being saturated and satiated with emotion and sensation, I went to bed and slept the sleep of the saved and thankful.

I was opening my boxes on the 10th when the telephone at my bedside rang. It was the First Sea Lord. His voice sounded odd. He gave a sort of cough and gulp, and at first I could not hear quite clearly. 'Prime Minister, I have to report to you that the *Prince of Wales* and the *Repulse* have both been sunk by the Japanese – we think by aircraft. Tom Phillips is drowned.' 'Are you sure it's true?' 'There is no doubt at all.' So I put the telephone down. I was thankful to be alone. In all the war I never received a more direct shock. The reader of these pages will realize how many efforts, hopes, and plans foundered with these two ships. As I turned over and twisted in bed the full horror of the news sank in upon me. There were no British or American capital ships in the Indian Ocean or the Pacific except the American survivors of Pearl Harbor, who were hastening back to California. Over all this vast expanse of waters Japan was supreme, and we everywhere were weak and naked.

I went down to the House of Commons as soon as they met at eleven that morning to tell them myself what had happened.

I have bad news for the House which I think I should pass on to them at the earliest moment. A report has been received from Singapore that HMS *Prince of Wales* and HMS *Repulse* have been sunk while carrying out operations against the Japanese in their attack on Malaya. No details are yet available except those contained in the Japanese official communiqué, which claims that both ships were sunk by air attack.

I may add that at the next sitting of the House I shall take occasion to make a short statement on the general war situation, which has from many points of view, both favourable and adverse, undergone important changes in the last few days.

1950

---

*What was it like to be a prisoner of the Japanese? We cannot properly put together a book of this sort without addressing the question. Noël Barber, a long marinated chief foreign correspondent, has pieced together a story of what happened in Singapore and, not for the first time, we can only be left gobstruck with admiration for the unbelievable courage people showed in the face of hardly credible brutality.*

*I have chosen this extract to highlight just two people from the many one could have chosen: first Norman Coulson, a water engineer, who kept an aspirin in his tightly clenched hand so that when the Japanese threw him back into his cell after a ghastly session of torture, he could give it to Freddy Bloom, a woman who edited the women's camp paper, and who shared his cell, because she had toothache. The other story concerns Robert Scott – later Sir Robert of the Foreign Office – who survived all the brutality that the Japanese could inflict on him and lived to witness the execution of Lieutenant Colonel Sumida – despite his disapproval of war crimes trials in principle. In his view the Japanese really had minds like fourteen-year-old schoolboys and were thus not answerable to ordinary rules of conduct or punishable under customary rules of law. Sumida, he told the court, who had been responsible for so much torture, had only been behaving in 'his own Japanese way'. Sumida, on being sentenced to hang, sent Scott a message thanking him for the fairness of his evidence.*

---

## SINISTER TWILIGHT

### NOEL BARBER

For three and a half years thousands of men, women and a handful of children were interned on the island of Singapore. None of the civilians had the remotest chance of making a dash for freedom from a speck in the ocean as escape-proof – and as evil – as Devil's Island. And though it was hope and faith that sustained the majority, it was hard even to have any hope in those first months when it seemed that nothing on land, in the skies and on the oceans could arrest the all-victorious Japanese. 'We never really lost hope,' Tim Hudson remembered later, 'but it was damned difficult when you tried to analyse the reasons for hoping.'

Life was wretched. Malnutrition caused many deaths. So did the peculiar Japanese indifference to illness, so that, for example, chronic diabetics died simply because the Japanese refused to issue the insulin which existed in Singapore. Others died as the added privations advanced old age. The frail Mrs Graham-White, who had introduced the half-naked survivors of the *Empress of Asia* at Freddy Bloom's wedding 'reception', quietly faded away because she did not have any hidden reserves of stamina to sustain her. Tommy Kitching died of a malignant disease which he had probably contracted before internment. Yet Lady Thomas – who was afforded no privileges of any sort – managed to survive despite the severe dysentery from which she had been suffering.

In the soldiers' camp at Changi military barracks (as distinct from the civilians in Changi jail) the long and terrible trek to the Siamese railway of death soon began. The lucky ones stayed in Changi, for those who were sent to work camps died in their thousands. Yet both soldiers and civilians managed to keep their sense of humour – and, occasionally, so did the Japanese. When Captain H. L. Greener, an education officer, was interrogated by Lt. Yamaguchi, the following light-hearted conversation (of which Greener made a note immediately afterwards) took place.

YAMAGUCHI: Is it wise, do you think, to appoint a man with only one eye [Wavell] to watch over all India?
GREENER: India can be fixed firmly with the glass eye. With the other he will watch the Japanese. (Japanese laughter.)
YAMAGUCHI: Are the Australians not worried that there are so many Americans in Australia, making advances to their women while they are away at the war?
GREENER: They do not seem to worry. You see, we have great confidence in our women. (Laughter.)
Y: It is said that they are marrying many of your girls. There will be perhaps none left when you get back. Is that not bad?
G: Oh no. Those Americans will stay in Australia and we wish to increase our population.
Y: And who will your young men marry?
G: We shall send for some girls from America. It is only fair. (Laughter.)
Y: We are told the Americans in India have better conditions than the British, and they are stuck up.
G: People are often stuck up when they have more money.
Y: But will not such jealousy impair your war effort?
G: In the last war there was much jealousy. American and British troops used to fight in the estaminets in France. Yet won the war together.
Y: I cannot believe there is affinity of spirit between the Allied Nations sufficient to win the war.
G: Do you believe that there is much affinity of spirit between the Germans and the Italians? (Loud and prolonged mirth.)

Everybody made the best of a bad job, not only to bolster morale, but in a practical manner. Gardens started sprouting.

Plays and concerts were produced. A school was started for the children in the civilian camp. Cicely Williams had never worked so hard doctoring the sick. Freddy Bloom became editor of the women's camp paper, while beyond the wall that separated men from women, clandestine short-wave radio sets went into operation, giving the camp a daily bulletin of what was happening in the rest of the world. The radios were miraculously contrived out of bits and pieces often smuggled into the camp with the help of the Chinese in Singapore who rallied magnificently to the aid of the internees. Many of the Chinese were discovered and tortured. Scores paid for their loyalty with their lives. Yet there always seemed to be another man eager to help, ready to step into the shoes of the one who had mysteriously disappeared.

Contact between the city and the camp was not difficult if one had nerve and courage. At first many Europeans were at liberty. But even when men like Buckeridge were interned after six months (to join Tim Hudson in a cell with flaking walls bearing the roughly painted sign 'Hudson's Bay') the Japanese needed to send small but regular parties of Europeans into Singapore for a variety of reasons, and though they always went under guard, sometimes the soldiers could be bribed, while others were so lazy it was easy to deceive them.

One man who had to make frequent trips to the city was Norman Coulson, a PWD water engineer who had flatly refused to leave with the ill-fated Nunn party. The water system at Changi was constantly in need of repairs and replacements – no doubt helped by a little sabotage – and Coulson, as the only expert, was detailed to buy the spare parts in Singapore. Before long he was in touch with the Chinese underground, and – through go-betweens – with Leslie Hoffman, who was daily operating the short-wave radio he had concealed from the Japanese. In the hope that the news would seep into Changi, the British in India were broadcasting hours of morale-boosting personal items from wives, relatives, and friends of those in camp. Hoffman faithfully wrote down the simple, poignant messages – many telling a man in prison the one item of news he most wanted to know – that the wife he had evacuated was safe. The problem now arose of how to smuggle the news into camp, and Hoffman had to act with the utmost discretion, for almost immediately after capitulation he had been interrogated and beaten up by the Kempetei; and though he had been released after some weeks, he was still under suspicion. However, he and Coulson contrived an ingenious plan. Hoffman wrote the notes on rice paper. These were then delivered to a Chinese plumber, and each time Coulson visited Singapore he was able to hide the precious messages in the pipes and joints he bought from the plumber for the ancient pumps at Changi. In all Hoffman sent several thousand messages into Changi. It was then a simple matter (comparatively simple, that is) to relay the messages from the men's to the women's camp. (So efficient was the camp smuggling that, though Freddy Bloom was only allowed to see Philip once for a few minutes in three and a half years, they kept in touch with smuggled messages, and even managed to exchange Christmas gifts.)

For some the black deeds of the Kempetei started early. While most civilians were settling down in camp as best they could, Rob Scott was taken from Sumatra in handcuffs and kept in solitary confinement for eight and a half months in a cell with no light or running water. Each day he was taken to the Kempetei headquarters in the YMCA building for cross-examination. At first sessions lasted fourteen hours a day, but as Scott laconically noted, 'later the interpreter got tired'. The Japanese demanded to know the most incredible details – everything from the name of Scott's grandfather to a list of Shakespeare's plays – this last wildly irrelevant topic because the Japanese had discovered a slip of paper on which Scott had written the quotation, 'Seeking the bubble reputation even in the cannon's mouth', and seized upon it as a code. During these months the Japanese used bluster, threats – 'even beer on some occasions' – but no actual physical violence. And then in February 1943, 'I was suddenly released to the comparative paradise of ordinary internment.'

The indefatigable Scott was not idle for long. Soon he was playing a leading role in the secret camp news organization – a committee of five which co-ordinated the operation of the increasing number of hidden short-wave receivers. The identities of the committee of control and of the camp operators, scouts, messengers, were known to only a few, and even inside the organization many did not know the identities of their colleagues. It worked with astonishing efficiency for many months – until the fatal day of 10 October 1943.

On this day – known in Singapore as the 'Double Tenth' – a large force of Kempetei and Japanese troops without warning raided the camp. Scott remembers that 'I had the dubious honour of being the first to be arrested'. Every inch of the camp was searched and inevitably the Japanese discovered several indiscreet diaries of war news and camp activities. These were not fatal, but then, in the cell of one of the key men in the committee – a man who had operated a radio set – the Japanese discovered notes of a BBC news bulletin. The man was arrested. At first he feigned ignorance, but after weeks of torture he revealed the names of his colleagues – including Scott, Coulson and Hoffman. It was a disaster of the first magnitude to the camp, for about fifty internees, including two women – Freddy Bloom and Cicely Williams – were rounded up, together with a similar number of Asians in Singapore.

Some were released after a few days of questions; others were incarcerated for more than a year, and in this terrible period thirteen men died in the Kempetei cells of disease after torture. One was tortured to death. One man committed suicide rather than face the prospect of more torture. A man in Scott's cell cut his tongue out in front of Scott so that he could never betray his colleagues. Many who suffered diabolical torture were innocent of any 'crime'. One man was arrested, never questioned, and kept for five months until he died of dysentery and medical neglect. As the torture proceeded, the waves of suffering spread to the entire camp. Rations were cut, even for children. Games, concerts, plays, lectures, school lessons were forbidden for months.

Soon after the Double Tenth the Kempetei swooped on the old house on stilts in Serangoon where Leslie Hoffman was living. As luck would have it, Leslie was not listening in that night and he had concealed the radio so well that the Japanese were never able to find it. Nonetheless he had been betrayed, and the Kempetei were convinced the set existed. For months Hoffman was brutally tortured – he was accused of being 'a Rob Scott spy' – but as with Scott, all the sadistic tortures the Kempetei could invent never broke him. Despite months in the cages, often starved for days at a time, beaten daily for weeks at a time, he never divulged the name of a single accomplice.

Freddy Bloom and Cicely Williams spent several months in one tiny cage which they shared with several men. They had no beds. Indeed, the sole item of 'furniture' consisted of a toilet – in full view of the men and the guard who watched them unceasingly through the bars. They had no protection against lice and mosquitoes. The only way to get any water for drinking or washing was to flush the lavatory. Night after night they were grilled, refused sleep, denied food. For several weeks Norman Coulson shared their cage. Day after day the man who had smuggled the news into camp was flogged with such severity that, in Freddy's words, 'his back and legs were as raw as liver in a butcher's shop'. After each beating, when the guards threw his limp body back into the cage, Freddy and Cicely cleaned his mangled flesh with the aid of one small handkerchief they had secreted, dipping it into the lavatory water to make some sort of cold compress.

Coulson must have been a man of extraordinary courage for Freddy remembers that one morning, just as he was about to be taken out for grilling, he said to her with a grin, 'You don't look your usual cheery self this morning!' Freddy told him not to worry – but she had suddenly got a raging toothache. Hours later, when a bleeding Coulson was dumped back in the cage, and the women tried to wash his wounds, he held out a tightly-clenched fist to Freddy. It contained one tablet of aspirin which a Japanese had given him, but instead of crunching it to ease his intolerable pain, Coulson had kept it for Freddy's toothache.

The most vicious torture of all, however, appears to have been reserved for Rob Scott, and his punishment included one week in which he was never allowed to sleep, lie down or relax, and during which he was on half rations for the first four days, and given no food for the rest of the time. When not being questioned he had to squat, Japanese fashion, in front of the sentry, who could see at a glance everything inside the cage. During questions he was usually forced to kneel on a rack, sometimes tied by a wrist to a window, with his arm fully extended. Japanese sentries doubled his legs under him and jumped on the soles of his feet until the open wounds exposed the ligaments and bones. He was flogged repeatedly. He would be called out of his cell about 11 p.m. – 'my interrogator preferred working at night' – put on a rack for a couple of hours in silence, then questioned for twenty minutes and beaten up for an hour. At last it would be over, and by 2.30 in the morning, Scott would be sent back to his cell. Then would come the worst torture of all.

Tottering with fatigue and pain, he would be called out again only half an hour later – to go through the entire procedure once more. At the end of 'one hectic session' he was told he had been sentenced to death and compelled to write a farewell letter to his wife. 'I was then in such a state that the sentence left me unmoved, even when he announced the date and place, and brought in the sword with which I was to be beheaded, making me run my finger along the blade to test its keenness. In a way I welcomed the prospect, and regretted the reprieve twenty-four hours later, because it meant that the examination would be continued.'

Some died after torture – including Coulson and Hugh Fraser, the acting Colonial Secretary, who had driven out to Bukit Timah to make the first arrangements for surrender. Yet the fact remains that though Rob Scott had been singled out as the arch-criminal, the Kempetei were never able to break either his spirit or his body. It was not only a question of bravery; a man needed reasoning; an understanding of the way the Japanese mind worked; and Rob Scott, with his lucid brain, was one of the few men able to analyse afterwards just how he had been able to keep on living, and indeed how he had been able to outwit the Kempetei in the physical and mental battle that lasted for over twelve months.

Scott realized immediately that behind the Double Tenth arrests lay a Japanese suspicion that the civilian camp harboured a big spy, sabotage and counter-propaganda organization in radio contact with India. Early on this absurd suspicion became almost a certainty in their minds, and because of his background Scott was cast in the role of master spy. 'I was the super criminal.' They firmly believed this. From time to time they even flattered Scott. He was, said the Kempetei, 'more dangerous than a division of the British Army'. His name 'was known to every schoolboy in Japan'.

Scott, however, knew the mentality of the Kempetei. He likened them, in his brilliant unpublished report, to 'spoilt boys of fourteen, headstrong, selfish, brutal'. They had 'the schoolboy's imagination. As his mind teems with images of fighter pilots, Red Indians round the corner, spies, hidden treasures, so the Kempetei seemed to live in a world of melodrama where everyone and everything was suspect, all foreigners were spies, and the wilder the story the more fascinatingly probable it became.' Nothing was too outrageous. At one time Scott was accused of running a secret radio station in a tomb in a Chinese cemetery during the very time he had been locked up in solitary confinement miles from the spot. And he discovered another trait which was to prove invaluable. 'Like children they are insensitive to criticism', so that in the wary battle of wits that followed day after day, night after night – a battle in which Scott, despite his suffering, had to be constantly on the alert to avoid traps – he found one sure line of defence. Whenever he was flattered, he would insist that he was unworthy of the honour of being 'the man who had turned the people of South East Asia against the Japanese'. Inevitably he would then be asked who *was* responsible. And if the interrogation then took a dangerous turn, if Scott felt the Kempetei were setting a trap for him, he always had one further line of defence: The Japanese themselves, he would say, were to blame. Time and again he made this point – which, of course was true – and it never failed to infuriate them. As he wryly noted later, 'Anti-Japanese criticism of this type was most useful in distracting them when questions began to get embarrassing. The immediate results for me were usually painful, so I used this device as a last resort. It never failed to work.'

As the months dragged on, Scott, despite his suffering, was able to realize that his tormentors were getting less and less sure of their ground. Many internees had been tortured into giving conflicting stories. They would say anything to avoid torture, and as Scott puts it, 'The Japanese had collected too much evidence and did not know what was true and what was false. I began to sense a lack of certainty and assurance, however much they blustered and shouted. It became, in my mind, a race with time; could I by denials convince them that they were after a mare's nest, or at any rate so discredit the evidence collected as to shake their faith in it before I collapsed? I won, but only by a short head.'

With typical modesty, Scott in his report glossed over the terrible suffering he endured. But it is a fact that by keeping a tight hold on his reason Scott was able to beat the Kempetei, even though after months of torture and neglect he was suffering from bacillary dysentery, oedema, scabies and many minor ailments. And in the end the Kempetei gave up. They sent him back to the civilian camp, convinced he was about to die. Scott, who at the capitulation had weighed fourteen stone six pounds, had shrunk to seven stone ten pounds, and even with all the care the British doctors in camp could lavish on him, it was months before he could walk. In camp, however, he was at least able to get some extra food to supplement the miserable rations doled out by the Japanese. A flourishing black market had sprung up, and internees could buy goods on credit, signing chits to be paid at the end of the war. The prices were fantastic – butter cost $430 a pound, jam $280 a jar, while a tin of powdered milk cost $700. Scott signed the chits cheerfully – and is convinced to this day that without the extra nourishment he would have died.

Slowly the years of agony rolled on until men and women, who could hardly remember anything other than the stifling atmosphere of the camp, suddenly began to sniff a new and heady scent – the scent of victory, of liberation. VE-Day came and went. On the secret radios – now operating again – news filtered through of the massive American naval victories in the Pacific, to be followed by the details of Hiroshima, so that almost before the prisoners realized what was happening, Cicely Williams, on one of her occasional medical visits to the men's camp, was startled to see a cheerful British soldier pat his Japanese guard on the back, whereupon the guard offered him a bar of chocolate.

Were the rumours of Japanese surrender true? asked Cicely Williams, whereupon the Tommy gave a reply that only a soldier could give.

'Don't worry, lady,' he grinned. 'The Emperor's signing on the dotted line next week.'

When freedom came on 5 September 1945, one of the first men to greet Rob Scott was Ian Morrison of *The Times*, who had arrived with the advance troops. Morrison had made no secret of his admiration for Scott, but in a curious way Scott could sense that his old friend was ill at ease. He seemed embarrassed. At last Morrison blurted out the truth. He had written a book about the fall of Singapore and it contained 'a sort of obituary notice' of Scott. For Morrison (in common with the Foreign Office) had for years assumed he had perished on the *Giang Bee*.

Scott managed a grin and said to Morrison, 'Don't worry – I'll write your obit for you!' Scott did. When Morrison was killed in the Korean war, Scott happened to be in London, and went straight to *The Times* and wrote Morrison's obituary notice.

To others, release came in different ways, but perhaps nothing was so typical of Chinese loyalty – and Chinese memory – as the moment when Tim Hudson stepped from internment to freedom.

Hudson had kept in fairly good health – though he had lost a great deal of weight – and he walked sturdily to the camp gates to savour the greatest moment of his life – a breath of fresh, free air. And he had barely moved outside before a small figure clutching a parcel elbowed her way out of the dense waiting crowd. She looked a little older – and she looked as though she, too, had suffered – but it was Mei Ling, carrying – just as she had done the night before Tim went into camp – a parcel of freshly-laundered clothes. 'They were still warm with the beautiful smell of a hot iron,' Tim remembers.

Rob Scott was involved in one last macabre incident that followed liberation, when Lt-Colonel Sumida, chief of the Kempetei, was tried in Singapore. Scott was called to give evidence, which 'I gave reluctantly because I did not hold with war crimes trials'. In fact Scott – as impartial and dispassionate as ever – went out of his way to show that the man responsible for so much torture had only been behaving in 'his own Japanese way'. Sumida was, however, sentenced to be hanged, whereupon he sent Scott a message 'thanking me for the fairness of my evidence'.

Rob Scott now did an extraordinary thing, which is best described in his own inimitable way. 'I thought that the least I could do, to close that chapter, was to go out and see him hanged. Which I did – rather closer than I meant to, as it began to pour with rain, and the only covered, sheltered spot in the prison yard was the scaffold, so I mounted it with the executioner, and stood to one side, an inch or so from the trapdoor, whilst it was sprung with Sumida on it.'

Of all people who might have been expected to require a long period of readjustment, Rob Scott comes high on the list, and there were some who doubted if he would ever be able to resume his brilliant career in the Foreign Service. Not at all. For some months Scott lay in a hospital in India. Though little more than a bag of bones, he began to fret so much for some work to do – above all wanted to get his impressions on paper while they were still fresh in his mind – that he persuaded the Foreign Office to send him a typist. When she arrived, Scott firmly grabbed the typewriter and told the young lady to go away and enjoy herself. He preferred to do his own typing; and it was in hospital that he wrote his two lucid reports – one on the sinking of the Giang Bee, the other on his torture – that summed up so brilliantly the problems involved between the different races.

Predictably, Rob Scott had a meteoric rise in the Foreign Service, becoming Minister at the British Embassy in Washington, followed by spells of duty as British Commissioner-General in South East Asia, Commandant of the Imperial Defence College, and finally Permanent Secretary at the Ministry of Defence until he retired in 1963 – retired being a comparative term, for he still serves on countless committees. He received a knighthood and a string of letters after his name. Now Sir Robert lives in an old disused railway station near Peebles in Scotland, which he has transformed into a delightful split-level house set amidst the rolling countryside he loves so much.

1968

John Hersey was educated at Yale and became one of America's best war correspondents. His novel A Bell for Adano won the Pulitzer Prize in 1944, and he was commended by the secretary of the Navy for bravery in helping the wounded when working as a war correspondent on Guadalcanal.

In May 1946 the New Yorker sent him to the Far East to find out what had really happened at Hiroshima. When his story came back the magazine made a historic decision; it threw out everything except the advertisements and Hersey's 30,000 words. Here, we give Chapter One, in which a totally disparate group of human beings have the dubious honour of being chosen by fate as victims of the first atomic bomb ever to be used in war.

## HIROSHIMA

### JOHN HERSEY

At exactly fifteen minutes past eight in the morning, on 6 August 1945, Japanese time, at the moment when the atomic bomb flashed above Hiroshima, Miss Toshiko Sasaki, a clerk in the personnel department at the East Asia Tin Works, had just sat down at her place in the plant office and was turning her head to speak to the girl at the next desk. At that same moment, Dr Masakazu Fujii was settling down cross-legged to read the Osaka Asahi on the porch of his private hospital, overhanging one of the seven deltaic rivers which divide Hiroshima; Mrs Hatsuyo Nakamura, a tailor's widow, stood by the window of her kitchen watching a neighbour tearing down his house because it lay in the path of an air-raid defence fire lane; Father Wilhelm Kleinsorge, a German priest of the Society of Jesus, reclined in his underwear on a cot on the top floor of his order's three-storey mission house, reading a Jesuit magazine, *Stimmen der Zeit*; Dr Terufumi Sasaki, a young member of the surgical staff of the city's large, modern Red Cross Hospital, walked along one of the hospital corridors with a blood specimen for a Wassermann test in his hand; and the Reverend Mr Kiyoshi Tanimoto, pastor of the Hiroshima Methodist Church, paused at the door of a rich man's house in Koi, the city's western suburb, and prepared to unload a handcart full of things he had evacuated from town in fear of the massive B29 raid which everyone expected Hiroshima to suffer. A hundred thousand people were killed by the atomic bomb, and these six were among the survivors. They still wonder why they lived when so many others died. Each of them counts many small items of chance or volition – a step taken in time, a decision to go indoors, catching one street-car instead of the next – that spared him. And now each knows that in the act of survival he lived a dozen lives and saw more death than he ever thought he would see. At the time none of them knew anything.

The Reverend Mr Tanimoto got up at five o'clock that morning. He was alone in the parsonage, because for some time his wife had been commuting with their year-old baby to spend nights with a friend in Ushida, a suburb to the north. Of all the important cities of Japan, only two, Kyoto and Hiroshima, had not been visited in strength by B-*san*, or Mr B, as the Japanese, with a mixture of respect and unhappy familiarity, called the B29; and Mr Tanimoto, like all his neighbours and friends, was almost sick with anxiety. He had heard uncomfortably detailed accounts of mass raids on Kure, Iwakuni, Tokuyama, and other nearby towns; he was sure Hiroshima's turn would come soon. He had slept badly the night before, because there had been several air-raid warnings. Hiroshima had been getting such warnings almost every night for weeks, for at that time the B29s were using Lake Biwa, north-east of Hiroshima, as a rendezvous point, and no matter what city the Americans planned to hit, the Super-fortresses steamed in over the coast near Hiroshima. The frequency of the warnings and the continued abstinence of Mr B with respect to Hiroshima had made its citizens jittery; a rumour was going around that the Americans were saving something special for the city.

Mr Tanimoto is a small man, quick to talk, laugh, and cry. He wears his black hair parted in the middle and rather long; the prominence of the frontal bones just above his eyebrows and the smallness of his moustache, mouth, and chin give him a strange, old-young look, boyish and yet wise, weak and yet fiery. He moves nervously and fast, but with a restraint which suggests that he is a cautious, thoughtful man. He showed, indeed, just those qualities in the uneasy days before the bomb fell. Besides having his wife spend the nights in Ushida, Mr Tanimoto had been carrying all the portable things from his church, in the close-packed residential district called Nagaragawa, to a house that belonged to a rayon manufacturer in Koi, two miles from the centre of town. The rayon man, a Mr Matsui, had opened his then unoccupied estate to a large number of his friends and acquaintances, so that they might evacuate whatever they wished to a safe distance from the probable target area. Mr Tanimoto had no difficulty in moving chairs, hymnals, Bibles, altar gear, and church records by pushcart himself, but the organ console and an upright piano required some aid. A friend of his named Matsuo had, the day before, helped him get the piano out to Koi; in return, he had promised this day to assist Mr Matsuo in hauling out a daughter's belongings. That is why he had risen so early.

Mr Tanimoto cooked his own breakfast. He felt awfully tired. The effort of moving the piano the day before, a sleepless night, weeks of worry and unbalanced diet, the cares of his parish – all combined to make him feel hardly adequate to the new day's work. There was another thing, too: Mr Tanimoto had studied theology at Emory College, in Atlanta, Georgia; he had graduated in 1940; he spoke excellent English; he dressed in American clothes; he had corresponded with many American friends right up to the time the war began; and among a people obsessed with a fear of being spied upon – perhaps almost obsessed himself – he found himself growing increasingly uneasy. The police had questioned him several times, and just a few days before he had heard that an influential acquaintance, a Mr Tanaka, a retired officer of the Toyo Kisen Kaisha steamship line, an anti-Christian, a man famous in Hiroshima for his showy philanthropies and notorious for his personal tyrannies, had been telling people that Tanimoto should not be trusted. In compensation, to show himself publicly a good Japanese, Mr Tanimoto had taken on the chairmanship of his local tonarigumi, or Neighbourhood Association, and to his other duties and concerns this position had added the business of organising air-raid defence for about twenty families.

Before six o'clock that morning, Mr Tanimoto started for Mr Matsuo's house. There he found that their burden was to be a tansu, a large Japanese cabinet, full of clothing and household goods. The two men set out. The morning was perfectly clear and so warm that the day promised to be uncomfortable. A few minutes after they started, the air raid siren went off – a minute-long blast that warned of approaching planes but indicated to the people of Hiroshima only a slight degree of danger, since it sounded every morning at this time, when an American weather plane came over. The two men pulled and pushed the handcart through the city streets. Hiroshima was a fan-shaped city, lying mostly on the six islands formed by the seven estuarial rivers that branch out from the Ota River; its main commercial and residential districts, covering about four square miles in the centre of the city, contained three-quarters of its population, which had been reduced by several evacuation programmes from a wartime peak of 380,000 to about 245,000. Factories and other residential districts, or suburbs, lay compactly around the edges of the city. To the south were the docks, an airport, and an island-studded Inland Sea. A rim of mountains runs around the other three sides of the delta. Mr Tanimoto and Mr Matsuo took their way through the shopping centre, already full of people, and across two of the rivers to the sloping streets of Koi, and up them to the outskirts and foothills. As they started up a valley away from the tight-ranked houses, the all-clear sounded. (The Japanese radar operators, detecting only three planes, supposed that they comprised a reconnaissance.) Pushing the handcart up to the rayon man's house was tiring, and the men, after they had manoeuvred their load into the driveway and to the front steps, paused to rest awhile. They stood with a wing of the house between them and the city. Like most homes in this part of Japan, the house consisted of a wooden frame and wooden walls supporting a heavy tile roof. Its front hall, packed with rolls of bedding and clothing, looked like a cool cave full of fat cushions. Opposite the house, to the right of the front door, there was a large, finicky rock garden. There was no sound of planes. The morning was still; the place was cool and pleasant.

Then a tremendous flash of light cut across the sky. Mr Tanimoto has a distinct recollection that it travelled from east to west, from the city toward the hills. It seemed a sheet of sun. Both he and Mr Matsuo reacted in terror – and both had time to react (for they were 3,500 yards, or two miles, from the centre of the explosion). Mr Matsuo dashed up the front steps into the house and dived among the bedrolls and buried himself there. Mr Tanimoto took four or five steps and threw himself between two big rocks in the garden. He bellied up very hard against one of them. As his face was against the stone he did not see what happened. He felt a sudden pressure, and then splinters and pieces of board and fragments of tile fell on him. He heard no roar. (Almost no one in Hiroshima recalls hearing any noise of the bomb. But a fisherman in his sampan on the Inland Sea near Tsuzu, the man with whom Mr Tanimoto's mother-in-law and sister-in-law were living, saw the flash and heard a tremendous explosion; he was nearly twenty miles from Hiroshima, but the thunder was greater than when the B29s hit Iwakuni, only five miles away.)

When he dared, Mr Tanimoto raised his head and saw that the rayon man's house had collapsed. He thought a bomb had fallen directly on it. Such clouds of dust had risen that there was a sort of twilight around. In panic, not thinking for the moment of Mr Matsuo under the ruins, he dashed out into the street. He noticed as he ran that the concrete wall of the estate had fallen over – toward the house rather than away from it. In the street, the first thing he saw was a squad of soldiers who had been burrowing into the hillside opposite, making one of the thousands of dug-outs in which the Japanese apparently intended to resist invasion, hill by hill, life for life; the soldiers were coming out of the hole, where they should have been safe, and blood was running from their heads, chests and backs. They were silent and dazed.

Under what seemed to be a local dust cloud, the day grew darker and darker.

At nearly midnight, the night before the bomb was dropped, an announcer on the city's radio station said that about two hundred B29s were approaching southern Honshu and advised the population of Hiroshima to evacuate to their designated 'safe areas'. Mrs Hatsuyo Nakamura, the tailor's widow who lived in the section called Nobori-cho and who had long had a habit of doing as she was told, got her three children – a ten-year-old boy, Toshio, an eight-year-old girl, Yaeko, and a five-year-old girl, Myeko – out of bed and dressed them and walked with them to the military area known as the East Parade Ground, on the north-east edge of the city. There she unrolled some mats and the children lay down on them. They slept until about two, when they were awakened by the roar of the planes going over Hiroshima. As soon as the planes had passed, Mrs Nakamura started back with her children. They reached home a little after two-thirty and she immediately turned on the radio, which, to her distress, was just then broadcasting a fresh warning. When she looked at the children and saw how tired they were, and when she thought of the number of trips they had made in past weeks, all to no purpose, to the East Parade Ground, she decided that in spite of the instructions on the radio, she simply could not face starting out all over again. She put the children in their bedrolls on the floor, lay down herself at three o'clock, and fell asleep at once, so soundly that when planes passed over later, she did not waken to their sound.

The siren jarred her awake at about seven. She arose, dressed quickly, and hurried to the house of Mr Nakamoto, the head of her Neighbour-hood Association, and asked him what she should do. He said that she should remain at home unless an urgent warning – a series of intermittent blasts of the siren – was sounded. She returned home, lit the stove in the kitchen, set some rice to cook, and sat down to read that morning's Hiroshima Chugoku. To her relief, the all-clear sounded at eight o'clock. She heard the children stirring, so she went and gave each of them a handful of peanuts and told them to stay on their bedrolls, because they were tired from the night's walk. She had hoped that they would go back to sleep, but the man in the house directly to the south began to make a terrible hullabaloo of hammering, wedging, ripping, and splitting. The prefectural government, convinced, as everyone in Hiroshima was, that the city would be attacked soon, had begun to press with threats and warnings for the completion of wide fire lanes, which, it was hoped, might act in conjunction with the rivers to localize any fires started by an incendiary raid; and the neighbour was reluctantly sacrificing his home to the city's safety. Just the day before, the prefecture had ordered all able-bodied girls from the secondary schools to spend a few days helping to clear these lanes, and they started work soon after the all-clear sounded.

Mrs Nakamura went back to the kitchen, looked at the rice, and began watching the man next door. At first she was annoyed with him for making so much noise, but then she was moved almost to tears by pity.

Her emotion was specifically directed toward her neighbour, tearing down his home, board by board, at a time when there was so much unavoidable destruction, but undoubtedly she also felt a generalized, community pity, to say nothing of self-pity. She had not had an easy time. Her husband, Isawa, had gone into the army just after Myeko was born, and she had heard nothing from or of him for a long time, until, on 5 March 1942, she received a seven-word telegram; 'Isawa died an honourable death at Singapore.' She learned later that he had died on 15 February, the day Singapore fell, and that he had been a corporal. Isawa had not been a particularly prosperous tailor and his only capital was a Sankoku sewing machine. After his death, when his allotments stopped coming, Mrs Nakamura got out the machine and began to take in piecework herself, and since then had supported the children, but poorly, by sewing.

As Mrs Nakamura stood watching her neighbour, everything flashed whiter than any white she had ever seen. She did not notice what happened to the man next door; the reflex of a mother set her in motion toward her children. She had taken a single step (the house was 1,350 yards, or three-quarters of a mile, from the centre of the explosion) when something picked her up and she seemed to fly into the next room over the raised sleeping platform, pursued by parts of her house.

Timbers fell around her as she landed, and a shower of tiles pommelled her; everything became dark, for she was buried. The debris did not cover her deeply. She rose up and freed herself. She heard a child cry, 'Mother, help me!' and saw her youngest – Myeko, the five-year-old – buried up to her breast and unable to move. As Mrs Nakamura started frantically to claw her way towards the baby, she could see or hear nothing of her other children.

In the days right before the bombing, Dr Masakazu Fujii, being prosperous, hedonistic, and at the time not too busy, had been allowing himself the luxury of sleeping until nine or nine-thirty, but fortunately he had to get up early the morning the bomb was dropped to see a house guest off on a train. He rose at six, and half an hour later walked with his friend to the station, not far away, across two of the rivers. He was back home by seven, just as the siren sounded its sustained warning. He ate breakfast and then, because the morning was already hot, undressed down to his underwear and went out on the porch to read the paper. This porch – in fact, the whole building – was curiously constructed. Dr Fujii was the proprietor of a peculiarly Japanese institution, a private, single-doctor hospital. This building, perched beside and over the water of the Kyo River, and next to the bridge of the same name, contained thirty rooms for thirty patients and their kinsfolk – for, according to Japanese custom, when a person falls sick and goes to a hospital, one or more members of his family go and live there with him, to cook for him, bathe, massage, and read to him, and to offer incessant familial sympathy, without which a Japanese patient would be miserable indeed. Dr Fujii had no beds – only straw mats – for his patients. He did, however, have all sorts of modern equipment: an X-ray machine, diathermy apparatus, and a fine tiled laboratory. The structure rested two-thirds on the land, one-third on piles over the tidal waters of the Kyo. This overhang, the part of the building where Dr Fujii lived, was queer-looking, but it was cool in summer and from the porch, which faced away from the centre of the city, the prospect of the river, with pleasure boats drifting up and down it, was always refreshing. Dr Fujii had occasionally had anxious moments when the Ota and its mouth branches rose to flood, but the piling was apparently firm enough and the house had always held.

Dr Fujii had been relatively idle for about a month because in July, as the number of untouched cities in Japan dwindled and as Hiroshima seemed more and more inevitably a target, he began turning patients away, on the ground that in case of a fire raid he would not be able to evacuate them. Now he had only two patients left – a woman from Yano, injured in the shoulder, and a young man of twenty-five recovering from burns he had suffered when the steel factory near Hiroshima in which he worked had been hit. Dr Fujii had six nurses to tend his patients. His wife and children were safe; his wife and one son were living outside Osaka, and another son and two daughters were in the country on Kyushu. A niece was living with him, and a maid and a manservant. He had little to do and did not mind, for he had saved some money. At fifty he was healthy, convivial, and calm, and he was pleased to pass the evenings drinking whisky with friends, always sensibly and for the sake of conversation. Before the war, he had affected brands imported from Scotland and America; now he was perfectly satisfied with the best Japanese brand, Suntory.

Dr Fujii sat down cross-legged in his underwear on the spotless matting of the porch, put on his glasses, and started reading the Osaka *Asahi*. He liked to read the Osaka news because his wife was there. He saw the flash. To him – faced away from the centre and looking at his paper – it seemed a brilliant yellow. Startled, he began to rise to his feet. In that moment (he was 1,550 yards from the centre), the hospital leaned behind his rising and, with a terrible ripping noise, toppled into the river. The Doctor, still in the act of getting to his feet, was thrown forward and around and over; he was buffetted and gripped; he lost track of everything, because things were so speeded up; he felt the water.

Dr Fujii hardly had time to think that he was dying before he realized that he was alive, squeezed tightly by two long timbers in a V across his chest, like a morsel suspended between two huge chopsticks – held upright, so that he could not move, with his head miraculously above the water and his torso and legs in it. The remains of his hospital were all around him in a mad assortment of splintered lumber and materials for the relief of pain. His left shoulder hurt terribly. His glasses were gone.

Father Wilhelm Kleinsorge, of the Society of Jesus, was, on the morning of the explosion, in rather frail condition. The Japanese wartime diet had not sustained him, and he felt the strain of being a foreigner in an increasingly xenophobic Japan; even a German, since the defeat of the Fatherland, was unpopular. Father Kleinsorge had, at thirty-eight, the look of a boy growing too fast – thin in the face, with a prominent Adam's apple, a hollow chest, dangling hands, big feet. He walked clumsily, leaning forward a little. He was tired all the time. To make matters worse, he had suffered for two days, along with Father Cieslik, a fellow-priest, from a rather painful and urgent diarrhoea, which they blamed on the beans and black ration bread they were obliged to eat. Two other priests then living in the mission compound, which was in the Nobori-cho section – Father Superior LaSalle and Father Schiffer – had happily escaped this affliction.

Father Kleinsorge woke up about six the morning the bomb was dropped, and half-an-hour later – he was a bit tardy because of his sickness – he began to read Mass in the mission chapel, a small Japanese-style wooden building which was without pews, since its worshippers knelt on the usual Japanese matted floor, facing an altar graced with splendid silks, brass, silver, and heavy embroideries. This morning, a Monday, the only worshippers were Mr Takemoto, a theological student living in the mission house; Mr Fukai, the secretary of the diocese; Mrs Murata, the mission's devoutly Christian housekeeper; and his fellow-priests. After Mass, while Father Kleinsorge was reading the Prayers of Thanksgiving, the siren sounded. He stopped the service and the missionaries retired across the compound to the bigger building. There, in his room on the ground floor, to the right of the front door, Father Kleinsorge changed into a military uniform which he had acquired when he was teaching at the Rokko Middle School in Kobe and which he wore during air-raid alerts.

After an alarm, Father Kleinsorge always went out and scanned the sky, and this time, when he stepped outside, he was glad to see only the single weather plane that flew over Hiroshima each day about this time. Satisfied that nothing would happen, he went in and breakfasted with the other Fathers on substitute coffee and ration bread, which, under the circumstances, was especially repugnant to him. The Fathers sat and talked a while, until, at eight, they heard the all-clear. They went then to various parts of the building. Father Schiffer retired to his room to do some writing. Father Cieslik sat in his room in a straight chair with a pillow over his stomach to ease his pain, and read. Father Superior LaSalle stood at the window of his room, thinking. Father Kleinsorge went up to a room on the third floor, took off all his clothes except his underwear, and stretched out on his right side on a cot and began reading his *Stimmen der Zeit*.

After the terrible flash – which, Father Kleinsorge later realized, reminded him of something he had read as a boy about a large meteor colliding with the earth – he had time (since he was 1,400 yards from the centre) for one thought: A bomb has fallen directly on us. Then, for a few seconds or minutes, he went out of his mind.

Father Kleinsorge never knew how he got out of the house. The next things he was conscious of were that he was wandering around in the mission's vegetable garden in his underwear, bleeding slightly from small cuts along his left flank; that all the buildings round about had fallen down except the Jesuits' mission house, which had long before been braced and double-braced by a priest named Gropper, who was terrified of earthquakes; that the day had turned dark; and that Murata *san*, the housekeeper, was near by, crying over and over, 'Shu Jesusu, *awaremi tamai!* Our Lord Jesus, have pity on us!'

On the train on the way to Hiroshima from the country, where he lived with his mother, Dr Terufumi Sasaki, the Red Cross Hospital surgeon, thought over an unpleasant nightmare he had had the night before. His mother's home was in Makaihara, thirty miles from the city, and it took him two hours by train and tram to reach the hospital. He had slept uneasily all night and had wakened an hour earlier than usual, and, feeling sluggish and slightly feverish, had debated whether to go to the hospital at all; his sense of duty finally forced him to go, and he had started out on an earlier train than he took most mornings. The dream had particularly frightened him because it was so closely associated, on the surface at least, with a disturbing actuality. He was only twenty-five years old and had just completed his training at the Eastern Medical University, in Tsingtao, China. He was something of an idealist and was much distressed by the inadequacy of medical facilities in the country town where his mother lived. Quite on his own, and without a permit, he had begun visiting a few sick people out there in the evenings, after his eight hours at the hospital and four hours' commuting. He had recently learned that the penalty for practising without a permit was severe; a fellow-doctor whom he had asked about it had given him a serious scolding. Nevertheless, he had continued to practise. In his dream he had been at the bedside of a country patient when the police and the doctor he had consulted burst into the room, seized him, dragged him outside, and beat him up cruelly. On the train, he just about decided to give up the work in Mukaihara, since he felt it would be impossible to get a permit, because the authorities would hold that it would conflict with his duties at the Red Cross Hospital.

At the terminus, he caught a street-car at once. (He later calculated that if he had taken his customary train that morning, and if he had had to wait a few minutes for the street-car, as often happened, he would have been close to the centre at the time of the explosion and would surely have perished.) He arrived at the hospital at seven-forty and reported to the chief surgeon. A few minutes later, he went to a room on the first floor and drew blood from the arm of a man in order to perform a Wassermann test. The laboratory containing the incubators for the test was on the third floor. With the blood specimen in his left hand, walking in a kind of distraction he had felt all morning, probably because of the dream and his restless night, he started along the main corridor on his way toward the stairs. He was one step beyond an open window when the light of the bomb was reflected, like a gigantic photographic flash, in the corridor. He ducked down on one knee and said to himself, as only a Japanese would, 'Sasaki, *gambare!* Be brave!' Just then (the building was 1,650 yards from the centre), the blast ripped through the hospital. The glasses he was wearing flew off his face; the bottle of blood crashed against one wall; his Japanese slippers zipped out from under his feet – but otherwise, thanks to where he stood, he was untouched.

Dr Sasaki shouted the name of the chief surgeon and rushed round to the man's office and found him terribly cut by glass. The hospital was in horrible confusion: heavy partitions and ceilings had fallen on patients, beds had overturned, windows had blown in and cut people, blood was spattered on the walls and floors, instruments were everywhere, many of the patients were running about screaming, many more lay dead. (A colleague working in the laboratory to which Dr Sasaki had been walking was dead; Dr Sasaki's patient, whom he had just left and who a few moments before had been dreadfully afraid of syphilis, was also dead.) Dr Sasaki found himself the only doctor in the hospital who was unhurt.

Dr Sasaki, who believed that the enemy had hit only the building he was in, got bandages and began to bind the wounds of those inside the hospital; while outside, all over Hiroshima, maimed and dying citizens turned their unsteady steps toward the Red Cross Hospital to begin an invasion that was to make Dr Sasaki forget his private nightmare for a long, long time.

Miss Toshiko Sasaki, the East Asia Tin Works clerk, who is not related to Dr Sasaki, got up at three o'clock in the morning on the day the bomb fell. There was extra housework to do. Her eleven-month-old brother, Akio, had come down the day before with a serious stomach upset; her mother had taken him to the Tamura Pediatric Hospital and was staying there with him. Miss Sasaki, who was about twenty, had to cook breakfast for her father, a brother, a sister, and herself, and – since the hospital, because of the war, was unable to provide food – to prepare a whole day's meals for her mother and the baby, in time for her father, who worked in a factory making rubber ear-plugs for artillery crews, to take the food by on his way to the plant. When she had finished and had cleaned and put away the cooking things, it was nearly seven. The family lived in Koi, and she had a forty-five-minute trip to the tin works, in the section of town called Kannon-machi. She was in charge of the personnel records in the factory. She left Koi at seven, and as soon as she reached the plant, she went with some of the other girls from the personnel department to the factory auditorium. A prominent local Navy man, a former employee, had committed suicide the day before by throwing himself under a train – a death considered honourable enough to warrant a memorial service, which was to be held at the tin works at ten o'clock that morning. In the large hall, Miss Sasaki and the others made suitable preparations for the meeting. This work took about twenty minutes.

Miss Sasaki went back to her office and sat down at her desk. She was quite far from the windows, which were off to her left, and behind her were a couple of tall bookcases containing all the books of the factory library, which the personnel department had organized. She settled herself at her desk, put some things in a drawer, and shifted papers. She thought that before she began to make entries in her lists of new employees, discharges, and departures for the Army, she would chat for a moment with the girl at her right. Just as she turned her head away from the windows, the room was filled with a blinding light. She was paralysed by fear, fixed still in her chair for a long moment (the plant was 1,600 yards from the centre).

Everything fell, and Miss Sasaki lost consciousness. The ceiling dropped suddenly and the wooden floor above collapsed in splinters and the people up there came down and the roof above them gave way; but principally and first of all, the bookcases right behind her swooped forward and the contents threw her down, with her left leg horribly twisted and breaking underneath her. There, in the tin factory, in the first moment of the atomic age, a human being was crushed by books.

1972

# THE SWEET BREATH
# OF FEAR

SALUTE
OUR
SOLDIER

"Salute the Soldier" Week in the
Prime Minister's Constituency,
June 10-17.

Timothy Corsellis was a Leading Aircraftman in the RAF when he wrote 'News Reel of Embarkation'; he went on to become a 2nd officer in the Air Transport Auxiliary, but died in action in 1941. He was a friend of the RAF poet Nigel Weir.

## NEWS REEL OF EMBARKATION

### TIMOTHY CORSELLIS

Where are you going to, laughing men?
For a holiday on the sea?
Laughing, smiling, wonderful men,
Why won't you wait for me?

God, how I love you, men of my race,
As you smile on your way to a war.
How can you do it, wonderful face,
Do you not know what's before?

Laugh, laugh, you soldier sons,
Joke on your way to the war,
For your mothers won't laugh at the sound of the guns
And the tales of the filth and the gore.

Smile and joke, young sailor Jack,
For it's the same old story.
There'll be no jokes when you come back,
And bloody little glory.

The bombing of Monte Cassino remains one of the great moral issues of the war: was it sacrilege by the Allies – or a regrettable necessity dictated by the iron imperatives of war? Harold Nicolson said he would rather his son died than that the monastery should be destroyed (unaware that his son was indeed there). 'Works of art are irreplaceable,' he declared in an axiom which others may feel was the reverse of the truth. 'Human lives are replaceable.' What did the fighting men dug in below the monastery in a torrrent of rain, snow and mud, not to say bullets and bombs, feel about it? Raleigh Trevelyan, who was there, gives us an eloquent answer.

## CASSINO

### RALEIGH TREVELYAN

We turn now to those who were actually doing the fighting in the 'torrents of rain and snow'. Who saw the guts of their comrades scattered on that same snow and mud. Who were expecting to die just like that, at any moment. Who remembered their families in Marysville, Ohio, in Lostwithiel, Cornwall, in Waikari, South Island New Zealand, in Birsilpur, Rajputana. And for that matter in Greifenburg, Pomerania. And who wanted to see their families again. An historian or thesis-writer who has not experienced what it is like to be told, under the equivalent of a sentence of death, that you are about to go on a patrol across seemingly impossible country, which could at best result in a bullet through your face or groin, cannot possibly appreciate the feelings of the ordinary soldier, unaware moreover of disagreements, jealousies and strain at top level, trusting that there is sanity in the things he has been asked to do, and trying to believe that what seems like ghastly confusion does really have a purpose behind it. If most of the American top brass agreed with [General Mark] Clark about the monastery not being occupied, that feeling did not permeate into the lower ranks. Harold Bond, a lieutenant in the Texan Division, the 36th Infantry, has written: 'All of us were convinced that the abbey was a German strongpoint, and that it was being used by them for the excellent observation it gave of all our positions.' And then: 'The tired infantrymen, fighting for their lives near its slopes, were to cry for joy as bomb after bomb crumbled it into dust.'

Sergeant Evans of the 2nd Battalion of the London Irish was in the plain below. 'It just had to be bombed. Oh, it was malignant. It was evil somehow. I don't know how a monastery can be evil, but it was looking at you. It was all-devouring if you like – a sun-bleached colour, grim. It had a terrible hold on us soldiers. I don't think I was convinced that the Germans were firing from there, but it was such a wonderful observation post. We thought it had to be destroyed. We just didn't know how the place could be taken otherwise. I am sure what I thought was shared by ninety per cent of the lads in our division.' Sergeant Jenkins of the same regiment earlier on had been in the 1st Battalion's Intelligence on Monte Cassino. 'I had a pair of captured German periscope binoculars. You could see the Germans walking around the base of the building, and the road coming down. You could see small trucks. You couldn't see them going into the monastery because you couldn't see any exits or entrances.'

Lieutenant Bruce Foster of the 60th Rifles one morning had been to call on a Guards battalion, camped in a dreary olive grove. 'Since you ask me what I felt about the monastery, I'll ask you something. Can you imagine what it is like to see a person's head explode in a great splash of grey brains and red hair, and have the blood and muck all over you, in grey brains and red hair, and have the blood and muck all over you, in your mouth, eyes, ears? And can you imagine what it is like when that head belonged to your sister's fiancé? I knew why it happened, I was positive, it was because some bloody fucking Jerry was up there in that fucking bloody monastery directing the fire that killed Dickie, and I know that still; to hell with all those Pontius Pilates who pretend they were so bloody innocent and had nothing to do with the bombing. Christ, Dickie was the finest, most upright man you or I would ever meet. I am just glad that he died quickly, which is more than a lot of other poor fuckers did up there. It drove me mad to see those chaps at HQ poring over coloured maps and never dreaming of going up to the front line to see what conditions were really like.'

1981

*Keith Douglas won all his education by scholarship and published his first poetry at the age of sixteen. He fought in a crusader tank from Alamein to Tunisia, and arranged for his poetry to be published before D-Day – keenly aware that it might be his last chance. He was killed in Normandy on 9 June 1944 – the third day after the Allied landings. 'Vergissmeinnicht' is particularly poignant because it deals with the death of a German soldier.*

## VERGISSMEINNICHT

### KEITH DOUGLAS

Three weeks gone and the combatants gone,
Returning over the nightmare ground
We found the place again, and found
The soldier sprawling in the sun.

The frowning barrel of his gun
Overshadowing. As we came on
That day, he hit my tank with one
Like the entry of a demon.

Look. Here in the gunpit spoil
The dishonoured picture of his girl
Who has put: *Steffi Vergissmeinnicht*
In a copybook gothic script.

We see him almost with content
Abased, and seeming to have paid
And mocked at by his own equipment
That's hard and good when he's decayed.

224

But she would weep to see today
How on his skin the swart flies move;
The dust upon the paper eye
And the burst stomach like a cave.

For here the lover and killer are mingled
Who had one body and one heart.
And death who had the soldier singled
Has done the lover mortal hurt.

1943

---

Enoch Powell became a Professor of Greek at the age of twenty-five and was a brigadier at the age of thirty-two. Despite all his glittering political achievements, however, his two volumes of poetry published before the war are not so well known. The poem we publish here has a measured authority which characterizes all his work.

## THE NET LIKE A WHITE VAULT

ENOCH POWELL

The net like a white vault, hung overhead
Dewy and glistening in the full moon's light,
Which cast a shadow-pattern of the thread
Over our face and arms, laid still and white
Like polished ivories on the dark bed.
The truck's low side concealed from us the sight
Of tents and bivouacs and track-torn sand
That lay without; only a distant sound
Of gunfire sometimes or, more close at hand,
A bomb, with dull concussion of the ground,
Pressed in upon our world, where, all else banned,
Our lonely souls eddied like echoing sound
Under the white cathedral of the net,
And like a skylark in captivity
Hung fluttering in the meshes of our fate,
With death at hand and, round, eternity.

1951

Paul Scott never made much money in his lifetime and devoted his last years to an almost obsessional degree on his Raj Quartet – since made into a television series and enjoyed by millions. When he wrote 'Tell us the Tricks' he was still an obscure soldier.

## TELL US THE TRICKS

PAUL SCOTT

Say, soldier! Tell us the tricks,
    the tackle of your trade;
The passage of your hours;
    the plans that you have made –
Of what do you think – what consider?
Tell us of the slow process,
That gradual change
    from man to soldier –?

And what can I say, what reply?
    There is no answer.
The tale is hidden in the eye.
The soldier's here – the man is not:
Man's voice was lost;
The sex decayed
By the bitter bayonet – the chattering shot
The growth delayed.
The brief days of youth,
And its forgotten past,
Cannot be commanded to appear,
We hope they may at last
    – some other time – some different year.

Vernon Scannell is one of our most regarded living poets. He has published ten volumes of verse and wears a number of literary garlands (The Heinemann Award for Literature, the Cholmondeley Poetry Prize among them). He has been a professional boxer and chief fiction reviewer for The Listener and the New Statesman. He was an honoured adviser and speaker in the 1985 BBC television series Soldiers, a History of Men in Battle. Yet while all he said was accurate as far as it went, he omitted to reveal that during the North African campaign he had deserted from a battle and been sentenced to three years' imprisonment. He has now told his story in a new book called Argument of Kings, where he appears as John Bain. That is his real name; he took the name Vernon Scannell to distance himself from his wartime record. For myself, I am prepared to hear the case against Scannell/Bain; but only from someone who served with him there in that hot and lethal place impregnated as it was with what he calls 'the faintly sweet breath of corruption and fear'.

## ARGUMENT OF KINGS

### VERNON SCANNELL

The battalion soon reached the foot of the hills and began to climb up to where the fighting had been going on. They had been marching for about twenty minutes when the first dead Seaforths were seen.

John was nudged into awareness when Hughie said, 'There's one poor bastard's finished with fuckin'-an'-fightin'.'

The soldier was lying on his stomach, his head turned away from John's regard so his face could not be seen. There was no sign of a wound. He might have been asleep except that his stillness was that absolute, immovable stillness of the dead, that total cancellation of any possibility of movement. Yet the dead were not inanimate things. They were not like stones or burnt-out vehicles or discarded equipment. They remained human and vulnerable and pathetic.

Soon more dead were seen, scattered on the hillside like big broken dolls, and when John's platoon reached the now deserted enemy slit-trenches the area was littered with corpses. The rocks and sand had lost their earlier greyness and were now a pale yellowish brown in the morning sun. Already the flesh of the dead soldiers, British and enemy, was assuming a waxy theatrical look, transformed by the maquillage of dust and sand and the sly beginnings of decay.

B Company was ordered to halt and stand easy.

'Can't see any wounded,' Hughie said. 'The meat-wagons must've got them away down one of them tracks on the left flank.'

John did not answer. He thought he could already smell the sweet feculence of the dead.

'You all right, Johnny?'

He nodded. 'Yeah, I'm okay.' But he was feeling strange and Hughie must have seen some outward sign of the sick, slightly feverish condition that seemed to generate an inward shivering and veil his surroundings with a transparent yet elusively transforming tegument of, not so much unreality, as a changed, harder and sharper reality. Then he saw that the other men in his section and from the other platoons must have been given the order to fall out because they were moving among the dead bodies, the Seaforths' corpses as well as the German, and they were bending over them, sometimes turning them with an indifferent boot, before they removed watches, rings and what valuables they could find. They seemed to be moving with unnatural slowness, proceeding from one body to another, stooping, reaching out, methodical and absorbed.

Hughie had gone. He must have joined the scavengers.

John Bain watched this scene for a few moments. Then he turned away and started to walk back down the slope towards the foot of the hills where they had dug in on the previous night. No one attempted to stop him. No voice called out, peremptory and outraged. He walked unhurriedly but quite steadily, not looking back, his rifle slung on his right shoulder. And still no one shouted. It was as if he had become invisible. He plodded onwards and downwards. The sun was strong now and he felt the heat biting through his KD shirt. Sweat was soaking his hair under the steel helmet. He did not look back but kept his eyes down, seeing no more than a few yards in front of him. If there were any sounds his ears did not register them. He moved without any sense of physical exertion as if he had been relieved of a great burden and could enjoy an easy, almost floating sense of effortlessness as he walked onwards, down to the level ground and on to a rough track.

1987

---

*There were of course many different ways of serving one's country in North Africa. Venal Vera, according to that fecund witness, Anon, had a colourful war out there; and a rather useful one.*

---

## VENAL VERA

### ANONYMOUS

They call me Venal Vera, I'm a lovely from Gezira,
The Fuhrer pays me well for what I do.
The order of the battle, I obtained from last night's rattle
On the golf course with a Brigadier from 'Q'.

I often have to tarry on the back seat of a gharry,
It's part of my profession as a spy,
While his mind's on copulation I'm exacting information
From a senior GSO from GSI.

When I yield to the carresses of the DDWS's
I get from them the low-down on the works,
And when sleeping in the raw with a major from G4
I learn of Britain's bargain with the Turks.

On the point of the emission, in the 23rd position,
While he quavered with exotic ecstacy,
I heard of the location of a very secret station
From an over-sexed SO from OS3.

So the old Colonels and the Majors, and the whisky-soaked
    old stagers
Enjoy themselves away from England's shore,
Why bring victory nearer when the lovelies of Gezira
Provide them with a lovely fucking war?

---

*'A Soldier – His Prayer'* has a curious history. It was blown by the wind into a slit trench at El Agheila during a heavy bombardment. No one knows who wrote it; but it was destined to become one of the best known of all war poems.

---

## A SOLDIER – HIS PRAYER

ANONYMOUS

Stay with me, God. The night is dark,
The night is cold: my little spark
Of courage dies. The night is long;
Be with me, God, and make me strong.

I love a game. I love a fight.
I hate the dark; I love the light.
I love my child; I love my wife.
I am no coward. I love Life,

Life with its change of mood and shade.
I want to live. I'm not afraid,
But me and mine are hard to part;
Oh, unknown God, lift up my heart.

You stilled the waters at Dunkirk
And saved Your Servants. All your work
Is wonderful, dear God. You strode
Before us down that dreadful road.

We were alone, and hope had fled;
We loved our country and our dead,
And could not shame them; so we stayed
The course, and were not much afraid.

Dear God, that nightmare road! And then
That sea! We got there – we were men.
My eyes were blind, my feet were torn,
My soul sang like a bird at dawn!

I knew that death is but a door.
I knew what we were fighting for:
Peace for the kids, our brothers freed.
A kinder world, a cleaner breed.

I'm but the son my mother bore,
A simple man, and nothing more.
But – God of strength and gentleness,
Be pleased to make me nothing less.

Help me, O God, when Death is near
To mock the haggard face of fear,
That when I fall – if fall I must –
My soul may triumph in the Dust.

---

*We still know much less about the war in Russia than about those theatres of war where our own troops were engaged; but the fragmentary evidence we do have suggests that the fighting there outdid anything we experienced ourselves in its scale and bitterness. It also clearly elicited uncounted stories of heroism, most never recounted. The Stalingrad diary of Lieutenant Anton K. Dragan for 21 September 1942 does something to fill the gap in our imagination.*

---

## STALINGRAD DIARY

### LIEUTENANT ANTON K. DRAGAN

21 September 1942

The Germans had cut us off from our neighbours. The supply of ammunition had been cut off; every bullet was worth its weight in gold. I gave the order to economize on ammunition, to collect the cartridge-pouches of the dead and all captured weapons. In the evening the enemy again tried to break our resistance, coming up close to our positions. As our numbers grew smaller, we shortened our line of defence. We began to move back slowly towards the Volga, drawing the enemy after us, and the ground we occupied was invariably too small for the Germans to be able easily to use artillery and aircraft.

We moved back, occupying one building after another, turning them into strongholds. A soldier would crawl out of an occupied position only when the ground was on fire under him and his clothes were smouldering. During the day the Germans managed to occupy only two blocks.

At the crossroads of Krasnopiterskaya and Komsomolskaya Streets we occupied a three-storey building on the corner. This was a good position from which to fire on all comers and it became our last defence. I ordered all entrances to be barricaded, and windows and embrasures to be adapted so that we could fire through them with all our remaining weapons.

At a narrow window of the semi-basement we placed the heavy machine-gun with our emergency supply of ammunition – the last belt of cartridges. I had decided to use it at the most critical moment.

Two groups, six in each, went up to the third floor and the garret. Their job was to break down walls, and prepare lumps of stone and beams to throw at the Germans when they came up close. A place for the seriously wounded was set aside in the basement. Our garrison consisted of forty men. Difficult days began. Attack after attack broke unendingly like waves against us. After each attack was beaten off we felt it was impossible to hold off the onslaught any longer, but when the Germans launched a fresh attack, we managed to find means and strength. This lasted five days and nights.

The basement was full of wounded; only twelve men were still able to fight. There was no water. All we had left in the way of food was a few pounds of scorched grain; the Germans decided to beat us with starvation. Their attacks stopped, but they kept up the fire from their heavy-calibre machine-guns all the time.

We did not think about escape, but only about how to sell our lives most dearly – we had no other way out.

The Germans attacked again. I ran upstairs with my men and could see their thin, blackened and strained faces, the bandages on their wounds, dirty and clotted with blood, their guns held firmly in their hands. There was no fear in their eyes. Lyuba Nesterenko, a nurse, was dying, with blood flowing from a wound in her chest. She had a bandage in her hand. Before she died she wanted to help to bind someone's wound, but she failed . . .

The German attack was beaten off. In the silence that gathered around us we could hear the bitter fighting going on for Mamayev Kurgan and in the factory area of the city.

How could we help the men defending the city? How could we divert from over there even a part of the enemy forces, which had stopped attacking our building?

We decided to raise a red flag over the building, so that the Nazis would not think we had given up. But we had no red material. Understanding what we wanted to do, one of the men who was severely wounded took off his bloody vest and, after wiping the blood off his wound with it, handed it over to me.

The Germans shouted through a megaphone: 'Russians! Surrender! You'll die just the same!'

At that moment a red flag rose over our building.

'Bark, you dogs! We've still got a long time to live!' shouted my orderly, Kozhushko.

We beat off the next attack with stones, firing occasionally and throwing our last grenades. Suddenly from behind a blank wall, from the rear, came the grind of a tank's caterpillar tracks. We had no anti-tank grenades. All we had left was one anti-tank rifle with three rounds. I handed this rifle to an anti-tank man, Berdyshev, and sent him out through the back to fire at the tank point-blank. But before he could get into position he was captured by German tommy-gunners. What Berdyshev told the Germans I don't know, but I can guess that he led them up the garden path, because an hour later they started to attack at precisely that point where I had put my machine-gun with its emergency belt of cartridges.

This time, reckoning that we had run out of ammunition, they came impudently out of their shelter, standing up and shouting. They came down the street in a column.

I put the last belt in the heavy machine-gun at the semi-basement window and sent the whole of the 250 bullets into the yelling, dirty-grey Nazi mob. I was wounded in the hand but did not leave go of the machine-gun. Heaps of bodies littered the ground. The Germans still alive ran for cover in panic. An hour later they led our anti-tank rifleman on to a heap of ruins and shot him in front of our eyes, for having shown them the way to my machine-gun.

There were no more attacks. An avalanche of shells fell on the building. The Germans stormed at us with every possible kind of weapon. We couldn't raise our heads.

Again we heard the ominous sound of tanks. From behind a neighbouring block stocky German tanks began to crawl out. This, clearly, was the end. The guardsmen said goodbye to one another. With a dagger my orderly scratched on a brick wall: 'Rodimtsev's guardsmen fought and died for their country here.'

# A CROWD IS
# NOT COMPANY

Robert Kee wrote A Crowd is not Company in 1945 and 1946, fresh from the prisoner of war camp where he had spent the previous three years. It was published then as a novel for two reasons. The first, hard though it is to believe now, was that in those days people simply did not want to read war books. On the other hand publishers wanted to find new young writers, and so, with the encouragement of Graham Greene, then working at the publishers Eyre and Spottiswoode, he published it as a novel. There was a second reason: certain events in it were embroidered; certain characters were run together to make composites. Yet the main thrust of the book is verisimilitude.

Kee crashed on the Dutch coast when piloting a Hampden Bomber; he describes in the preface how he had sat in the lavatory that day and thought that this would be his last trip. He had thought that on every previous occasion, but this time it turned out that he was right. His description of the actual texture of life in prison camp has seldom if ever been equalled. And, as he remarks in his preface, there was a sense in which everything that has happened since is secondary to it: 'I have lived what would conventionally be regarded as a reasonably full life and enjoyed many important human emotions, happy and sad. And yet, re-reading this book, everything that has happened to me since seems somehow secondary to what happened then. . . It is in this way, I think, that those who have been through a war are divided from those who have not: the most impressive thing in their life can seem already to have happened.'

---

## A CROWD IS NOT COMPANY

### ROBERT KEE

I cannot write fully about the years that followed. Although at the time they were made up of an apparently infinite chain of familiar days, I can think of them now only as a whole. The only real characteristic of each day was that it was the same as the day before and to give any account of such days in strict sequence would make as tedious reading as it made tedious living. Now it is possible to summarize the main features of that life in a single chapter.

You adjusted yourself to prison life. Unnatural conditions became natural and as time passed it was more and more difficult to believe that there was any other life beyond that which went on inside the wire. Certainly it was an adjustment which you fought against. It was claustrophobic to feel that the outside world, which reason told you was still there, was in fact disappearing. But adjustment went on all the same because it was the only way of making yourself tolerate a condition which you loathed. So the outside world faded.

Of course you could never forget about it. Sometimes you would see people who lived in it walking past the camp. News of public events poured in ceaselessly through the German loudspeakers and the secret wireless. Letters arrived from home. But all these things somehow had their centre inside the wire. It was as if they were all specially created to be viewed from there.

As soon as prisoners had been poured into the particular patch of ground which was to be their camp, all this activity materialized from nothing; and it materialized in every camp regardless of the nationality of the prisoners. It was quite spontaneous, for the Germans instigated nothing although they would sometimes co-operate in an elementary way by allowing wood for goalposts or permitting the construction of a theatre. The ceaseless thrust and bustle came from something deep and primeval in man. The restless indifferent force of human energy, responsible alike for beauty and ugliness, comedy and tragedy, saintliness and crime, had to find its own level inside the wire.

But if the determining force in human existence was unaltered, the peculiarities of environment – shortage of food, absence of women, lack of space, remoteness of the outside world – did produce corresponding peculiarities of behaviour. Some tendencies in human behaviour were encouraged, others repressed, and the results were both pleasant and unpleasant. Strange twists were given to the normal body of human nature, revealing that such freak developments are potentially in all of us all the time.

The only beneficial peculiarity of the environment was the sense of detachment from the outside world. In the first place people developed a greater objectiveness than they had ever done while they were living in it. The formation of liberal thought by those who normally might have taken a pride in never bothering to think at all was remarkable. But more significant than this was the general increase in sensibility. There were no cinemas or pubs or dances so that we were forced to find pleasure in the ordinary things which surrounded us, the sky and books and the changing seasons. Many people seemed to become aware of such things for the first time in their lives. 'I never realized that sunsets could be so lovely.' 'This classical music has much better tunes than dance music and I don't seem to get tired of them nearly so easily.' 'At home you hardly know whether it's raining from one day to the next, but here you feel better every time the sun comes out.' 'I never used to read poetry at all but I've just found out that it says all the things I've often felt but never been able to express.' 'I didn't realize Dickens was so funny.' Naïve unsophisticated statements such as these marked a regeneration which perhaps must be experienced by more than a handful of prisoners if we are to care enough about civilization to want to save it.

As people became more intensely aware of the pleasures of beauty they wanted to create it for themselves, and another new source of happiness was discovered. Commercial travellers began to paint, stockbrokers to act and footballers to write poetry. Perhaps none of it was very good, but it was at least the beginning of something true in the lives of people who had been educated to falsity. Certainly not everybody in the camp found pleasure in books or music or poetry or nature, but many people who normally would never have had anything to do with such things were forced by their environment to look into them and found there greater wealth than they had ever known before.

I often used to wonder whether we should carry these new springs of happiness away with us when we emerged. I certainly intended to. If we could find a heightened sense of beauty in the world of a prison camp, I thought, surely we could find it in the great free world of which we dreamed? I cursed myself for having made such a feeble thing of life before being shot down. I determined that it should not happen again and it seemed impossible that it should, for this time I should carry with me the foundation of happiness which I had found behind the wire. I used to despise the people who wrote me letters from England showing that they found the world drab and depressing. They seemed silly and childish and so much less wise than us who really did live in a drab and depressing world and yet found happiness in it. I laughed when I read of the things which they considered important: political creeds, literary cliques, careerist intrigues.

Looking back now I wonder at my arrogance. The very fact that I had only properly discovered a foundation of happiness when separated from the world should have shown me that the tendency of the world was to flood and destroy such a thing. I should have known that no amount of understanding can carry any individual for long against the swirling crowds of social existence, and that soon after rejoining them I too should be stampeding with them. The fact that I was in a prison camp at all should have made clear to me the ruthlessness and irresistibility of the stampede.

All the other peculiar effects of camp environment were bad. In so far as material conditions were more unpleasant, so human beings were more unpleasant. It is not my experience that physical hardship 'brings out the best in a man'. Changes of character brought about by the fluctuation of material conditions were so marked that they were noticeable even at the time from within the camp. As the weekly parcel issue decreased from one to a half you began to notice who took more than his share of the butter or the jam and though you felt mean for noticing it you went on being mean. You were glad when someone suggested that the butter or the jam should be cut up into rations even though you did see the hard selfishness in his eyes as he said it and felt sick because you knew that normally he was neither hard nor selfish. When there were no Red Cross parcels at all you began to notice that people sized up the rations of margarine before they helped themselves, and though you despised them for it you were none the less sharp to do it yourself. A roster for crusts had to be started as these contained more bread than the average thin slice. After some weeks without Red Cross parcels, people began to arrive early at meals so that they could size up and take the largest of the scrupulously rationed helpings of potatoes, or the thickest of the apparently identical slices of bread. Though the differences were minute they were capable of calling forth the highest passions: great content if you did well, or jealousy and despair if you did badly. You loathed it when you saw other people behaving like this and yet you could no more control it in yourself than you could any other automatic physical reflex. And it was small compensation to be able to loathe yourself.

Life was not quite a state of nature or a question of the survival of the fittest, but in times of no food parcels the partition separating us from that state was unpleasantly thin and even at the best of times it was thin enough to be able to hear most of what went on on the other side. The general shortage of comforts and of everything which kept us just above the lowest level of life was sufficiently great to make individuals cling on to what they had with something like fanaticism. Improvised cooking utensils, the contents of the three-monthly clothing parcel, a few nails, bits of wood for shelves, were objects around which a sacred ring was drawn. There was an unspoken religious respect for another man's possessions far stronger than the respect for property in normal society and correspondingly more unpleasant. If you wished to borrow such things you instinctively made it clear that you intended no blasphemy.

The effect of overcrowding was the disastrous one of turning you against all humanity. Your mind became numbed to everything about human beings except that they pressed close around you all the time, that they slept above or below you, that you could never turn your head without seeing some evidence of their closeness – their clothes or their books or their photographs – that they made it impossible for you ever to be alone. Although this was no fault of theirs you hated them for it. Certainly you did not quarrel with them all the time. Superficially you were usually on good terms with them as individuals and sometimes there was even an elementary sense of comradeship. But underneath you did not think of them as individuals. They were the crowd whose heads you could not see over. And the crowd was not company.

Of all the various forms of starvation and near starvation at work, sex starvation was the most complete. Officers did not go out of the camp to work and they had no contact with women. Some were prisoners for four or five years. 'What did you do about sex?' It is the question everybody asks and it is difficult to give a satisfactory answer because everybody wants a definite or even a sensational one. I think most prisoners would say that the sex problem worried them less than they had expected it to, but that is not to say that it did not worry most people some of the time and some people all the time. A restraining factor was undoubtedly the poorness of the food. But there was sufficient sex feeling left over to need an outlet and this was often more than could be successfully sublimated into a mere exuberance of energy in reading or games or any other form of camp activity.

I think there was very little practised homosexuality. The reason for this was a simple one: that it was highly impractical. The natural British attitude to sex made any open homosexual conduct such as was supposed to exist at the French Stalags inconceivable, while the lack of any privacy made public school secrecy impossible. As a result such homosexuality as there was usually took a repressed form. There were a

237

few couples whose friendship was of long standing and who were always seen about together. There were a few people who 'took an interest' first in one young man and then another. There were a few young men who developed female characteristics, unconsciously perhaps at first but certainly consciously when they became aware of the power that these gave them. (There was a long correspondence in a camp newspaper about the evil effects which female parts in a play had on such people.) There was a good deal of schoolboy teasing and even bullying which probably had its origins in sex. But it is useless to start deciding which aspects of behaviour did or did not have their origin in sex. Even in normal society it is boring and, after a while, meaningless to trace everything to a common source, especially when the detail is elaborate. It was just that in camp the link between sex and behaviour was often cruder and more obvious than in ordinary life. As with all the other special effects of camp environment, those produced by sex starvation were not organically different but merely the ordinary trends aggravated and emphasized.

All these twists given to human character by the conditions of camp life were noticeable in varying degrees throughout the years. And in normal life too they stand always within call. 'Is man no more than this?' says Lear, standing on the heath with his two companions and watching the madman. 'Consider him well . . . Here's three on's are sophisticated; thou art the thing itself; unaccommodated man is no more but such a poor, bare, forked animal as thou art.' It is a truth which I can never now forget as I go about a world in which human beings apparently have themselves under control. The smooth-phrased BBC announcer, the amusing don, the self-confident politician, the jargon-perfect critic, the editor of the literary magazine – all are reducible within a few months to a bewildered defensive creature with hollow cheeks and desperate eyes whose only cares will be to see that he gets his fair share of the potato ration, that nobody steals his bed boards, and that he exchanges his cigarette ends for food or vice versa at the best possible price. Whenever I hear a man being witty or sensible or kindly or civilized I think: the qualities which now seem so much a part of this man could be stripped away at any time, and there would be left just a man who suffered and who fought with his suffering like an animal.

Such thoughts need not be pessimistic. But they should make us modest. They should also make us determined to prevent the conditions which bring out this aspect of our nature.

There was one practical advantage which our miniature world had over the world outside the wire. It was possible to escape from it. Those who spend their lives looking for some practical escape from the ordinary world eventually have to accept the fact that there is no escape except through death or the imagination. In a prison-camp the world you wanted to get to was visible all the time and, although you did not live in it, you knew that it was only a matter of some barbed wire and a few yards away. Of course there were some people who, as in the ordinary world, were content with their lives and therefore had no wish to escape. Others realized that it was only a matter of patience to wait for the guaranteed escape which would be provided by the end of the war, and as the war dragged on more and more people became converted to this view. But the lust for escape was a powerful one and the fact that escape was possible made the idea a great stimulus whether you got away or not.

Not only was the world into which you wanted to escape there for you to see but you also knew that it was a practical possibility to reach it. There was nothing magic or even electric about the barbed wire. It could be cut or climbed or dug under. So satisfactory was this knowledge that many people were content with nothing else. It was possible to spend all day wandering happily round and round the camp musing on the possibility of a hole cut in the wire here, a tunnel dug there, or an assault with scaling ladders somewhere else. And all the time you knew that you would never take the risk of getting shot which this involved or have the necessary patience to carry it out.

Many people took this game of make-believe to fantastic lengths and went through the whole elaborate business of a preparation for escape without the slightest real intention of ever carrying it out.

Impractical plans absorbed imaginative people for weeks. There was the chemist who toyed with the possibilities of making synthetic gas for a balloon, the aerodynamic expert who planned to construct a glider out of bed boards, and the dog-lover who wanted to make himself a dog-skin out of an Irvin flying suit and crawl out as one of the guards' Alsatians. The orthodox visualized themselves cutting through the wire or bringing off some unprecedented bluff at the main gate. All schemes involved weeks and sometimes months of furtive planning, decisions on route and disguise, invention of a suitable story for travelling purposes and sometimes even the learning of a new language. Generally speaking, the longer the period of planning for an escape the more satisfactory it was for the prospective escaper. For weeks he would live in a world by himself, conscious as he watched the humdrum routine of his fellow prisoners that he was destined for higher things and happy in the knowledge that he was not as other men. Each night as he lay in bed he would imagine himself catching the train from the local station – such reveries usually assumed the initial achievement of getting outside the camp – or stalking the frontier guards among the mountains with Switzerland a few hundred yards away across the snow . . . Then the welcome at the British Embassy, the flight back to England, the smiles and the cheering and the medals, the pressing of Button A in the telephone box: 'Hullo, I'm back.' And at some point it would all become as real as it was ever to become again, as the happy escaper slid into dreams until morning. For weeks it would go on like this and then suddenly one day you would notice him just lying in the sun instead of studying his map, or reading a novel instead of his German grammar. 'How's that scheme of yours coming on?' you might ask him and he would reply with just a little too much nonchalance to sound natural: 'Oh, I had to give it up; we had good reason for thinking that the goons were on to it.' or 'It's too late now really: the mountains are impassable at this time of year . . . perhaps next spring . . . .' And you would know that at last he had called his own bluff.

It is difficult to assess the amount of self-deceit involved in such unreal escapes. It was often obvious from the start that they would never lead to anything and this made those who were more settled openly contemptuous. They regarded such activity as a schoolboy game of cloaks and daggers. So it was, but that in itself was no real explanation. The state of mind of day-dream escapers was not simple and they both believed in their plans and knew quite well that they would never carry them out at the same time. Certainly there would have been no satisfaction in such behaviour if the would-be escaper had not for a time at any rate believed in himself.

Of course not all escape schemes were unreal. Many hundreds of successful escapes were made by prisoners during the war. But even in the most matter-of-fact and determined plans there was always an element of unreality. Everyone engaged on an escape scheme enjoyed the furtiveness necessary for good security: the concealment of tell-tale evidence under coats a few feet away from unsuspecting sentries, the private knowledge kept from other members of the hut. They enjoyed too the almost unlimited scope for invention and strategy, and the personal romanticizing in bed at night. It was the schoolboy's dream come true. Here were all the ingredients of an exciting life and nothing to pay. If you played spies or conspirators anywhere else your life was at stake. But here, if you were caught preparing an escape, the worst that could happen to you was fourteen days solitary confinement with books and writing materials, and it was often a pleasant change to spend a fortnight by yourself after months of compulsory association.

It was this element of unreality which made tunnelling the most popular scheme for escape. It gave easily the best value. While a wire or a gate scheme might take a few weeks if spun out to the maximum, tunnels were sometimes under construction for six months. During that time the pleasures of furtiveness were open to all concerned, and to these was added the satisfaction of hard physical work and the stimulus of a mild sense of danger while actually working under the earth. There was even one tunnel which, after it had reached its original destination outside the wire, was continued twenty or thirty yards to further cover. There it was saved further prolongation by discovery by the Germans before anyone had escaped at all. Several tunnels were completed but discovered before they could be used because the escapers were 'waiting for the thaw' or 'for the berries to appear on the hedgerows', and sometimes individuals would fail to go through with attempts (which others carried out) because 'their boots were being mended' or 'they had sprained an ankle playing basketball'.

It was only at the last moment that the unreal nature of an escape project was finally determined. Then of course it seemed to have been predetermined all the time. 'I knew he'd never try it: he never really wanted to get out.' 'It was a commonsense scheme and he wanted to get out: it was bound to work.' But it was not as simple as that. It was just that at the moment of climax when the escape had to be attempted or abandoned, it became if attempted something quite different from what it had been in the planning. It became a decisive and dangerous piece of initiative and the escaper got the credit of it having been that all the time.

So, year after year, abnormal influences jostled with the normal and all were considered normal. Sometimes rain lashed the tarred roofs of the huts until they glistened like the skin of a seal. Sometimes all life seemed stilled in the aquarium silence of a July sun. Always, outside the wire, the bored guards relieved each other at two hourly intervals while, inside, prisoners did the washing-up or quarrelled or went to sleep. And always, inside and outside, people dreamed of the end of the war.

1947

---

Though nothing remotely compensated for the loss of their liberty, the RAF prisoners of war in Stalag Luft VI organized their unwelcome and unending days of captivity with admirable resource. They were part of what came to be called the barbed wire university – where the only qualification for entry was to have faced death. They studied law and medicine, banking and farming, Latin and Greek. The timetable overleaf shows just how seriously they went about it. They took – and passed – exams set for them by the Red Cross Educational Section at Oxford. They thus helped fit themselves for peace; but first and foremost, they saved themselves from the prisoner's worst enemy: boredom.

| CLASS ROOMS | TIMES | Monday | Tuesday | Wednesday | Thursday | Friday | Saturday | Sunday |
|---|---|---|---|---|---|---|---|---|
| **B 11 Barrack** | 0000-1000 | MATHS I. ELEM. | MATHS II. ELEM. | MATHS. I. ELEM. | MATHS II ELEM | MATHS I. ELEM. | MATHS. II. ELEM. | |
| | 1000-1100 | ← CHARTERED INSTITUTE OF SECRETARIES → | | | | | MATHS. IV ELEM | |
| | 1100-1200 | FRENCH I | FRENCH II | FRENCH I | FRENCH II | FRENCH I | FRENCH II | TYPOGRAPHY |
| | 1300-1400 | ENG.GRAMMER I | GERMAN | ENG.GRAMMER II | GERMAN | ENG.GRAMMER I | GERMAN | ENG.GRAMMER II |
| | 1400-1500 | MATHS.III ELEM. | MATHS III ELEM. | MATHS III ELEM. | ENG.GRAMMER III | CHEMISTRY | ENG GRAMMER III | FRENCH III |
| | 1500-1600 | ENG. LIT. | ENG. HIST. | ENG. LIT. | ENG. HIST. | HEAT,LIGHT&SOUND | COMMERCE II | MAG. & ELECTRI. |
| | 1600-1700 | CANADIAN AGRICULTURE | CHEMISTRY | EUROPEAN HIST. | ENG.GRAMMER IV | EUROPEAN HIST. | HEAT.LIGHT&SOUND | MATHS IV ELEM. |
| | 1800-1900 | ECONOMICS | MECHANICS | COMMERCE I | ECONOMICS | MECHANICS | HOTEL MANAGEMENT | BOTANY |
| | 1900-2000 | FRENCH III | ENG.GRAMMER IV | MAG.&ELECTRICITY | FRENCH III | BOTANY | ENG. LIT. | AGRICULTURE |
| **C 13 Barrack** | 0900-1000 | MUSIC | MOTOR TRADE | ELEM.SHORTHAND | MUSIC | INTERNAL COMBUSTION ENGINE | GERMAN | |
| | 1000-1100 | MECHANICAL DRAWING | AGRICULTURE BANKERS | INSURANCE | MECHANICAL DRAWING | INSURANCE | AGRICULTURE | |
| | 1100-1200 | (DRAWING) | (BANKERS) | LAW | (DRAWING) | N.A.L.G.O | ITALIAN | FRENCH |
| | 1300-1400 | INTERNAL COMBUSTION ENGINE | NAVIGATION I | FRENCH | N.A.L.G.O. ELEM. | ADVANCED | N.A.L.G.O. ELEM. | LAW |
| | 1400-1500 | NAVIGATION II | GERMAN | CANADIAN AGRICULTURE | NAVIGATION II | ITALIAN | NAVIGATION I | INSURANCE |
| | 1500-1600 | INSURANCE | LAW | N.A.L.G.O. ELEM. | N.A.L.G.O | BANKERS.ELEM | NAVIGATION I | SPANISH |
| | 1600-1700 | SPANISH | MECH.DRAWING | MATRICULATION DRAWING | ADVANCED | MOTOR TRADE | INSURANCE | CANADIAN AGRICULTURE |
| | 1800-1900 | SHIPPING | N.A.L.G.O | SHIPPING | CANADIAN AGRICULTURE | SHIPPING | N.A.L.G.O | SHIPPING |
| | 1900-2000 | N.A.L.G.O. ELEM | ADVANCED | ITALIAN | MATHS | SPANISH | ADVANCED | SHORTHAND, SPEED |
| **Mid.D. Barrack** | 0000-1000 | FRENCH | LATIN | LATIN | FRENCH | GERMAN | LATIN | |
| | 1000-1100 | ← ENGLISH LITERATURE B.A. → | | | | | | |
| | 1100-1200 | ← PERIODS FOR B.Sc. (Econ) → | | | | | | |
| | 1300-1400 | ← PERIODS FOR EXAMINATIONS → | | | | | CALCULUS | B.Sc.(General) |
| | 1400-1500 | | | | | | SPANISH | ENGLISH LIT. |
| | 1500-1600 | | | | | | ART | ENGLISH LIT. |
| | 1600-1700 | | | | | | ART | FRENCH |
| | 1800-1900 | LATIN | FRENCH | B.Sc.(General) | GERMAN | HISTORY | GERMAN | SPANISH |
| | 1900-2000 | GREEK | GERMAN | GREEK | HISTORY | GREEK | B.Sc.(General) | GREEK |
| **Fiction Library** | 0900-1000 | NAVIGATION III | NAVIGATION IV | METALLURGY | NAVIGATION III | RADIO II | ELEM. MATHS. | |
| | 1000-1100 | MUSIC | ENGINEERING CALCULUS | CALCULUS | ELEM.MATHS | ELEM MATHS | TECH.ELECTRICITY | |
| | 1100-1200 | GERMAN | ELEM MATHS | RADIO I | RADIO IV | SHORTHAND | METALLURGY | RADIO III |
| | 1300-1400 | ← FICTION LIBRARY → | | | | | | |
| | 1400-1500 | | | | | | | |
| | 1500-1600 | | | | | | | TECH ELECTRICITY |
| | 1600-1700 | | | | | | | MUSIC |
| | 1800-1900 | BUILDING | ARCHITECTURE | BUILDING | ARCHITECTURE | BUILDING | SALES | BUILDING |
| | 1900-2000 | | | | | | | |
| **Hairdressers Shop** | 0900-1000 | | | | | | | |
| | 1000-1100 | ← WORK PERIOD → | | | | | | |
| | 1100-1200 | | | | | | | |
| | 1300-1400 | | | | | | | |
| | 1400-1500 | | | | | | | |
| | 1500-1600 | | | | | | | |
| | 1600-1700 | | | | | | | |
| | 1800-1900 | ART ADVANCED LIFE | ART BASIC LIFE STILL LIFE | ART ADVANCED LIFE | ART BASIC LIFE STILL LIFE | ART BASIC LIFE | ART STILL LIFE | ART ADVANCED LIFE |
| | 1900-2000 | | | | | | | |

# IN THE MOOD

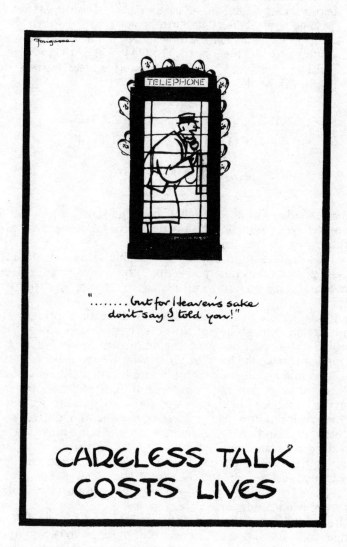

"........ but for Heaven's sake
don't say I told you!"

CARELESS TALK
COSTS LIVES

'Next to a letter from home,' declared General James Doolittle commanding the US Air Force in 1944, 'Captain Miller, your organization is the greatest morale-builder in the European Theatre of Operations.' Glenn Miller was then just forty years old, and despite a personality that had all the charisma of a high school maths teacher, had created a kind of music that spoke directly to the hearts and minds of millions of serving men and women as no other did. He had joined the army because he felt there was a job he could do for Americans away fighting that no one else could, and built around him a great new band. The young people of Great Britain were as enraptured by the Glenn Miller sound as their American counterparts; till now though, they had only been able to hear it on scratchy 78 rpm records. Then, on 13 July 1944, at 8.30 p.m., without a word of warning, the band broadcast live on the BBC for the first time. It was a revelation, as Laurie Henshaw of the Melody Maker reported.

## GLENN MILLER ON THE AIR

### LAURIE HENSHAW

It's happened. Adolph, on behalf of swing fans, take a bow! You've violated a few treaties since the early Thirties, but you won't be razzed for ripping this barrier aside.

In 1934, in retaliation for a long-standing AFM edict, the Ministry of Labour placed an embargo against the engagement of American orchestras in this country. And it's taken a major war to tear this ban apart.

But now it's happened, and British bandleaders' preserves, guarded from foreign encroachment for the past decade, have been gaily trampled upon, but I bet the selfsame British leaders will be the first to stampede to shake the hand of a man whom they've been copying since the Glenn Miller tone colour and 'In the Mood' became famous.

Why don't the papers tell us these things? Miller should have been given the headlines; the doodle-bugs could have taken second place.

The only indication readers had that a major air offensive was about to start was the bland announcement that at 8.30 on Thursday evening (13 July) the American Band, Supreme Allied Command, would broadcast. Thinking this was a field day for Sousa, I nearly missed the airing; and how many 'MM' readers did the same? The announcement wasn't even in the Radio Times, which told us that we were going to hear the ill-fated and short-lived 'Sitting on a Fence'.

The great Glenn was introduced by twenty-year-old BBC compère Jean Metcalf, and proved to have a most pleasing voice and microphone manner – all this and a Captaincy, too. Jazz has definitely grown out of the musical ranks.

Miller announced that Sgt Ray McKinley would kick the tunes rolling with a drum intro to 'American Patrol'.

Ray hit out, and the rest of the personnel, including such well-known names as Mel Powell (ex-Goodman piano), Zeke Zarchy (ex-Goodman trumpet), Carmen Mastren (ex-Tommy Dorsey guitar), and Bobby Nichols (ex-Vaughn Monroe trumpet) rocked into the first number.

Twenty-year-old Mel Powell took the first solo spot, and 20,000 British jazz pianists dropped in their tracks. Powell tolled the death-knell to the esteem of a lot of self-opinionated young men.

An interesting trumpet solo by Zeke Zarchy was also featured in this number.

Jean announced that Miller had brought over a special arrangement of Gershwin's 'Summertime'. Although played in more commercial vein, this was good. Twenty fiddles bolstered up the background harmonies and Miller should know there are twenty since he hired them. To me they sounded full enough to be the string section of the London Symphony Orchestra.

A comedy swing number followed entitled 'Juke Box Saturday Night', wherein the boys chanted a rhyme about Harry James (the trumpet even did the James chorus of 'Ciribiribin', and it was a grand burlesque), and a vocal team did a playful skit on the Ink Spots, even to the stock guitar intro, and the phony tenor voicing on the arch demon of the coloured quartet.

Dorothy Carless sang next and made a good job of 'I Couldn't Sleep a Wink Last Night'.

A blues followed with the Basic English title 'It Must Be Jelly 'Cos Jam Don't Shake Like That'. The number rode all right, with thrilling solo spots by tenor and trumpet, and the rhythm section merged like mad.

Bruce Trent then sang 'Without a Song' and has certainly improved since he's been 'Student Prince-ing' round the country. But whether his thick sort of voice is right against the Miller bunch – ah, that's another story.

Finally, Dave Rose's 'Holiday for Strings' was dressed up in a new setting by arranger Sgt Jerry Gray. Miller's symphony section plucked their pizzicato passages most precisely, and the full sax and brass sections did some smooth things on their own account.

Thus ended a half-hour's broadcast. And the Captain himself announced that he'll be back next Thursday. The radio remains switched on for a week: we won't nearly miss him a second time.

Whether Miller's broadcasts are continued depends on his Army commitments, and also, maybe, to listeners' reactions. We don't have to be assured that 'MM' readers will do their part to see that the BBC finds out what's wanted!

*Ray Sonin* [Editor of the *Melody Maker*] *adds*: Henshaw has reported the airing quite accurately, and the general effect was one of superb musicianship and teamwork.

Mel Powell was undoubtedly the solo man of the broadcast, but Zeke Zarchy's trumpet didn't impress me personally, nor would I say the band

245

was always up to the terrifically high wax standard associated with Miller.

Two things stood out a mile from this broadcast and explain the difference between crack US and crack home-grown bands. America has arrangers of genius and section leaders who can really inspire their teams.

Did I hear you say that America also had the musicians and the leaders? Perhaps you're right.

---

One of the most bizarre effects of the war, little examined till recently, was the exposure of many thousands of black GIs to British life. At that time the colour bar was still a fact of life in America and black GIs were put in separate all-black units. The British in those days knew nothing about black people; many indeed had never even seen one. The great waves of immigration from the West Indies and West Africa lay far ahead. So the British could only judge on what little they knew. They sympathized with black GIs first, out of a natural penchant for the under-dog; second, because frankly the blacks had plenty of money to spend and were good for business; third, because their perception of blacks was then obtained almost entirely from Hollywood films, where they were invariably cast as easy-going, simple-minded, good-humoured bit players. However, there was a problem: very few black servicewomen indeed came to Britain, and the only female company was that of white British girls. This caused all sorts of problems, not least with white GIs from the southern states. It must be said in all truth that many British girls took a fancy to these black GIs without reservation and indeed with gusto.

---

## WHEN JIM CROW MET JOHN BULL: BLACK AMERICAN SOLDIERS IN WORLD WAR II BRITAIN

### GRAHAM SMITH

The US Army's attitude to the prospect of its black soldiers having sexual relations with white British women provided another of the home front's nice ironies. In general the Army's advice to the soldiers was that interracial dating was bound to take place and they were to tolerate this. Thus while the British were cautioning citizens not to become too friendly with the blacks because that would not happen in the United States, and to defer to the American attitude, the American Army command was saying that black/white associations must be respected because they were going to happen in Britain.

Insofar as there was a basic instruction to American troops on the social issue it was Eisenhower's letter to General Lee of 5 September 1942 which said that everyone in the European Theatre must recognize that interracial relationships would take place on 'a basis mutually acceptable to the individuals concerned and there must be no official attempt to curtail this'. Lee was to ensure that this was transmitted to every officer in the theatre, and there is no doubt that many conscientious officers made sure the message, unpalatable to many though it was, went right down the line. If black and white liaisons were tolerated in Britain, the Army authorities were anxious that this image should not be for export. Sometime in the second half of 1943 *Life* magazine showed pictures of black soldiers in London night clubs dancing with white girls. This was regarded as 'material . . . calculated to unduly inflame racial prejudice both overseas and in the UNITED STATES [sic]'. The result was a War Department censorship regulation prohibiting the passing for any purposes of amateur photographs 'showing negro soldiers in poses of intimacy with white women or conveying "boyfriend-girlfriend" implications'. On 7 March 1945 because of the 'vigorous protest' in Europe Eisenhower requested that this ban be lifted for such photographs intended for the soldiers' personal use as opposed to those meant for publication.

Despite all the prohibitions, white girls did go out with black soldiers, and these relationships had important repercussions. Arguably it was the most explosive aspect of the American presence, with four consequences all closely linked to each other. In the first place it was a major cause of the disturbances between black and white Americans, some of which resulted in deaths. Secondly, it affected British attitudes towards the blacks: most disliked the miscegenation they saw. Thirdly, females were largely blamed for 'chasing' the blacks and consequently British and white American opinions of British women were influenced. Lastly, there were several hundred illegitimate 'brown babies' born to English mothers, a problem which remained unsolved for some time in the post-war period.

Disturbances at Leicester and Bristol indicated that sexual rivalry was a major reason, if not *the* major reason, for the clashes between black and white Americans, and this scenario was repeated in varying degrees up and down the country. Black women being few in number, all GIs were competing for the favours of a finite number of white women in Britain. That this would cause trouble was obvious at an early stage in the American presence. Professor Gilbert Murray, an Oxford don and a member of the BBC's 'Brains Trust', reported at the end of June 1942 that American whites were 'taking a threatening attitude' towards the blacks and were talking of 'lynching any whom they find dancing with white girls'. Murray went on to note that an 'American colonel said in so many words that the great ambition of every one of these blacks was to rape a white woman.'

The words of the [American] white soldiers themselves shed some light on the depth of feeling. From Northern Ireland a quartermaster corporal forecast trouble:

It seems that several outfits of coloured troops preceded us over here and have succeeded pretty well in salting away the local feminine pulchritude . . . the girls really go for them in preference to the white boys, a fact that irks the boys no end, especially those of the outfit that come from the north. No doubt there will be some bloodshed in the near future.

Sheer gut response seems to have been the principal driving force of the white soldiers' outrage. 'I've seen nice looking English girls out with American Negro soldiers as black as the ace of spades', wrote a first lieutenant from Wellingborough. 'I have not only seen the Negro boys dancing with white girls, but we have actually seen them standing in doorways *kissing the girls goodnight.*' On occasions white vehemence went hand in hand with popular mythology in an attempt to rationalize why the blacks got on so well with the locals: 'The lower classes of white girls . . . seem to prefer the coloured troops to white. "The good Lord was extra kind to the negro – so they say".' A member of a military police battalion in Liverpool did not mince words: 'Honey you should see how the "old women" like to go around with negroes here. Perhaps they like to go around with them because they have immense Penises.'

British civilians were not immune to the rumours and reports of the sexual activity of the black GIs, especially in view of the likely principal stereotype about black people that was held in Britain at that time, namely that blacks were less sexually inhibited and capable of giving greater sexual satisfaction than white men. This attitude was typified by a civilian from Leamington Spa who felt in June 1944 that it was 'horrible to see the white girls running round with the blacks but they do say once a black never a white, don't they?' A local fellow in Somerset was even blunter. His view, when he witnessed girls looking into a black GI camp, was that these maids 'prick-mazed they be, prick-mazed'.

In broad terms blacks were welcomed and liked in Britain during the war years. The one exception to this general pattern was when the sexual factor came to the fore. What is of interest, however, is that few people saw any intellectual gulf between their broad acceptance of blacks and their particular dislike of miscegenation. The implication is that separation between the races at the sexual level was the accepted norm of society and this could therefore be totally detached from the other aspects of black behaviour. The popular view was that blacks, especially in view of their part in the war effort, could be accepted by whites as brothers but never as spouses.

Concern about the racial problem continued in high places through-out the war. Harry Haig, the Southern Regional Commissioner, felt strongly enough about black troops and promiscuity to meet Herbert Morrison and Frank Newsam at the Home Office in November 1943, when he expressed anxiety that 'coloured troops were inclined to misconstrue ordinary politeness shown to them by English women'. The Home Secretary's response was to blame the American authorities who had considered it 'politically necessary that a reasonable proportion of coloured troops should be sent to this country'. Comparable views emerged when Winston Churchill renewed his interest in the black Americans in the autumn of 1943. His correspondence with the Duke of Marlborough and James Grigg revealed concerns about VD, brown babies and rape. The War Minister reported to the Premier that some of the cases of association were because white women were sympathetic to the black soldiers but others were 'of a far more mundane and vicious nature' and called for measures 'more stringent than education'.

It is important to remember at this point that white GIs were far more numerous in Britain than the blacks and that there was plenty of criticism of their sexual behaviour too; but most concern did settle on the black perspective of the problem. Home Intelligence reports verified this as did the Mass Observation survey of August 1943, which revealed that one in seven people disapproved of mixed marriages even though about 25 per cent of observers had become more friendly towards blacks, partly as a result of meeting American troops.

It was at this point that the British did a little more intellectual side-stepping, albeit unconsciously. Even the sternest critics thought the blacks in Britain were 'behaving well', were aware that there were few black women in Britain, and could see that some of the rape cases raised a lot of doubts. Almost as if to dissociate the blacks from charges of sexual extravagance and keep their records clean, the British now began to pin the responsibility for the sexual liaisons on British women. They were only happening, was the implicit argument, because women of all ages were relentlessly pursuing the black GIs. The Ministry of Information reported 'furtive tales of sexual excesses . . . Young irresponsible girls from homes where there is little parental control are said to find coloured men tremendously fascinating and frequently accost them.' Whether this was true was immaterial, but clearly this attempt at understanding the stituation rebounded to the blacks' disadvantage. Under pressure British girls began to drop their black boyfriends.

It is interesting here to turn from the general to the particular and return to the men of the black ordnance aviation company at Scout Dyke Army Base in the West Riding of Yorkshire. They did find at least their wine and women in Huddersfield and a discussion about this opened up in the local paper, the *Huddersfield Examiner*. The correspondence would be quite remarkable even today but its frankness in times of war was refreshing at the very least. It is worth quoting at length because of the many issues related to the black American presence in Britain which were raised. The debate began on Monday 20 September 1943 after the publication of an article about the conduct of a 'small minority' of local girls. They were allegedly having sex with the black GIs – in shop doorways, quiet streets, open spaces and in vehicles drawn up alongside the pavements. After the investigation the reporter concluded that 'if blame is to be attached anywhere it should not be put on the shoulders of our coloured guests . . . the main responsibility lies with a small fraction of misguided young women in Huddersfield, some of them, I am sorry to say, nothing more than unscrupulous sponging "gold diggers".' A Josephine Rickett rushed to the defence of her young Yorkshire contemporaries:

> The negro soldiers, though as a rule well-behaved, do whistle after our girls, stop them in the street, speak to them as they walk through the town, and invite them to go for drinks. Some (please note only some) of the girls tempted by the large quantity of money possessed by these negroes (as compared to our own troops) have agreed and gone for drinks with them. This, agreed, is not always the case but it could be that these girls are afraid of offending the negroes . . . they are taught in the church to treat the negroes exactly as they treat our own people. They are told to be friendly toward the negro soldier, and yet when they go out with them, they invoke a torrent of abuse from all quarters . . . . If these [black] men are not strong enough to resist the wiles and temptations of mere children, then, they are not fit to fight for this country against the most desperate enemy she ever had.

One of the black GIs responded at length to the debate, demonstrating just how alien a place he had found England. Half a crown, he admitted, was a cheap price for a double scotch and girls could be tempted by this, but it was the fact that the pubs seemed so central to all entertainment that puzzled this GI.

> We do not criticize your local 'pubs' for we happen to realize that is your life. Would it be asking too much of the local populace to realize that we are actually bored because it has nothing to offer? . . . we are a very small contingent of soldiers, thousands of miles from home, who have made . . . the best of our position and get what little pleasure that may be had in this locality . . . . Please do not for a minute harbour the hallucination that we have no race pride, that we wouldn't glory in the possibility of spending our 'hard earned' finance on young ladies of our own race. It hasn't occurred to you that no-one will ever be able to fill the void that the absence of Negro girls has created . . . whistling at girls, offering them the opportunity of sharing a drink is not confined to the American Negro, but applied to men of all races, creeds or colours – yes, even the British Tommy . . . . How many soldiers of any given race would resist the wiles and temptations of what is termed 'the camp follower' regardless of her age . . . who could not be regarded as an 'innocent virgin' or a typical English lady . . . you will find that just a 'cold shoulder' will relieve you of unwanted negro companionship. We, too, are a very reserved race.

At the beginning of the black American presence 'even the nicest type of female' enjoyed the company of black troops, wrote a British naval officer. It was obvious that many young girls found the blacks fascinating, appreciating their attentiveness and good manners.

It is almost possible to pin-point exactly when the British ceased to view the black soldiers' relations with the local girls with equanimity. This change occurred about March or April 1943. During the last six months of 1942 favourable Home Intelligence reports on black GIs outnumbered the unfavourable ones by almost two to one. From mid-1943 to the end of 1944 this pattern was almost the exact reverse, with most of the unfavourable comments relating to sex. Colonel Rowe, the Liaison Officer at the War Office, felt as early as January 1943 that the tide of opinion was turning, helped along by the added pressure from white GIs, with the result that almost the whole weight of public opinion was now against those girls who continued to go with the black troops. The birth of the first brown babies in the spring of 1943 simply added fuel to a fire already well alight.

Added to the disapproval of British people, many white Americans too saw British women who dated blacks as prostitutes or people of loose morals, and not the least of the problems for the black GIs and their partners was that such judgements had very practical results. Whenever white GIs discovered girls who had consorted with blacks the girls were completely ostracized; and because whites could bring more pressure to bear on English girls, blacks were now in a 'catch-22' situation – cut off from normal relationships they were left to pay for their sex (with the attendant danger of venereal disease), or accept the favours of very young girls who often looked older than their years. Both alternatives merely served to bring them more condemnation from British citizens.

The problem of very young girls chasing the black American soldiers certainly was not easy to solve. Their behaviour was considered by many as quite brazen and disgusting, and beyond any measure of parental control. The issue gave the press some good headline opportunities. 'Midland Girls haunt coloured men's barracks' blared one provincial newspaper. The *Spectator* in August 1943 was more circumspect, though no less emphatic:

> There is no doubt that girls today are laying themselves out to attract these men, especially overseas troops, and coloured men in particular, who do not understand the fact that white girls are ready and anxious to give themselves, as they undoubtedly do, for money and to have a good time . . . frequently girls of thirteen and fourteen have attached themselves to coloured soldiers.

Explanations are not hard to find. Family life was inevitably shattered by the war with so many males, fathers as well as husbands and fiancés, absent from home, and much routine industrial work to be done. One woman, in answer to Mass Observation, believed that the fascination for blacks came from 'unhappy little girls whose cramped lives at home and work seem to have driven them into a welter of sexual excitement'.

Despite all the adverse publicity (or perhaps because of it) many girls remained faithful to the black Americans right to the end of the war. An incredible scene occurred at Bristol towards the end of August 1945 which must have underlined many of the fears that British citizens had experienced during the war. Hundreds of screaming girls aged seventeen to twenty-five besieged the barracks where black soldiers were preparing to go back to the US, singing a Bing Crosby hit 'Don't Fence Me In'. Barriers were broken down and later the gates of the railway station were rushed. 'To hell with the US Army colour bars! We want our coloured sweethearts' was the cry, while one rain-soaked eighteen-year-old said, 'We intend to give our sweeties a good send-off. And what's more, we intend going to America after them.'

There was no question of the black soldiers being forgotten after their departure. After the war General Weaver recounted a rhetorical question put to him by an English prelate. 'How could you believe, my dear cousins from overseas, that we will ever forget our magnificent amalgamation when we view the great crop of little brunettes you have left behind?' In truth the real problem of the brown babies could not be dealt with so flippantly.

1987

# A BIT OF A WAR
# GOING ON

"EVERY SHILLING'S
A SHELL!"

KENSINGTON WAR WEAPONS WEEK
May 17th — 24th

At precisely fifteen minutes past midnight on 6 June 1944, the greatest armada the world has ever known began its assault on the French coastline. D-Day – the longest day of the year, as luck would have it – had begun. Cornelius Ryan has pieced together a lively, moving and often even comical account of this bizarre and stupendous day, as the following extract will quickly indicate. The notion that a piper should actually splash along the surf, playing 'The Road to the Isles' in that maelstrom, takes a bit of believing – but is absolutely true. And the story of Charles Lynch of Reuters standing on the beach, waving his fist at the pigeons which were to take his messages back to London, but which had turned and fled, takes some believing too. But that he actually shouted 'Traitors! Damn traitors!' is also beyond all reasonable doubt. Ryan prints a fascinating appendix in which he describes the peacetime occupations of the D-Day veterans – British, American and Canadian – whom he interviewed as they were when the book came out in 1960. Thus, telegraphist John Webber, who tells the story of the amazingly blasé Royal Marine captain, had become an ophthalmic optician. Piper W. Millen, the man who played the mad pipes as the men leapt ashore, was a male nurse. Lieutenant Taylor who remarked that this bloody job was impossible – but nevertheless did it – was a tobacconist. Frogman Jones, who told the terrible story of the landing craft that overturned with the men lifted into the air as if in a slow motion cartoon, was by then a building contractor. And so on. All, indeed, were to all intents and purposes now ordinary men; but all men who had lived through an extraordinary day.

## THE LONGEST DAY

### CORNELIUS RYAN

Now on this great and awful morning the last phase of the assault from the sea began. Along the eastern half of the Normandy invasion coast, Lieutenant-General Dempsey's British Second Army was coming ashore, with grimness and gaiety, with pomp and ceremony, with all the studied nonchalance the British traditionally assume in moments of great emotion. They had waited four long years for this day. They were assaulting not just beaches but bitter memories – memories of Munich and Dunkirk, of one hateful and humiliating retreat after another, of countless devastating bombing raids, of dark days when they had stood alone. With them were the Canadians with a score of their own to settle for the bloody losses at Dieppe. And with them, too, were the French, fierce and eager on this homecoming morning.

There was a curious jubilance in the air. As the troops headed towards the beaches the loudspeaker in a rescue launch off Sword roared out 'Roll Out the Barrel'. From a rocket-firing barge off Gold came the strains of 'We Don't Know Where We're Going'. Canadians going to Juno heard the rasping notes of a bugle blaring across the water. Some men were even singing. Marine Denis Lovell remembers that 'the boys were standing up, singing all the usual Army and Navy songs'. And Lord Lovat's 1st Special Service Brigade commandos, spruce and resplendent in their green berets (the commandos refused to wear tin helmets), were serenaded into battle by the eerie wailing of the bagpipes. As their landing-boats drew abreast of Admiral Vian's flagship HMS *Scylla*, the commandos gave the 'thumbs-up' salute. Looking down on them, eighteen-year-old Able Seaman Ronald Northwood thought they were 'the finest set of chaps I ever came across'.

Even the obstacles and the enemy fire now lacing out at the boats were viewed with a certain detachment by many men. On one LCT, Telegraphist John Webber watched a Royal Marine captain study the maze of mined obstacles clotting the coastline, then remark casually to the skipper, 'I say, old man, you really must get my chaps on shore, there's a good fellow.' Aboard another landing-craft a 50th Division major stared thoughtfully at the round Teller mines clearly visible on top of the obstacles and said to the coxswain, 'For Christ's sake, don't knock those bloody coconuts down or we'll all get a free trip to hell.' One boatload of 48th Royal Marine commandos were met by heavy machine-gun fire off Juno and men dived for cover behind the deck superstructure. Not the adjutant, Captain Daniel Flunder. He tucked his swagger stick under his arm and calmly paraded up and down the foredeck. 'I thought,' he explained later, 'it was the thing to do.' (While he was doing it, a bullet ploughed through his map case.) And in a landing-craft charging for Sword Major C. K. 'Banger' King, just as he had promised, was reading *Henry V*. Amid the roar of the diesels, the hissing of the spray and the sound of gunfire, King spoke into the loud-hailer, 'And gentlemen in England now a-bed/Shall think themselves accurs'd they were not here . . . .'

Some men could hardly wait for the fighting to begin. Two Irish sergeants, James Percival 'Paddy' de Lacy, who had toasted De Valera hours before for 'keepin' us out of the war', and his buddy, Paddy McQuaid, stood at the ramps of an LST and, fortified by good Royal Navy rum, solemnly contemplated the troops. 'De Lacy,' said McQuaid, staring hard at the Englishmen all around them, 'don't you think now that some of these boys seem a wee bit timid?' As the beaches neared, De Lacy called out to his men, 'All right, now! Here we go! At the run!' The LST ground to a halt. As the men ran out, McQuaid yelled at the shell-smoked shore-line, 'Come out, ye bastards, and fight us now!' Then he disappeared under water. An instant later he came up spluttering. 'Oh, the evil of it!' he bellowed. 'Tryin' to drown me before I even get up on the beach!'

Off Sword, Private Hubert Victor Baxter of the British 3rd Division revved up his Bren gun carrier and, peering over the tip of the armoured plating, plunged into the water. Sitting exposed on the raised seat above him was his bitter enemy, Sergeant 'Dinger' Bell, with whom Baxter had been fighting for months. Bell yelled, 'Baxter, wind up that seat so you can see where you're going!' Baxter shouted back, 'Not bloody likely! I can see!' Then, as they swept up the beach, the sergeant, caught up in the excitement of the moment, resorted to the very thing that had begun the feud in the first place. He slammed down his fist again and again on Baxter's helmet and roared, 'Bash on! Bash on!'

As the commandos touched down on Sword, Lord Lovat's piper, William Millin, plunged off his landing-craft into water up to his armpits. He could see smoke piling up from the beach ahead and hear the crump of exploding mortar shells. As Millin floundered towards the shore, Lovat shouted at him, 'Give us "Highland Laddie", man!' Waist-deep in the water, Millin put the mouthpiece to his lips and splashed on through the surf, the pipes keening crazily. At the water's edge, oblivious to the gunfire, he halted and, parading up and down along the beach, piped the commandos ashore. The men streamed past him, and mingling with the whine of bullets and the screams of shells came the wild skirl of the pipes as Millin now played 'The Road to the Isles'. 'That's the stuff, Jock,' yelled a commando. Said another, 'Get down, you mad bugger.'

All along Sword, Juno and Gold – for almost twenty miles, from Ouistreham near the mouth of the Orne to the village of Le Hamel on the west – the British swarmed ashore. The beaches were choked with landing-craft disgorging troops, and nearly everywhere along the assault area the high seas and underwater obstacles were causing more trouble than the enemy.

The first men in had been the frogmen – 120 underwater demolition experts whose job it was to cut thirty-yard gaps through the obstacles. They had only twenty minutes to work before the first waves bore down upon them. The obstacles were formidable – at places more densely sown than in any other part of the Normandy invasion area. Sergeant Peter Henry Jones of the Royal Marines swam into a maze of steel pylons, gates and hedgehogs and concrete cones. In the thirty-yard gap Jones had to blow he found twelve major obstacles, some of them fourteen feet long. When another frogman, Lieutenant John B. Taylor of the Royal Navy, saw the fantastic array of underwater defences surrounding him, he yelled out to his unit leader that 'this bloody job is impossible'. But he did not give it up. Working under fire, Taylor, like the other frogmen, methodically set to work. They blew the obstacles singly, because they were too large to blow up in groups. Even as they worked, amphibious tanks came swimming in among them, followed almost immediately by first-wave troops. Frogmen rushing out of the water saw landing-craft, turned sideways by the heavy seas, crash into the obstacles. Mines exploded, steel spikes and hedgehogs ripped along the hulls, and up and down the beaches landing-craft began to flounder. The waters offshore became a junkyard as boats piled up on top of one another. Telegraphist Webber remembers thinking that 'the beaching is a tragedy'. As his craft came in Webber saw 'LCT's stranded and ablaze, twisted masses of metal on the shore, burning tanks and bulldozers'. And as one LCT passed them, heading for the open sea, Webber was horrified to see 'its well deck engulfed in a terrifying fire'.

On Gold Beach, where frogman Jones was now working with the Royal Engineers trying to clear the obstacles, he saw an LCT approach with troops standing on the deck ready to disembark. Caught by a sudden swell, the craft swerved sideways, lifted and crashed down on a series of mined steel triangles. Jones saw it explode with a shattering blast. It reminded him of a 'slow-motion cartoon – the men, standing to attention, shot up into the air as though lifted by a water spout . . . at the top of the spout bodies and parts of bodies spread like drops of water.'

Boat after boat got hung up on the obstacles. Of the sixteen landing-craft carrying the 47th Royal Marine commandos in to Gold Beach, four boats were lost, eleven were damaged and beached and only one made it back to the parent ship. Sergeant Donald Gardner of the 47th and his men were dumped into the water about fifty yards from shore. They lost all their equipment and had to swim in under machine-gun fire. As they struggled in the water, Gardner heard someone say, 'Perhaps we're intruding, this seems to be a private beach.' Going into Juno the 48th Royal Marine commandos not only ran foul of the obstacles, they also came under intense mortar fire. Lieutenant Michael Aldworth and about forty of his men crouched down in the forward hold of their LCT as shells exploded all about them. Aldworth shoved his head up to see what was happening and saw men from the after hold running along the deck. Aldworth's men yelled out, 'How soon do we get out of here?' Aldworth called back, 'Wait a minute, chaps. It's not our turn.' There was a moment's pause and then someone inquired, 'Well, just how long do you think it will be, old man? The ruddy hold is filling full of water.'

The men from the sinking LCT were quickly picked up by a variety of craft. There were so many boats around, Aldworth recalls, that 'it was rather like hailing a taxi in Bond Street'. Some men were delivered safely on to the beaches; others were taken out to a Canadian destroyer, but fifty commandos discovered themselves on an LCT which had unloaded its tanks and was under instructions to proceed directly back to England. Nothing the infuriated men could say or do would persuade the skipper to change his course. One officer, Major de Stackpoole, had been wounded in the thigh on the run-in, but on hearing the LCT's destination he roared, 'Nonsense! You're all bloody well mad!' With that he dived overboard and swam for shore.

For most men the obstacles proved to be the toughest part of the assault. Once they were through these defences, troops found the enemy opposition along the three beaches spotty – fierce in some sectors, light and even non-existent in others. On the western half of Gold men of the 1st Hampshire Regiment were almost decimated as they waded through water that was at places three to six feet deep. Struggling through the heaving sea line abreast, they were caught by heavy mortar bursts and criss-crossing machine-gun fire that poured out from the village of Le Hamel, a stronghold occupied by the tough German 352nd Division. Men went down one after another. Private

Charles Wilson heard a surprised voice say, 'I've bought it, mates!' Turning, Wilson saw the man, a strange look of disbelief on his face, slide beneath the water without another word. Wilson ploughed on. He had been machine-gunned in the water before – except that at Dunkirk he had been going the other way. Private George Stunell saw men going down all around him too. He came across a Bren gun carrier standing in about three feet of water, its motor running and the driver 'frozen at the wheel, too terrified to drive the machine on to the shore'. Stunell pushed him to one side and with machine-gun bullets whipping all around drove up on to the beach. Stunell was elated to have made it. Then he suddenly pitched headlong to the ground; a bullet had slammed into a tin of cigarettes in his tunic pocket with terrific impact. Minutes later he discovered that he was bleeding from wounds in his back and ribs. The same bullet had passed cleanly through his body.

It would take the Hampshires almost eight hours to knock out the Le Hamel defences, and at the end of D-Day their casualties would total almost two hundred. Strangely, apart from the obstacles, troops landing on either side encountered little trouble. There were casualties, but they were fewer than had been anticipated. On the left of the Hampshires, men of the 1st Dorset Regiment were off the beach in forty minutes. Next to them the Green Howards landed with such dash and determination that they moved inland and captured their first objective in less than an hour. Company Sergeant-Major Stanley Hollis, killer of ninety Germans up to now, waded ashore and promptly captured a pillbox single-handed. The nerveless Hollis, using grenades and his Sten gun, killed two and captured twenty in the start of a day that would see him kill another ten.

On the beach to the right of Le Hamel it was so quiet that some men were disappointed. Geoffrey Leach of the RAMC saw troops and vehicles pouring ashore and found that there was nothing 'for the medicos to do but help unload ammunition'. To Marine Denis Lovell, the landing was like 'just another exercise back home'. His unit, the 47th Royal Marine commandos, moved quickly off the beach, avoided all enemy contact, turned west and set out on a seven-mile forced march to link up with the Americans near Port-en-Bessin. They expected to see the first Yanks from Omaha Beach around noon.

But this was not to be – unlike the Americans on Omaha, who were still pinned down by the rugged German 352nd Division, the British and the Canadians were more than a match for the tired and inferior 716th Division with its impressed Russian and Polish 'volunteers'. In addition, the British had made the fullest possible use of amphibious tanks and armoured vehicles. Some, like the 'flail' tanks, lashed the ground ahead of them with chains that detonated mines. Other armoured vehicles carried small bridges or great reels of steel matting which, when unrolled, made a temporary roadway over soft ground. One group even carried giant bundles of logs for use as stepping-stones over walls or to fill in anti-tank ditches. These inventions, and the extra-long period of bombardment that the British beaches had received, gave the assaulting troops additional protection.

Still some strong pockets of resistance were encountered. On one half of Juno Beach men of the Canadian 3rd Division fought through lines of pillboxes and trenches, through fortified houses, and from street to street in the town of Courseulles before finally breaking through and pushing inland. But all resistance there would be mopped up within two hours. In many places it was being done with quickness and dispatch. Able Seaman Edward Ashworth, off an LCT which had brought troops and tanks in to the Courseulles beach, saw Canadian soldiers march six German prisoners behind a dune some distance away. Ashworth thought that this was his chance to get a German helmet for a souvenir. He ran up the beach and in the dunes discovered the six Germans 'all lying crumpled up'. Ashworth bent over one of the bodies, still determined to get a helmet. But he found 'the man's throat was cut – every one of them had had his throat cut', and Ashworth 'turned away, sick as a parrot. I didn't get my tin hat.'

Sergeant Paddy de Lacy, also in the Courseulles area, had captured twelve Germans who had come almost eagerly out of a trench, their arms raised high above their heads: De Lacy stood staring at them for a moment; he had lost a brother in North Africa. Then he said to the soldier with him, 'Look at the super-blokes – just look at them. Here, take them out of my sight.' He walked away to make himself a cup of tea to soothe his anger. While he was heating a canteen of water over a Sterno can a young officer 'with the down still on his chin' walked over and said sternly, 'Now look here, Sergeant, this is no time to be making tea.' De Lacy looked up and, as patiently as his twenty-one years of Army service would allow, replied, 'Sir, we are not playing at soldiers now – this is real war. Why don't you come back in five minutes and have a nice cup of tea?' The officer did.

Even as the fighting was going on in the Courseulles area, men, guns, tanks, vehicles and supplies were pouring ashore. The movement inland was smoothly and efficiently handled. The beachmaster, Captain Colin Maud, allowed no loiterers on Juno. Most men, like Sub-Lieutenant John Beynon, were a little taken aback at the sight of the tall, bearded officer with the imposing bearing and the booming voice who met each new contingent with the same greeting, 'I'm chairman of the reception committee and of this party, so get a move on.' Few men cared to argue with the custodian of Juno Beach; Beynon remembers he had a cudgel in one hand and the other held tight to the leash of a fierce-looking Alsatian dog. The effect was all he could have hoped for. INS correspondent Joseph Willicombe recalls a futile argument he had with the beachmaster. Willicombe, who had landed in the first wave of Canadians, had been assured that he would be allowed to send a twenty-five-word message via the beachmaster's two-way radio to the command ship for transmission to the US. Apparently no one had bothered to so inform Maud. Staring stonily at Willicombe, he growled, 'My dear chap, there's a bit of a war going on here.' Willicombe had to admit that the beachmaster had a point.

Correspondents on Juno had no communications until Ronald Clark of United Press came ashore with two baskets of carrier pigeons. The correspondents quickly wrote brief stories, placed them in the plastic capsules attached to the pigeons' legs and released the birds. Unfortunately the pigeons were so overloaded that most of them fell back to earth. Some, however, circled overhead for a few moments – and then headed towards the German lines. Charles Lynch of Reuter's stood on the beach, waved his fist at the pigeons and roared, 'Traitors! Damned traitors!' Four pigeons, Willicombe says, 'proved loyal.' They actually got to the Ministry of Information in London within a few hours.

All along Juno the Canadians suffered. Of the three British beaches theirs was the bloodiest. Rough seas had delayed the landings. Razor-edged reefs on the eastern half of the beach and barricades of obstacles created havoc among the assault craft. Worse, the naval and air bombardment had failed to knock out the coastal defences or had missed them altogether, and in some sectors troops came ashore without the protection of tanks. Opposite the towns of Bernières and St Aubin-sur-Mer men of the Canadian 8th Brigade and the 48th Marine commandos came in under heavy fire. One company lost nearly half its men in the dash up the beach. Artillery fire from St Aubin-sur-Mer was so concentrated that it led to one particular horror on the beach. A tank, buttoned up for protection and thrashing wildly up the beach to get out of the line of fire, ran over the dead and the dying. Captain Daniel Flunder of the commandos, looking back from the sand dunes, saw what was happening and oblivious of the bursting shells ran back down the beach shouting at the top of his voice, 'They're my men!' The enraged Flunder beat on the tank's hatch with his swagger stick, but the tank kept on going. Pulling the pin on a grenade, Flunder blew one of the tank's tracks off. It wasn't until the startled tankers opened the hatch that they realized what had happened.

Although the fighting was bitter while it lasted, the Canadians and the commandos got off the Bernières–St Aubin beaches in less than thirty minutes and plunged inland. Follow-up waves experienced little difficulty and within an hour it was so quiet on the beaches that Leading Aircraftman John Murphy of a barrage balloon unit found that 'the worst enemy was the sand lice that drove us crazy as the tide came in.' Behind the beaches street fighting would occupy troops for nearly two hours, but this section of Juno, like the western half, was now secure.

The 48th commandos fought their way through St Aubin-sur-Mer and, turning east, headed along the coast. They had a particularly tough assignment. Juno lay seven miles away from Sword Beach. To close this gap and link up the two beaches, the 48th was to make a forced march towards Sword. Another commando unit, the 41st, was to land at Lion-sur-Mer on the edge of Sword Beach, swing right and head west. Both forces were expected to join up within a few hours at a point roughly half-way between the two beach-heads. That was the plan, but almost simultaneously the commandos ran into trouble. At Langrune, about a mile east of Juno, men of the 48th found themselves in a fortified area of the town that defied penetration. Every house was a strongpoint. Mines, barbed wire and concrete walls sealed off the streets. From these positions heavy fire greeted the invaders. Without tanks or artillery the 48th was stopped cold.

On Sword, six miles away, the 41st after a rough landing turned west and headed through Lion-sur-Mer. They were told by the French that the German garrison had pulled out. The information seemed correct – until the commandos reached the edge of the town. There artillery fire knocked out three supporting tanks. Sniper and machine-gun fire came from innocent-looking villas that had been converted into blockhouses, and a rain of mortar shells fell among the commandos. Like the 48th the 41st came to a standstill.

Now, although no one in the Allied High Command knew about it yet, a vital gap six miles wide existed in the beach-head – a gap through which Rommel's tanks, if they moved fast enough, could reach the coast and, by attacking left and right along the shore, could roll up the British landings.

Lion-sur-Mer was one of the few real trouble-spots on Sword. Of the three British beaches, Sword was expected to be the most heavily defended. Troops had been briefed that casualties would be very high. Private John Gale of the 1st South Lancashire Regiment was 'cold-bloodedly told that all of us in the first wave would probably be wiped out'. The picture was painted in even blacker terms to the commandos. It was drilled into them that 'no matter what happens we must get on the beaches, for there will be no evacuation . . . no going back'. The 4th commandos expected to be 'written off on the beaches', as Corporal James Colley and Private Stanley Stewart remember, for they were told their casualties would run as 'high as eighty-four per cent'. And the men who were to land ahead of the infantry in amphibious tanks were warned that 'even those of you who reach the beach can expect sixty per cent casualties'. Private Christopher Smith, driver of an amphibious tank, thought his chances of survival were slim. Rumour had increased the casualty figure to ninety per cent and Smith was inclined to believe it, for as his unit left England men saw canvas screens being set up on Gosport Beach and 'it was said that these were being erected to sort out the returned dead'.

For a while it looked as though the worst of the predictions might come true. In some sectors first-wave troops were heavily machine-gunned and mortared. In the Ouistreham half of Sword, men of the 2nd East Yorkshire Regiment lay dead and dying from the water's edge all the way up the beach. Although nobody would ever know how many men were lost in this bloody dash from the boats, it seems likely that the East Yorks suffered most of their two hundred D-Day casualties in these first few minutes. The shock of seeing these crumpled khaki forms seemed to confirm the most dreadful fears of follow-up troops. Some saw 'bodies stacked like cordwood' and counted 'more than 150 dead'. Private John Mason of the 4th commandos, who landed half an hour later, was shocked to find himself 'running through piles of dead infantry who had been knocked down like nine-pins'. And Corporal Fred Mears of Lord Lovat's commandos was 'aghast to see the East Yorks lying in bunches. . . . It would probably never have happened had they spread out.' As he charged up the beach determined to make 'Jesse Owens look like a turtle', he remembers cynically thinking that 'they would know better the next time'.

Although bloody, the beach fight was brief. Except for initial losses, the assault on Sword went forward speedily, meeting little sustained opposition. The landings were so successful that many men coming in minutes after the first wave were surprised to find only sniper fire. They saw the beaches shrouded in smoke, nursing orderlies working among the wounded, flail tanks detonating mines, burning tanks and vehicles littering the shore-line, and sand shooting up from occasional shell bursts, but nowhere was there the slaughter they had expected. To these tense troops, primed to expect a holocaust, the beaches were an anticlimax.

In many places along Sword there was even a bank holiday atmosphere. Here and there along the seafront little groups of elated French waved to the troops and yelled, '*Vive les Anglais!*' Royal Marine Signalman Leslie Ford noticed a Frenchman 'practically on the beach itself who appeared to be giving a running commentary on the battle to a group of townspeople'. Ford thought they were crazy, for the beaches and the foreshore were still infested with mines and under occasional fire. But it was happening everywhere. Men were hugged and kissed and embraced by the French, who seemed quite unaware of the dangers around them. Corporal Harry Norfield and Gunner Ronald Allen were astonished to see 'a person all dressed up in splendid regalia and wearing a bright brass helmet making his way down to the beaches'. He turned out to be the mayor of Colleville-sur-Orne, a small village about a mile inland, who had decided to come down and greet the invasion forces.

Some of the Germans seemed no less eager than the French to greet the troops. Sapper Henry Jennings had no sooner disembarked than he was 'confronted with a collection of Germans – most of them Russian and Polish "volunteers" – anxious to surrender'. But Captain Gerald Norton of a Royal Artillery unit got the biggest surprise of all: he was met 'by four Germans with their suitcases packed, who appeared to be awaiting the first available transportation out of France'.

Out of the confusion on Gold, Juno and Sword, the British and the Canadians swarmed inland. The advance was business-like and efficient and there was a kind of grandeur about it all. As troops fought into towns and villages examples of heroism and courage were all around them. Some remember a Royal Marine commando major, both arms gone, who urged his men along by shouting at them to 'get inland, chaps, before Fritz gets wise to this party'. Others remember the cocky cheerfulness and bright faith of the wounded as they waited for the field ambulance men to catch up with them. Some waved as the troops passed, others yelled, 'See you in Berlin, mates!' Gunner Ronald Allen would never forget one soldier who had been badly wounded in the stomach. He was propped up against a wall calmly reading a book.

Now speed was essential. From Gold troops headed for the cathedral town of Bayeux, roughly seven miles inland. From Juno the Canadians drove for the Bayeux-Caen highway and Carpiquet Airport, about ten miles away. And out of Sword the British headed for the city of Caen. They were so sure of capturing this objective that even correspondents, as the London *Daily Mail's* Noel Monks was later to recall, were told that a briefing would be held 'at point X in Caen at 4 p.m.' Lord Lovat's commandos marching out of the Sword area wasted no time. They were going to the relief of General Gale's embattled 6th Airborne troops holding the Orne and Caen bridges four miles away and 'Shimy' Lovat had promised Gale that he would be there 'sharp at noon'. Behind a tank at the head of the column Lord Lovat's piper Bill Millin played 'Blue Bonnets over the Border'.

For ten Britishers, the crews of the midget submarines X20 and X23, D-Day was over. Off Sword Beach Lieutenant George Honour's X23 threaded through waves of landing-craft streaming steadily in towards the shore. In the heavy seas, with her flat superstructure almost awash, all that could be seen of the X23 were her identifying flags whipping in the wind. Coxswain Charles Wilson on an LCT 'almost fell overboard with surprise' when he saw what appeared to be 'two large flags apparently unsupported' moving steadily towards him through the water. As the X23 passed, Wilson couldn't help wondering 'what the devil a midget sub had to do with the invasion'. Ploughing by, the X23 headed out into the transport area in search of her tow-ship, a trawler with the appropriate name of *En Avant*. Operation Gambit was over. Lieutenant Honour and his four-man crew were going home.

The men for whom they had marked the beaches marched into France. Everyone was optimistic. The Atlantic Wall had been breached. Now the big question was, how fast would the Germans recover from the shock?

1982

---

The Chaplains' Department had the highest casualty percentage in the British Army. One padre in ten would be a casualty before the war was over. These were the sobering statistics the Reverend R.G. Strutt took with him as he left training centre. The reason was simple: army chaplains would bring Christ's message where it mattered most – in the front line. Strutt was gazetted to an assault division preparing for D-Day, went through battle school with them, and landed with them in France at 4 a.m. on the morning of 6 June 1944. The Regimental Aid Post was set up in a coach-house in the middle of an orchard.

## THE PARSON IN BATTLEDRESS

### REV. R.G. STRUTT

Our attack began early in the morning and I began work with the doctor at about 4.30 a.m. We worked hard all the morning, writing casualty cards, making sweet tea, bandaging and noting the dose and time of administering drugs. The counter-attack came and was repulsed and we worked on hard all the afternoon. I then got down to the gruesome business of burying the dead. The bodies were brought to a coach-house, and with a couple of men I searched them for their personal effects. These were put into canvas bags with one of the identity discs. Graves had been dug, and with a handful of terribly tired men I conducted the burial services. At 1.30 the following morning I was filling in the last grave. When it was light again I erected the crosses and forwarded the details with the map references on triplicate forms to the Graves Commission, who would, months later, locate the graves, open permanent cemeteries and erect permanent memorials. Bodies of others who had been missing were located during the next few days on the scene of the fighting, and these were collected, identified and given proper burial. The number was heartbreaking. It included the man whom I had looked upon as my particular pal in the battalion. Caen was a great victory. At what cost – and now, as the Peace Conference fights its way through amendments, to what purpose?

By now the routine was sweat, blood, weather, mortar fire, broken sleep and acute discomfort. We hung on doggedly, hoping to be given a break soon with a hot shower. The shower and a night's sleep did materialize but we were soon back again suffering under a hail of fire from mortar, 88 and 'moaning minnies'.

We moved to a house with a concrete cellar at one stage of the advance. The 'recce' party did not speak too highly of it. There was blood all over the walls and bodies in the gardens. It wasn't so bad. I went on ahead with a corporal before the main party arrived and we found that the blood on the walls was merely remnants of a couple of chickens which had probably been too near a grenade. There were feathers as well as blood. The dead German on the garden path was not a pretty sight – a hand grenade had exploded near him and he was somewhat untidy. We were careful about moving him because of experience of cunning booby traps. There were electric cables hanging loose from the house and so we tied a loose end to his foot, went upstairs and, from the shelter of the house wall, tugged the wire until we had moved him his own length. He did not explode. We wrapped him in a curtain and made a slit trench into a grave for him. We laid our own dead ready for removal to a burial ground and then swept the house ready for the Regimental Aid Post to move in.

While my battalion was holding on this sector I managed to get some days at B echelon writing letters to next of kin. My biggest batch was 93 letters.

After nearly two months of pretty constant contact with the enemy we passed into reserve. Glorious relaxation! The library which I had bought in London was available and I was able to hold Communions and services in comparative peace away from the smell of death, decayed cattle and the nausea of wet khaki.

Being in reserve was a limited paradise and soon we were wanted again. We moved forward to some wooded country near Vire, set up the Regimental Aid Post in the lee of an inland cliff, and before long received a most unpleasant barrage of fire. This went on spasmodically during the afternoon and at about 5.30 the Aid Post was hit. The doctor and his orderlies were all hit except two and myself. Although none was serious, it did mean evacuation. The doctor would hang on until a reinforcement could be procured. I set about the usual routine for evacuation and prepared the jeep for a couple of stretcher cases and a 'walking-wounded' man. I was in the open on my way to one of the wounded fellows when I heard the next lot coming. I could do nothing; there was no cover; an explosion, a shower of dust, 'my head', pain – I was conscious but losing grip. So this is what death may be like! A crisis called for a prayer. All crises do and it was quite natural to pray. 'Whatever happens Lord, I am with you.'

The doctor crawled to me and got me into a trench. My head was covered in field dressings. I felt sick. Consciousness was coming and going. The jeep had not left and another stretcher was put aboard. I was on it. With my head cradled in the arms of a fellow who had become a Christian under my ministry, I began the long journey back to the base hospital. On 6 August 1944, two months after landing, I was put aboard a Dakota for the flight to England. Hit on Sunday, and operated upon on Tuesday, given penicillin drip and every attention, my paralysed body came back to life. After a short spell of light duty, I was invalided out on the day before VE-Day 1945.

'The Chaplains' Department has the highest casualty percentage in the British Army and one out of every ten of you will be a casualty before the war is over. . . .' I wonder who the others were!

1964

---

*While the Allies fought desperately for a foothold on the continent of Europe, the home front had to face a new terror.*

*Of all the calamities that befell London during the war few had more emotional clout than the destruction of the Guards Chapel by a flying bomb on Sunday, 18 June 1944. It was not a particularly beautiful building, nor even a very old one, but it was a living embodiment of the Guards mystique and here, in peacetime, hung their colours, some shrouded in net, dating back to the days of the Crimea. Sunday morning matins there, as we read, drew many worshippers who were not actually part of the Guards establishment and none had a more poignant story to tell than the young ATS subaltern Elizabeth*

Sheppard-Jones, who made her way across the park to worship there that morning.

She was never to walk again. Her testimony carries across the decades: 'There was a noise so loud it was as if all the waters and winds in the world had come together in mighty conflict and the Guards Chapel collapsed upon us in a bellow of bricks and mortar.'

## THE GUARDS CHAPEL

### NORMAN LONGMATE

Sunday morning matins at the Guards Chapel was a fashionable occasion, but not restricted to what was later called 'the Establishment'. The nurses of St Giles Hospital, Camberwell, frequently joined the congregation, though that morning they were too busy coping with flying-bomb casualties. The Chaplain General to the Forces had preached there two months earlier on Easter Sunday. Many of the congregation had noticed that 'his voice shook a little as he spoke to them of "our loved chapel"' and afterwards he had 'confided to a friend, his impression of a strange unfamiliar sadness and doom over-shadowing the sacred precincts.'

Among those present on the morning of Sunday, 18 June 1944, was a young ATS subaltern, Elizabeth Sheppard-Jones, who had walked across the park to the service with a girlfriend.

We sat near the back of the chapel and watched the people come in . . . I . . . remember some of the people I saw, in particular a young Canadian Lieutenant who eagerly surveyed his surroundings as if to memorize the details that he might write them down in his next letter home. . . . In the gallery . . . a band of Guardsmen began to play . . . instead of an organ. . . . We sang the opening hymn. My mind must have wandered during the reading of the first lesson . . . I dare say I was thinking about my forthcoming leave. . . . 'Here endeth the first lesson,' the Guards' colonel who had been reading it must have said. The congregation rose to its feet. In the distance hummed faintly the engine of a flying bomb. 'We praise thee, O God: we acknowledge Thee to be the Lord,' we, the congregation, sang. The dull buzz became a roar, through which our voices could now only faintly be heard. 'All the earth doth worship Thee: the Father everlasting.' The roar stopped abruptly as the engine cut out. . . . The Te Deum soared again into the silence. 'To Thee all Angels cry aloud, the Heavens, and all the Powers therein.' Then there was a noise so loud it was as if all the waters and the winds in the world had come together in mighty conflict and the Guards Chapel collapsed upon us in a bellow of bricks and mortar . . . One moment I was singing the Te Deum and the next I lay in dust and blackness, aware of one thing only – that I had to go on breathing.

While Miss Sheppard-Jones was struggling to free herself, Dr R. V. Jones was hurrying to the site down Birdcage Walk.

I had . . . been used to the flying bomb. I knew its warhead was going to be about a ton. I knew what a ton of high explosive could do. . . . [But] it struck me then how very different the academic appreciation of explosions was from the actuality. The Guards Chapel was about 150 yards from my office and by the time I'd got down to the . . . Chapel they were just carrying out the first dead. . . . One lasting impression I had was the whole of Birdcage Walk was a sea of fresh pine tree leaves, the trees had all been stripped and you could hardly see a speck of asphalt for hundreds of yards.

Also rapidly on the scene was the Chief Warden of Westminster, who had been nearby at the Rutherford Street incident:

The whole floor was covered by debris, which blocked the portico entrance; on both sides the debris rose to ten feet, lessening in the centre. Apart from some movement at the east (altar) end there was a ghostly stillness over the whole scene. I appreciated at once that the incident was a rescue job from first to last. Doubling the length of the barrack square to the officers' mess, I spoke over the telephone to the Deputy Heavy Rescue Officer at Control, gave him a word picture of the scene and suggested Heavy and Light Rescue Parties, mobile cranes and ambulances. Two senior Rescue Officers with parties, ambulances and cranes were quickly on the scene and rescue operations then put in hand continued without a break for 48 hours.

So far the casualties at most incidents had proved less than expected – but not this time, as William Sansom graphically described:

To a first aid party that soon arrived the scene in its subsiding dust looked vast and boxlike, impenetrable; sloping masses of the grey walls and roof shut in the wounded; the doors were blocked; the roof crammed down; it was difficult to find any entrance; but there was one – behind the altar. From then on it became a matter for nurses and doctors to scramble up and down and in between the large intractable slopes and walls of chunked concrete – the same as in a low-tide rock formation, but here gritty and powdered everywhere with the lung-choking dust. These rocks of material had to be man-handled off casualties. While doctors were plugging morphia, and nurses and first aid personnel were feeding bicarbonate solution and wrapping on . . . dressings, all rescue services, together with soldiers from the barracks . . ., the King's Guard had just been dismounted and were waiting for dismissal in the barrack square . . ., began prising up the debris-blocks and carrying out those freed.

Among those still lying beneath the debris was Elizabeth Sheppard-Jones:

I felt no pain, I was scarcely aware of the chunks of massed grey concrete that had piled on top of me, nor did I realize that this was why breathing was so difficult. My whole being was concentrated in one tremendous effort of taking in long struggling breaths and then letting them struggle out again. It may have been an hour later, perhaps two or three or more, that . . . I was suddenly aware that somewhere far above me, above the black emptiness, there were people, living helpful people whose voices reached me, dim and disembodied as in a dream. 'Please, please, I'm here,' I said, and I went on saying it until my voice was hoarse and my throat ached with the dust that poured down it. . . . Someone frantically scraped away the rubble from around my head. . . . Somewhere not far away from me someone was screaming, screaming, screaming, like an animal caught in a trap. . . . My eyes rested with horror on a blood-stained body that, had my hands been free, I could have reached out and touched . . . the body of a young soldier whose eyes stared unseeingly at the sky. . . . I tried to convince myself that this was truly a nightmare, one from which I was bound soon to wake up. I think I must have been given a morphia injection for I still felt no pain, but I did begin to have an inkling that I was badly injured. I turned my freed head towards a Guardsman who was helping with the rescue work, and hysterically I cried out: 'How do I look? Tell me how I look!' . . . 'Madam,' he said, 'you look wonderful to me!'

Much later, at St Mary's Hospital, Miss Sheppard-Jones learned the truth. 'My spine was fractured and my spinal cord damaged . . . I was paralysed from the waist down.' That morning's walk across St James's Park had been the last she was ever to take. It was even longer before she knew the fate of her friend, whose father after a long search found his daughter's body 'on a mortuary slab. . . . Her neck had been broken, probably by the same piece of masonry that had broken my back.'

Sensibly enough, lunch was served as usual in the officers' mess, but in an atmosphere of deep gloom. 'One was so anxiously looking all the time at the door to see who was coming in,' remembers one man who had missed the service, thanks to an unexpected duty. He waited in vain for the friend beside whom he should have sat in chapel. 'No one had seen him that morning. . . . Had he been there? He had.' Long before the final casualty figures were known, news of the disaster had spread through London. The Prime Minister had spent the morning in bed at Chequers working on his boxes, but his wife, who had been to London to visit their daughter Mary, serving with an anti-aircraft battery in Hyde

Park, returned with the sad news. 'The battery has been in action,' Mrs Churchill told her husband, 'and the Guards Chapel is destroyed.' 'I gave orders at once,' Churchill later wrote, 'that the Commons should retire again to the Church House, whose modern steel structure offered somewhat more protection than the Palace of Westminster.' Others were equally alarmed by what had happened. Every top civil servant or society hostess knew someone in the Brigade who might have been at Wellington Barracks that morning. Mrs Robert Henrey, remembering the two young officers she had met on the train from Sevenoaks the previous evening, observed how 'the news of this catastrophe . . . cast a gloom over London, for it was the first major tragedy occasioned by this new weapon in the heart of the town.' 'All day,' wrote Jane Gordon, 'we kept hearing of more people we knew who had been killed,' and around 2.30 she was telephoned by the distraught wife of the young officer, so proud of being promoted major, with whom they had played bridge only two nights before. Her reaction, even after visiting Wellington Barracks for herself, was incredulity. 'This couldn't have happened to Dick. Why . . . we four had shared so many Blitz evenings . . . . It was only yesterday we were laughing on top of a bus.' But happened it had, for at last on Tuesday night their dead friend's body was recovered, one of the last bodies to be dragged from the rubble.

The Guards Chapel incident was by far the worst of the whole flying-bomb campaign. One hundred and nineteen people, mainly servicemen, were killed, and 102 seriously injured, some of whom later died; 39 others escaped with minor injuries.

Everyone agreed that the Civil Defence services had worked superbly well, and there had been no interruption from curious passers-by or anxious relations, since, as the chief warden of Westminster explained a year later in *ARP Review*, 'the barrack railings and Military Guard formed an effective barrier against the crowds which collected . . . and the barrack square was an ideal place for parking vehicles and loading casualties.' Civilians and military had worked side by side in harmony. 'The Incident Officer's headquarters and later the Incident Enquiry Point . . . were set up in the Guardroom and during darkness Royal Engineers and NFS supplied lighting over the whole incident.'

Among those who heard of the destruction of the Guards Chapel late that day was the writer James Lees-Milne, who was told of it at his club.

After dining we walked through Queen Anne's Gate, where a lot of windows with old crinkly blown glass panes had been broken. In St James's Park crowds of people were looking at the Guards Chapel across Birdcage Walk, now roped off. I could see nothing but gaunt walls standing, and gaping windows. No roof at all. While I watched four stretcher-bearers carry a body under a blanket, the siren went, and everyone scattered. I felt suddenly sick. Then a rage of fury welled inside me. For sheer damnable devilry what could be worse than this awful instrument?'                                           1981

The V1 struck down the august and the obscure with insane impartiality. Lotte Kramer was born in Germany of Jewish parents and was brought to England in 1939 by the Quakers. During the war she worked in a laundry, where no doubt she met Cissie, or someone very much like her.

## CISSIE

### LOTTE KRAMER

Her name was Cissie
And she mangled sheets,
Her hair was peroxide yellow;
She crooned about love
With a smoker's cough
While the sweat slipped down her belly.
She could tell a tale
Full of sex and ale
As the mangle wheeled her story;
And her laughter roared
As her bosom soared
When she slapped the sheets to glory.
In a war-time pub
Some GI pick-up
Cheered the Monday morning queues,
But below her pride
Of the good-time night,
Were a lonely woman's blues.
For once in a while
A black eye would smile
From her puffy face, full of sweat;
And we knew it meant
Her old man had spent
The infrequent night in her bed.
So she rolled and roared,
As she laughed and whored
Till one day she clocked-in no more:
No GI or mate
Kept her out so late –
But a Buzz-bomb had struck her door.

1974

*Arnhem, the brilliant, unorthodox idea that so nearly came off, provided some of the best writing to come out of the war. The street fighting had an intimacy and ferocity seldom equalled, and the stories that came out of it are better than any fiction. The glider pilot who had a bullet enter through his right temple and exit through his left leaving two neat little holes, but who was nevertheless going on working in the kitchen, and was last seen making rude signs from the back of the ambulance, is rightly described as a miracle man. At the time it was first published in 1945, Arnhem Lift was pseudonymous for security reasons; we now know it was written by a gallant Dutchman called Louis Hagen.*

## ARNHEM LIFT – DIARY OF A GLIDER PILOT

LOUIS HAGEN

Sunday

At stand to, next morning, I was asked about the success of our patrol to Div. HQ. What was meant by this was had we brought back any cigarettes? I was considered a complete failure, and to minimize my humiliation, I suggested that they should try smoking the long leaves which hung from the roof of the outdoor building at the back of our house. These were obviously tobacco leaves. Someone cried out, 'Dutch tobacco! Famous the whole world over!' I thought of the terrible disappointment they would feel after they'd smoked the stuff. Their resentment would come back to roost on me. An argument arose about tobacco in general. Someone said that the really good Dutch tobacco came from the colonies, another said that this grown in Holland was the real stuff. Some claimed they had smoked it already. I left them squabbling, knowing that they would find out only too soon. They started to dry the leaves over an open fire, and soon everyone was rolling the result in the palms of their hands and stuffing their pipes. The kitchen had to be evacuated almost at once, but some enthusiasts, who were suffering particularly, kept on smoking this filthy concoction till our first cigarette issue in Nijmegen.

The small arms fire and sniping this morning was worse than anything we had had before. It was doubly effective now. It came from the row of houses across the plantation, as well as from the wood. Our special enemy was the burnt-out house, directly opposite us. This was a sniper's paradise, and Jerry was using some kind of apparatus to throw hand grenades from behind the house against our façade and barricaded windows. These continuous explosions right under our noses were really very uncomfortable. Our barricades of the windows and doors had to be re-done every time the blast of a grenade threw them back into the room. There is nothing more irritating than a grenade bouncing into a furnished room and rolling perhaps under the bed, where it can't be fished out and thrown back before it explodes.

The solution to our troubles would have been simply to knock the building flat, but we had no mortar bombs at all, and the Piat bombs we had collected could not be spared for a job of this sort.

I changed my Bren gun position from the attic into the front room of the second floor. I started to give them bursts any time I could detect the slightest movement. Smithy was beside me, sniping with his rifle through a hole in the wall near the window. The crackling of small arms fire was like a bonfire. The Germans had probably detected our firing positions. We could hear the thud of the bullets on the outside wall, and the shape of each window was outlined and filled in by a pattern of bullet holes on the wall behind us. Each time they hit the edge of the windows, a spray of chips, splinters and plaster made us jump aside. They seemed to be giving Smithy and me all their attention.

Suddenly, Smithy shouted, 'I've been hit.' His whole wrist and hand were soaked in blood. He lay on the floor, whilst I tried to tie a bit of rag round the wound to stop the bleeding. Then we both crawled across the room to the door, and I shouted for someone to help him down the stairs into the Officers' Room. I had to stay up there as the Bren was too valuable for our defence to be left inactive.

I poked my barrel through the hole that Smithy had left, and started firing at some movement I detected. Then a sudden terrific bang . . . I thought this was my turn. My hand was covered with blood, and I withdrew the gun quickly. I wiped the blood away, expecting to find a serious injury as I could feel no pain at all, and discovered that a splinter had just penetrated a vein and this was causing the bleeding. And then I noticed my Bren barrel, and realized how incredibly lucky I had been. A bullet had entered the flash eliminator that widens the barrel at the end, split it open and by some miracle ricocheted off again, instead of going into me. The good old gun still worked, but I had to exchange barrels at the earliest opportunity. Anyhow, after a few minutes, the signal for my morning session in the attic was heard from the top of the street, and, calling to Lt X, I fetched the Piat and went up the stairs, quite confident and taking my time. By now we knew the slow and careful approach of our old friend, the German self-propelled gun.

This morning though, they had a surprise for us. They manoeuvred two of them into position. One on each side of the road. The terrific small arms attack seemed to show that they were working up for real business. We were glad we had fetched those twenty bombs last night, as with two SP's firing shells incessantly as they advanced, we had to lay a screen across the road. This was our only hope of stopping them. They stopped dead for a while, just out of range, and then retired slowly. The small arms activity died down to normal, and we knew we had repelled them again, anyhow for the moment.

It suddenly became a pleasant Sunday morning. Our regular Arnhem hotpot was simmering, the Red Cross appeared on the streets, and everyone came down for a breather to see how the food was getting on and how the others were. Eating our food, the reaction from the heavy attack made us quite gay, and we compared our near misses. Everybody boasted and produced proof. I thought I had a pretty good story to tell, but when I saw some of the others, I knew that this morning's battle honours were not mine. Like all of us, Tony wore a sort of false bosom under his battle smock. This consisted of all his personal belongings and ammunition. A bullet had passed through this bosom, into his water bottle, smashed up the pin of a hand grenade in his top pocket and passed out again. His first reaction had been fear that he was mortally wounded, for water from his bottle was trickling down his body, and he naturally thought this must be blood. After examining himself, he removed all his belongings and got an even worse fright when he pulled out a live grenade minus the pin. He had thrown it away before he realized what he was doing, and the fright (though of course he said it was the explosion) knocked him for six. Anybody who survived an experience like that deserved to get out alive, and Tony did.

The next of this morning's heroes was Fitz. His private bullet, which he now thinks of with great affection, entered his false bosom and ripped his smock and the tunic underneath it three-quarters of the way across his chest, just above the heart. There were many minor escapees like myself with my Bren gun. I fetched this down proudly and passed it round the kitchen. Then Vic discovered that my left epaulette had been split across by a bullet. I felt I could now join the other two on equal terms. As a matter of fact, none of us could hold a candle to our private miracle man. This glider pilot was the pride of our street, because by all the laws of nature he ought to have been dead, and instead he was doing kitchen fatigues quite happily.

A bullet had entered his right temple and exited through his left, leaving behind it a couple of neat little holes. He wasn't even knocked out of the fight by this, and had to be ordered sternly not to take part in combatant duties. Not only did he remain working in the kitchen all the time we were in our house, but he was able to retreat with us across the Rhine. The last we saw of him was sitting perkily in the back of an ambulance in Belgium, making rude signs at us as he passed. An MO, whom we told about it later, said that this was possible, as the front part of the brain governs the emotions, and an injury to it does not necessarily cause any organic change. He explained that the work done by the damaged part of the brain would be taken on temporarily by another part. And he added that quite often people injured in this way become very cheerful and feel stimulated. This, of course, does not last for long, but would account for the way our miracle man behaved.

Sunday afternoon was fairly quiet, but towards dusk the firing increased sharply. Before we knew what was happening it developed into the first direct assault on our position. Somehow Jerry had crossed the road from the wood into the next house. I hadn't seen it happen, so they might have come from the plantation in our rear. The first thing I saw were the tops of German helmets moving along the space between the two houses. There were some kind of verandas in front of the houses, which only gave them very slight cover. I had to get a firing line from my attic to them, which meant removing several tiles, and by the time I got into position, they were firing at us with an automatic gun. I could take my time aiming and getting ready as it was very unlikely that they would detect me. After my first burst the German who was firing disappeared and his gun toppled over on to the veranda. Either myself or someone else firing in the same direction had hit one or more of them. I started looking round for new victims. It was getting dark now and difficult to make out what was going on. Right underneath me next door only about three yards away, a window was pushed open and I saw people moving inside the room. So the Germans were here! This room had always been empty and lately the whole house had been evacuated to strengthen the top corner position. They were trying to get out of the window into our house and I could not fire at them from where I was as they were too close underneath me. I ran from my attic to a side window on the second floor to lob a hand grenade into the room. I heard it break some glass and a few seconds later it exploded. When my eyes got used to the darkness again, I could still see movement in the room; I lobbed another grenade and still I could see movement in the room after it had exploded. I couldn't make out why I had not killed everyone in there and threw, one after another, my remaining store of grenades. And still there was movement in the room. I was just going to run down and fetch some more hand grenades to deal with this apparent wave of Germans, when a controlled and quiet voice called up to me: 'What do you think you are doing? Trying to kill us all?' My heart stood still for a moment. Then I realized what I had been doing. I was certain I had killed and injured many of them; it was the worst moment of the whole seven days, and I wished I was dead myself. I jumped down the stairs out of the house and across to the other one through the window and into the room. Everything looked quite normal there, except for the miracle man lying on the bed with a bandage round his head and the Lieutenant and three others sitting on the floor. I told them that it was I who had thrown the grenades, and where were the casualties? he said: 'Oh, it was you, was it? Thank God, you didn't know your job – At such short distance you should have waited four seconds until you threw; that gives another three seconds until the grenade explodes. As it was, we lobbed them out of the window as fast as you threw them. They all exploded just outside, and you're a fool not to have noticed it.' I was never more grateful for being a fool!

The others had been fighting hard all round the house as the enemy had tried to get at us from every side. It began to get quieter and it seemed as if they had had enough. Next morning we found several bodies, amongst them my Jerry machine gunner.

I was called to the Officers' Room, and Capt. Z told me to wake him at 1 a.m., as he had to report to the Brigadier at 2 a.m. I was to go with him to Div. HQ, so I made my bed, and Lt X, who was duty officer for that period, promised to wake me in time. It was hell to get up at this hour of the morning for I had only had two hours' sleep. The light was dim and it was peaceful and warm. Capt. Z's full rosy cheeks and the regular vibrations of the ends of his moustache made a picture of peace and content. I could hardly bring myself to wake him. I shook him gently, but soon realized that sterner measures would have to be used. I pulled the sheets and eiderdown off him, shook him roughly and shouted at him, 'Capt. Z, you have to get up to go to the Div. HQ.' 'Who's giving orders here?' he replied. 'The Brigadier, sir, and it's nearly half-past one.'

We arrived in the cellar at Div. HQ; the little room of the Intelligence people was very crowded, and none took any notice of us. Everyone was half asleep and could hardly keep their eyes open. I reported the glider pilot section under Capt. Z present and pointed out our position and that of the enemy on the map. There were no orders for the next day, except to carry on as usual, and a bit of encouragement by telling us that we had been doing well. We went on another scrounge and returned with a few Piat bombs and several hundred rounds of rifle ammo.

1945

*War reporting found the BBC at its professional best. Its correspondents – men like Richard Dimbleby, Godfrey Talbot and Wynford Vaughan Thomas – became household names. Here, Vaughan Thomas does not conceal his pleasure at broadcasting from the very seat till recently occupied by William Joyce, otherwise known as Lord Haw-Haw. Note too that at this climax of the war, the notion that Hamburg had been laid waste still seemed undiluted good news. The notion that something appalling had happened there – even measured against the rough yardstick of wartime horrors – had not yet registered.*

## WAR REPORT

### WYNFORD VAUGHAN THOMAS

4 May 1945. 'This is Germany calling. Calling for the last time from Station Hamburg, and tonight you will not hear views on the news by William Joyce, for Mr Joyce – Lord Haw-Haw to most of us in Britain – has been most unfortunately interrupted in his broadcasting career, and at present has left rather hurriedly for a vacation, an extremely short vacation if the Second British Army has anything to do with it, maybe to Denmark and other points north. And in his place this is the BBC calling all the long-suffering listeners in Britain who for six years have had to put up with the acid tones of Mr Joyce speaking over the same wave-length that I'm using to talk to you now.

'I'm seated in front of Lord Haw-Haw's own microphone, or rather the microphone he used in the last three weeks of his somewhat chequered career; and I wonder what Lord Haw-Haw's views on the news are now? For Hamburg, the city he made notorious, is this evening under the control of the British Forces, and we found a completely and utterly bomb-ruined city.

'We thought Bremen was bad, but Hamburg is devastated. Whole quarters have disintegrated under air attacks. There are miles upon miles of blackened walls and utterly burnt-out streets, and in the ruins there are still nearly a million people and 50,000 foreign workers living in the cellars and air-raid shelters. Today you don't see a single civilian on the streets; as soon as we came in we imposed a forty-eight hour curfew, and there's a Sunday quiet over the whole city; all that stirs in the streets is a British jeep or an armoured car, or a patrol of British Tommies watching that the curfew is strictly enforced.

'The docks are even more devastated than the town, the great shipyards of Bloem and Voss are a wilderness of tangled girders, and in the middle of this chaos fourteen unfinished U-boats still stand rusting on the slipways. Work on them finally stopped two months ago; after that date Hamburg was a dead city.

'Rummaging through Lord Haw-Haw's desk we found a revealing time-table he drew up for his work, for 10 April 1945, and at the end of it is the glorious item: '1450–1510 hrs. a pause to collect my wits.' Well – he and the citizens of Hamburg have now got plenty of time to collect their wits, for tonight the sturdy soldiers of the Devons, the famous Desert Rats, are on guard over Haw-Haw's studios, the Allied military authorities are now running his programme, and instead of "Germany Calling", the colonel in charge gives you now the new call-sign of "Station Hamburg". This is Radio Hamburg, a station of the Allied Military Government. [*Same announcement in German.*] And from Hamburg we take you back to London.'

1946

*And finally, in this section, a magnificently eccentric testimonial to Bovril from Monty. How on earth do we manage without him?*

### HEADQUARTERS: 21 ARMY GROUP

26 March 1945

Dear Miss Storey

Thank you for your letter of 23 March. I am sure you will be glad to know that the assaulting troops that crossed the Rhine in the moonlight on Friday night, 23rd March, all had a drink of Bovril before starting. Mr Churchill much enjoyed a cup of it when touring the area on 24 March.

Yrs sincerely

B. L. Montgomery

Field-Marshal

# COULD IT
# HAPPEN HERE?

*There have been other descriptions of the fundamentally indescribable experience of going into Belsen for the first time. I have chosen that by Alan Moorehead because he makes an honourable though doomed attempt to set it in a logical framework.*

## GLIMPSES OF GERMANY – BELSEN

### ALAN MOOREHEAD

Just before you get to the main entrance of Belsen concentration camp – or rather the place where the camp used to be before the British burned it down – you come on a farmhouse. I suggested to the others in my party that we should turn in there and eat lunch before – rather than after – we visited the camp.

While the table was being set for us in the dining-room we were interested to know from the farmer what he thought of Belsen. 'I don't know very much about it,' he said. 'Each morning I had to drive up there with a cart full of vegetables – swedes and turnips mostly – and one of the SS guards took the horse and cart from me at the gate. After a bit the cart and horse were returned to me and I drove away. I was never allowed inside, and I didn't want to go in anyway. I knew something horrible was going on, but I didn't ask about it lest I should find myself inside.'

We finished the meal and drove up to the gate with a special pass which General Dempsey had given the correspondents: from the first Dempsey was very keen that we should see Belsen and write about it. Although the British had only captured the place from the Germans a few days before, they seemed to have things well organized. Hungarian guards were still spaced along the barbed wire fence, good-looking men who jumped eagerly to attention when an army vehicle came by. At the gate British soldiers were on guard. There were notices in English: 'Danger Typhus', 'Car Park', 'Powder Room', 'Inquiries' and so on.

A young army doctor and a captain from the Pioneers were in charge. The Captain's job was supervising the counting and burial of bodies. Possibly as a form of immunization from the grisly work he appeared to be in particularly jovial spirits.

'I love doing this,' he said, picking up the metal syringe filled with anti-louse powder. 'Come on.'

A squirt up each sleeve. One down the trousers. Two more squirts down the back and front of the shirt and a final shot on the hair. It was rather pleasant.

'We collected the local burgomeisters from the surrounding villages this morning and took them round the camp,' the doctor said.

'How did they take it?'

'One of them was sick and another one wouldn't look. They all said they had never dreamed that this was going on.'

We were now walking down the main driveway towards the first of the huts and administrative buildings. There were large crowds of civilian prisoners about, both those who strolled about in groups talking many different languages and those who sat silent on the ground. In addition there were many forms lying on the earth partly covered in rags, but it was not possible to say whether they were alive or dead or simply in the process of dying. It would be a day or two before the doctors got around to them for a diagnosis.

'There's quite a different air about the place in the last two days,' the doctor said. 'They seem much more cheerful now.'

'And the burial rate has gone down considerably,' the captain added. 'I'm handling just under three hundred a day now. It was five hundred to start with. And we are evacuating five hundred every day to the Panzer training school. It has been made into a hospital. Would you like to see the SS boys?'

We saw the women guards first. A British sergeant threw open the cell door and some twenty women wearing dirty grey skirts and tunics were sitting and lying on the floor.

'Get up,' the sergeant roared in English.

They got up and stood to attention in a semi-circle round the room, and we looked at them. Thin ones, fat ones, scraggy ones and muscular ones; all of them ugly, and one or two of them distinctly cretinous. I pointed out one, a big woman with bright golden hair and a bright pink complexion.

'She was Kramer's girlfriend,' the sergeant growled. 'Nice lot, aren't they?'

There was another woman in a second room with almost delicate features, but she had the same set staring look in her eyes. The atmosphere of the reformatory school and the prison was inescapable.

Outside in the passageway there was a large blackboard ruled off in squares with white lines. Down the left-hand side of the board was a list of nationalities – 'Poles, Dutch, Russians' and so on. Spaced along the top of the board was a list of religions and political faiths – 'Communist, Jew, Atheist'. From the board one might have seen at a glance just how many prisoners were in the camp from each nation, and how they were subdivided politically and religiously. However, most of the numbers appeared to have been rubbed off, and it was difficult to make out the totals exactly. Germans seemed to make up the majority of the prisoners. After them Russians and Poles. A great many were Jews. As far as one could decipher there had been half a dozen British here, one or two Americans. There had been something like fifty thousand prisoners altogether.

As we approached the cells of the SS guards the sergeant's language became ferocious.

'We have had an interrogation this morning,' the captain said. 'I'm afraid they are not a pretty sight.'

'Who does the interrogation?'

'A Frenchman. I believe he was sent up here specially from the French underground to do the job.'

The sergeant unbolted the first door and flung it back with a crack like thunder. He strode into the cell, jabbing a metal spike in front of him.

'Get up,' he shouted. 'Get up. Get up, you dirty bastards.' There were half a dozen men lying or half lying on the floor. One or two were able to pull themselves erect at once. The man nearest me, his shirt and face spattered with blood, made two attempts before he got on to his knees and then gradually on to his feet. He stood with his arms half stretched out in front of him, trembling violently.

'Get up,' shouted the sergeant. They were all on their feet now, but supporting themselves against the wall.

'Get away from that wall.'

They pushed themselves out into space and stood there swaying. Unlike the women they looked not at us, but vacantly in front, staring at nothing.

Same thing in the next cell and the next, where the men who were bleeding and were dirty were moaning something in German.

'You had better see the doctor,' the Captain said. 'He's a nice specimen. He invented some of the tortures here. He had one trick of injecting creosote and petrol into the prisoner's veins. He used to go around the huts and say "Too many people in here. Far too many." Then he used to loose off the barrel of his revolver round the hut. The doctor had just finished his interrogation.'

The doctor had a cell to himself.

'Come on. Get up,' the sergeant shouted. The man was lying in his blood on the floor, a massive figure with a heavy head and bedraggled beard. He placed his two arms on to the seat of a wooden chair, gave himself a heave and got half upright. One more heave and he was on his feet. He flung wide his arms towards us.

'Why don't you kill me?' he whispered. 'Why don't you kill me? I can't stand any more.'

The same phrases dribbled out of his lips over and over again.

'He's been saying that all morning, the dirty bastard,' the sergeant said. We went out into the sunshine. A number of other British soldiers were standing about, all with the same hard, rigid expressions on their faces, just ordinary English soldiers, but changed by this expression of genuine and permanent anger.

The crowds of men and women thickened as we went further into the camp. The litter of paper and rags and human offal grew thicker, the smell less and less bearable. At the entrance soldiers were unloading trucks filled with wooden latrines but these had not yet been placed about the camp, so many hundreds of half-naked men and women were squatting together in the open, a scene such as you sometimes see in India – except that here it was not always possible to distinguish men from women and indeed to determine whether or not they were human at all.

We drove through the filth in cars and presently emerging on to an open space of yellow clayey soil we came on a group of German guards flinging bodies into a pit about a hundred feet square. They brought the bodies up in handcarts and as they were flung into the grave a British soldier kept a tally of the numbers. When the total reached five hundred a bulldozer driven by another soldier came up and started nudging the earth into the grave. There was a curious pearly colour about the piled up bodies and they were small like the bodies of children. The withered skin was sagging over the bones and all the normal features by which you know a human being had practically disappeared. Having no stomach for this sort of thing I was only able to look for a second or two, but the SS guards and even the British soldiers there appeared to have grown used to the presence of death and able to work in its presence without being sick.

'The doctors are doing a wonderful job,' the Captain said: 'They are in the huts all day sorting out the living bodies from the dead, and it's not easy sometimes to tell the difference. Of course there are a lot who are just hopeless and they are simply left. But they are saving a lot now. We have got in all the food we want – two meals a day at 10 and 6. Come on and have a look at one of the huts. We will go to the women first.'

It was a single storey rectangular building, I suppose about a hundred feet long. Wooden bunks ran in tiers up to the ceiling and there was a narrow passage just wide enough to allow you to pass through. Since the majority of the women there were too weak to move and had no attention whatever, the stench was nauseating. Hurrying through, handkerchief to nose, one saw nothing but livid straining faces and emaciated arms and legs under the filthy bedclothes on either side. Many were using their last strength to moan feebly for help. These animals were piled one on top of the other to the ceiling, sometimes two to a bunk.

An old hag, somewhat stronger than the others, was standing at the further door. 'I'm twenty-one,' she whispered. 'No, I don't know why they put me in here. My husband is a doctor at the front – I'm German but not Jewish. I said that I did not want to enlist in the women's organization and they put me in here. That was eighteen months ago.'

'I've had enough of this,' I said to the Captain.

'Come on,' he said. 'You've got to go through one of the men's huts yet. That's what you're here for.'

It was, if anything, more rancid than the one I had seen, but this time I was too sick with the stench to notice much except the sound of the voices: 'Doctor, Doctor.'

As we returned towards the entrance the people around us were noticeably better in health than those at the pits and the huts. As they were able to walk some instinct drew the people away from the charnel houses and up and out towards the entrance and the ordinary sane world outside. It was all like a journey down to some Dantesque pit, unreal, leprous and frightening. And now that one emerged into the light again, one's first coherent reactions were not of disgust or anger or even, I think, of pity. Something else filled the mind, a frantic desire to ask: 'Why? Why? Why? Why had it happened?' With all one's soul one felt, 'This is not war. Nor is it anything to do with here and now, with this one place at this one moment. This is timeless and the whole world and all mankind is involved in it. This touches me and I am responsible. Why has it happened? How did we let it happen?'

We stood there in a group, a major from the commandos, a padre, three or four correspondents, having at first nothing to say and then gradually and quietly asking one another the unspoken question.

Was it sadism? No, on the whole, not. Or, if it was sadism, then it was sadism of a very indirect and unusual kind. Relatively little torture was carried out at this camp. The sadist presumably likes to make some direct immediate act which inflicts pain on other people. He could not obtain much satisfaction from the slow process of seeing people starve.

Then again the Germans were an efficient people. They needed manpower. Can one imagine anything more inefficient than letting all this valuable labour go to rot? The prisoners in Belsen were not even obliged to work. They were simply dumped in here and left to make what shift they could with a twice daily diet of turnip stew. Incidentally this lack of work probably led to the break-up of the prisoners' morale as much as anything.

The Germans, too, had a normal fear of disease spreading among themselves. And yet they let these thousands of bodies lie on the ground. It's true that there was not a great deal of typhus in the camp, but it had already broken out when the German commanders approached the British and offered to cede the camp under the terms of a truce.

It was not torture which had killed the prisoners. It was neglect. The sheer indifference of the Nazis. One began to see that the most terrible thing on earth is not positive destruction nor the perverse desire to hurt and destroy. The worst thing that can happen to you is for the master to say, 'I do not care about you any more. I am indifferent'. Whether you washed or ate or laughed or died – none of this was of any consequence any more because you as a person had no value. You were a slug on the ground, to be crushed or not to be crushed, it made no difference.

And having become attuned and accustomed to this indifference, the guards were increasingly less affected by the suffering of the people around them. It was accepted that they should die. They were Russians. Russians die. Jews die. They were not even enemies. They were disease. Could you mourn or sympathize with the death throes of a germ?

Now here is where the evidence of Kramer, the camp commandant, comes in. To consider Kramer calmly I think we have first got to rid ourselves temporarily of our memory of that published picture of him shuffling across the yard in shackles. And we have to forget for a moment the title he was given through the world, 'The Monster of Belsen'. A friend of mine, a trained intelligence officer and interrogator in the British army, went into the whole question very carefully with Kramer and this was Kramer's statement:

'I was swamped. The camp was not really inefficient before you crossed the Rhine. There was running water, regular meals of a kind – I had to accept what food I was given for the camp and distribute it the best way I could. But then they suddenly began to send me trainloads of new prisoners from all over Germany. It was impossible to cope with them. I appealed for more staff, more food. I was told this was impossible; I had to carry on with what I had. Then as a last straw the Allies bombed the electric plant which pumped our water. Cartloads of food were unable to reach the camp because of the Allied fighters. Then things really got out of hand. In the last six weeks I have been helpless. I did not even have sufficient staff to bury the dead, let alone segregate the sick.'

Thus Kramer.

'But how did you come to accept a job like this?' he was asked. The reply: 'There was no question of my accepting it. I was ordered. I am an officer in the SS and I obey orders. These people were criminals and I was serving my Führer in a crisis by commanding this camp. I tried to get medicines and food for the prisoners and I failed. I was swamped. I may have been hated, but I was doing my duty.'

There was some truth in this last. Not only were the prisoners fond of hurling missiles at Kramer since we arrived, but his own guards turned on him as well. Kramer asked the British authorities that he should be segregated. He was told that in this event he would have to be shackled and to this he agreed.

Who then was responsible for Belsen and, for that matter, all the other camps? The SS guards? They say they were ordered. They hated the work but disobedience to Kramer meant death. Kramer says he was in precisely the same position. And so presumably do all the other Kramers above him until you reach Himmler. What does Himmler say? Himmler says he is serving his Führer. The Führer, of course, was innocent and knew nothing about the vulgar details (quite a number of Germans assured us of that). But – we can imagine Himmler saying – it was vital to protect the Führer from his enemies inside the Reich – the Jewish bolsheviks who would have cheerfully murdered him. At this dire crisis for Germany and the Party one could not be too nice about the details – possibly some people were treated a little too harshly. But one could not afford to take chances. The Nazis were perfectly prepared to treat these prisoners with humanity, but the enemies of Germany made this impossible. They destroyed communications, they blocked the food supply. Naturally the camps suffered.

But the people of Germany? Why had they allowed this thing to be? Why had they not protested? The average German answers: in the first place we did not know these camps existed. Secondly, how could we have protested? What possibly could we have done? The Nazis were too strong.

Very well then, why did you not protest when the Nazis were rising to power?

They answer: How could we foretell that the Nazis would end this with horror? When they first came to power they embarked on a programme that was excellent for Germany: new roads, modern buildings and machines. It seemed rational and good at the beginning. When we realized that Hitler was turning to war it was already too late. By then the Nazis had claimed our children. They were Nazified in the schools. A parent would be denounced by his own child if he spoke against the Nazis. Little by little we were overwhelmed and in the end it was too late. There was no point at which we could have effectively protested. Why did not foreign countries which had the power check the Nazis soon enough? If only you had attacked us before the Nazis become too strong.

And so the blame is thrown back upon the world. No one anywhere is willing to take responsibility. Not the guard or the torturer. Not Kramer. Not Herr Woolf. [The German arms manufacturer whose opinions are paraphrased above.] They were all ordered. Not Himmler or Hitler (the end justified the means); they were fighting to rid the world of the terrible menace of Jewish bolshevism – they were ordered by their high sense of duty. Not the German people. They too had to obey. And finally not the world. Is England Germany's keeper?

That is the line of argument which we have heard as observers of this final eclipse of Germany. I write it here not because I accept or reject it, but because we are still too close to the scene to do much more than report personally and directly; and it seems a pity to give way to the downright childishness of saying that all Germans are natural black-hearted fiends capable of murdering and torturing and starving people at the drop of the hat.

If I were compelled to make some sort of direct line at this moment I would say – Yes, all mankind is in some way responsible for Belsen, but in varying degrees. Herr Woolf, for example, is a cultured European. Surely he could have seen a little more clearly than, say, the average German workman, what the Nazi party was going to mean and have made some protest in time. Clearly, too, the Germans generally and the leading Nazis most particularly are far more embroiled in this monstrosity than anyone else. The Junkers and the Wehrmacht power-through-war class – they too are utterly compromised. But the degree of guilt varies enormously both inside and outside of the Nazi Party, inside and outside of Germany. Probably the least of all to blame is the unpolitical boy who was put into uniform and forced to come here into the German battlefield to support the tardy conscience of the world. And die for it.

There is only one thing possible that one can do for him now – be vigilant to snap the long chains that lead to the future Belsens before they grow too strong. A shudder of horror went round the world when the news of these concentration camps was published, but only, I think, because of the special interest and the special moment in the war. We were engrossed with Germany and it is perhaps not too subtle to say that since Germany was manifestly beaten, people wanted to have a justification for their fight, a proof that they were engaged against evil. From the German point of view Belsen was perfectly mistimed. Worse camps like Auschwitz existed in Poland and we took no notice. Dachau was described in the late Thirties and we did not want to hear. In the midst of the war three-quarters of a million Indians starved in Bengal because shipping was wanted in other parts, and we were bored.

The last living patient has been evacuated from Belsen. The hateful buildings have been burned down. The physical evidence of all those horrible places will soon have been wiped out. Only the mental danger remains. The danger of indifference.

1945

*The experience of Germans at the hands of the Russians in East Germany was the other side of the coin. The Martyrdom and Heroism of the Women of East Germany was published in Munich by a Roman Catholic organization called Christ Unterwegs in 1955. It collates the testimony of many different witnessses, here a South German nun in Breslau.*

## THE MARTYRDOM AND HEROISM OF THE WOMEN OF EAST GERMANY

Breslau, Monday, 7 May 1945, the day of the capitulation:
The Russians occupied the town. We had as yet no idea that the coming night would hold greater terror and dangers for us than bombs and shells. In the course of the day the Russians were given permission to do all the looting they wanted to. Several Russians came to the house at intervals and wanted us to give them food, etc. During the afternoon some of them tried to get hold of some of our girls, but the latter fortunately managed to escape. We began to dread what might happen during the evening and the night. Some of the women of the neighbourhood sought shelter with us. At about eleven o'clock at night, a crowd of Russians came to the house and, after smashing the front door with their boots, entered. There were about twenty of them, and they promptly started ransacking all the rooms and removed all the food supplies, suitcases, and anything else they found, and put them on a lorry which was standing in front of the house. Then they started searching for the girls, who had meanwhile hidden. They flashed their electric torches on all the beds in the cellar. A Russian civilian grabbed hold of my wrists and dragged me to the cellar-door. I put up a fierce

resistance, and he then tried to drag me into the cellar by my veil, but got hold of my shawl instead, and so I managed to escape in the darkness. Unfortunately, however, he then seized hold of one of our girls, who had been trying to protect me and for this reason had not run away. Six of the Russians then fell upon the poor girl and violated her. I shall never forget this dreadful incident as long as I live, for the poor girl sacrificed herself for my sake. It was about one o'clock at night by the time these monsters left the house.

Towards morning other hordes arrived, but they were only out to steal wireless-sets and clocks and watches, etc., and did not molest us personally. We gladly gave them all we had, so long as they left us in peace. As evening approached once more, we were seized with fear and terror. We all said the Rosary together and many other prayers asking for the Lord's protection for the coming night. We could hear defenceless women and children screaming for help nearby, and their screams were a sign to us to go into hiding as fast as we could. Again and again we said the Psalm, 'Out of the depths have I cried unto thee, O Lord', and our prayers were answered, for during this second night we were not molested at all, and when morning came we gave thanks to the Lord for His Mercy. Small parties of Russians came to the house again and again in the course of the day, but all they wanted was a drink, and they did not molest us in any way.

It was about seven o'clock in the evening when the gang that had raided the house the first night appeared again. Most of the nuns fled and ran to a house in School Alley, as we had arranged. I ran out of the house on to Luther Square, however, as I had caught sight of about twelve cars and several officers of high rank standing there. Calling for help as loudly as I could, I remained standing in front of our ruined building, and thereupon a general and four officers and two women in uniform came up to me. The general spoke German fluently and, accompanied by the four officers and the two women, he then went into the convent with me and ordered all the Russians to clear out of the building. He got hold of one of the marauders, an officer, by the arm and asked me whether the man had come to the convent on a previous occasion. I told him he had, and thereupon he apparently reprimanded the man fairly sharply and made him walk out of the building in front of him. The general then turned to me and said, 'This officer won't molest you again.'

I thanked him for his kindness, and he then asked me about our work. He also told me that the Russians had found 80,000 litres of wine at the former headquarters of the German commander of the fortress, and that there was not much he could do to prevent the licentious behaviour of the soldiers, since practically all of them were drunk.

The general had just departed and I had gone back into our yard, when I suddenly turned round and saw to my great horror that the officer whom the general had reprimanded was pursuing me, with a revolver in his hand. He was only about ten yards behind me. I ran across the yard as fast as I could and through a back-door and down a small alley, until I reached the house in School Alley to which the rest of the nuns had fled when the Russians had come to the convent and I had gone to get help. As the Russian officer lost track of me, he had all the houses in the vicinity searched, much to the distress of the inhabitants. Again and again we heard him shouting with rage. In the meantime I had rejoined the rest of the nuns, who were hiding in a loft over the house. Several young women were also hiding there, as one could not be too careful. Suddenly we heard angry voices and the sound of heavy boots tramping about in the apartments underneath us. Next minute they were already climbing up the steps to the loft.

I can hardly describe our emotions at this moment. We held our crucifixes in our hands and made the act of contrition, for we knew that if they found us it would mean our death. One of the nuns climbed up to the dormer-window and was determined to jump out of it, rather than fall into the hands of the Russians alive. There was an uncanny silence in the loft. We held our breath as we heard the Russians carrying on a loud argument outside the loft. 'In our need and distress the Lord hath spread out his wings over us!' The Russians failed to find the entrance to the loft and tramped down the steps again, shouting and cursing.

It was eleven o'clock at night by the time we ventured out on to the street and went along to the babies' home to ask for shelter there. They very kindly took us in and hid us on the third floor, where we spent the rest of the night. Cries of help re-echoed through the stillness of the night, and we prayed for all those who were in danger. Next morning things were fairly quiet. Now and again small parties of Russians came to the house for the purpose of looting, but the officer who had pursued me did not reappear, so apparently the general had sent them away after all, otherwise he would most surely have turned up again.

The next day was a very sorrowful one for us. At about three o'clock in the afternoon we heard a shot in the garden. Next minute, one of the older girls came running into the house and told us that there was a nun lying on the ground at the far end of the garden, and that there was a Russian standing over her. Our Reverend Father, the Prelate, who had just arrived from Rosenthal in order to see how we were faring, ran out into the garden and called out to the Russian in Polish. The latter made off as fast as he could, leaving his bicycle and a suitcase behind.

It was indeed a sad sight which met our eyes. Poor Mother Felizitas, the oldest of our nuns, lay there in the grass, dead. The Russian had shot her in the heart. Reverend Father gave her the Extreme Unction, and then we carried her body to the mortuary, where it had to remain for three days, as the Russian commandant issued an order to this effect and a commission was to investigate the case. But, of course, nothing was done in the matter. We dug a grave under the large cross in our garden and there we interred Mother Felizitas. As it was impossible to obtain a coffin, we had to wrap her body in sheets. Reverend Father officiated at the funeral and preached a very moving sermon at the graveside.

Dear Mother Felizitas was seventy-eight when she died. Her life was one of sacrifice. For forty years she was in charge of the boilers in our laundry and kitchen. She served our Order faithfully for almost sixty years and has, no doubt, received her reward in Heaven for her untiring devotion. During the three days in which her body lay in the mortuary we had a certain amount of protection against the Russians, for whenever any of them came to the house we told them that one of their comrades had shot one of our nuns. Just as we were in the act of filling up the grave after the funeral some young Russians again appeared on the scene. One of the girls, who was the first to spot them, jumped into the grave, which was still open, in order to protect herself, but I am sure dear Mother Felizitas would forgive her for doing so.

Gradually, the number of cases of assault by Russians decreased. Only on one other occasion did a Russian pursue me, but he abandoned his chase on catching sight of a young girl. I hid in the garden, underneath a big currant-bush, and remained there for a long time until the danger was over.

The nuns of our Order at the convent in Rosenthal and the girls there had similar experiences to ours. The nuns hid the girls again and again and tried to prevent the Russians from getting hold of them. One night, which was particularly dreadful, Reverend Father stood with his back to the wall and his arms stretched out for two hours repeating in Polish again and again, 'Only over my dead body', whilst he and the nuns prevented the Russians from gaining access to the girls. We all of us owe so very much to this noble priest, who, despite his age, was always with us in the hours of our greatest need and distress. How gladly would we compensate him for all the misery he himself was obliged to endure for having endeavoured to help others.

# MOST IGNOMINIOUS
# OF DEATHS

CARELESS TALK
COSTS LIVES

*Thanks to Doctor Eugen Dollman, Hitler's interpreter we are able to be voyeurs at the final meeting between the Führer and the Duce. It was, even by their standards, a banal affair and not without its element of farce, as when Mussolini's guzzling son Vittorio downs his third slice of cake. Probably both dictators knew perfectly well that the writing was on the wall; Hitler had escaped the Generals' plot that very day, but, progenitor of Blitzkrieg and genocide though he was, still had the courtesy to send for Mussolini's coat so that he would not catch cold. As we shall see, each man met his end within the year, his mistress beside him.*

## THE TEA PARTY

### DOKTOR EUGEN DOLLMANN

The day [20 July 1944] dawned humid and sultry. There was nothing pleasurable about the train journey, which was constantly interrupted by air-raid warnings . . .

At last the train drew slowly into Görlitz. Gone were the gorgeous red carpets, the flags, garlands and military bands of former times. The only concomitants of this dismal reception were a grey-blue sky, a few scattered rain-drops and the mournful rustle of fir and pine.

The Führer of the Greater German Reich was standing on the platform with his paladins behind him, as of yore. He wore a long black cape, and his cap was pulled low over his face. That was all I saw as I leapt out and stationed myself beside him before the visitor from Lake Garda could descend from his carriage. It was part of my interpreter's duties to do this, and I always comforted myself with the thought that if the war went badly I might be able to find a job with the railways.

A moment later we were face to face with Benito Mussolini.

'Duce, a few hours ago I experienced the greatest piece of good fortune I have ever known!'

Hitler extended his left hand, and I saw that he was wearing his right arm in a sling.

It was about 3.30 p.m.

We soon learned the nature of Hitler's good fortune when he gave a brief account of how he had escaped assassination by a hair's breadth at 12.50 p.m. that day. Mussolini shook hands with Göring, Ribbentrop, Bormann and – needless to say – Heinrich Himmler, who was convulsed with agitation. Himmler soon set off with Hitler and Bormann on the short trip from the station to the Wolf's Lair, while Mussolini had to content himself with Göring . . . . Before long we were standing in front of the ruins of the so-called Tea-house where the midday conference had taken place. It was a room measuring sixteen feet by forty-one, and in its centre stood a map-table long enough to accommodate five people standing side by side. The whole place was a picture of havoc and devastation.

The two dictators sat down, one on an upturned box and the other on a rickety chair, looking vaguely like the characters from some Shakespearian tragedy. The man who had just cheated death delivered a monologue while Mussolini rolled his staring eyes to and fro as only he knew how. Divine providence was invoked. It was claimed that . . . since [the Führer] was so manifestly a darling of the gods, joint victory was assured. The frightful chaos surrounding us, the scent of death and destruction and the sight of the man who had escaped it virtually unscathed – was this not confirmation of the miracle to come? Being a guest and a true son of the South with a truly Latin fondness for signs and omens, Benito Mussolini needed no convincing of this . . .

We at last adjourned for the traditional tea-party, which was a positively ghoulish affair. Mussolini's son, the fat and foolish Vittorio, who disliked conferences as much as he liked his stomach, appeared from somewhere, and we assembled round a large tea-table in one of the huts which had not been damaged by the explosion. I sat in my usual position between the dictators, and the exalted Italian and German guests distributed themselves round us. The table was laid with painstaking neatness and tended by the usual blue-eyed SS boys in white jackets. But for the conversation of the Germans present, no outside observer would have guessed that only the intervention of the gods had made the tea-party possible at all. As it was, they all talked, led by Göring, Dönitz, Ribbentrop and Keitel. It suddenly occurred to them why ultimate victory had so far eluded their grasp: the whole thing was a conspiracy on the part of the generals. Conversation reverted to the generals again and again, and Göring, with an air of probity which matched his spotless white uniform, announced in deadly earnest that the same treacherous generals had secretly been withdrawing their best combat troops from the front line.

There were going to be big changes. Dönitz affirmed this on behalf of his blue-jackets, Ribbentrop on behalf of his diplomats – who came in for some scathing remarks from Göring, even on this solemn occasion – and Martin Bormann, the éminence grise, on behalf of the Party.

Absolved of all responsibility now that the generals had conveniently shouldered it for them, they noisily proclaimed their faith in ultimate victory. I looked round the table during this demonstration of loyalty. Mazzolini and Anfuso were exchanging amused glances, Graziani was vainly trying to impress Keitel with the story of his escape from assassination at Addis Ababa, Vittorio Mussolini was busy with his third slice of cake, and his father was nervously crumbling a piece of the same cake and moulding it into little figures. I turned to Hitler, thinking to engage him in conversation with his friend, but abandoned the idea at once. Watching him as he sat huddled in his chair like some inanimate idol, dull eyes gazing into infinity, I felt sure that, whatever the next few moments brought forth, it would not be polite tea-table conversation.

Minutes of uneasiness and apprehension elapsed before the storm finally burst. Outside, a light rain pattered unceasingly on the window-panes. All eyes were fixed on the motionless figure who alone could break the spell.

Then it came.

'Never have I felt more strongly that providence is at my side – indeed, the miracle of a few hours ago has convinced me more than ever that I am destined for even greater things and shall lead the German people to the greatest victory in its history. But I shall crush and destroy all the treacherous creatures who tried to stand in my path today. Traitors in the bosom of their own people deserve the most ignominious of deaths – and they shall have it! I shall wreak vengeance – inexorable vengeance – on all who were involved in this, and on their families, if they aided them. I shall exterminate this whole brood of vipers once and for all! Exterminate them, yes, exterminate them. . . .'

The vision of revenge faded, leaving Hitler staring into the distance with an even paler face and eyes drained of fire.

With the unerring instinct of his race, the Duce realized that it was up to him to seize the initiative and save the situation. He laid his hand on Hitler's and looked into his eyes with a gentle, endearing smile, and Hitler abruptly awoke from his reverie. Someone opened the outside door. The rain had stopped, and Hitler told me to send for the Duce's coat. I must have looked surprised, because he told me that a fresh east wind generally sprang up in the late afternoon. The Duce was used to a soft climate, and Hitler did not want him to risk catching cold. I sent someone for the coat, secretly reflecting that a cold was the least of Mussolini's worries – and ours.

I handed the Duce his plain grey-green army greatcoat and was rewarded with raised eyebrows. When I translated his host's solicitous remarks, his proud response was in the spirit of the Caesars: '*Caro Dollmann, un Duce in un momento come questo non prende un raffreddore!*' (At a time like this, a Duce does not catch colds!) – but he put his coat on all the same . . .

Adolf Hitler accompanied us back to Görlitz station. One pale and ageing man, with his cap pulled even lower over his face, extended his left hand to another pale and ageing man. The two incongruous friends gazed deep into each other's eyes once more, as in the days of their glory, but the light in those eyes was extinguished, almost as though they guessed that this was their last meeting.

---

*Mussolini's end was, if anything, more inglorious than Hitler's. As Max Gallo tells us, his plunge from absolute power was even more brutal. One day he was Mussolini, surrounded by an apparently devoted court; forty-eight hours later he was constrained to put on a soldier's heavy cap smelling of coarse wool, to lie on the bed of a truck, and act the drunken trooper in front of twenty German soldiers. As all the world now knows, he was shot by Partisans and his body hung upside down for everyone to see in Milan. There was perhaps this touch of humanity in the respective ends of the two dictators: each died with his mistress – though while Eva Braun's body was never definitely found, Clara Patacci dangled upside down with Mussolini for the crowd to spit on.*

# MUSSOLINI'S ITALY

## MAX GALLO

At six-thirty that morning, in the little lakeside village of Domaso, two Partisan leaders, Bill (Urbano Lazzaro) and Pedro (Pier Luigi Bellini delle Stelle), were roughly roused out of sleep by messengers: a German column had been spotted heading for Dongo, a village about three miles to the south. A few minutes later Bill and Pedro were on their way to Dongo and the little village of Musso. They heard a few volleys of automatic arms and then everything was silent again. The column had stopped at a road-block set up by Partisans and the Fifty-second Garibaldi Brigade, and there had been some exchanges of shots between the Partisans and an armoured car. A peasant in his field fell, mortally wounded by one of the volleys from the car. He died a few minutes later: the last victim of Fascism in Italy.

Not long afterwards the Germans asked for a parley.

On this 27 April Marshal Zhukov's troops had reached Berlin and shells were falling without interruption on the bunker housing the Führer. Officers and soldiers of the *Wehrmacht* had no further wish to die beside this Italian lake a few days before the inescapable defeat of their Reich.

The Partisans bluffed magnificently: more barricades sprang up rapidly along the road taken by the German officers sent to negotiate with the leaders of the Garibaldi Brigade. On the nearby embarkment armed men had taken up very prominent positions. The German captain contemplated this impressive deployment with disquiet. Finally Pedro dictated his terms to the captain as he stood facing the German in the road:

1) Only German vehicles and soldiers would be permitted to pass through. All Italians and all civilian vehicles in the column must be surrendered.

2) All the German cars and trucks would submit to inspection at Dongo.

'I should like a half-hour in order to confer with my officers,' the captain said. He walked down the road past the motionless heavy trucks until he came to the armoured car. He could be seen in discussion with men in civilian clothes. In a few minutes he announced that he agreed to the Partisans' conditions. The military convoy started up and the German soldiers punctiliously saluted the Partisans.

The armoured car and a few civilian vehicles still stood in the middle of the road. A long argument with the Partisan leader began . . . . Colonel Casalinuovo sprang out of the armoured car and stood face to face with the Partisan, shouting: 'Well, are you going to pass us through or not? Be careful: we're prepared for anything and we will never surrender! Let us through or it will be the worse for you.'

At three-fifteen the armoured car tried to run through the barrier. It met a curtain of gunfire, and the car was halted by the explosion of a grenade beneath it. Soon the hierarchs were prisoners . . . . There was not a sign of Mussolini. The prisoners were taken to Dongo. In the middle of the road, near the blackened, half-overturned armoured car, a young Militiaman writhed in agony, his face shattered . . . .

The Partisans checked each soldier's papers individually and in-spected the trucks. Suddenly a Partisan summoned Bill. He said that he had seen Mussolini in a German uniform. Bill went up to the truck pointed out by his comrade. Inside, just behind the cab, a man lay outstretched, his helmet over his face and the collar of his German army overcoat turned up. Just a drunken soldier, the other Germans in the truck said.

'Camerata! – Comrade!' Bill shouted. There was no reply. 'Eccellenza! – Your Excellency!' Still no reply. Bill shouted more forcefully: 'Cavaliere Benito Mussolini!'

The man made a barely visible movement. Bill removed his helmet. There was a shaven skull, a skull that Italians had seen so many times that they would recognize it among a thousand. Mussolini lay quite still. Bill removed Mussolini's sun-glasses and turned down his coat collar. Still Il Duce did not move. Bill removed the automatic rifle that was between Mussolini's knees. Still there was neither a movement nor a word from Il Duce. Was it fear, was it panic that paralysed him? No doubt; but perhaps he was beyond both those emotions and merely numb.

The plunge had been too brutal. Less than forty-eight hours ago he was still Mussolini, surrounded by apparently devoted men, and now here he was constrained to put on a soldier's heavy cap, smelling of coarse wool, constrained to lie on the bed of a truck and act the drunken trooper in front of twenty private soldiers of the Wehrmacht who sat openly staring at the clandestine stowaway at their feet. He was Il Duce, whom Chamberlain and Hitler had taken by the hand, whom the Pope had received; he was Il Duce, the peer of the greatest, with the kings, the marshals, the heads of states round him, and the crowd like a sea beneath the balcony of Palazzo Venezia; and he was a hunted man in a corner of a foreign truck, less than any of these foreign soldiers.

Bill had to help him to his feet: they stood face to face. A crowd had gathered round the truck, for the news had run like a powder train through the village: 'They got Mussolini!' The crowd began to shout;

now the German soldiers in the truck were frightened, and they surrendered their weapons.

Bill and Mussolini were face to face. Quite spontaneously the political commissar of the Fifty-second Garibaldi Brigade announced: 'I arrest you in the name of the Italian people.' Then Bill and another Partisan took Mussolini by the armpits and helped him down to the road. They made a passage through the yelling crowd and took Mussolini to the town hall, where the mayor said reassuringly: 'Don't worry, you will not be harmed.'

'I am sure of that,' Mussolini said slowly, 'the population of Dongo is generous.'

In a few minutes the hierarchs from the armoured car also arrived at the town hall. When they saw Mussolini, they stood at attention and said together: '*Salve* [hail], Duce.'

Mussolini nodded in reply. He could hear the shouts from the crowd outside and from time to time he looked toward the door with anxious eyes, as if he feared to see it smashed at any minute by men determined to kill him. Little by little, however, as he saw that he was being treated with consideration, he seemed to recover his self-control; he argued, answered various questions, tried to justify himself. Matteotti? He had had nothing to do with that. The war? All the doing of the Germans.

The documents in his black bag were checked, but they seemed to contain nothing of major importance. At the bottom of the bag the searchers found some sterling and drafts on Swiss banks for several million lire.

By now it was dark in Dongo, but there was no lull in activity. The Partisan leaders conferred. Theirs was a grave responsibility: they wanted at all costs to prevent a summary execution and at the same time they wanted to keep Mussolini out of the Allies' hands: Il Duce should be tried by the Italians. That night Mussolini was taken to Germanesino; then, in order to keep his place of detention secret, his head was covered and in blinding rain he was taken to a peasant house in Bonzanigo in the commune of Mezzagra. There he was joined by Claretta Petacci.

She had been arrested at Dongo in her brother's car: he had claimed to be the Spanish consul in Milan. Mussolini had asked Pedro, the Partisan leader, to convey his greetings to her, and Claretta had succeeded in persuading Pedro to allow her to rejoin Il Duce. Together he and she, in that evening of 27 April 1945, clambered up the mountain road that led to the house of a peasant, De Maria. They were given the bedroom on the second floor, and two young armed Partisans were posted at the door.

It was cool and rainy.

Late in the evening the news of the capture reached the high command of the Corps of Volunteers for Freedom (CVL). As of 25 April, Article V of the code of justice promulgated by the Committee of National Liberation provided the death penalty for Mussolini and the hierarchs as for any Fascist taken armed. For Il Duce and the hierarchs there was no salvation.

But a race got under way. The Partisans, especially on the extreme left (Communists and Socialists), were afraid that the British and Americans would get hold of the Fascist leaders and save them from the ultimate penalty. In addition, one of the clauses of the 8 September armistice stipulated that Il Duce was to be turned over to the Allies. But the whole left Resistance approved when Sandro Pertini, a Socialist, exlaimed: 'Mussolini deserves to be shot like a mangy dog!'

Meanwhile the Allies were driving northward, and quick action was imperative. An American officer of Italian origin, Captain Daddario of the staff of the United States Fourth Army, had already reached Milan from Switzerland, and Graziani had managed to surrender to him (and thus to escape execution). The CVL leaders decided to precipitate matters: most of them were Socialists and Communists. Colonel Valerio (later Walter Audisio, a Communist deputy) obtained from Captain Daddario and the Resistance military authorities (General Cadorna) the passes and other papers necessary to his mission.

Though the American captain was not informed of the colonel's purpose, General Cadorna was aware of it. But at that time he was primarily concerned with the German divisions that were withdrawing northward in good order. Besides, like every Italian in the Resistance, he did not want Mussolini to be handed over to the Allies, not so much out of fear that he would escape punishment as out of concern for national independence and dignity. The matter of Mussolini was the business of Italians. The Italian people was a mature people that stood in no need of lessons from the Allies. Such was Cadorna's thinking. Hence he kept his hands off: he did not assist Valerio's mission, but he did not impede it.

Valerio left Milan in a FIAT 1500 at two-thirty in the morning of 28 April, followed by a truck carrying fifteen reliable Partisans. The first stop was Como, which they reached during the morning. There Valerio learned that two men had left Como, under the auspices of the town's CLN, to identify the prisoners and bring them back to Como. And the Allies' advance guard was entering the town even as Valerio was leaving it with his men.

Valerio raced along the lake-side road, even crashing a road-block erected by the Partisans. About one-thirty in the afternoon he and his men reached Dongo. The fifteen Partisans from Milan lined up in front of the town hall. Pedro, the local commander of the *Garibaldini*, tried to question Valerio's orders for the execution of the Fascist chiefs. Valerio had decided even to execute Claretta Petacci, and he was adamant. 'I am not the one who sentenced her,' he said. 'She was condemned earlier. Remember, I am carrying out an order and you ought not to meddle. I know what I am doing and I am the one who will decide what I have to do.'

The fate of Mussolini and Claretta Petacci was now sealed. Valerio and some of his men went to De Maria's house. 'I have come to liberate you,' he told Mussolini, 'let's make it fast.'

His manner admitted of no reply. Without a word Claretta and Mussolini followed the group of Partisans. Mussolini was wearing a workman's heavy cap; Claretta was clinging to him. After a short car trip, Valerio got out in front of the gateway of a villa. 'Hurry up,' he said, 'get into that corner.'

Stunned, his back to the wall, Mussolini stared. Suddenly Valerio said in a tight voice: 'By order of the high command of the Corps of Volunteers for Freedom I am instructed to do justice for the Italian people.' Mussolini almost collapsed and Claretta threw her arms round him.

'He must not die,' she said.

'Back where you were,' Valerio replied. She went back.

There was one volley, then a second. Mussolini and Claretta Petacci were dead. It was 28 April 1945.

Two Partisans stayed with the bodies while Valerio went back to Dongo, where the fifteen hierarchs were waiting in the park along the parapet that overlooks the lake. When Valerio tried to put Marcello Petacci among them, they raised a unanimous protest. 'Get out, get out! Not with us, that one's a traitor! He should not be shot with us.'

Marcello was removed. Someone cried 'Viva l'Italia' and a few others gave the Fascist salute. 'Half turn,' the commander of the firing squad shouted. The doomed men faced the lake, whose water mirrored the April sky, with its shifting fantasies of blue areas and dark clouds clinging to the steep slopes of the mountains rising above the shore.

'Fire!' They fell, their twisting bodies resting on one another. 'Fetch Petacci,' Valerio ordered.

Petacci struggled and managed to work free, running through the narrow streets like a maddened animal; then he leaped into the lake and everyone began to fire at him. It did not take many shots to make him sink.

The rest of the bodies were slung into Valerio's truck: Mussolini's and Claretta's were on top of the others. The truck got back to Milan the next day, 29 April. All seventeen corpses were thrown on the sidewalk of Piazza Loreta beside the garage in which the Germans had shot fifteen hostages on 14 August 1944. Soon all Milan was crowding round to view them. People wanted to see, to be reassured by the gruesome spectacle, to see and to touch: some trampled the bodies, others spat on them, shoved a mocking sceptre into Mussolini's hands, made jokes. 'Petacci,' someone shouted, and someone else held up her corpse to show it . . . . A Partisan had the idea of hanging all the bodies by the feet from the rafters of the garage for everyone to see. A placard with the victim's name chalked on it was attached to each corpse.

And this profanation of death seemed to serve as a magic ceremony, collective and primitive: the end of a bewitchment, the resolve to understand that in truth Il Duce and his hierarchs had been only men.

Men even poorer than the rest, even viler, for their bodies were there, offered to sneers and obscene gestures, hanged head down. And the crowd pressed in and revenged itself on them – a huge crowd of the jubilant, the hateful, and the merely curious, all discovering from these poor shapes of men reduced to bloody puppets that Il Duce and his hierarchs had had neither enough champions nor enough personal courage to save their bodies from the gallows. Thus 29 April 1945 concluded in violence what 23 March 1919 had inaugurated in violence.

1973

---

*The Last Days of Hitler shows Hugh Trevor-Roper (later Lord Dacre) at his most magisterial and incisive. As an intelligence officer at the time he was given the task of uncovering step by step the last few weeks of Hitler's life. When the book first came out in March 1946 it was heaped with accolades. A.J.P. Taylor said it was an 'incomparable book, by far the best written on any aspect of the second German war'. Trevor-Roper proved – to the satisfaction of most reasonable men – that Hitler had killed himself in the bunker. It is curious to note that Hitler's death had an immediate effect on his entourage: they began to smoke again – an indulgence forbidden them during the Führer's lifetime.*

---

## THE LAST DAYS OF HITLER

### HUGH TREVOR-ROPER

When Von Bulow left the Bunker, Hitler was already preparing for the end. During the day the last news from the outside world had been brought in. Mussolini was dead. Hitler's partner in crime, the herald of Fascism, who had first shown to Hitler the possibilities of dictatorship in modern Europe, and had preceded him in the stages of disillusion and defeat, had now illustrated in a signal manner the fate which fallen tyrants must expect. Captured by Partisans during the general uprising of northern Italy, Mussolini and his mistress Clara Petacci had been executed, and their bodies suspended by the feet in the market-place of Milan to be beaten and pelted by the vindictive crowd. If the full details were ever known to them, Hitler and Eva Braun could only have repeated the orders they had already given: their bodies were to be destroyed 'so that nothing remains'; 'I will not fall into the hands of an enemy who requires a new spectacle to divert his hysterical masses.' In fact it is improbable that these details were reported, or could have strengthened an already firm decision. The fate of defeated despots has generally been the same; and Hitler, who had himself exhibited the body of a field-marshal on a meat-hook, had no need of remote historical examples or of a new and dramatic instance, to know the probable fate of his own corpse, if it should be found.

In the afternoon, Hitler had had his favourite Alsatian dog, Blondi, destroyed. Professor Haase, his former surgeon, who was now tending the wounded in his clinic in Berlin, had come round to the Bunker and killed it with poison. The two other dogs belonging to the household had been shot by the sergeant who looked after them. After this, Hitler had given poison capsules to his two secretaries, for use in extremity. He was sorry, he said, to give them no better parting gift; and praising them for their courage, he had added, characteristically, that he wished his generals were as reliable as they.

In the evening, while the inhabitants of the two outer bunkers were dining in the general dining-passage of the Führerbunker, they were visited by one of the SS guard, who informed them that the Führer wished to say goodbye to the ladies and that no one was to go to bed till orders had been received. At about half-past two in the morning the orders came. They were summoned by telephone to the Bunker, and gathered again in the same general dining-passage, officers and women, about twenty persons in all. When they were assembled, Hitler came in from the private part of the Bunker, accompanied by Bormann. His look was abstracted, his eyes glazed over with that film of moisture which Hanna Reitsch had noticed. Some of those who saw him even suggested that he had been drugged; but no such explanation is needed of a condition upon which more familiar observers had often commented. He walked in silence down the passage and shook hands with all the women in turn. Some spoke to him, but he said nothing, or mumbled inaudibly. Ceremonies of silent handshaking had become quite customary in the course of that day.

When he had left, the participants in this strange scene remained for a while to discuss its significance. They agreed that it could have one meaning only. The suicide of the Führer was about to take place. Thereupon an unexpected thing happened. A great and heavy cloud seemed to roll away from the spirits of the Bunker-dwellers. The terrible sorcerer, the tyrant who had charged their days with intolerable melodramatic tension, would soon be gone, and for a brief twilight moment they could play. In the canteen of the Chancellery, where the soldiers and orderlies took their meals, there was a dance. The news was brought; but no one allowed that to interfere with the business of pleasure. A message from the Führerbunker told them to be quieter; but the dance went on. A tailor who had been employed in the Führer's headquarters, and who was now immured with the rest in the Chancellery, was surprised when Brigadeführer Rattenhuber, the head of the police guard and a general in the SS, slapped him cordially on the back and greeted him with democratic familiarity. In the strict hierarchy of the Bunker the tailor felt bewildered. It was as if he had been a high officer. 'It was the first time I had ever heard a high officer say "good evening",' he said; 'so I noticed that the mood had completely changed.' Then, from one of his equals, he learned the reason of this sudden and irregular affability. Hitler had said goodbye, and was going to commit suicide. There are few forces so solvent of class distinctions as common danger, and common relief.

Though Hitler might already be preparing for death, there was still one man at least in the Bunker who was thinking of life: Martin Bormann. If Bormann could not persuade the German armies to come and rescue Hitler and himself, at least he would insist on revenge. Shortly after the farewell ceremony, at a quarter-past three in the morning of 30 April, he sent another of those telegrams in which the neurosis of the Bunker is so vividly preserved. It was addressed to Dönitz at Ploen; but Bormann no longer trusted the ordinary communications, and sent it through the Gauleiter of Mecklenburg. It ran:

> DÖNITZ! – Our impression grows daily stronger that the divisions in the Berlin theatre have been standing idle for several days. All the reports we receive are controlled, suppressed, or distorted by Keitel. In general we can only communicate through Keitel. The Führer orders you to proceed at once, and mercilessly, against all traitors. – BORMANN

A postscript contained the words: 'The Führer is alive, and is conducting the defence of Berlin.' These words, containing no hint of the approaching end – indeed seeming to deny its imminence – suggest that Bormann was reluctant even now to admit that his power would soon be over, or must be renewed from another, less calculable, source.

Later in the same morning, when the new day's work had begun, the generals came as usual to the Bunker with their military reports. Brigade-führer Mohnke, the commandant of the Chancellery, announced a slight improvement: the Schlesischer railway station had been recaptured from the Russians; but in other respects the military situation was unchanged. By noon the news was worse again. The underground railway tunnel in the Friedrichstrasse was reported in Russian hands; the tunnel in the Vostrasse, close to the Chancellery, was partly occupied; the whole area of the Tiergarten had been taken; and Russian forces had reached the Potsdamer Platz and the Weidendammer Bridge over the River Spree. Hitler received these reports without emotion. At about two o'clock he took lunch. Eva Braun was not there; evidently she did not feel hungry, or ate alone in her room; and Hitler shared his meal, as usually in her absence, with his two secretaries and the cook. The conversation indicated nothing unusual. Hitler remained quiet, and did not speak of his intentions. Nevertheless, preparations were already being made for the approaching ceremony.

In the morning, the guards had been ordered to collect all their rations for the day, since they would not be allowed to pass through the corridor of the Bunker again; and about lunchtime Hitler's SS adjutant, Sturmbannführer Guensche, sent an order to the transport officer and chauffeur, Sturmbannführer Erich Kempka, to send two hundred litres of petrol to the Chancellery garden. Kempka protested that it would be difficult to find so large a quantity at once, but he was told that it must be found. Ultimately he found about 180 litres and sent it round to the garden. Four men carried it in jerricans and placed it at the emergency exit of the Bunker. There they met one of the police guards, who demanded an explanation. They told him that it was for the ventilating plant. The guard told them not to be so silly, for the plant was oil-driven. At this moment Hitler's personal servant, Heinz Linge, appeared. He reassured the guard, terminated the argument, and dismissed the men. Soon afterwards all the guards except those on duty were ordered to leave the Chancellery, and to stay away. It was not intended that any casual observer should witness the final scene.

Meanwhile Hitler had finished lunch, and his guests had been dismissed. For a time he remained behind; then he emerged from his suite, accompanied by Eva Braun, and another farewell ceremony took place. Bormann and Goebbels were there, with Burgdorf, Krebs, Hewel, Naumann, Voss, Rattenuber, Hoegl, Guensche, Linge, and the four women, Frau Christian, Frau Junge, Fräulein Krueger, and Fräulein Manzialy. Frau Goebbels was not present; unnerved by the approaching death of her children, she remained all day in her own room. Hitler and Eva Braun shook hands with them all, and then returned to their suite. The others were dismissed, all but the high-priests and those few others whose services would be necessary. These waited in the passage. A single shot was heard. After an interval they entered the suite. Hitler was lying on the sofa, which was soaked with blood. He had shot himself through the mouth. Eva Braun was also on the sofa, also dead. A revolver was by her side, but she had not used it; she had swallowed poison. The time was half-past three.

Shortly afterwards, Artur Axmann, head of the Hitler Youth, arrived at the Bunker. He was too late for the farewell ceremony, but he was admitted to the private suite to see the dead bodies. He examined them, and stayed in the room for some minutes, talking with Goebbels. Then Goebbels left, and Axmann remained for a short while alone with the dead bodies. Outside, in the Bunker, another ceremony was being prepared: the Viking funeral.

After sending the petrol to the garden, Kempka had walked across to the Bunker by the subterranean passage which connected his office in the Hermann Goering Strasse with the Chancellery buildings. He was greeted by Guensche with the words, 'The Chief is dead'. At that moment the door of Hitler's suite was opened, and Kempka too became a participant in the funeral scene.

While Axmann was meditating among the corpses, two SS men, one of them Hitler's servant Linge, entered the room. They wrapped Hitler's body in a blanket, concealing the bloodstained and shattered head, and carried it out into the passage, where the other observers easily recognized it by the familiar black trousers. Then two other SS officers carried the body up the four flights of stairs to the emergency exit, and so out into the garden. After this, Bormann entered the room and took up the body of Eva Braun. Her death had been tidier, and no blanket was needed to conceal the evidence of it. Bormann carried the body into the passage, and then handed it to Kempka, who took it to the foot of the stairs. There it was taken from him by Guensche; and Guensche in turn gave it to the third SS officer, who carried it too upstairs to the garden. As an additional precaution, the other door of the Bunker, which led into the Chancellery, and some of the doors leading from the Chancellery to the garden, had been hastily locked against possible intruders.

Unfortunately, the most careful precautions are sometimes unavailing; and it was as a direct result of this precaution that two unauthorized persons in fact witnessed the scene from which it was intended to exclude them. One of the police guards, one Erich Mansfeld, happened to be on duty in the concrete observation tower at the corner of the Bunker, and noticing through the opaque, sulphurous air a sudden, suspicious scurrying of men and shutting of doors, he felt it his duty to investigate. He climbed down from his tower into the garden and walked round to the emergency exit to see what was afoot. In the porch he collided with the emerging funeral procession. First there were two SS officers carrying a body wrapped in a blanket, with black-trousered legs protruding from it. Then there was another SS officer carrying the unmistakable corpse of Eva Braun. Behind them were the mourners – Bormann, Burgdorf, Goebbels, Guensche, Linge, and Kempka. Guensche shouted at Mansfeld to get out of the way quickly; and Mansfeld, having seen the forbidden but interesting spectacle, returned to his tower.

After this interruption, the ritual was continued. The two corpses were placed side by side, a few feet from the porch, and petrol from the can was poured over them. A Russian bombardment added to the strangeness and danger of the ceremony, and the mourners withdrew for some protection under the shelter of the porch. There Guensche dipped a rag in petrol, set it alight, and flung it out upon the corpses. They were at once enveloped in a sheet of flame. The mourners stood to attention, gave the Hitler salute, and withdrew again into the Bunker, where they dispersed. Guensche afterwards described the spectacle to those who had missed it. The burning of Hitler's body, he said, was the most terrible experience in his life.

Meanwhile yet another witness had observed the spectacle. He was another of the police guards, and he too came accidentally upon the scene in consequence of the precautions which should have excluded him. His name was Hermann Karnau. Karnau, like others of the guard who were not on duty, had been ordered away from the Bunker by an officer of the SS Escort, and had gone to the Chancellery canteen; but after a while, in spite of his orders, he had decided to return to the Bunker. On arrival at the door of the Bunker, he had found it locked. He had therefore made his way out into the garden, in order to enter the Bunker by the emergency exit. As he turned the corner by the tower where Mansfeld was on duty, he was surprised to see two bodies lying side by side, close to the door of the Bunker. Almost at the same time

302

they burst, spontaneously it seemed, into flame. Karnau could not explain this sudden combustion. He saw no one, and yet it could not be the result of enemy fire, for he was only three feet away. 'Possibly someone threw a match from the doorway,' he suggested; and his suggestion is essentially correct.

Karnau watched the burning corpses a moment. They were easily recognizable, though Hitler's head was smashed. The sight, he says, was 'repulsive in the extreme'. Then he went down into the Bunker by the emergency exit. In the Bunker, he met Sturmbannführer Franz Schedle, the officer commanding the SS Escort. Schedle had recently been injured in the foot by a bomb. He was distracted with grief. 'The Führer is dead,' he said; 'he is burning outside'; and Karnau helped him to limp away.

Mansfeld, on duty in the tower, also watched the burning of the bodies. As he had climbed the tower, after Guensche had ordered him away, he had seen through a loophole a great column of black smoke rising from the garden. As the smoke diminished, he saw the same two bodies which he had seen being brought up the stairs. They were burning. After the mourners had withdrawn, he continued to watch. At intervals he saw SS men come out of the Bunker and pour more petrol on the bodies to keep them alight. Some time afterwards he was relieved by Karnau, and when Karnau had helped him to climb out of the tower, the two went together to look at the bodies again. By now the lower parts of both bodies had been burned away and the shinbones of Hitler's legs were visible. An hour later, Mansfeld visited the bodies again. They were still burning, but the flame was low.

In the course of the afternoon a third member of the police guard sought to watch the spectacle of the burning bodies. His name was Hans Hofbeck. He went up the stairs from the Bunker and stood in the porch; but he did not stay there. The stench of burning flesh was intolerable and drove him away.

Late that night Brigadeführer Rattenhuber, the head of the police guard, entered the Dog-bunker where the guards were spending their leisure, and spoke to a sergeant of the SS Escort. He told him to report to his commanding officer, Schedle, and to pick three trustworthy men to bury the corpses. Soon afterwards Rattenhuber returned to the Dog-bunker and addressed the men there. He made them promise to keep the events of the day a holy secret. Anyone talking about them would be shot. Shortly before midnight Mansfeld returned to duty in the tower. Russian shells were still falling, and the sky was illuminated by flares. He noticed that a bomb crater in front of the emergency exit had been newly worked upon, and that the bodies had disappeared. He did not doubt that the crater had been converted into a grave for them; for no shell could have piled the earth around it in so neat a rectangle. About the same time, Karnau was on parade with the other guards in the Vossstrasse, and one of his comrades said to him: 'It is sad that none of the officers seems to worry about the Führer's body. I am proud that I alone know where he is.'

That is all that is known about the disposal of the remnants of Hitler's and Eva Braun's bodies. Linge afterwards told one of the secretaries that they had been burned as Hitler had ordered, 'till nothing remained'; but it is doubtful whether such total combustion could have taken place; 180 litres of petrol, burning slowly on a sandy bed, would char the flesh and dissipate the moisture of the bodies, leaving only an unrecognizable and fragile remainder; but the bones would withstand the heat. These bones have never been found. Perhaps they were broken up and mixed with the other bodies, the bodies of soldiers killed in the defence of the Chancellery, and the body of Fegelein, which were also buried in the garden. The Russians have occasionally dug in that garden, and many such bodies have been unearthed there. Perhaps, as Guensche is said to have stated, the ashes were collected in a box and conveyed out of the Chancellery. Or perhaps no elaborate explanation is necessary. Perhaps such investigations as have been made have been somewhat perfunctory. Investigators who left Hitler's engagement diary unobserved in his chair for five months may easily have overlooked other relics which were more deliberately concealed. Whatever the explanation, Hitler achieved his last ambition. Like Alaric, buried secretly under the riverbed of Busento, the modern destroyer of mankind is now immune from discovery.

While these last rites and pieties were being observed by guards and sentries, the regents of the Bunker were busy with more practical matters. Having set the bodies alight and paid their last summary respects, they had returned to safety underground, there to contemplate the future. Once again, as after Hitler's first leave-taking, a great cloud seemed to have been lifted from their spirits. The nightmare of ideological repression was over, and if the prospect before them remained dark and dubious, at least they were now free to consider it in a business-like manner. From this moment nobody seems to have bothered about the past or the two corpses still sizzling in the garden. That episode was over, and in the short space of time remaining they had their own problems to face. As the tragically-minded guard observed, it was sad to see everyone so indifferent to the Führer's body.

The first evidence of the changed atmosphere in the Bunker was noticed by the secretaries, who had been dismissed during the ceremony, but who now returned to their stations. On arrival they learned the details from Guensche and Linge; but it was not from such second-hand information only that they knew that Hitler was dead. Everyone, they observed, was smoking in the Bunker. During Hitler's lifetime that had been absolutely forbidden; but now the headmaster had gone and the boys could break the rules. Under the soothing influence of nicotine, whose absence must have increased the nervous tension of the past week, they were able to consider the administrative problems which the Führer had left them to face.

1947

# HUMBLE THANKS
# TO ALMIGHTY GOD

# LETTER TO HIS SON

## HAROLD NICOLSON

8 May 1945 from Sissinghurst

The normality continued in the morning. I attended a meeting of the *Institut Français* and lunched at the Beefsteak. By that time things began to liven up. There was some cheering in the streets and crowds in Leicester Square. But when I had finished my luncheon, I found a very different scene. The whole of Trafalgar Square and Whitehall was packed with people. Somebody had made a corner in rosettes, flags, streamers, paper whisks and, above all, paper caps. The latter were horrible, being of the comic variety. I also regret to say that I observed three Guardsmen in full uniform wearing such hats: they were not Grenadiers; they belonged to the Coldstream. And through this cheerful, but not exuberant, crowd I pushed my way to the House of Commons. The last few yards were very difficult, as the crowd was packed against the railings. I tore my trousers in trying to squeeze past a stranded car. But at length the police saw me and backed a horse into the crowd, making a gap through which, amid cheers, I was squirted into Palace Yard. There I paused to recover myself, and seeing that it was approaching the hour of 3 p.m., I decided to remain there and hear Winston's broadcast which was to be relayed through loudspeakers. As Big Ben struck three, there was an extraordinary hush over the assembled multitude, and then came Winston's voice. He was short and effective, merely announcing that unconditional surrender had been signed, and naming the signatories. (When it came to Jodl [The Chief of Hitler's Operational Staff of the Wehrmacht], he said 'Jodel'[1].) 'The evil-doers,' he intoned, 'now lie prostrate before us.' The crowd gasped at this phrase. 'Advance Britannia!' he shouted at the end, and there followed the Last Post and *God Save the King* which we all sang very loud indeed. And then cheer upon cheer.

I dashed back into the House and into the Chamber. After the roar and heat outside it was like suddenly entering an Oxford quadrangle on Eights Week night. Cool and hushed the Chamber was, with P.J. Grigg answering questions as if nothing unusual were impending. The clock reached 3.15, which is the moment when the Questions automatically close. We knew that it would take Winston some time to get to the House from Downing Street in such a crowd. We therefore made conversation by asking supplementary questions until 3.23. Then a slight stir was observed behind the Speaker's chair, and Winston, looking coy and cheerful, came in. The House rose as a man, and yelled and yelled and waved their Order Papers. He responded, not with a bow exactly, but with an odd shy jerk of the head and with a wide grin. Then he started to read to us the statement that he had just made on the wireless. When he had finished reading, he put his manuscript aside and with wide gestures thanked and blessed the House for all its noble support of him throughout these years.

Then he proposed that 'this House do now attend at the Church of St Margaret's, Westminster, to give humble and reverend thanks to Almighty God for our deliverance from the threat of German domination'. The motion was carried, and the Serjeant at Arms put the mace on his shoulder and, following the Speaker, we all strode out. Through the Central Lobby we streamed, through St Stephen's Chapel, and out into the sunshine of Parliament Square. We entered St Margaret's by the West door which was furthest away from us, and that meant a long sinuous procession through a lane kept open for us through the crowd. I had expected some jeers or tittering, since politicians are not popular and in the mass they seem absurd. But not at all. Cheers were what we received, and adulation. The service itself was very short and simple, and beautifully sung. Then the Chaplain to the Speaker read in a loud voice the names of those who had laid down their lives: 'Ronald Cartland; Hubert Duggan; Victor Cazalet; John Macnamara; Robert Bernays' – only the names of my particular friends registered on my consciousness. I was moved. The tears came into my eyes. Furtively I wiped them away. 'Men are so emotional,' sniffed Nancy Astor, who was sitting next to me. Damn her.

Then back we streamed into the House and adjourned for the day. Winston made a dash for the smoking-room. When he was passing through Central Hall the crowd there broke into loud clapping. He hesitated and then hurried on. A little boy dashed out: 'Please, sir, may I have your autograph?' Winston took a long time getting out his glasses and wiping them. Then he ruffled the little boy's hair and gave him back his beastly little album. 'That will remind you of a glorious day,' he said, and the crowd clapped louder than before. In the smoking-room Kenneth Pickthorn produced a bottle of champagne and we clinked glasses.

I went on to a party at Chips Channon's. Why did I go to that party? I should have been much happier seeing all the flood-lighting and the crowds outside Buckingham Palace. But I went and I loathed it. There in his room, copied from the Amalienburg, under the lights of many candles, were gathered the Nurembergers and the Munichois celebrating our victory over their friend Herr von Ribbentrop. I left early and in haste, leaving my coat behind me. A voice hailed me in Belgrave Square. It was Charles, seventh Marquess of Londonderry, Hitler's friend. As we walked towards his mansion in Park Lane, he explained to me how he had warned the Government about Hitler; how they would not listen to him; how, but for him, we should not have had the Spitfires and 'all this', waving a thin arm at the glow above a floodlit Buckingham Palace, at the sound of cheering in the park, and at the cone of searchlights which joined each other like a maypole above our heads.

Enraged by this, I left him in Park Lane and walked back through the happy but quite sober crowds to Trafalgar Square. The National Gallery was alive with every stone outlined in flood-lighting, and down there was Big Ben with a grin upon his illumined face. The statue of Nelson was picked out by a searchlight, and there was the smell of distant bonfires in the air. I walked to the Temple and beyond. Looking down Fleet Street one saw the best sight of all – the dome of St Paul's rather dim-lit, and then above it a concentration of searchlights upon the huge golden cross. So I went to bed.

That was my victory day.

# I SHALL BE
# ALL RIGHT

The war ended in tears for Pierre Clostermann, the brilliant and brave Free French pilot from whom we have already heard. Did he weep for his 'Grand Charles', the plane he would never fly again? Or for his dead comrades? Or for his lost youth? Maybe a little of each. He went on to become the youngest member of the Chambre des Députés and a devoted supporter both of Anglo-French unity and a united Europe.

Pilot Officer Michael Scott was not so fortunate. He was lost over the North Sea on his first operational sortie on 24 May 1941. He loved music, and recorded in his diary for 1941 the pieces he had heard; most recently Schubert's great Ninth symphony in C major. 'Now,' he wrote to his father in the letter he would receive only after his son was dead, 'I am off to the source of Music.' His papers are in the Imperial War Museum, one set among the many thousands held there. Let his last letter stand for them all.

## THE DOOR CLOSES

### PIERRE CLOSTERMANN

27 August 1945

I had applied for immediate demobilization and it had been granted. I had that morning gone to say my farewells to Broadhurst and to the RAF. The New Zealander Mackie was then commanding 122 Wing. I had made a point of going to HQ at Schleswig in my 'Grand Charles'. Coming back I had taken him high up in the cloudless summer sky, for it was only there that I could fittingly take my leave. Together we climbed for the last time straight towards the sun. We looped once, perhaps twice, we lovingly did a few slow, meticulous rolls, so that I could take away in my finger-tips the vibration of his supple, docile wings.

And in that narrow cockpit I wept, as I shall never weep again, when I felt the concrete brush against his wheels and, with a great sweep of the wrist, dropped him on the ground like a cut flower.

As always, I carefully cleared the engine, turned off all the switches one by one, removed the straps, the wires and the tubes which tied me to him, like a child to his mother. And when my waiting pilots and my mechanics saw my downcast eyes and my shaking shoulders, they understood and returned to the Dispersal in silence.

I sat next to the pilot of the Mitchell which was to take me back to Paris. As he taxied towards the runway he passed in front of the aircraft of the Wing, smartly lined up wing-tip to wing-tip, as if for an inspection. By them stood the pilots and the mechanics, waving.

Slightly to one side stood my 'Grand Charles', my old JF-E, with its red spinner, the black crosses of our victories under the cockpit, compact, determined and powerful-looking with its big motionless four-bladed propeller, which would never again be started by me. It was like the turning of a page in a book.

To the accompaniment of the strident howl of its American engines, the Mitchell gathered speed and rose into the air. I glued my face to the window for a last glimpse behind our tail of Lübeck airfield, of the tiny glittering crosses on the grass, growing smaller and indistinct in the evening mist. The pilot, embarrassed, turned his head the other way.

It was all over. No more would I see my flight of Tempests line up behind my 'Grand Charles', clumsy looking on their long legs, offering the yawning hole of their radiators to the wind from their propellers, with the trustful faces of their pilots leaning out of the cockpits, waiting for my signal.

But pride welled up within me when I thought of you, my planes, and above all of you, my dear RAF friends, whom I had had the privilege of knowing and living amongst, with your uniforms the colour of your island mists.

---

## FAREWELL LETTER TO HIS FATHER

### PILOT OFFICER M. A. SCOTT

KILLED IN ACTION. 24–5–41. Bomber Command, aged 25.

Torquay
21/8/40

Dear Daddy,

As this letter will only be read after my death, it may seem a somewhat macabre document, but I do not want you to look on it in that way. I have always had a feeling that our stay on earth, that thing we call 'Life', is but a transistory stage in our development and that the dreaded monosyllable 'Death' ought not to indicate anything to be feared. I have had my fling and must now pass on to the next stage, the consummation of all earthly experience. So don't worry about me; I shall be all right.

I would like to pay tribute to the courage which you and mother have shown, and will continue to show in these tragic times. [They had three serving sons.] It is easy to meet an enemy face to face, and to laugh him to scorn, but the unseen enemies Hardship, Anxiety and Despair are very different problems. You have held the family together as few could have done, and I take off my hat to you.

Now for a bit about myself. You know how I hated the idea of War, and that hate will remain with me for ever. What has kept me going is the spiritual force to be derived from Music, its reflection of my own feelings, and the power it has to uplift the soul above earthly things. Mark [his brother lost at sea in January 1942] has the same experiences as I have in this, though his medium of encouragement is Poetry. Now I am off to the source of Music, and can fulfil the vague longings of my soul in becoming part of the fountain whence all good comes. I have no belief in a personal God, but I do believe most strongly in a spiritual force which was the source of our being, and which will be our ultimate goal. If there is anything worth fighting for, it is the right to follow our own paths to this goal and to prevent our children from having their souls sterilized by Nazi doctrines. The most horrible aspect of Nazism is its system of education, of driving instead of leading out, and of putting State above all things spiritual. And so I have been fighting.

All I can do now is to voice my faith that this war will end in Victory, and that you will have many years before you in which to resume normal civil life. Good luck to you!

# ACKNOWLEDGEMENTS

'Entertainers Friendly and Hostile', an extract from *Phoney War on the Home Front* by E. S. Turner (Michael Joseph, 1961), is reprinted by permission of Michael Joseph Ltd copyright ©; 1961 E. S. Turner: the poem 'Officers' Mess' by Gavin Ewart, from *Horizon, More Poems from the Forces* (Routledge and Kegan Paul 1942), is reprinted by permission of Gavin Ewart; the poem 'Mess' by Walter Andrewes from *Penguin New Writing*, 17, edited by John Lehmann (Penguin Books, 1943), copyright © Walter Andrewes, is reprinted by permission of Penguin Books; '14487348 Green', an extract from *The Boy Who Shot Down An Airship* by Michael Green (Heinemann, 1988) is reprinted by permission of William Heinemann Ltd; the poem 'Naming of Parts' by Henry Reed, from *A Map of Verona* (Cape, 1970), is reprinted by permission of BBC Books; the advertisement for Rose's Lime Juice, which was published in *Keep Mum!* by George Begley (Lemon Tree Press, 1975), is reprinted by permission of Allen Synge & Co; 'What Would Christ Have Done?', an extract from *Phoney War on the Home Front* by E. S. Turner (Michael Joseph, 1961), is reprinted by permission of Michael Joseph Ltd copyright © 1961 E. S. Turner; the extracts from *This England 1940-1946* (New Statesman, 1946), edited by Michael Barsley, are reprinted by permission of the New Statesman; 'Living Below Standard', an extract and table from *Our Towns*, by the Women's Group on Public Welfare in association with the National Council of Social Service (Oxford University Press, 1943), is reprinted by permission of Oxford University Press; the extract from *Return via Dunkirk* (Hodder & Stoughton, 1947) by John Austin is reprinted by permission of the author and Hodder & Stoughton Ltd; the extract from *The Diary of Virginia Woolf* (Chatto & Windus, 1984), edited by Anne Olivier Bell, is reprinted by permission of the Executors of the Virginia Woolf Estate, and Chatto & Windus and The Hogarth Press; the extracts from Harold Nicolson's *Diaries and Letters 1939-1945* (Collins, 1967) is reprinted by permission of William Collins Sons & Co Ltd; the extract from *Postscripts* (Heinemann, 1940), by J. B. Priestly, is reprinted by permission of William Heinemann Ltd; 'My First Big Show over France' and 'The Door Closes' extracts from *The Big Show* by Pierre Closterman (Chatto & Windus, 1951) is reprinted by permission of Chatto & Windus and the Hogarth Press; the poems 'Combat Report', 'Missing' and 'For Johnny', from *For Johnny* by John Pudney (Shepheard-Walwyn), are reprinted by permission of David Higham Associates Ltd; the extract from *Boy in the Blitz* by Colin Perry (Leo Cooper, 1972) is reprinted by permission of Colin Perry and Leo Cooper Ltd; the poem 'Air Raid Across the Bay at Plymouth', from *Collected Poems* by Stephen Spender (Faber & Faber, 1954) is reprinted by permission of Faber & Faber Ltd; the extract from *Their Finest Hour* (Allen & Unwin, 1940), edited by Allan A. Michie and Walter Graebner, is reprinted by permission of Unwin Hyman Ltd; the poem 'Night Raid' by Desmond Hawkins, from *Poetry in Wartime* (Faber & Faber), is reprinted by permission of David Higham Associates; 'Publish or Perish' an extract from *Friends of Promise* by Michael Shelden (Hamish Hamilton, 1989) is reprinted by permission of Hamish Hamilton Ltd copyright © 1989 Michael Shelden; the extract from *Invasion 1940* by Peter Fleming (Hart-Davis, 1957) is reprinted by permission of Grafton Books; the poem 'Steel Cathedrals' by Dirk van den Bogaerde (Dirk Bogarde), which originally appeared in *Poetry Review*, is reprinted by permission of the Peters Fraser & Dunlop Group Ltd and Poetry Review; the extract from *Britain's Internees in the Second World War*, by Mirian Kochan (Macmillan), is reprinted by permission of Macmillan, London and Basingstoke; the poem 'Refugees' by Louis MacNeice, which originally appeared in Horizon (March, 1941) and was later published in *The Collected Poems of Louis MacNeice* (Faber & Faber, 1966), is reprinted by permission of Faber & Faber Ltd; the extract from *The Queen Mother*, by Ann Morrow (Panther, 1985), is reprinted by permission of Grafton Books; the extract from *Bomber Command* by Max Hastings (Michael Joseph, 1979) is reprinted by permission of Michael Joseph Ltd, Max Hastings copyright; the poem 'The Death of the Ball Turret Gunner' by Randall Jarrell, from *The Complete Poems of Randall Jarrell* (Faber & Faber, 1971), is reprinted by permission of Faber & Faber Ltd; the extract 'Fire Over Cologne' by Carl Olsson, from *From Hell to Breakfast* (Allen & Unwin, 1943), is reprinted by permission of Unwin Hyman Ltd; the English translation of the extract 'Paris under the Occupation' by Jean-Paul Sartre, was published in *French Writing on English Soil* (Sylvan Press), edited by J. G. Weightman, and is reprinted by permission of the Sartre Estate and Edns Gallimards; the extract from *Children in Bondage*, by Save the Children Fund (Longman, 1942), is reprinted by permission of Save the Children Fund and the Longman Group UK Ltd; the extract from *Wodehouse at War* by Iain Sproat, (Milner, 1981), is reprinted by permission of Iain Sproat; the extract from *Pursuit* by Ludovic Kennnedy (Collins, 1974) is reprinted by permission of William Collins Sons & Co. Ltd; the poem 'Destroyers in the Arctic' by Alan Ross, from *Blindfold Games* (Collins Harvill), is reprinted by permission of Alan Ross; the extract from *My Name Is Frank* by Frank Laskier (Allen & Unwin) is reprinted by permission of Unwin Hyman Ltd; the poem '48-Hour Pass (for A.C.H.)' by J. D. James, from *Poetry from Oxford in Wartime* (Fortune Press), edited by William Bell, is reprinted by permission of the Estate of J. D. James; the poem 'Oxford Leave' by Gavin Ewart, from *Horizon, More Poems from the Forces* (Routledge & Kegan Paul 1942), is reprinted by permission of Gavin Ewart; the poem 'Oxford in Wartime', by Mary Wilson, is reprinted by permission of Hutchinson & Co. Ltd; the extract from *Women in Wartime* by Jane Waller and Michael Vaughan-Rees (Macdonald Optima, 1987) is reprinted by permission of Jane Waller and Michael Vaughan-Rees; the extract from *War Factory* by Celia Fremlin (1943, repr. Cresset) is reprinted by permission of Celia Fremlin; the extract from *Home Front* by James Lansdale Hodson (Gollancz, 1944) is reprinted by permission of the Peters Fraser & Dunlop Group Ltd; the extract from *Day of Infamy* by Walter Lord (Longman) is reprinted by permission of Holt, Rinehart & Winston Inc.; the extract from *The Second World War, Vol. III: The Grand Alliance* by Winston S. Churchill (Cassell, 1950) is reprinted by permission of Cassell PLC; the extract from *Sinister Twilight* by Noel Barber (Collins, 1968; new edn., Arrow Books) is reprinted by permission of Curtis Brown & Farquharson and Arrow Books; the extract from *Hiroshima* by John Hersey (Penguin, 1972), is reprinted by permission of Penguin Books Ltd; the poem 'News Reel of Embarkation' by Timothy Corsellis from *Poems from the Forces* (Routledge & Kegan Paul); edited by Keidrych Rhys, is reprinted by permission of Routledge; 'Cassino' an extract from *Rome 44* by Raleigh Trevelyan (Secker & Warburg, 1981) is reprinted by permission of Martin Secker & Warburg Ltd; the poem 'Vergissmeinnicht' by Keith Douglas, from *Selected Poems* (Faber & Faber) is reprinted by permission of the estate of Keith Douglas; the poem 'The Net Like A White Vault' from *Dancer's End* by Enoch Powell (Falcon Press, 1951) is reprinted by permission of the Rt. Hon. Enoch Powell, MBE; the poem 'Tell Us the Tricks' by Paul Scott is reprinted by permission of the Estate of Paul Scott; the extract from *The Argument of Kings* by Vernon Scannell (Robson, 1987) is reprinted by permission of Robson Books; the poem 'A Soldier – His Prayer' by an unknown soldier in the Eighth Army, from *Poems from the Dessert* (Harrap), is reprinted by permission of the Harrap Publishing Group Ltd; the extract from *A Crowd Is Not Company* by Robert Kee (Eyre & Spottiswoode, 1947) is reprinted by permission of David Higham Associates Ltd; 'Glenn Miller on the Air', an extract from *Next to a Letter from Home* by Geoffrey Butcher (Sphere, 1986) is reprinted by permission of Mainstream Publishing; the extract from *When Jim Crow Met John Bull* by Graham A. Smith (Tauris, 1987) is reprinted by permission of I. B. Tauris & Co.; the extract from *The Longest Day* by Cornelius Ryan (Gollancz, 1982) is reprinted by permission of Victor Gollancz Ltd; the extract from *Hamptonians at War*, written and published by the pupils and staff of Hampton Grammar School, is reprinted by permission of the headmaster of Hampton School; 'The Guards Chapel', an extract from *The Doodlebugs* by Norman Longmate (Hutchinson, 1981; Arrow pbk) is reprinted by permission of Norman Longmate; the poem 'Cissie' by Lotte Kramer, which first appeared in *Contemporary Review* (Vol 224, 1974), is reprinted by permission of *Contemporary Review*; the extract from *Arnhem Lift* by Louis Hagen (Pilot Press, 1945 is reprinted by permission of Louis Hagen; the broadcast war report by Wynford Vaughan Thomas which later appeared in *War Report* (BBC dispatches: AEF, 1944-5) (Oxford University Press, 1946) is reprinted by permission of BBC Books; Viscount Montgomery of Alamein's letter to Bovril, which was published in *Keep Mum!* by George Begley (Lemon Tree Press, 1975), is reprinted by permission of Allen Synge & Co.; the extract 'Glimpses of Germany: Belsen', from *Eclipse* by Alan Moorehead (Hamish Hamilton, 1945), is reprinted by permission of the Estate of Alan Moorehead and Hamish Hamilton Ltd; the extract from *Mussolini's Italy* by Max Gallo (Abelard-Schuman, 1973) is reprinted by permission of Blackie & Son Ltd; the extract from *The Last Days of Hitler* by Hugh Trevor-Roper (Macmillan Press, 6th Edn 1987) is reprinted by permission of Macmillan, London and Basingstoke; the farewell letter by GS (Scott, Pilot Officer), which is held by the Imperial War Museum, is reprinted by permission of his sister, Flora Scott.

Every effort has been made to trace the holders of copyright material used in this anthology. We apologise for any omissions in this respect, and on notification we undertake to make the appropriate acknowledgement in subsequent editions.

# BREAD AND BUTTER LETTER

I should like to thank first Leo Cooper, the military publisher, who generously gave me the run of his extensive and fascinating library of war books, as well as much practical advice. Michael Conway, founder of the 1940s Association, proved the almost perfect foil to this solid start by providing me with a wealth of unexpected wartime oddities: pamphlets, advertisements, booklets, notebooks, as well as books published at the time and now well-nigh forgotten. I am also indebted to Rod Suddaby, Keeper of the Department of Documents at the Imperial War Museum, for his unstinted help.

The staff at the London Library were as helpful as ever; and I was lucky enough to have the help of two excellent booksellers: in London, Mary MacIntosh of the Elgin Bookshop, who conjured up new or recent books in a trice; and in the country Dick Batstone of Batstone Books, who provided me with enough secondhand books on the war to start a small library of my own. My daughter Amanda Smith researched with her customary zing, and typed the commentary for good measure. At Pavilion Books I am as ever grateful to Colin Webb, Managing Director, whose idea the book was, and to Jillie Norrey for proving such a steadfast editor. I should also like to thank Steve Dobell for his careful copy editing, Tom Sawyer for the design and John Gorham for the jacket, and Martin Noble for clearing the permissions. Once again I have to thank Oscar Turnill for putting the manuscript through his seasoned and expert scrutiny, thus saving me from many slips, solecisms, and howlers. Finally I should like to thank my old friend Kenneth Jenkins, formerly Lieutenant K.A.Q. Jenkins of the East Surrey Regiment, and an unfailing fountain of lore on all military matters. The book is dedicated to him as a small token of my thanks.

# INDEX OF AUTHORS, TITLES AND SOURCES